Inland Waterways BOAT LISTING

compiler
Douglas E. Maas

Foreword by David Stevenson
contributions from
David Daines, Mary Matts, Audrey Buxton
photographs by
Douglas Maas, Harry Arnold and the Boat Owners
illustrations by Frank Munns
and the contributions of
numerous Boat Owners and the Project's well-wishers

Inland Waterways Books
Narborough, Leicestershire
1997

First published in 1997 by
Inland Waterways Books
8 Clover Close, Narborough, Leicester LE9 5FT

© Douglas E. Maas, 1997

All rights reserved

Printed by Alfred Willday & Son Ltd.
Unit 1, Duns Lane, Leicester LE3 5LX

ISBN 0 9530034 0 X

FOREWORD

by David Stevenson
(formerly Chairman, the Inland Waterways Association)

Fifty years ago, you would have seen me, with Ian Allan Spotters' books in hand on the overbridge at the east end of Southampton Central (as it was then) station looking eagerly eastwards towards the mouth of the tunnel, below the town's (now city's) impressive and relatively new Civic Centre buildings, for the first billow of smoke that would indicate the approach of a Weymouth bound express headed by a Lord Nelson or King Arthur class locomotive. Would it have a nameplate that was not already underlined in my 'Southern' notebook?

Little did I realise then that the line of this tunnel closely followed that of the tunnel that had originally been built for the Southampton and Salisbury Canal, which caused the later tunnel builders some problems! Nor indeed, at this stage of my life, did I have any real interest in waterways and I lived some way from any completed or active canals anyway. A pity, because I might then have appreciated at an early age that I was witnessing the passing of an era, for the canals then still carried considerable numbers of trading boats, bearing the names of such legendary firms as Fellows, Morton and Clayton and Samuel Barlow & Co. I might even have become aware that the Inland Waterways Association had been formed that year to advocate 'the Retention, Conservation, Restoration and Development of the Inland Waterways for the fullest possible commercial and recreational use'.

Names and numbers have a fascination for many which adds to the pleasures of travel, whether by boat, train or other means. Doug Maas has produced a much needed book which details the boats which now cruise the waterways, some still, I am pleased to say, for commercial purposes. However, the vast majority are owned privately or are in hire fleets, so that the pleasures of the waterways can be enjoyed by an ever growing number of people. These boats carry a fascinating variety of names, many with personal or humorous connections; others bear the names of well known places on the canal system, whilst hire fleets often name their boats in classes in similar manner to the railways of yore. Whether you are an old canal hand, an ex train-spotter like me, a young boy or girl experiencing the waterways for the first time or simply find all names of interest, I believe you will find *Inland Waterways Boat Listing* a mine of interesting information.

My copy will certainly be kept close to the helm of *Black Swan*.

David Stevenson

For Marilyn, my wife,
for her good advice which I should have taken

INTRODUCTION

Why bother?

Many people enjoy lists for their own sake. Making them, reading them, studying them, updating them, using them for various purposes. Those people are probably the loco spotters, librarians, archivists and stamp collectors of this world. I suppose I tend to lean, just a bit, in that direction.

Some lists laboriously built up might be just lists for their own sake. More likely they will be an adjunct to a hobby or job. So it is with me. My interest in waterways and boats goes back to about age nine. Arthur Ransome (the children's author of Swallows and Amazons and other tales of the English lakes, the Norfolk Broads and East Coast sailing) gave me a love of boats, landscape and a bit of outdoor adventure. Parents were persuaded to a Broads holiday and that did the trick. Determination followed - at age ten - to become a boat builder or to sail the oceans in at least a three-masted square-rigger. Or both.

For some reason, I can only hazily remember a very early visit to Foxton locks for its gigantic bunch of wild flowers which I was required to collect for a school competition. Alhough a later experience involving being lowered on a stretcher from the top of the ruins of the inclined plane boiler house as part of an ambulance exercise is very clearly recalled!

Demands of teenage tended to put waterways on one side. A pity. Though whenever there were boats to see, I stopped and saw. As David Stevenson indicates in his Foreword, railways somehow link with boats, and I followed L.T.C. Rolt (a few years after him) to the Talyllyn Railway where I spent six blissfully happy years, volunteering amid the steam and the narrow guage.

A weekend drive - utilising a very old car but a brand new driving licence - led myself and a friend quite accidentally to Braunston. The towing path seemed to lead along in an interesting fashion, worth following. So, as many have done, we found ourselves at the locks. Not alone. A pair of boats, the like of which I could not recall seeing before, were rising in the bottom lock. A man and a woman doing the work. Plus a dog sitting on top. We were young but keen photographers. A 2.$^{1}/_{4}$" square colour slide film was expensive and, usually, one carefully taken shot per subject was the rule. Now, looking back at no less than *seven* pictures I took of those boats and the surroundings, must have meant that a considerable impression was made. My interest had been re-kindled. The now faded colour slides have been made into prints and as I look at them while writing this, I actually recall very little detail. Certainly not the boat names. But one of the pictures shows the boats passing the third lock by the Admiral Nelson and the butty to have been *Satellite*. The picture is reproduced on the back cover of this book, together with a modern view of the same scene with my own boat, *Aldebaran* (the far one), in the same lock. Of course the scenario was complete when I bought and read, quite recently, David Blagrove's *Bread Upon the Waters* which includes many vivid descriptions of life at Braunston, in particular the goings-on at the Admiral Nelson around 1961-62, exactly the same period as the visit described above.

For most readers of this book there is likely to have been a similar "moment" when boats and the waterways grabbed hold of their lives, never to let go. Messing about in boats, holidays on boats, simply looking at boats and perhaps just waiting for that "moment". We all want to know a bit more about boats. Or so it seems to me.

There are the experts, of course. Overall-clad and never "happier" than when nursing (or cursing) a vintage engine into life. The preservers of boats (and canals) who derive their life's pleasure and whole meaning of existence from restoration projects and who give the rest of us constant pleasure as we look upon the results of their labours. There are those who build and maintain boats for a living and whose advice is usually an essential life-line to amateurs like me. Many are those for whom the waterways are a draw for a wide variety of other reasons (millions of them, BW say) but their scene could not be complete without the boats. And of course the multitude of people for whom boats are simply a way of life - whether spare time or whole time - who are, in the main, ready with a bit of advice, an entertaining anecdote, a merry quip as we pass port to port, even the tall story or two in the canalside local after a hard day at the locks.

So why bother with a list of boats?

There are already excellent books about boats. If your interest is largely about historic working boats, or steam driven boats, or sailing barges, you will find a multitude of publications devoted to these subjects. The number of general and technical waterway books and books about the history of boats, from *Narrow Boat* onwards, is very large. I have neither the experience nor competence to even begin thinking of adding to their number.

But I can gather information and produce *Lists*! Hopefully interesting lists!

When embarking on this project, it seemed to me that boat owners might be persuaded to co-operate by providing their own information about their boats. The resulting list could be of interest, in different ways, to everyone. The "expert" who is surely always on the lookout for something new to learn, or a reference to check. The keen boater who is, in any event, always curious about other boats. The holidaymaker who - in most cases - has a ready interest and who may well be thirsty for knowledge. What better way than to see a boat in passing and being able to "look it up". (Perhaps not quite as good as getting into conversation with a willing owner). And of course - as so many people have already said - it's better than an Ian Allan Loco Spotters book for offering a splendid pastime - ticking off the boats seen. I say "better" because there's lots of extra information within this list to learn from along the way.

Once all these possibilities had matured in my mind there seemed no choice but to "have a go". Research for such a book is a long and expensive business. Getting the message to boat owners. A message that will persuade them to co-operate by filling in a questionnaire, at the same time assuring them that there is no ulterior motive. And a message that explains what is wanted. Some principles had to be laid down. What precisely did I want the book to be? Here are the broad principles which have been followed:

> For reasons which quickly become clear, the book should not aim to try to be fully comprehensive - it would be impossible to get more than a fraction of boats on our inland waterways described by their owners. Future editions might develop the theme with larger numbers.

> All descriptions must be the story as told by the owners, subject only to the requirements of editing for length, clarity, etc. A basic description including name, number, type, size and colour was clearly essential in each case. To make the book generally readable, editing would exclude repetitious items - "steel construction", "tongue and groove lining", "Calor gas cooking" and the like are usually items which have been left out. Exceptional features, especially visible ones, have been included. Entry length is often determined by the age of a boat or the adventures it has had. So, sometimes, historic craft tend to take more space on the basis that just about everyone is interested in their history, though in a book like this a full history is seldom possible. Specialist books, museums, etc. are the appropriate source of further information.

> The area to be covered seemed easy at the outset. As boats cruised the connected inland system, dedicated "spotters" might see them anywhere. But what about the Lancaster, Monmothshire & Brecon, Scotland, River Medway, Norfolk Broads and many other detached waterways? Even Ireland? Certainly a narrow boat I know, normally based on the Ashby canal, is enjoying an extended stay across the water. Difficult decisions were, to be frank, simply avoided by welcoming all entries except those for boats which were clearly more intended for salt water than fresh. This has resulted in only a few representative examples from some waterways. Maybe future (or separate) editions will cover these and other specialisms more comprehensively.

> The "volume" of boats, to make the book of interest in other ways, would be made up by adding to the "main" entries with "one-line" entries giving little more than name/number/size/colour. This would avoid the temptation and danger of making assumptions about information which might be wrong and the risk of including descriptions which might displease owners for various reasons.

Whatever else the book would be it was certainly NOT going to have any similarity to a list of boats for sale or to a holiday hire brochure. Readers may, as an incidental, find something useful in this connection.

So, the Project was embarked upon. I acknowledge below the colossal help and encouragement which has come from all quarters. It needs to be said and repeated that such a list can never be perfect, complete or totally accurate. As soon as it is started, it becomes out of date. But nevertheless I hope readers will use it and enjoy it. Whether as a reference book, or as a "boat-spotting" book or just as a quite enjoyable read. Even, maybe, to help inspire the name for a new boat.

In particular I would like to think that the book did not simply stand alone but that it becomes a part of an ongoing project which produces future volumes from time to time, becoming ever more comprehensive and useful. A good basis for that now exists but for it to happen readers should say that it should happen, seek to promote the use of the book and - most important - encourage a good supply of future entries from other boat owners.

I do hope the *Inland Waterways Boat Listing* enhances your pleasure, however you enjoy our waterways and their boats.

Douglas Maas
Aldebaran, May 1997

PUTTING SOMETHING BACK

Whether enjoying cruising or simply taking a walk along the towing path or watching the boats go by, I am always conscious of the great debt I owe to those who have gone before. For that reason, when inviting entries for this book, I pledged that - given a reasonable success - some of the proceeds would be put back into something interesting and useful for the benefit of the future of our waterways and those who use them. I look forward to being able to do that and, no doubt, whatever it is it will have a relevance to the *Listing* Project and will be made known. Watch this space, as they say.

ACKNOWLEDGEMENTS

Those who had the vision - out of the necessity which is progress - to construct our inland waterway system and those who operated it under indescribably tough working conditions deserve my thanks for enabling me to enjoy my interest and pleasure now. Stating the obvious? Well, why not? Equal thanks to the countless enthusiasts who, for 50 years, have moved mountains to ensure the survival of the system. Close on their heels are the writers and producers of numerous books and articles without which my knowledge would be perilously close to nil. Similarly to the many "boating people" - professional and amateur - with whom we all exchange knowledge and experience of the cut and the river over the years.

Specifically for this book, I must first thank those who buy it. You'll be pleased to know you're reducing the deficit! Equal and special thanks to every boat owner who, quite voluntarily, has taken trouble to fill in the Questionnaire about their boat - often with painstaking detail - and send it to a perfect stranger! Without your faith in the project it would have fallen at the first hurdle. And a particular note of gratitude to those many entrants who added some words of encouragement to their entry, which helped spur me on during endless lonely hours at the word processor. I hope justice has been done to your entry - there could be a "next time" in which we can improve and amend, perhaps adding new adventures.

I must add that "spreading the word" involved circularising many hundreds of waterway clubs, societies and businesses, asking them to pass on information to members and customers and indeed to include their own boats and hire fleets. Special thanks to those who did decide to help in this way - many magnificently.

Many individuals deserve my very special thanks in no small measure. My IWA Leicestershire Committee colleagues, with whom it is a privilege to serve, for their ready willingness to "test" the Questionnaire; in particular David Stevenson, for his inspiring Foreword and John Croot for some good advice and the list of "Barney Boats". From elsewhere Brian Holmes and John Toy for their magnificent generosity in providing their own painstakingly compiled long lists for me to use as I wished (John for working boats and Brian for boats in general). They saved me much time and effort. Others, too many to name individually, have provided countless other bits and pieces of information so useful in completing the jigsaw.

I needed some expert help to do justice to an explanation about historic working boats and was indeed fortunate to bump into David Daines at Shackerstone Steam Fair. Not only has he enthusiastically encouraged the idea of the *Listing* and sees useful developments for the future but also eagerly took up the challenge of writing two original pieces on his subject which appear exclusively in the *Listing*. Frank Munns has contributed good technical advice and in particular the line illustrations which add that extra attractiveness to the book. These are examples of my promise not to allow the *Listing* to become too "dry". Others include a selection of photographs - quite a few of mine but also some sent in by boat owners - plus those needed to help illustrate working boat types, by Harry Arnold (Waterway Images). Equally, I am indebted to Mary Matts for one of her delightfully descriptive pieces of writing (not for readers of a nervous disposition) and to Audrey Buxton for a relevant poem.

Administering such a project - with its thousands of bits of paper, envelopes, labels and postage stamps, plus proof reading and checking that all is well, packing and despatching, transport and miscellaneous support - is a vital task of colossal proportions. Therefore, without the generous help of Mary, Cliff, Pam, Anne and Bernard in this department the whole thing could have sunk without trace. Many, many thanks.

Marilyn, my wife, has put up with two years of boat fitting overlapped by a year of book writing (among other things). I love her and thank her for doing so.

My grateful acknowledgements are due to the commercial waterway press and their staff who have seen fit to give some help in publicising this curious exercise and equal thanks to IWA and NABO who have done likewise in their magazines.

A bit of advertising in this book was seen to be a "good idea" as it would help to finance a more comprehensive volume. I thank those firms who have put a degree of faith in the success of the book by buying the small amount of advertising space which was on offer and I am sure their messages will "stand out"! Similarly, I thank those waterway businesses who have decided to stock the book on their retail shelves; prior to mid-April 1997 these were Batterdale Books of Hatfield, Cowroast Marinas, Foxton Boat Services Ltd., Middlewich Narrow Boats, Nantwich Canal Centre, Sileby Mill Boatyard, Stoke Bruerne Museum.

In this connection, my particular thanks go to Laurence Cook, manager of Stoke Bruerne Museum for hospitably allowing the book launch there on 5th July and to British Waterways staff generally following my various requests for assistance.

Finally, I sincerely thank Peter Willday and his staff, the book's printers, for their endless good advice and for producing what I am sure will be an excellent volume technically, despite my endless lists of worries and queries.

PHOTOGRAPHS

Photographs are by the compiler, except:
those used to illustrate some working boat types, and *Symbol* are
by Harry Arnold (Waterway Images);
some photographs used to illustrate particular boat entries have been supplied by
the boat entrants (on the front cover, these illustrate *Pegasus* - top left,
Stokie No. 1 - first under title, *Papaneek* - second under title)

List of Contents

Abbreviations	inside front cover
Foreword David Stevenson	3
Introduction	5
Putting Something Back	8
Acknowledgements	9
List of Contents	11
What Next?	12
Using the *Listing*, including "Essential Note"	13
The *Inland Waterways Boat Listing*	from 15
Historic Narrow Boats David Daines	41
Boatwife's Lament A H Buxton	72
Names for Boats Douglas Maas	120
I Name This Ship David Daines	122
Icy Christmas Mary Matts	179
The "List Man" Strikes Again	192
Location Glossary	193
Some Last Thoughts	198

WHAT NEXT?

YOU could participate in this *Listing* Project. If you think the book is interesting and useful, consider the second edition! A future edition (or even separate smaller editions) could only happen if this one is reasonably popular and successful and if the proportion of "full entries" was much greater. Existing entries will need updating as required and discrepancies ironed out.

It follows that some positive communication from readers would be helpful if not essential!

1. You could simply let it be known that you like the book (many have already said they've liked the idea), or say that you don't, or make suggestions about how you would like to see it improved.

2. You could recommend it to others (or give copies as presents!) so that any small profit could finance a second edition. Suggest your own local boatyard/chandler/bookshop stocks it.

3. Lots of new entries will be needed. Spread the idea to boat owners (show them this book). Incidentally, the high cost of advertising for entries has to be passed on in the book price. Large numbers of "word of mouth" entries will help to keep the price of future editions down!

4. Note discrepancies and errors carefully when "boat spotting" and tell us about them (see "Essential Note" on page 13).

5. If your boat is listed in this book you may want to update the entry in future. We would contact you anyway so please tell us about any change of address.

Therefore it is all an easy matter of keeping in touch! Any information you send will be carefully noted, collated and used as necessary for any future edition. Names and addresses received in response to 3 and 5 above will likewise be carefully stored and used to send out information at the appropriate time.

Thank you for your interest and for any assistance you can give.

Please use the following to make contact by post or phone:

INLAND WATERWAYS BOOKS
8 CLOVER CLOSE, NARBOROUGH
LEICESTER LE9 5FT

TELEPHONE: 0116 - 2750746

USING THE *LISTING*

ESSENTIAL NOTE

It is vital to differentiate the "full entries" from the "one-line" brief entries. The former have been supplied by the boat owners and, with the exception of a degree of editing for length, the avoidance of some repetition and the use of abbreviations, they consist largely of what the owners themselves want to say about their craft. The full entries have been subject to several checking stages and, hopefully, will be entirely accurate.

In much larger numbers, the "one-line" entries are included for general interest - in particular for the benefit of those readers who find "boat-spotting" a good pastime. Also perhaps to form a basis from which any future edition of the *Listing* will be compiled. However it is as well to understand the circumstances in which many (not all) of these are collected. Mostly by observation. Perhaps from a stationary boat or lock side. But maybe by the steerer of a moving boat (with note pad or tape recorder) so long as safety permits. Most (but not all) records include licence numbers. Some include estimates of length and colours, *given in italics*. Other bits of information are sometimes also included. But when all these records are merged together in compiling the list some possible discrepancies turn up! And it is usually impossible to go back for another look!

It could be as much fun spotting the discrepancies, putting them right (and even telling the *Listing* about them) as simply ticking the "good" entries.

For example, a fairly frequent discrepancy might be simple duplication. Perhaps two records have been made of the same boat but only one records the licence number or, after several transcribings, an error has crept in. Take *Renton* for example. There are two entries. Is it one boat or two? We're fairly sure it is only one but cannot be certain and therefore have included both records. Time and further observations will confirm. Observations may not be perfect and *Charley Girl* just might have become *Chorley Girl* (though probably not) or, even more easily, *Meadow Sweet* might really be *Meadowsweet*. A simple error could move a boat around in the alphabet, so its worth checking.

Get as much satisfaction from spotting errors as otherwise. If you collect a few, keep a note (include licence number) and send it to us. We'll be very pleased.

USING THE MAIN ENTRIES
(AND THE BRIEF ENTRIES WHERE APPROPRIATE)

There can be variations in the extent of information available but in general the following order is used (note abbreviations given inside front cover and in the Location Glossary):

BOAT NAME Listed strictly alphabetically with only these provisos: "St." and "Saint" are listed together; "The ..." is always counted but just in case the record made doesn't include that word it might be worth checking for the second word in the name; "&" is ignored when placing names in alphabetical order. If there is a boat number shown, say, as "2" or "II" this is generally ignored for the purpose of the alphabet. But the word "TWO" would be considered part of the name and be treated alphabetically.

LICENCE NUMBER (mostly available). Common prefixes are B = Bridgewater, N = Nene, M = Medway. SSR = Small Ships Register. Others can be worked out!

ADDITIONAL EXTERNAL WORDING Shown in CAPITAL letters. Repetitions of "Registered at ...", phone numbers, etc. are not included.

USE Mostly not given if private, residential or continuous cruising. Otherwise such descriptions as Hire, Restaurant, Hotel, Working, Commercial, Camping, etc. are used.

WHAT THE BOAT IS Not spelled out but abbreviated in most cases. See abbreviations list. In particular note that "NbT" or NbTug" could be either an historic "Traditional" or "Tug" narrow boat or a modern boat constructed in that style. The date of building and remainder of the entry will generally make all clear.

CONSTRUCTION The assumption is made that a boat described as "Nb.." is all steel and "Grp" refers to a river/canal cruiser of that material. If these descriptions are inadequate a full description is given. "Composite" refers to iron hull with wooden (elm) bottom.

SIZE 99% of full entries have been supplied in feet and inches. If metric, then metric is given. Length is always given in full entries *(estimated in italics in some brief entries)*. Generally "beam" is not given if between 6'10" and 7' although sometimes that latter dimension appears significant and is therefore included. Otherwise beam ('b') is given. Similarly "draught" ('d') is not shown unless it appears exceptional for the type of craft, e.g. very shallow or over 30" for a narrow boat.

COLOURS Simplicity has not been easy to achieve but some abbreviations (see list) have been used for the most common colours. Specific shades, when given, have been included.

BUILDER/FIT-OUT, ETC. These details follow 'B:' starting with year then builder/fit-out and other information as appropriate. If the full location of a builder/fitter-out is not given, check the Location Glossary at the end of the book.

PROPULSION Generally the full information given by the owner is included. But please note that the words "diesel", "petrol", "marine" and the like are rarely used as they would become very repetitive. The assumption is made that inboard engines use diesel and outboards use petrol. Information is given if otherwise.

BASE is shown as owner has indicated - either a specific or a more general location, as preferred. Additional information about many locations is given in the Location Glossary at the end of the book.

OTHER INFORMATION about name, history, features and events generally follows.

ACCESSION NUMBER at the end of each main entry helps with administration.

INFORMATION SOUGHT BY OWNER, ETC. A number of entries include the owner's appeal for information about a boat's history, sister vessels or other responses, etc. Any reader may send a letter to an entrant via the Publisher who will forward it. Simply write the letter, then place in a sealed envelope, with a postage stamp and write as the first line of the address:

BOAT NAME and ACCESSION NUMBER *(both are essential)*

Place this in another envelope, stamped and addressed to:

Inland Waterways Books, 8 Clover Close, Narborough, Leicester LE9 5FT

The publisher will be pleased to address and forward such correspondence.

Inland Waterways BOAT LISTING

19th HOLE 53593
4 CHEERS 52317
4 DIAMONDS 54840

A

In which we meet a boat with a split personality, one which was named by mistake, lots of winners, wheels on the water, go exploring (by hotel, too), a visit to Peru and preparing for a new millennium

AARDVARK 73991
AARDVARK 91516
ABACUS 73057
ABBA ROSE 49063
ABEL TASMAN 51695
ABER No.1 71965 Lg Woolwich Town Cl motor. Ex GUCC/BW
ABERGAVENNY CASTLE 64912 Hotel Boat Butty and **ROSE OF BRECON** 64911 Hotel Boat Motor 50′ lt blue/yel. B: 1975 Hancock & Lane, f/o Willow Wren. Lister SR3 (*Rose*). Base Cambrian Cruisers, Mon & Brec canal. Purpose built hotel boat pair for this canal. 018423
ABIGAIL *NbT 70′ blue/red*
ABIGAIL 62906
ABIGAIL 66510
ABILEA 102933
ABILITY 49752
ABILITY 67862
ABLE BAKER 73196
ABOPA 50200
ABORIGINE 77446
ABOYNE 62370 Lg Woolwich Town Cl butty. Ex GUCC/ BW/WW/BL
ABRAHAM 101273
ABRAXAS 54281 BARROW-UPON-SOAR NbT 47′6″ dk blue/mar. B: 1994 Mel Davis Boatbuilders, f/o Nimbus Narrowboats. Beta (Kubota) 33.5bhp. Base Barrow-upon-Soar. 21349
ABSOLUTE 51387

ABSOLUTELY 53606
ABSOLUTELY 74143
ACCORD 82874
ACHERNAR Sm Woolwich Star Cl motor. Ex GUCC/BW
ACHILLES "Star" class butty, originally composite (steel sides, elm bottom). Commercial contract work. 70′, b 7′ cabin awaiting restoration - no decoration. B: circa 1935 Harland & Wolff Ltd. for GUCCCo. Butty to *Collingwood*, *Yeoford* or other motors. Base Birmingham Gas Street basin - normally operates BCN and other Midlands canals. After commercial carrying ceased about 1970 boat adapted for camping ("camping afloat") in mid 1970s but is currently an empty shell awaiting further restoration. 034990
ACHILLES 1927 PULBOROUGH Dinghy double hull 10′6″, b 4′6″, d 6″ orange/wh. B: 1975 by Tabor, Taplow. 4hp Seagull ob. Base R.Arun - Pulborough, Sussex. Used to explore "unknown" rivers, streams, abandoned canals of England, France in connection with writing of owner's book - *(Pleasure Boating in the Victorian Era* - Phillimore, 1983). Was first twin hull boat to navigate R.Arroux (tributory of R.Loire) from Igornay to Digoin since P G Hamerton's canoe voyage in 1866 (see pp 42-51 in aforementioned book). 20176
ACHILLES 62277
ACHILLES 79317
ACHILLES III 66277
ACORN G&J MADDOX NORTHWICH GP12 NbT 50′ dk grm/mar. B: 1991 Cheshire Steel Craft (Geoff Pilling), owner f/o. Perkins D3 152. Base Hesford Marine. Recessed rear panels; trad pine/ mahogany fit-out. 2096
ACORN 50312
ACORN 70568
ACORN 78168
ACTIS   Sm Woolwich Star Cl butty.   Ex GUCC/BW
ACTIVE *NbC 40′ blue/red*

15

ACTIVE 74528
ACTON BELL 70798 NbC 45' red/yel. B: 1978 Hancock & Lane. Lister. Base New Mills Marina, Peak Forest Canal. 22385
ADA GARTH 50142
ADAGIE 61530
ADAGIO 48719
ADAGIO 49593
ADAGIO 51925
ADAGIO 104407
ADAGIO B1143
ADAGIO II 64145
ADAMANT *conv. steamer 60'*
ADAMS APPLE *see VICTORIA*
ADAM'S ARK 70574
ADAM STUART 2 69137
ADASTRA 80764
ADDERLEY MV BW-NW
ADDERLEY 74770
ADELAIDE *NbT blue/mar 55'*
ADELICIA 78914
ADENUFF 54786
AD LIB FROLIC 79236
ADMIRAL FREWEN 76402 NbC 50' red/grn
ADMIRAL HAWKE 79315
ADMIRALS YARN B0480
ADOLPHUS 61278
ADRIAN 53872
ADRIAN 73117
ADRIANA *NbC 50' blue/red*
ADRIANA 45254
ADRIANA 48349
ADVENTURER 46150
ADVENTURER 50700
ADVENTURER 62083
ADVENTURER 66307
ADVENTURER 74061
ADVENTURER 101200
ADVENTURER 103434
AEGEAN GLORY 100894
AEGIR 67614
AEMELIUS 69202
AEOLUS 76442
AFENJACK 54929
AFON BRAINT 75910
AFRICAN QUEEN 54427
AFRICAN QUEEN 77267
AFRICAN ROOTS 67779
AFTERNOON DELIGHT 91407
AFTER U 101249
AGAPE 102008
AGATE 64236
AGNAR 71752
AGNES No.13 52756
AGNES BLOMFIELD 66245
AGNES PURSEY 73467
AGRICOLA TOWER 68420
AHAB 73351
AIDA 72704
AILEEN 31548
AILSA 67135
AIMEE 62159
AIMEE B 60511
AINTREE MV BW-NW

AIRE Crane boat 18.59m BW-NE
AIRE Grp 30' wh/brown
AIRE 61633
AIREDALE 50482
AIREDALE H 61968
AISLING 49246
AIYONI 65278
AJAX 46568
AJAYCEE 47559
A.J.TELGATE 52323
AKAPULERAN 60026
AKOND OF SWAT *362952 NbT 50' red/grn*
ALACRITY 46761
ALAN A DALE Tug 9.55m BW-NE
ALAN & MARGARET 054676 SANDBACH Nb 50' red/blue. B: 1995 Dave Massey Wincham Wharf. Base Wincham Wharf. Wheelhouse. A new concept in luxury all weather cruising; Ensign 2000 a new boat for a new millennium. 24834
ALANNA 53678
ALASKA 67150
ALBA MOON II WARGRAVE Grp 24', d 14" ivory. B: 1992 Fulwood Cruisers Ltd. 15hp Honda ob petrol. Base Wargrave on Thames. 20133
ALBANA 79334
ALBAN LOOM 79348
ALBANNACH 68415
ALBATROSS 46852
ALBATROSS 50943
ALBATROSS 52274
ALBATROSS 61736
ALBATROSS 72719
ALBERT Motor. Ex 'Ovaltine'
ALBERT *NbT 50' blue/red*
ALBERT 48357
ALBERT 49503
ALBERT 53420
ALBERT 73079
ALBERT 74450
ALBERT No.1 74881
ALBERTINE Hire. NbC 60' red/grn. Base Rose Narrowboats, Brinklow, N.Oxford canal. 026718
ALBERT OWL 47505
ALBERTTO 45841
ALBION 45995
ALBION 49902 Nb BCN Tug 55', dk blue/cr. B: 1989-90 Les Allen & Son, f/o 1995 Richard Willmington. Russell Newbery DM2 2-1 reduction, 26"x18" prop. Base Brewood. Used commercially on contract work, towing, etc. on BCN 1990-1995; now pleasure only. Name not derived from West Bromwich Albion but from Albion Junction on BCN (appropriate for a BCN tug). 22405
ALBION 54897
ALCAREM B1547
ALCEDO 60394 NbC 32' grn/yel. B: 1981-83 shell: Arcrite Fabrications for Harborough Marine, f/o Roger & Pamela Barsted, Lichfield Boat Club (HM Classic Boat Club No. 1014). 1.5L Thornycroft 90. Base Inglemere, T&M. 23573
ALCEDO ATTHIS 47886
ALCESTIS 52723
ALCHEMIST 68751

ALCHEMY 31823
ALCHEMY 69849
ALCHEMY 71164
ALCHERA 500712 R.A. AND W. EVANS, FENNY STRATFORD NbT 42' dk blue/red. B: 1995/6 Tim Tyler, Hixon, f/o Aynho Wharf Boatbuilders. Beta Marine 1305 (Kubota). Base Fenny Stratford. *Alchera* means "dreamtime" in Aborigine lore. 20120
ALCOR No.4 70078 Sm Woolwich Star Cl motor. Ex GUCC/BW
ALDAVE B1015
ALDEBARAN 52645 *NbT 55' blue/graining*
ALDEBARAN 54489 STOKE GOLDING NbST 53' grn/red. B: 1994/5 Midland Canal Centre, Stenson, f/o by owners (help with tecnicals by Ashby Narrowboat Co.). Lister 4cyl Alpha 36hp. Base Stoke Golding. Started life on back of an envelope and design has been followed almost exactly. Story of the fit-out, starting with a blunt screwdriver, a rusty saw, a hammer and a bag of nails, is the subject of slide presentation: *The Adventures of the Pea Green Boat*. *(This book compiler's boat).* 21225
ALDER Yarwoods Tree Cl motor. Ex FMC
ALDERLEY ROSE 66044
ALDFORD Pontoon narrow ramped BW-NW
ALDGATE Lg Woolwich Town Cl motor Ex GUCC/BW
ALEIDA Tug. Boat Museum
ALE & HEARTY 83213
ALERT 78891
ALEXAN III 65396 *NbC 30' red/grn*
ALEXANDER 62685
ALEXANDER 70339
ALEXANDER B1278
ALEXANDRA Inspection craft. Boat Museum
ALEXANDRA JAYNE 53274
ALEXANDRIAN 52609
ALEXAS 69885
ALEXIS 53635
ALEX THEKI 103871
ALFANNE 63390
ALFHEIM 72651
ALFORD 89310
ALFRED 46041
ALFRED LEROY MILFORD BOAT HOUSE MILLBROOK GUILDFORD Cruising restaurant. 45', b 13'6" grn/red. B: 1979 Hancock & Lane/ Guildford Boat House. Base Guildford, R.Wey. Named after boat house owner in 1890's. First cruising restaurant in the area. 016334
ALGRIVE 61962
ALHODES 64683
ALICANAS 52919
ALICE *NbC 40' red/blue*
ALICE 48817
ALICE 52992
ALICE 53314
ALICE 53375
ALICE 71448
ALICE 73824
ALICE 78721
ALICE II 48306

ALICE V . River cruiser clinker built mahogany on steamed oak 6.3m, b 2.4m varnished mahogany/lt blue deck paint. B: (?)1959 Stanley Goodwin & Son, Kidderminster; 1988 f/o and engine change by present owner. Yanmar 1GM10 (originally Stuart-Turner 8hp 2 stroke). Base Marlow on Thames. *(Owner believes this boat is unique on Thames and would like to know of any sister vessels elsewhere in Britain - see page 14)*. 20177
ALICE ELIZABETH 53094
ALICE JEAN 50235
ALICE LOUISE 50884
ALICE MARIA 51900
ALICE MAUD 47399
ALICE OF MARCH 73311
ALICE ROSE 75044
ALICIA 51943
ALICIA 62492
ALIKA 69663
ALIMANDA 79977
ALIMERA DOS 87422
ALINA 54771
ALISMA 66825
ALISON 048701 DEBDALE WHARF NbT 40' navy/burgundy. B: 1990 Delph Marine, owner f/o ongoing. Re-con (D.T. Thomas Marine) BMC 1.5. Base Debdale Wharf marina. 24886
ALISON *NbT 42' mar/blue*
ALISON 70177
ALKAID 53691
ALKALI 69943
ALL BOYS 68375
ALLEGHENY *Dutch barge narrow beam 56' bl/wh*
ALL OR NOTHING 76762
ALL RIGHT NOW 48203
ALLISA 62028
ALLOUETTES 100344
ALMA MARY 54616
AL MAMOON 76904
ALMANAC Barney(24) 1973 52'
ALMERIMAR DOS *Grp 21'*
ALMIRA 64618 STOKE ON TRENT NbC 39', d 18" lt blue. B: 1971 G Faulkner Cosgrove. BMC 1500. Base Stoke on Trent Boat Club. Distinctive hull unique to builder who produced boats for limited period. Integral steel strakes running whole length are unusual, gunwhales higher than norm. Owned by same family from new, over 10,000 hours covered. 23690
ALMO'S DREAM 48677 *NbT 50' mar/wh/blue*
ALMOST 46899
ALONDRA 60941
ALONDRA 60942
ALONG SHORTLY *NbC 20' red*
ALONSO 45407
ALPE 69702
ALPERTON Lg Woolwich Town Cl butty. Ex GUCC/BW/WW
ALPHA 91370
ALPHA CENTAUR 74814
ALPHA JULIET 72469
ALPHEUS 63492

17

ALPINE CHOUGH 52796
ALPINE SWIFT 500600
ALRON 69924
ALSO ABEY 50693
ALTA 500085
ALTAIR 066832 Hire. NbC 50′ grn/red. BMC 1.5. Base Evesham Marina, R.Avon. 0371047
ALTERNATIVE 48273
ALTIUM PETIMUS 79398
ALTO CIRRUS 64185
ALTON 102 Large Woolwich Town class working Nb - commercial carrying when available 71′6″ dk blue/lt blue. B: 1936 Harland and Wollf. Petter PD2. Base Upper Peak Forest canal. 25942
ALTO STRATUS 78303
ALUCIO 48531
ALVECHURCH Motorboat 12m BW-LAP
ALVICO 70136
ALVON 73958
ALZARK 48207
ALZAZOLA BLU 79110
AMADEUS 50519
AMADEUS 74099
AMALFI-D 45138
AMANDA 52174
AMANDA 54101 SSR66238 NbT 40′ grn/mar. B: 1992 Marque Narrowboats, owner f/o. FMK 3. (Has cruised Chelmer canal/R.Blackwater/ R.Crouch/R.Thames involving sea passage). Residential/continuous cruising. 23543
AMANDA 68906
AMARANTH B1593
AMARANTHUS 69679
AMARETO B1626
AMARILLO 61794
AMARYLIS 60527
AMARYLLIS Cruiser. Boat Museum
AMARYLLIS 47997
AMAZING GRACE 45851
AMAZING GRACE 050792 MOUNTSORREL NbT 62′ blue/grey/dk blue. B: 1991 Colecraft, private f/o. 2.5L Leyland mounted port side of engine room, connected by lorry prop shaft and two couplings. Base Mountsorrel, R.Soar. Trad furnished boatmans cabin. Built in pirana pine stained glass fronted dressers. 25967
AMAZON QUEEN 54338
AMBER 50073
AMBER 60425
AMBER 74266
AMBER II 62068
AMBERGATE 77305 HARRISON & ROBERTS LANGLEY MILL NbT 62′ grn/ orange. B: 1982 Les Allen & Sons; f/o mostly DIY. Gardner 3LW. Base Langley Mill. 261065
AMBERLEY 61628
AMBITION 53619 NbT 60′ blue/red
AMBITION 79544
AMBITION TOO NbT 60′ bl/crm
AMBLE 46103
AMBLER 54123
AMBLESIDE 46235
AMBOSELI 51088 NbT 55′ brown
AMBROKE 53487

AMBUSH (& Viktoria) Commercial boats
AMELIA 47457
AMELIA 51040
AMELIA 67634
AMELIA 76129
AMELIA ELLEN 70207
AMELIA JANE 49603
AMERAN 50761
AMERTON Power boat 12m BW-CATM
AMETHYST Hire. NbC 56′ blue/red. Base The Wyvern Shipping Co, Linslade, GU. 00439
AMETHYST 51012
AMETHYST 52968
AMETHYST 60426
AMETHYST 75173
AMIE EM 77324
AMIK 45459 M21974 Grp trailable Nb 23′ red/grn. B: 1990 Wilderness Beaver, self f/o. Honda 9.9 4 stroke ob. Based Tonbridge, R.Medway. Picture of beaver on sides. 21216
AMINGTON Flat 16m BW-CATM
A-MIRAGE 093610 Caraboat. Grp cruiser hull, caravan type top 4.87m, b 2.7m wh/yel. B: 1970 Caraboat Ltd. Honda 7.5hp ob. Base Venetian Marina Village in the Summer and at owners home in Winter. Boat makes people smile as the wheels remain visible when in water. Internal steering. 64 of the type were made between 1969-1973. Believe only 21 now left (not all afloat). 21275
AMITY 500438
AMMELENIA 52272
AMNESIA 77179
AMOR 51614
AMORICA 67531
AMOS NbTug 60′ grey
AMOS Barney(9) 1971 32′
AMPSON AQUA 70269
AMSTERDAM 500335
AMY 49727
AMY 53176
AMY 61889
AMY 68448
AMY 82977
AMY CLAIRE 49994
AMY EM 77324 NbC 50′ grn/red. B: 1981 Ken Cordell, Whixall. BMC 1500. Base Aynho Wharf. Built as project after owner's wife died. Originally Mary Caroline, then Lucy. Present name since 1993. Mooring bitts said to be off L&L short boat. Art deco style female heads on cabin sides. 23660
AMY LILIAN 49491
AMY THE PUP 77822
ANAGRAM 500899
ANASTASIA 52152 MACCLESFIELD NbT 45′ mar/Donegal grn. B: shell 1989 Mike Gration Greentour Ltd., f/o by owner and launched 1992. Russell Newbery DM1 1930s design single cylinder 9hp. Base Macclesfield Canal. 21299
ANA XENIA 73938
ANCHILLA 47925
ANCHOR 76656
ANCHORS AWAY 64212
ANDANTE 76211 NANTWICH NbT 40′ Oxford blue/wh. B: 1982 Canal Transport Services

(Denis Cooper), Norton Canes. Thornycroft BMC 1.5, PRM gbox. Base Nantwich. 20129
ANDANTE 45571 SSR 37609 CLEVELAND Grp trail boat 7m coffee/crm. B: hull 1987 Wilderness Beaver, owner f/o completed 1989. Petrol ob. Trailed. Won "Best boat trailed to rally" IWA Glascon 1989; "Best ob powered boat" - IWA Waltham Abbey 1989; fit-out featured in *Waterways World* 1989; cruises French canals every Summer. 21364
ANDANTE 74004 F C & E J WRIGHT BETWEEN BRIDGE 88 & 89 GU NbT 47' brown/cr. B: 1989 R&D Fabrications. Mitsubishi 4 cyl; Thornycroft marinisation. Base Milton Keynes Marina. 23599
ANDANTE 54112 WARWICK NbST 55' grn/mar. B: 1994 Colecraft, f/o Kate Boats. Kubota BV1905. Base Kate Boats, Warwick. 21318
ANDANTE *NbC 40' wh/blue*
ANDANTE *50' blue*
ANDANTE 46261
ANDANTE 47839
ANDANTE 51649
ANDANTE 60477
ANDANTE 61915
ANDANTE 67080
ANDANTE 69743
ANDANTE 79413
ANDANTE 94278
ANDANTE B1035
ANDANTINO 49284 NbST/C 54'9" dk blue/burgundy. B: 1990 J. Paling trading as "Ironstone". Perkins 4108 4 cyl (1.76litre). Base Trent Lock area. 23658
ANDANTINO 51958
ANDARI 63444
ANDELAINE 46920
ANDERTON 66118
ANDIAN HAZELNUT 66124
ANDORA 46815
ANDRABEC *60063 NbC 30' grn/red*
ANDREA-C 102691
ANDREBEC 60063
ANDRELEIGH 51073
ANDREW 50471

ANDREW N 71836
ANDRINA 69047 Twin Nb 59', b 13'7" blue. B: *right side* 1979 West Riding Boat Co, Wakefield; *left side* 1992 Ironworks, Nazeing, Essex. Base Southern wide system. Owner explains: right side has been owned since 1982. Retirement to be cruising in Europe - solution was a duplicate hull built and both fitted out as one boat. Enlarged side doors/hatches for access. Hulls bolt together and can be separated (1 hour) for maintenance, road transport and getting past jammed lock gates by moving the boat in two halves. 21315
ANDROMEDA 45870
ANDROMEDA 60295
ANDROMEDA 67745
ANDURIL No 96 - NORTON CANES. A M & J LARGE & CO. BIRMINGHAM NbT 70' blue/crm. Wooden superstructure. B: 1970/71 Malcolm Braine, Norton Canes. Mercedes OM 636 x2 hp. Base Nunn's Acre Boathouse, Goring on Thames. 22386
ANDY 68692
ANDY 95152
ANGARHAD 76887
ANGEL 211 Lg Woolwich Town Cl. butty. Ex GUCC/BW
ANGEL Barney(40) 70'
ANGELA 69918
ANGELA JANE 1 66783
ANGELA JANE 2 66786
ANGELEEN 75976
ANGELMIST 45360
ANGELO 52255
ANGELO 79221
ANGEL OF ISLINGTON 66646
ANGELUS *Dutch barge grn/red*
ANGLA *62062 NbC 50' grey/bl/yel*
ANGLIA 62062
ANGLO LEAKING 76669
ANGLO LISTING NbC 50' red/grn
ANGRY BULL 65650
ANGUS 104076
ANHINGA 48370
ANISE 500463

ASHBY NARROW BOATS
at THE ASHBY CANAL CENTRE

Boats are our business - they have been for nearly 25 years

Call in to our premises at bridge 26 and see how our reputation has been earned (by offering value for money with friendly service)

Boatbuilding*Repairs*Refits*Repaints*Blacking*Brokerage*Chandlery

**WILLOW PARK, STOKE GOLDING,
NUNEATON, WARKS CV13 6EU   TEL/FAX: 01455 212636**

ANITU 48279
ANJEU 48186
ANJOU 80297
ANKER Piling boat 12m BW-LAP
ANLUCE *Grp Wanderer 55 40' crm*
ANN 50058
ANNA 68877
ANNA 71659
ANNA B0234
ANNA DINN 52044
ANNA LAETITIA 68900
ANNA LEONE 76947
ANNA LISA 77418
ANNA MARIE 46286
ANNABELLE 46182
ANNABELLE 46367
ANNABELLE 48855
ANNABELLE 67739
ANNA OF THE FIVE TOWNS 72457
ANN BOLEYN 69299
ANNE 69867 River Cl motor. Ex BW
ANNE 68051
ANNE 76075
ANNE BOLEYN *NbT 60' blue*
ANNE BOLEYN 74764
ANNE BULLEN 66480
ANNE ELIZABETH 54402
ANNE HENSHALL 61751
ANNE-MARIE 50007 No 9 THE SHOEMAKE FAMILY LOCKSBOTTOM NbT 65' Dk grn/burgundy/ivory. Commissioned 1989: shell by John White, Liverpool; f/o Nigel Flynn Construction Ltd, Maidenhead; launched 1991. Lister-Petter STW/3 (last one installed in boat 1989). Based Bourne End Moorings, Berkhamsted. F/o is by a master carpenter/interior designer: solid oak panelling, full size bath, gold plated taps, washable white leather, hand glazed tiles, diesel generator, etc. 22407
ANNE MARIE 74236
ANNE PAGE 92734
ANNEKA 52123
ANNETTE 47671
ANNIE 31549
ANNIE 45141 B0269
ANNIE 47868
ANNIE 61653
ANNIE 75225
ANNIE 75503 THRUPP NbST 45' Oxford blue/red. B: 1987 Colecraft Engineering, owner f/o. Mitsubishi. Base Thrupp Wide, Oxford Canal. *Annie* was name shared by both owners' mothers. 22396
ANNIE 77687
ANNIE JO 77112
ANNIE LEAH 73493
ANNIE MAY 45694
ANNIE MAY 74100
ANNIE PAGE 52562
ANNIE ROSE *Trailboat*
ANNIE ROSE 31886
ANN MARIE 73233
ANN MARIE III 69150
ANNTON 47255

ANODYNE *NbT 70' red/grn*
ANODYNE 49444
ANONA B 50290
ANONDINE 76101
ANONIMITY 48641
A NONNY MOUSE 68532
ANOTHER COUNTRY 45849
ANOTHER GEM 52547
ANOTHER STINT 51749
ANOVA 68829
ANSON PARTIES AFLOAT BIRMINGHAM & MIDLAND CANAL CARRYING Co. No.1 "Admiral" class commercial Nb converted in 1972 by B & MCCCo. to 46 seater trip boat 70', b 7' coach grn/chrome yel. B: circa 1958 Isaac Pimblott & Co. Ltd, Northwich for British Transport Commission (Waterways). Armstrong-Siddeley AS2 twin cyl 20bhp. Base Birmingham Gas Street basin. Preserves much of exterior look, especially bow, engine room and stern. Hold now provides all-weather covered accommodation, bar, toilet, wired for sound. Normally cruises BCN and Northern Stratford canal. 034989
ANSON 47510
ANSON 62276
ANSTON 73516
ANSTRUTHER 45521
ANSWER 46623
ANSWER TWO 69973
ANT Mtce boat - flat, dumb BW-NW
ANT *see WASP*
ANTARTIC *(spelling as on boat)*. 71238 Ice boat
ANTARES 62396 DIGLIS NbT steel hull, wood superstructure 50' grn/red. B: 1972 Rugby Boatbuilders. Lister SR3. Base Diglis Basin, Worcester. Adventurous cruises have included crossing the Dee Weir at Chester and to Farndon; Manchester Ship canal - Ellesmere Port to Manchester; 2 return tidal passages of R.Severn - Sharpness/Bristol. 261056
ANTARES 62591
ANTARTIC 71238
ANTELOPE 1452
ANTELOPE 48721
ANTELOPE 65432 FMC FLEET NO 287 REGISTERED AT BIRMINGHAM 1452 BCN 978 Motor Narrow Fly boat - rivetted iron construction 71'6", b 7'1", d 2'6" navy/wh. B: 1923 W J Yarwoods. Bolinder 1052 2 cyl. Base Stone, T&M. Original Josher motor fly boat; owned FMC 1923-47, BWB 1948-54, Willow Wren CCC (as *Grebe*) 1954-80, Taylor family 1980-date.25954
ANTELOPE *Grp 30' wh/bl*
ANTOINETTE 62149
ANTOM 500440
ANTONIO 102595
ANTONS LUCK 92710
ANTRIADES III B1429
ANTURIO 71646
ANVAL G5687 Grp cruiser 27', b 9'6" white. Built 1974 Appleyard Lincoln, Ely; f/o Buckden Marina, Buckden, Huntingdon. Perkins 4108. Base Huntingdon Boathaven R.Ouse. 23562
ANYA 68843

ANYA 69972
AOLEUS 70463
APACHE 75779
APERATEETH 101069 *Grp 21'*
APHELION 51652
APHRODITE 64869
APHRODITE 79859   Nb - copy of butty 49' (originally 45') Forest grn/Wineberry. B: 1980 by Whittle Boats (new bow section by Stenson Boatbuilders 1995). Owner f/o. Yanmar 1.5. Base Swarkestone Boat Club T&M. One of small number built 1979/80 as a butty copy; all had rounded bows which tended to push water. New bow gives cleaner lines and makes it unique amongst those built. Forward galley enables view out while slaving over hot stove.   20143
APHRODITE IX 64818
APOLLO 065498 APOLLO CANAL CRUISES LTD. SHIPLEY WHARF   Trip/Waterbus. Iron/steel Nb motor. 57', b 7'2", d 3' grn/red. B: 1929 Crichtons Saltney Dock nr Chester for Midlands & Coast Company (rare example of this co's boats); 1936 converted to motor by Harris at Netherton; 1939 to Fellows, Morton & Clayton; 1946 to Ernest Thomas (Walsall) Ltd; 1951 shortened to 57' & re-named *DOT*; 1970? to M E Braine; 1971 converted by M E Braine (Pelsall) to trip boat for David Lowe (Apollo Canal Cruises). Lister HR W2M6R2 (1974).   01020
APOLLO   NbST. Hire. 60' dk grn/pale grn. B: & base Weltonfield Narrowboats.   00664
APOLLO 58 *Nb red/grn*
APPLE Motor.
APPLE 63348
APPLEBY 45933
APPLECROSS 62963
APPLEMINT 70739
APPOLLO 60086
APPOLLO 58 74737
APPY DAZE *NbT 50' grn*
APPY JACK 48927
APRIL 48200
APRIL DREAM 62036
APRIL ROSE 76467
APRIL STAR 61904
APSLEY   Motor boat 52'6" BW-OGU
AQUABELLE 60082
AQUA DANSEUR 30595
AQUALAINE 67668
AQUA PESKY 88655
AQUARELLE 75917
AQUARIGO 64468
AQUARIUS 47394
AQUARIUS 49640
AQUARIUS No 9 60088   Sm Woolwich Star Cl motor. Ex GUCC/BW
AQUARIUS 63305
AQUARIUS 78716
AQUARIUS 102104
AQUARIUS II 49432
AQUAROMA 64774
AQUA ROMA 74278
AQUARRA 72931
AQUATIC 45215

AQUAVELLA 62663
AQUAVISION 77855
AQUEDUCK 80396
AQUILA 48946
AQUILA 50614
ARA 68101   Sm Woolwich Star Cl butty. Ex GUCC/BW/WW
ARABELLA 63754
ARABELLA 73552
ARABESQUE 48796
ARABIA 340 Saltley Motor. Ex FMC/BW
ARABIAN NIGHTS 66763 Hire. Wide beam 45', b 10' grn/red. Lister. Base Evesham Marina, R.Avon.   0371027
ARAGORN 51427
ARAMANDA 45979
ARAMANDA 78306
ARAMANTUS 68464
ARAMAS 71180
ARAMIS 79639
ARAN 65552
ARATHORN 75370
ARAWAI 77224
ARBUTUS 67882
ARCADIA   NbST. Hire. 53' dk grn/pale grn. B: & base Weltonfield Narrowboats.   00663
ARCADIA 49369
ARCADIA 52363
ARCADIA 75271
ARCADY *NbC 60' grn*
ARCADY 65243
ARCARI 50347
ARCAS   Sm Woolwich Star Cl motor Ex GUCC BW-
ARCAS 83299
ARCHIBALD 62414
ARCHIDAMUS 52473
ARCHIMEDES 12 67024 Sm Woolwich Star Cl motor. Ex GUCC/BW
ARCHIMEDES 85118
ARCK 74859 Nb 50' grn/red. B: 1988 Springer. 1.5 BMC. Base Henwood Wharf, Solihull.   23554
ARCLID MV BW-NW
ARCTIC SKUA 51472
ARCTIC STAR B0793
ARCTIC TERN 49843
ARCTURUS Ricky Star Cl motor. Ex GUCC
ARCTURUS 100661
ARCTURUS *see SIRIUS*
ARDANZA *50718 NbT 55 Mar*
ARDEA *NbT 40' red/bl*
ARDEA 61764
ARDEN No 2 47524
ARDTGET 76036
AREADY 54583
ARFA-MO 49218
ARGANSA 50718
ARGEE BARGEE 66968
ARGEE BARGEE 70978
ARGO 214   Sm Woolwich Star Cl butty. Ex GUCC/BW/WW
ARGON BIRMINGHAM & MIDLAND CANAL CARRYING Co. No.2 "Star" class butty, composite (steel sides, elm bottom). Camping boat

What it's all about. Idyllic moorings, Shackerstone, Ashby canal

("Camping Afloat") 70′, b 7′. coach grn/chrome yel. B: circa 1935 Harland & Wolff Ltd. Woolwich for GUCCCo., adapted for camping 1977. Butty to *Collingwood.* Base Birmingham Gas Street basin. Starred in BBC TV "Canal Children" in 1976. Exterior preserves original look. Interior provides sleeping, cooking and living accommodation for up to 12 people "under canvas". Operates anywhere in system, incl. M.S.C. but mostly on long circuits of Midlands from B'ham.   034991
ARGUS 62336 Sm Woolwich Star Cl butty. Ex GUCC/BW/WW
ARGUS 50075
ARGUS 78871
ARGY BARGY 48582
ARGY BARGY 63954
ARGY BARGY 66154
ARIADNE 60384
ARIADNE 61195 Nb-centre w'house 43′ blue/white. B: 1978 David Parker, Penkridge. 1.5 BMC, hydraulic drive. Base Streethay Wharf, Coventry canal. Believed unique as other boats of this type are grp - this one is all steel with steel w'house canopy.   20114
ARIAL 78408
ARIEL 49552
ARIES Sm Ricky Star Cl. motor. Ex GUCC. Boat Museum
ARIES 48781
ARIES 48784
ARIES 60192
ARIES Barney(7) 1971 53′
ARISAIG 47088
ARISTOCAT 51201
ARISTOCRAT B1661

ARK 76199
ARK 81420
ARK ABE 45021
ARKADY Barney(5) 1970 45′
ARK MARINER 48589 B R KEMP NbC 55′ grn/red. B: 1990 Burden Blue Lias, f/o Blue Haven Marine. Base Braunston marina.   24837
ARK ROYAL 75783
ARKAROO 73659
ARKYD 30791
ARLEY Tug BW-NW
ARLEY 64881
ARMSWORTH 75987
ARNESS 102865
ARRIANADE 79483
ARROW Mtce boat 52′ BW-BBC
ARTEMIS 48805 NbT 55′ dk blue/red. B: 1990 TT Marine and Phoenix Narrowboats. Mitsubishi FMK. Base Welford. *Artemis* was Phoenix's exhibition boat in 1990 and featured on cover of Canal & Riverboat, Oct 1990.   20194
ARTEMIS 60604
ARTEMIS 73024 NbC 25′ blue/mar
ARTFUL OWL 50969
ARTHMARE Sea Otter 23′ grn
ARTHUR 72600
ARTHUR A BLAND Tug 10.67m
ARTHUR JOHN B 77763
ARTHUR VERDUN NbT 40′ blue/red
ARTICHOKE see OAK APPLE
ARTIFICER 48842
ARTYSANNE B1441
ARUNDEL 64615
ARWELL 66679
ARWEN 71073

22

ARWEN EVENSTAR 49720
ASCOT 104 63364 Lg Woolwich Town Cl motor. Ex GUCC/BW/WW
ASERET 50304
ASH No 3 69908
ASH BIRMINGHAM & MIDLAND CANAL CARRYING Co. No.4 "Tree" class butty, composite (steel sides, elm bottom). Camping boat ("Camping Afloat") 70', b 7'. coach grn/chrome yel. B: circa 1936 W J Yarwood & Co. Ltd. Northwich for Erewash Canal Carrying Co., adapted for camping 1978. Butty to *Yeoford.* Base Birmingham Gas Street basin. Interior provides sleeping, cooking and living accommodation for up to 12 people "under canvas". Operates anywhere in system but mostly on long circuits from Birmingham through Midlands. 034992
ASHANTI 50188
ASHBY 45872
ASHBY CASTLE 78538
ASHDOWNE 46151
ASHDOWN GIRL 50476
ASHLEA *NbC 45' blue/grey*
ASHLEY JACKSON 67199
ASHPERTON 72546
ASHRIDGE 73811
ASHTED 46055
ASHWELL 074327 G & A SMITH BLISWORTH NbT 62' blue/red. B: 1987 as 40'; lengthened to 50' in 1990 and to 62' in 1994; Colecraft, f/o by original owner and present owner on lengthening. Vetus M4. Base Gayton marina. 23596
ASHWOOD 69870
ASHWORTH 72291
ASKARI *see CLEOPATRA II*
ASKELADDEN 50913
ASLAN 49131 JEAN AND NEVILLE RILEY HATTON NbT. 45' blue. B: 1990 TT Marine. BMC 1.8 (Calcutt Marine). Base Grand Union, Hatton. Lion silhouette on cabin sides. 20119
ASLAN 47068 NbTug 45' red/grn. B: 1990 Eastwood Engineering, f/o previous owner. Petter B2 (1954). Base Southern GU. 24899
ASLAN 50749
ASLAN 70021
ASLAN 75120
ASLAND LASS 53684
ASMUND 51421
ASPEN 48735
ASPLEY 73904
ASPULL Iceboat. Boat Museum
ASPULL Tug BW-NW
ASTBURY 65490
ASTER 70041
ASTERIX 64186
ASTERIX 73917
ASTI 71376 EAST HADDON SAISONS Hire. NbT "Brum Tug" style 32' crm/grn. B: 1984 Brummagem Boats. Mitsubishi Vetus 3 cyl. Mounted in reverse direction with belt drive to prop. One of only 9 'Brum Tugs' in existence with belt drive and reversed engine saving cabin space. Base Welford. 009138

ASTLEY 78349
ASTON 51594
ASTON 62554
ASTON 78854
ASTON H ALL 71690
ASTRA 51985
ASTRAL ROVER OSPREY 502 Grp 19', b 6' wh/red. B: 1987 Wave Rider, Malden. Suzuki ob 25. Towed from home to Benson, R Thames. Osprey pictured on sides. 20142
ASTRID 53683
ATALANTA Sm Woolwich Star Cl butty. Ex GUCC
ATHELAS 89208
ATHELSTAN 72935
ATHENA 68960
ATHENA 71775
ATHENE NOCTUA 47009
ATHESIS *(Latin for R.Tees) NbT 50' mar/grn*
ATHESIS 74868
ATHOLL 54142
ATILLA 48060
ATLANTIC 71569
ATLAS Heritage craft 70' BW-BBC
AT LAST 100936
AT LAST B1419
AT LAST 64191 B1461
ATRED 75436
ATROPOS *NbT 45' blue*
ATRYBIAN 46837
AUBEPINE 65259
AUDACITY 69643
AUDENE 66365
AUDLEM MV BW-NW
AUDLEM PRIDE 53547
AUGUSTA 049498 No 172 LONGPORT WHARF NbT 62' red/grn. B: 1990 Stoke on Trent Boat Building Co Ltd. Russell Newbery. Base Cowroast marina. 21293
AUGUSTA 50662 NbC 30' blue/mar. B: 1991 Pat Buckle, Stibington. BMC 1.8L PRM g'box. Base Whilton marina. 23748
AUJON 70133
AUK MH82 80560 BW
AUKLAND 53017
AUKLAND 54018
AUNTIE BETTY II 52914
AUNT LUCY DARKEST PERU (plus pictures of Aunt Lucy). NbC 66', d 2'9" blue/wh. B: 1995 Mike Gration Greentour Ltd, f/o Dave Freeman, Lexden Swan Boat Services. MC42 by Duffields Marine. Base Pyrford Marina, Wey navigation. Decorative feature: the childrens character Paddington Bear was raised, according to the story, by his Aunt Lucy in Darkest Peru, who now lives in Home for Retired Bears in Lima. Pictures of Aunt Lucy are of an elderly lady bear dressed rather like the narrowboat working women of old but with a bowler hat too. 21310
AURIGA 53719 Sm Woolwich Star Cl motor. Ex GUCC/BW
AURORA 50587
AURORA 60128

AURORA 66107 NbC 40', b 7'2", d 18" grn/red. B: 1976 Simolda, owner f/o. Lister SP2. Base Robinsons Boat Yard Saville Town, Dewsbury. 23605
AURORA 71897
AURORA 73543
AURORA 79229
AURORA 85474
AURORA 96718
AURORA III 65861
AURORA Grp 30' wh
AUSTEND 30923
AUSTRALIA Commercial carrying working butty - forecabin boat - in livery as formerly operated under Captain Cargo Ltd. - red/grn/yel; iron composite construction. B: 1896 (believed correct) for Fellows Morton & Clayton Ltd. Base Coventry & GU canals. 031820
AUTOLYCUS 065833 NbT. 45' grn/red. B: 1979 Davison, Sawley. Leyland 1.5L. Base Midlands canals. 20100
AUTOLYCUS 67551
AUTUMN 67964
AUTUMN 71586
AUTUMN 75871
AUTUMN NbC 50' grn
AUTUMN BLISS 52120
AUTUMN GLORY 500405 DERBYSHIRE NbT 60' dk blue/mar. B: 1995 GT Boatbuilders, f/o Ian Nightingale and team at Nimbus Narrowboats. Greeves 27DM (Ruston Hornsby India Ltd) 2.5L 2 cyl 30hp, David Brown g'box 200M 2:1. Base Sawley Bridge marina. "First class fit-out". 25936
AUTUMN GOLD 79776
AUTUMN GOLD 80694
AUTUMN LEAVES 73794
AVALON 45737
AVALON 51451
AVALON 051707 NbT 58' Mercedes red/deep royal grn. B: 1992 Watercraft Boats Ltd. Perkins MC42. Base Gayton marina. Runner up for IWA 1992 Marion Munk Award for Best Boat. 23667
AVALON 51857
AVALON 61874
AVALON 63975
AVALON 64155
AVALON 64591
AVALON 65262
AVALON 67697
AVALON 74207
AVALON B1417
AVALON MIST 52669
AVANTI 52878
AVIMAR 76189
AVION 047433 NbC 40' dk blue/grey. B: 1989 Springer, self f/o 1990. 1800cc Thornycroft 4 cyl water cooled. Base High Line Yachting. F/o for pleasure use providing optimum use of space with 6 berths in 25 foot cabin. The name arose during a misunderstood phone call - should have been *Avalon* - but owner is pleased with the uniqueness of the "mistake". 251015
AVIS 60454 H WALKER FOXTON FELLOWS, MORTON & CLAYTON NbT conversion 70', d 3'4" grn/red. B: 1923 Yarwoods.

Climax. Base Foxton Boat Services. Ex FMC Motor (butty *Somerset*) used in northern fleet carrying dry goods from Liverpool to Birmingham. FMC No. 286, Reg. B'ham 1453. 22381
AVISTAR 69644
AVLA 52134
AVOCET 46300
AVOCET 63433
AVOCET 71245
AVOCET 75632
AVON Motor. Ex Mersey, Weaver & SCCCo./BW
AVON KENNET BOAT COMPANY NEWBURY Trip Boat. Wide Boat - Trad 70', b 11'6" red/grn. B: 1971/72 as purpose built passenger boat. 35hp Russell Newbery situated at extreme stern, separated from passenger accommodation by steel soundproof bulkhead. Base Newbury, K&A Canal. Bright and well painted side panels by the late Ian Lavendon of Newbury in traditional roses and castle design.
019455
AVON MV 16m BW-NE
AVON 62434
AVON 63952
AVON JUBILANT Powered general purpose work boat with cabin - commercial and navigation maintenance operated by Lower Avon Navigation Trust Ltd. 25', b 8' d 9"(unladen) blue. B: 1969 Seaborne Yacht Co, (boatbuilders) Kempsey, Worcester. Lister SR2 air cooled. Base Mill Wharf, Wyre Piddle, Lower Avon. Built on the instructions of C D Barwell at his expense for use by volunteers and others involved in maintenance of the navigation; ownership subsequently transferred to the Trust. 033908
AVON LASS 51379
AVON MIST 60431
AVON MIST 96299
AVON MONARCH 046131 Hire. NbT blue/red. BMC 1.5. Base Evesham Marina, R.Avon. 0371038
AVON SAPPHIRE 045961 Hire. NbC 50' grn/red. BMC 1.8. Base Evesham Marina, R.Avon. 0371034
AVON SWALLOW 066840 Hire. NbC 46' grn/red. BMC 1.5. Base Evesham Marina. 0371037
AVRINA 46778
AWANDRA 61314
AWAYAWHILE 60118
AWE Butty. Ex BW
AXE River Cl butty. Ex BW
AXE Hopper 21m BW-LAP
AYLESBURY BW-LON
AYLESBURY MERGANSER 60285
AYNHO 80616 Lg Woolwich Town Cl motor. BW-LON
AYR Lg Woolwich Town Cl butty. Ex GUCC/BW
AYR 54949
AZALIA 52614
AZANUTE 63191
AZOLLA 45303
AZURINA 61420
AZZURO 45550

B

An enemy target, a floating classroom, Royal connections, lots of Bantams, the world's oldest mud dragger, moving at a snail's pace, George's modesty screen, some fishy tales and a "double" blind date.

BAALBECK 68039
BABS 50877
BACARDI BLUES 73744
BACCHANALIA 61668
BACCHUS 48164
BACCHUS 67279
BACKWATER 77381 CAVERSHAM NbC 59'4" grn/red. B: 1982 Calcutt Boats. BMC 1.5. Originally *Wild Burdock* then *Jamyjosipipe*. 24879
BACOPA 61525
BACUP Wb motor. Boat Museum
BADACHRO 76325
BADGER 288 72505 Yarwoods motor. Ex FMC/BW
BADGER 60240 SILEBY MILL NbST 40' 2-tone blue. B: 1978-80 Sileby Boats; self-f/o. Lister SR2 2-cyl air cooled. Base Sileby Mill. Following f/o *Badger* was featured in *The Squire* magazine which remarked on the one-third of a mile of tongued-and-grooved timber 200 yards of electric cable, etc. 23755
BADGER 60126 P&S WRIGLEY & CO. REGENTS PARK NbT/ST 46' grn/magenta. B: 1980 Davison Bros on a Sager hull, Andy Burnett design. Base Sawley Bridge marina. 22478
BADGER 45331 MARPLE BADGER BOATS Hire. NbT 45' Oxford blue/grey. B: 1989 Warble Boat Builders on Colecraft hull. BL 1.8/ Thornycroft. Base Macclesfield Canal. Originally private use, now hirers benefit from high specification: drop cratch forming table, solar vents/battery charging, etc. 017342
BADGER 65330
BADGER 70582
BADGER 71982
BADGER 73151
BADGER 76585
BADGER 77025
BADGER 77522
BADGER 78280
BADGER 2 69289
BADGER II 63925
BADGER Dredger hydraulic 45' BW-NW
BAD JACK *73949 NbC 25' crm*
BADMOR 76330
BADSEY 68474 Lg Woolwich Town Cl motor. Ex GUCC/BW/WW
BAFA Barney(4) 1970 48'
BAGGERMAN VAN DEVA 79025
BAGGINS 80653
BAHT-AT 86219
BAILDON 64074
BAINTON 69769 SOUTHERN AND GENERAL PACKET BOAT CO. (original pair with *Berkhamsted*). Hire - camping. NbT working boat motor - Large Woolwich 71'6" dk grn/red. B: 1936 Harland & Wolff. Lister HB3. Base GUC Midlands. *Bainton's* history includes being sunk at Paddington Stop and being shot at by German fighters during the war. Has original wooden cabin frames, outer skin has been replaced. Refer *The George and the Mary* - Alan Faulkner. 23593
BAKERS DOZEN 53186
BAKEWELL 70258
BALA 89070 MV BW-NW
BALDOCK Lg Woolwich Town Cl motor. Ex GUCC/BW/WW
BALADOR 70718
BALCLUTHA 78747
BALDOCK 532
BALDRICK 47585
BALDRICK 66072
BALHAM 69838 Lg Woolwich Town Cl butty. Ex GUCC/BW/WW
BALLADORE 103187
BALLARD 52880
BALLOONS 60989
BALMORAL CASTLE 62097
BALOO *60460 NbC 30' grn/yel*
BALOO 74625
BALOO *NbT 40' blue*
BALOO TOO 65824 Residential. NbC 45' mar/grn. B: 1975 Springer/Bromsgrove Boatbuilders, Hanbury Wharf. Lister ST2. Base Droitwich Boat Centre, Hanbury Wharf. Former floating class room at Upland School, Worcester. Unusual forward roof hatch. 23584
BALTIC Ice breaker. Ex BCN
BALUNGA 64947

To be swallowed up by lift bridge, South Oxford canal

BAMBA 103595
BAMBI 79031
BANANAFISH 46079
BANBROOK 60645
BANBURY Lg Woolwich Town Cl butty. Ex GUCC/BW/WW
BANCROFT 50629
BANDIT 76400
BANDIT Barney(16) 1972 32'
BANGLE 79267
BANJAKA 94454
BANJANKA 79340
BANJER 85617 Narrow beam cruiser - plywood construction 18' crm/brown (almost GWR colours!) B: 1973 by present owners to plans of *Sea Tony* by Boat Plans of Poole, Dorset. Hull as designed but owners' cabin layout. Honda 9.9ob. Base NW canals. 22387
BANJO BOY 79584
BANROMA 84778
BANTAM II Tug. Boat Museum
BANTAM IV 71878 Bantam Pusher Tug 21', b 8'9", d 3'6" red/grn. B: 1949/50 E C Jones & Son, Brentford, Middx. Lister JP2 21bhp (original, with hand starting). Base as operational exhibit at London Canal Museum, Battlebridge Basin, Regent's canal. Fourth of 91 Bantam tugs built. Worked many years on gravel pits in Kent, Surrey. Restored by Chris Gibson for 10 years work on the Bristol Avon (cabin extended) and then donated by him to the Museum in 1994. Had to be transported to London partly by road because K&A not deep enough. Museum Trust received Transport Trust Prize in 1995 for restoration project. 0361014

BARBARA JOAN B0402
BARBARA MAY 61287
BARBARA MICHELLE 67686
BARBARA ROSE 52210
BARBARA ROSE N4296
BARBARELLA Grp bl/wh
BARBE 100630
BARBEL 64742
BARBEQUE 52357
BARBRA ANNE 77846
BARBU II 20130 Freeman 22 Grp cruiser. 22', b 7'2" wh/blue. B: 1969 John Freeman, Leics. Watermota based on 105E Ford Anglia 1100cc cross-flow engine. Base Guildford, R.Wey. Name from the Latin Barbus - fish. Mahogany veneers used all come from one log - every Freeman's woodwork is therefore unique. 20130
BARBY NbC 40' blue/grey
BARBY ROSE 75050
BARDOLPH 500370
BARGUS 60134
BARLEYCORN 46626
BARLEYCORN 65530
BARLEY FLY 67599 NbT red/grn
BARMERE Workboat dumb barge 72', b 14'6", d 5' bl. B: 1948 Yarwood's, Northwich. Base as exhibit, canal side, Sankey canal, St. Helens. First post war dumb barge of steel built for Manchester Ship Canal Co. to carry grain for Kellogs factory on Bridgewater canal at Stretford. Ceased working in 1974. 261070
BARMOUTH 65024
BARMY DAZE 104462
BARNABY 52635

Tug boat Bantam IV
[courtesy London Canal Museum

BANTAM Tug BW-NW
BANTAM 67 80098 Tug 4.9m BW-
BANYAN 70415
BANYANDAH 92759
BARBARA Seamaster cruiser. 20' wh/dk blue. B: about 1976 Peter White CBS, Frys Island, Reading. Base there. "Rescued as a sorry sight from the mud by present owner and both given new lease of life! Has since starred in a film role at Benson Marina". 21316
BARBARA 45833

BARNABY 73748
BARNABY 77187
BARNABY Grp 21'
BARNACLE BILL 49602
BARNES Lg Woolwich Town Cl butty. Ex GUCC/BW/WW
BARNES WALLIS 79100
BARNET Lg Woolwich Town Cl motor. Ex GUCC/BW
BARNEY 74889
BARNEY 77709

BARNHAM Lg Woolwich Town Cl motor. Ex GUCC/BW
BARN OWL 74838
BAR'N'OWL 49338
BARON 47295
BARON 66428
BARON *97589 Grp 18' blue/wh*
BAROS 50880
BAROSSA 53595 BAROSSA EMSWORTH NbC 48' mar/mid-blue. B: 1994 Colecraft, f/o Oxford Canal Boat Co. Beta Marine Kubota V1305. Base Willowtree marina GU (Paddington Arm). 23536
BARRACUDA 51578
BARRACUDA 63916
BARRACUDA 93407
BARROW Lg Woolwich Town Cl motor. Ex GUCC/BW
BARROW 12570
BART 500201 Wm OLDFIELD & Co COAL & LIME CARRIERS RIDDLESDEN WHARF Nb 58'6", d 2'6" grn. B: 1996, Roger Fuller, Five Towns Boat Building, f/o 1997 by owner. Ruston & Hornsby 3YC built 1993 - recovered from RB22 crane; Parsons 2:1 gearbox (1955) added. Base Granby Bridge, L&L. Boatman's cabin/engine room colour scheme based on Samuel Barlow Co Ltd. Paintwork Phil Speight. 261072
BARTHOLEMEW Crane boat 27.43m BW-NE
BARTOLEMEW DIAZ 71622
BARVIC PRINCE 50536
BASFORD 74762
BASILISK 47555
BASLOW 53088 A P & M I CLARKE HIGHER POYNTON MACCLESFIELD CANAL NbT 60' Dk grn/crm. B: 1993 GT Boats, Stafford (GT hull no. 57), f/o by owners ongoing. Perkins MC42. Base Marineville, Higher Poynton. 21294
BASRA 62509
BASSET 45862
BASUTO Clyde Puffer. Boat Museum
BATELEUR 46188
BATH 77743 Lg Woolwich Town Cl motor. Ex GUCC
BATHSHEEBA 62158
BAVIANDA 97985
BAYLEYDALE 54727
BAYLEYS MEADOW 45393
BAYLINER 50816
BAYWOOD 45027
BAZMART 80087
BB 82623
BBIT 51140
BEACHCOMBER 73462
BEACHLEY 55m BW-LON
BEACON 64062
BEACON 66745
BEAD 45306
BEAGLE 73554
BEAGLE 77238
BEAL MV 14.95m BW-NE
BEAM 46844
BEATRICE 49771
BEATRICE 50268

BEATRICE 101013
BEATTY 51196
BEATTY 60147
BEAU 70660
BEAU BRUMMEL 61939
BEAUFIGHTER II 68394
BEAUJOLAIS 72910
BEAUJOLAIS 72919
BEAULIEU 114
BEAULIEU 64479 Lg Woolwich Town Cl motor. Ex GUCC/BW/WW
BEAUMANOR 53543 NbT 54' dk blue/red stripe. B: 1993 Delph Marine, Birmingham, f/o by first owner. Perkins 4.108. Base Linslade, GU. Counter has welded "rope" pattern around it. 251003
BEAUMARIS CASTLE Hire. NbC 45' grn/yel. Electric propulsion. Base Castle Narrowboats, Gilwern. 00216
BEAUT 62798
BEAVER 52985
BEAVER 62637
BEAVER 72711
BEAVER 79573
BEAVER Dredger 43' BW-BBC
BEAVER *NbST 30' grn/red*
BEAVER-LEA Barney(29) 35'
BECKWOOD No 32 61409
BECKY 47467
BECKY 69597
BECKY ADDY 73774
BECKY DAWN 49849
BECRISMARSH 50774
BEDDINGTON BELLE *Nb centre cockpit grn*
BEDE 49244
BEDWORTH Lg Woolwich Town Cl butty. Ex GUCC/BW
BEE 48431
BEE *NbC 50' blue/yel*
BEECH Commercial carrying working motor in livery as formerly operated under Captain Cargo Ltd. - red/grn/yel; wooden construction. B: 1935 for Fellows, Morton & Clayton Ltd. Not currently in service. Base Coventry & GU canals. 031818
BEECH Tug 18' BW-BBC
BEECH 40113
BEECH 68301
BEECH 69909
BEECHCRAFT 54759
BEEFOR 51219
BEEJAY 102010
BEERSTALKER 52182
BEESTON Boat Museum
BEEZ TWO 61958
BEIDERBECKE 47736
BE-KALMER II 61526
BEKDALE H 71598
BELFAST 115 70032
BELGIAN CRUSADER 74739
BELGIUM 107 72736
BELINDA B 86185
BELLA 68524
BELLA II B0279
BELLA AMI 102306
BELLADONNA 66114

27

BELLAFLORS 67267
BELLANCA 68618
BELLATRIX 68363 Sm Northwich Star Cl motor. Ex GUCC/ Wulfruna Coal Co.
BELL BIRD 48560
BELLETTE Dolphin. Grp/wood centre cockpit cruiser 24' lt blue/wh. B: 1974 Brooklands Marine. Honda B100 4-stroke ob. Base Bossoms Boatyard, Binsey, R.Thames 21296
BELLWETHER 66753 CALCUTT NbC 57' Donegal grn/coral red. B: 1979 by Fernie 49'. Refit by Brummagem Boats 1984. Lengthened at bow in 1990 by Dave Thomas at Braunston. DIY fit-out of enlarged cabin 1991. 1.5L BL. Base Calcutt. Operated for hire with sister boat *Isabella* by Tillerman Boats, Upton-on-Severn 1979/80 then both sold. Original name not known but previous name was *La Valeur* when owned by a Birmingham publican. During idle period in Birmingham *Bellwether* sank while taking on water - hence 1984 re-fit. 21217
BELLWOOD 64205
BELMONT Butty in original but currently decayed condition awaiting restoration and proper display in "canal" setting during next few years by Leicestershire Museums Service at Snibston Discovery Park, Coalville. *Belmont* worked the Ashby, Fazeley, Coventry and GU canals. B: 1936 for GUCCCo., regd. at Brentford. Then, via BWB to Blue Line Carriers Ltd. in 1968. In

Belmont at Snibston Discovery Park, Coalville awaiting display in "canal" setting. Winding gear in background

1969 made last working journey with coal from Leics./Warwicks. coalfield to the jam 'ole in London. Stated at the time to be last narrowboat to carry a commercial load of coal and as such was well documented by BWB and canal media who photographed the journey. Thus featured on many post and Christmas cards in 1970s. *Belmont* has a very important local feature in the cabin - a 'modesty screen' is still present. This legal requirement for boat families came about as a result of the pioneering work by George Smith of Coalville who pushed through social reforms for boat people in the 1870s. 251000

BELMONT B1050
BEN 46425
BEN 64315
BEN 69086
BEN 69130 Nb unconverted BCN full length motor (unusual as mostly used tugs). 70', b 7', d 2'9" red/grn. B: 1934 Harris Brothers of Bumblehole. Lister CE 2 cyl. 16hp at 1200rpm (engine built 1938). Base GU canal. Originally cargo carrying boat for the Talbot Garage Company (Kidderminster) Limited, carrying coal for the carpet trade on the Staffs & Worcs canal. Subsequently worked for T&S Elements until late 1960s and would have pulled one or more "joeys". Converted for residential use late 1960's. Various owners. Present owner carrying out significant repair and restoration work to engine and hull. Small fore cabin built 1993. New back cabin built 1994, currently being fitted out. 23581
BEN 74226
BEN 74493
BEN 78158
BEN ANIA 74756
BEN GUNN 75421
BENA-RHIAMBA 79039
BENBOW 79711
BENEDICTA 69923
BENJAMIN 48124
BENSON II 53000
BENTLEY 52741
BENTLEY HOXTON 50403
BENTRUMAN 54364
BEOWULF 47756 No. 2 RAY MAYNARD HOLLOW HILL WHARF NbT 59'8" burnt coffee/ merchant fawn. B: 1991 Colecraft. Russell Newbery DM2 water cooled 18hp at 1000rpm. Base The Boatyard, Iver, Slough Arm, GU. 25923
BERD 47584
BERENGARIA 46560 SSR 49409 CAMBRIDGE CHARLES AND 'RONNIE' BOOTLE NbC 49' grn/ crm. B: 1989 P Buckle. 1.8 BL. Base Stibbington and overseas (eg Belgium). Sliding roof over saloon, moped carrier with 2 'drawbridge' ramps astern of taffrail. Much travelled - almost whole of UK connected system, then to continent in 1993 for Netherlands, Belgium and France, to date. 24843
BERGEN FJORD 51478
BERKELEY 74621
BERKHAMSTED 79376 SOUTHERN & GENERAL PACKET BOAT CO. (original pair with *Bainton*). Hire - camping. NbT working butty - Large Woolwich 71'6" dk grn/red. B: 1936 Harland & Wolff. Used for demolition of Long Itchington road bridge. Extended steel cabin replaced original extended wooden cabin. Also see *Bainton*. 23594

BERKLEY 71649
BERKSWELL Motorboat 12m BW-LAP
BERMONDSEY ROWES 45965
BERNADETTE 48808
BERRY BO 54032
BERTHA Iron drag boat designed by I.K.Brunel - the world's oldest working mechanically propelled steam boat used for dragging mud out of Bridgwater Docks. 54', b 14', d 2'6" black. B: 1844 Lunel of Bristol. Coal fired single cylinder steam. Exhibited Exeter Maritime Museum. 21244
BERTI *Grp 15' wh/blue*
BERTIE 100502
BERTIE No 4 49420
BERTIE WILLOWS *NbC 40' red/grn*
BERWICK 67121 NbC Grp top on steel hull 48' red/grn. B: 1975 C Marshal, owner f/o. SR3. Base L&L canal. 24783
BERWYN 49773
BERWYN 67712
BESORAH 54036
BESS 54459
BESS 77940
BESSIE B 53916
BESSIE B 54344
BETA *Nb 22'*
BETA 47875
BETARIG 68327
BETELGEUSE
BETH 70354
BETHAN 50845
BETHANY 52156
BETHANY 88861
BETHSAIDA 74162
BETJEMAN 49632
BETJEMIN *NbT 55' grn/red*
BETLEY 63371
BETRA 69977
BETSY 96253
BETTY 45696
BETTY 48350
BETTY 74809
BETTY B B0211
BETTY D 50222
BETTY ELLEN 75828
BETTY-JEAN 45916
BETTY JOHN B1475
BEULA-ELLEN 51854
BEULIEU 64479
BEVAN 78966
BEVAN *Gipsy 35*
BEVERLEY Lg Woolwich Town Cl butty. Ex GUCC/BW/WW
BEVERLEY 72646
BEVERLEY 74222
BEVERLY 49124
BEVERLY JANE 51032
BEWARE B0350

BEWICK SWAN 63093
BEWITCHED 045952 Hire. NbC 30' grn/red. BMC 1.5. Base Evesham Marina, R.Avon. 0371053
BEXFORD 73263
BEXHILL 70245 Lg Woolwich Town Cl motor. Ex GUCC/BW/UCC. *see* BRIGHTON
BEYOND 60168 Cabin cruiser - mahogany construction on oak frame 25'. B: 1966 J H Taylor, Chester. Volvo 3cyl. Base North Cheshire Cruising Club. Awarded IWA Burgee at Marple National Rally 1966 for best boat at 25'. 23588
B-FOUR 79586
BHAGA CHAL 52764
BICESTER 68903
BICESTER Lg Woolwich Town Cl motor. Ex GUCC/BW/WW
BIDEFORD Lg Woolwich Town Cl butty. Ex GUCC/BW/WW
BIENVENUE 46932
BIG JAX 73593
BIGMERE Wb unpowered. Boat Museum
BIG PENNY *NbC 50' blue*
BIG SHILLING 74623
BIG TITCH 54973
BIGAMIST 79136
BIGIFF 64734
BILANDO 67456
BILBO 45176
BILBO B 82494
BILBO BAGGINS 45848
BILBO BAGGINS 46934
BILBO BAGGINS 68913
BILBO BAGGINS B1670
BILKO 61096
BILL 45718
BILLIE *NbC stern wheelhouse 40' grn/red*
BILLIE 48303
BILL O'TOMS 50897
BILL ROY 67026
BILSTER 79448 Lg Woolwich Town Cl butty. Ex GUCC/BW/WW
BINGLEY Lg Woolwich Town Cl butty. Ex GUCC/BW/WW
BINGLEY 87431 MV BW-NW
BINNENSCHIP 45583
BINSEY 45400
BIRCH Tug 19'6" BW-OGU
BIRCH 67841
BIRCHILLS Joey. Ex E Thomas
BIRCHILLS No 2 Tug. Boat Museum
BIRD ISLAND Flat 11m BW-
BIRD OF DANCING 70515
BIRD OF DAWNING *NbC 40' grn/yel*
BIRDSWOOD *Trip boat, Froghall, Caldon canal*
BIRMINGHAM 121 Lg Woolwich Town Cl motor. Ex GUCC/BW. *see BISON*
BIRTHDAY GIRL 46061
BISCAYNE BAY 46436
BISON 60171 NbT 71', b 7', d 3' blue. B: 1923 W J Yarwood & Sons, Northwich for FM & C; framing for new superstructure by W H Walker Bros, Rickmansworth; converted to residential use in 1956. 2 cyl National (originally installed in GUCCCo *Birmingham*). Base Briar Cottage moorings, Lapworth. 24880
BISON 71570
BITTELL No 5 52495 Tug
BITTERN 63068
BITTERN 73347
BITTERN 75164
BITTERN Saltley motor. Ex FMC/BW/WW
BITTERN 89064 Tug BW-NW
BITZA B0837
BLABY Motor boat 37'11" BW-OGU
BLACK ADDER 74720
BLACK BEETLE Grp "Carribean" type cruiser 32', b 12' pale grn/bl hull. B: 1978 Alpha Craft, Brundall, Norfolk. 1.5 BMC. Base Benson, Oxon. Features wheelhouse/saloon with sliding canopy, armchairs, etc. 21249
BLACKBERRY WAY 54495 NbC 26' midnight blue. B: 1993 Springer. 1.5hp Honda - petrol. Base Gayton marina. 23557
BLACK BESS 54293
BLACKBIRD 64249
BLACKBIRD 67270
BLACKBIRD 78124
BLACK BRYONY 53200
BLACK CAT 61786
BLACK COUNTRY 500325
BLACKCOUNTRYMAN 74380
BLACKDEN GEM No.14 *NbT 50' red/grn*
BLACK DOG 60014
BLACKDOWN 75778
BLACK LABRADOR 45649
BLACK OPAL 64196
BLACK PIG 46102
BLACK PIG 46774
BLACK PIG 48216
BLACK PIG 52170
BLACK PIG 62056
BLACK PIG 69504
BLACK PIGLET 70374
BLACK PRINCE 75693
BLACK ROPE 66782
BLACK SEBASTIAN B0028
BLACK STORK 45941
BLACK SWAN 51241
BLACK SWAN 52751
BLACK SWAN 73147 JANET & DAVID STEVENSON SHARDLOW NbST 38' grn/bl. B: 1985 Springer, various fit-outs since. Leyland/BMC 1500. Base Langley Mill. Extensive cruising includes tideways, including Severn Estuary. 204
BLACK SWAN *NbC 30' red/blue*
BLACKTHORN *NbC 55' crm/blue*
BLACKTHORN 62552
BLACKTHORN 77738
BLAIR ATHOLL 75209
BLAISE 46404
BLAKE 73062
BLASTED FIRS 46946
BLEASDALE 73343
BLESSED 52080
BLESSLEA 46433
BLETCHLEY 61888 Lg Woolwich Town Cl motor. Ex GUCC/BW/WW

BLETCHYNDEN 68934
BLEW 1 45921
BLEW OVER 53345
BLIMEY 74640
BLIND DATE 2 054502 NbC 37'6" blue/bl. B: 1995 Mick Sivewright, Barbridge. Vetus 3 cyl 22hp. Base Marineville, Macclesfield canal. Heating by diesel stove. "Met on blind date, 10 years ago - hence name of boat; very happy with both". 25972
BLISS 50224
BLISS 77414
BLISS 103940
BLISS *NbT 60'*
BLISWORTH 76346
BLISWORTH 83895
BLISWORTH Motorboat 12m BW-LAP
BLOSSOM 65393 HINCKLEY AWCC - HINCKLEY BOAT CLUB - ASHBY CANAL ASSOCIATION NbC 35' red/grn. B: 1981 Springer. Yanmar 15hp twin. Base Hinckley Boat Club, Ashby Canal. 23646
BLOSSOM 47799 NbT 47' royal blue/lt blue. B: 1990 Stoke on Trent Boat Building Co Ltd. Thornycroft BMC 1.5. Base Fradley Junction. Nice unusual signwriting of name. 20154
BLOSSOM *79960 NbTug*
BLOSSOM 67109
BLOSSOM 72002
BLOSSOM 93767
BLUE BARBECUE 53658
BLUE BARROW 53221
BLUE BARROW 61172
BLUE BASS 60326
BLUE BAYOU 75484
BLUEBEARD 66350
BLUEBELL 49120
BLUEBELL 50128
BLUEBELL 52067
BLUEBELL *54323 NbT blue*
BLUEBELL 64706
BLUEBELL 67546
BLUEBELL 72877 NbT 47' blue/gold. B: 1986 Peter Nicholls, Napton. 1.5 BMC. Base Stoke Prior, Worcs. & Birmingham Canal. 22449
BLUEBELL 74040
BLUEBELL 74513
BLUEBELL 75269
BLUEBELL 75502
BLUEBELL 75559
BLUEBELL 79193
BLUEBELL II 50056
BLUEBELL Hire. NbC 40' blue/red. Base The Wyvern Shipping Co, Linslade, GU 00457
BLUEBELLE *NbT 55' blue/grey*
BLUE BELLE 45283
BLUE BELLE B0321
BLUEBELLS 50198
BLUEBERRY & CREAM 102308
BLUE BIRDS 71946
BLUECROSS 60346
BLUE CRYSTAL 051480 Hire. NbC 54' grn/red. BMC 1.8. Base Evesham Marina, R.Avon. 0371050
BLUE CRYSTAL 64992

BLUE DOLPHIN 61970
BLUE DOLPHIN 62687
BLUE ELEGANCE 62751
BLUE FISH 84603
BLUE FLAME 73287
BLUE FOX 61807
BLUE HALL 62921
BLUE HAYWOOD 54373
BLUE HAZE 75842
BLUE HAZE 95198
BLUE HORIZON 62631
BLUE ICE CREAM 51798
BLUE-JAY 76786
BLUE LADY 31581
BLUE LAGOON 76496
BLUE LAGOON 85636
BLUE MERLE 62342
BLUE MINK 61723
BLUE MINT 54775
BLUE MIST 31375
BLUE MIST 50062
BLUE MIST 104810
BLUE MOON 45959
BLUE MOON 49732
BLUE MOON 50320
BLUE MOON 78659
BLUE MOON 79897
BLUE MOON 97166
BLUE MOON B7965
BLUE NUN CORONET CANAL CARRYING CO. Hire. NbT 50' navy blue/crm. B: 1935 Harland & Wolff Little Woolwich iron butty; rebuilt 1996 by Industry Narrowboats to shape of Little Woolwich motor, with steel cabin and windows under clothed up front end. Ruston & Hornsby 2VSH (approx 1950 vintage). Base Welford. 0091060
BLUE OTTA 64801
BLUE PEARL 70717
BLUE PETER B0372
BLUE ROSE 75832
BLUE SEN II 73603
BLUE SHIREE 79324
BLUES IN THE NIGHT 51897
BLUE SKIES 76534
BLUESKY 66367
BLUE SPIRIT 52698
BLUE STAR 66462
BLUETHROAT 52388
BLUETIT 77316
BLUE VOLE 79161
BLUEYES *Cruiser 25'*
BLUE YONDER 500936
BLYTHE 81701 Piling boat 12m BW-LAP
BLYTH SPIRIT 60248
BOADICEA 49405
BOADICEA 6892
BOAT MATE 53376
BOAZ B0510
BOBBIES 68015
BOBBIN IV 91153
BOBBLES *Trailboat*
BOBBY ELLEN 72950
BOBBY OWLER *see PIRAAT*

BOBBYS GIRL 87670
BOBBYS GIRL 104290
BOBCAT *NbT grn/red*
BOB CAT 71769
BOBCAT 75659
BOB MAJOR 53303 *NbT mar/blue 45'*
BOBS DREAM *NbC 60' red/blue*
BOBTAIL 68779
BOBTAIL PRIDE 75077
BODEN 53252
BODGER 52583
BODGER 66716
BODGER 78111
BODGE TOO 48220
BODKIN 101006
BODVAR 72685
BO-JANGLES 62076
BOLERO *NbC 30' grn/red*
BOLERO 45112
BOLINAS 53532
BOLLIN 89243 MV 11.5m BW-NE
BONELLIS EAGLE 50156
BONNIE 69806
BONNIE & CLYDE 67961
BONNIE DAY 61708
BONNIE LADY B1634
BONNIE LASS 53907
BONNIE PRINCE 102853
BONOMY 101667
BOOJUM 52421 NbT 53'3" grn. B: 1992 Canal Craft shell, f/o by Larose Narrowboats Rochdale. Perkins MC42. Base Ashby Canal 21219
BOOMBRAT 66135
BOOMERANG 46122
BOOTES 60207
BOOTS 74424
BORDER LAD 70159
BORDER ROSE 74280
BORDESLEY Lg Woolwich Town Class butty. Ex GUCC/BW
BOREAS 45206
BORIS 97502
BORN FREE 51766
BOSK 66674
BOSLEY 53708
BOSLEY 87443 Tug BW-NW
BOSOBEL 62337
BOSSY BOOTS 52250
BOSSY LADY 53909
BOSUN 65879
BOSUN BELLE 2 64857
BOSWELL MV 11.5m BW-NE
BOSWORTH 46895
BOSWORTH 51646
BOSWORTH *NbT 55' blue*
BOUGHBREAK 70669
BOUGHTON 68918 NbC 45' grn/red. B: 1975/6 Rugby Boatbuilders. 1.5 BMC. Base Enslow, Oxford Canal. The name is believed to refer to "Boughton Engineering" who built steel shells under subcontract to Rugby Boatbuilders. 21359
BOUNCING BEN 65272
BOUNTY 64279
BOUNTY 65702

BOURNE 81751 Mtce boat 52' BW-BBC
BOURNEMOUTH 68096 122 (fleet no.). Ex working Big Woolwich Town Class 71'6" red/blue. B: 1937 Harland & Wolff, Woolwich. Conversion f/o: Willow Wren, Braunston; Kate Boats, Warwick. Original National 2 cyl. Base Burghfield Bridge, K&A Canal. Originally built for Grand Union Canal Carrying Co. 22495
BOWEHAIR 104331
BOWLAND 69444
BOWMONT 68129
BOWOOD 63565
BOWSTONES 60849
BRACKEN 52861
BRACKEN 60120
BRACKEN 76263
BRACKEN Grp grn/crm
BRACKLEY *(hotel boat with Ellesmere)*
BRACKLEY 64616
BRADDAN 51301
BRADSHAW Weedcutting boat BW-NW
BRAGANZA 68992
BRAHMS 66843
BRAIDLEY 62401
BRAIDLEY 75400
BRAMBLE 80428 Motor boat 35' BW-OGU
BRAMBLE 73217 NbT 45' dk blue/mar. B: 1986 John South/Starline, R.Avon, Glos. Vetus M414 32hp. Base Welton Wharf GU. 23729
BRAMBLE 500377 NbC 40' midnight blue. B: 1995 Liverpool Boats, owner f/o. Beta/Kubota. Base Ashby canal. 24779
BRAMBLE 45582
BRAMBLE 45651
BRAMBLE 51274
BRAMBLE 52546
BRAMBLE 60969
BRAMBLE No1 *NbT 55' grn/red*
BRAMBLING 66068
BRAMBLING No 2 48178
BRAMLEY 73325
BRAMLEY B1233
BRANDY 48862
BRANDY 76596
BRANDYSNAP 71754
BRANDY WINE 79409
BRANWELL No5 *NbT red/grn*
BRANWEN 60270
BRASS BUCKLE 77824
BRASS FARTHING B1290
BRAUNSTON 70759
BRAUNSTON TUNNEL 72667
BRAVEHEART 67541 *broad beam houseboat*
BRAW LASS 53167 Nb 50' grn/mar. B: 1993 Shepley Bridge Marina, Mirfield, Calder & Hebble. 35hp Beta-Kubota 4cyl. Base Warings Green, North Stratford Canal. 20200
BRAYTON MV 14.95m BW-NE
BREACH 102601 Nb Grp 17'6", b 6'10", d 9" grn/lt grn. B: March 1975 Wilderness Boats. Yamaha 9.9 hp 4 stroke. Trailed from home. (see Dec 96 Canal Boat) 22379
BREAD TRAY 75017
BREAK-AWAY 75793 THORNE NbT 47'

grn/red. B: 1988 TT Marine, later extended from 35' by Blue Water Marina. Isuzu 22hp/Dolphin. Base Snaygill, Skipton L&L. The name was hyphenated when boat was extended. 24904
BREAK TIME 54958
BREAM FELLOWS MORTON & CLAYTON NbT converted to residential 70', d 2'8" grn/red. B: 1932 Yarwoods Llster HA2. Base 3U/ Llangollen canals. First boat of "Fish" class built for FMC, commissioned 1932. Carried wheat and flour from Ellesmere Port to Birmingham until 1950s, then transferred to British Waterways maintenance fleet. During this period her cabin and engine room were cut off. It is believed they were converted to a tug which has now been united with parts of 3 other hulls to form another *Bream*. This *Bream* was eventually found sunk in Tixall Wide and was rebuilt as she is today by Keith Ball. 24918
BREAM 53621
BRECON CASTLE Hire. NbC 45' grn/yel. Electric propulsion. Base Castle Narrowboats, Gilwern. 00212
BRECON PRINCE 61332
BREDARN 63135
BREMEN 49037
BRENDON Mtce boat BW-NW
BRENDON 45935
BRENDON 46616
BRENIN NbC 20' red/grn
BRENIN 60986
BRENIN Barney(37) 1974 35' *(ex Rupert)*
BRENTFORD 70483
BRENTWOOD 53090
BRER FOX NbC 50' wh/grn
BRER FOX 61498
BREVE II 047270 NbC 55' wh cabin/royal blue with gold stripe (same livery as the Royal Yacht - not to be pretentious but because owner thinks it a lovely colour scheme! Crockery same colour. Owner is ex naval officer and prefers seagoing craft appearance). B: 1989 - hull by Graham Parker, Canal Craft, Penkridge, f/o J & D Matthias, Gailey Wharf. 1.8L BL, 1:3 reduction, Calcutt marine conversion. Base Victoria Dock, Gloucester. No well at bow for easier deck working and allows bunks under foredecking.21265
BREWOOD No 2 70474
BRIAN 51110 T.A. & M. BUXTON JOULE'S WHARF Residential (permanent cruising) NbST 65' dk blue. B: 1991 Stone Boatbuilding Ltd., self f/o. Bedford Astra marinised by Courtenay Marine Ltd. Base Audlem, SU Canal. Snails motif refer to "Brian" in Magic Roundabout and to Brian Artus of Stone Boatbuilding who took 12 months to build the hull! 20145
BRIAN 89573
BRI-ANN 51328
BRIANNE 46293
BRIAR ROSE 47874
BRIAR ROSE 77235
BRIDGEWATER BABE 52122
BRIDGNORTH 62325 NbC glass fibre superstructure on steel hull 42' red/grn. Entered service with Anglo Welsh hire fleet 1976(?).

B: Harborough Marine, partial refits by Anglo Welsh at Wootton Wawen and Aynho. Air cooled Lister SR2. Privately owned since 1992 - was then one of oldest A-W boats still in hire fleet. Base S.Oxford Canal. 21218
BRIDIE II 45918
BRIFFITT & PIECH NbT 40' grn/red
BRIGADIER 77938
BRIGHOUSE 89748 MV 14.95m BW-NE
BRIGHOUSE NAN 75371
BRIGHT EYES 47059
BRIGHTON Large Woolwich Working Nb Butty crm/burgundy. B: 1935 Harland & Wolff, Woolwich. Base R.Thames. Butty to *Nuneaton* (see entry). As a pair they are 2 of the 186 pairs built in 1930s for massive GUCCCo expansion programme. The 'Town' class were designed to carry 72 tons of cargo per pair on a draught of 4'3" at 6 knots. This was never achieved as planned dredging scheme never completed. *Brighton* originally butty to *Bristol*, carrying general cargoes. To British Transport Commission on nationalisation in 1948, then BW Board and later, lease to Willow Wren Canal Transport Services. When carrying ceased in 1970 *Brighton* went to Union Canal Carriers, mainly as camping boat paired with motor *Bexhill* and on R.Soar gravel traffic. Then to private ownership along with major surgery to bottom and footings plus new steel cabin fitted. Purchased by Narrowboat Trust in 1996 where further work being carried out. 022522
BRIGHTON ROCK 62316
BRIGHT WATER 93301
BRILLIANT 63205
BRILLIANT 71701
BRIMAR II 053759 RIVER SOAR NbT 57' dk grn/ red. B: 1994 Stowe Hill Marine, Weedon. Perkins MC42. Base R.Soar. 21285
BRIMFIELD 51787 NbT 50' midnight blue/red. B: 1991 GT Boatbuilders, Stafford, f/o: part Nimbus Narrowboats, Leicester, part by owner. 1.4L Thornycroft/Mitsubishi. Base Airedale Boat Club, Castleflatts, L&L canal. 20152
BRIMSTONE 45706
BRIMSTONE 71538
BRINCLIFFE 75064
BRINDARIAN 51181
BRINKLOW Motor boat 37'11" BW-OGU
BRISAS 83241
BRISTOL *see BRIGHTON*
BRITANNIA Hire. NbC 46' grn. B: 1980 Godalming Narrow Boats on Colecraft hull. BMC 1.5. Base Farncombe Boat House, R.Wey. 00377
BRITANNIA II M21573 Trip Boat. Wooden Jolly Boat - double diagonal planking with carvel skin of Honduras mahogany 27'. b 8', d 18" blue/crm. B: 1953 R.A.Newman & Sons Ltd, Hamworthy, Poole. Single Perkins P4(M). Base R.Medway, Tonbridge. Carries the HMY crest on bow - is one of the two 27' Jolly boats in service on the Royal Yacht between 1953 and 1980. 021497
BRITISH QUEEN 71045
BROADSTAIRS 500713 CLIFTON CRUISERS Hire. NbC 54' grn/crm. B: South West Durham

Steel Craft, f/o Clifton Cruisers. BL 1.8. Base Clifton Wharf, Rugby. 025673
BROCK 500424
BROCK BADGER 50256 MARPLE BADGER BOATS Hire. NbT 60' Mauritius blue/rustic red. B: 1991 Sagar Marine, Brighouse. Lister Alpha LPW4. Base Macclesfield canal. Originally privately owned high specification with twin chimneys, twin pigeon boxes, s/f stove, central heating, bath, bow thruster, etc. now available for hire. 017341
BROCTONIA *45307 NbT 55' grn/red*
BROGANS RUN 47953
BROKEN PROMISE 71182
BROLLY 65941
BRONTE *Push tug for Emily red*
BRONTY 53153
BROOKDALE 66722
BROOKES 53745
BROWNIE 51765
BROWNIE 70525
BRUCE TRAIL 54166
BRUIN 74851
BRUMMAGEM FLY *see COROLLA*
BRUNEL 73386
BRUNEL 78700
BRUNIE III 69753
BRUNSWICK 71716
BRYHER 62611
BRYNBELL 51493
BRYONY 47081
BRYONY TOO 501158 NbC 47' dk blue/brown. B: 1996 Liverpool Boats. Lombardini LDW1204 32bhp. Base Sherborne Wharf, Birmingham. Family coat of arms on cabin sides with motto "Hold Fast". Gas generator in bow locker plumbed in. 24864
BUBBLE 91962
BUBBLES 73374
BUCCANEER Hire. NbC 50' red/grn. Base Rose Narrowboats, Brinklow, N.Oxford canal. 026703
BUCCANEER 65197
BUCCANEER 71199
BUCCANEER 79126
BUCCANEER B1702
BUCKAROO Hire. NbT 34' red/grn. Base Rose Narrowboats, Brinklow, N.Oxford canal. 026696
BUCKAROO 65839
BUCKBY 77099
BUCKDEN No. 1 62467 Lg Woolwich Town Cl motor. Ex GUCC/BW/WW
BUCKS FIZZ 51329
BUCKSHEE 80111
BUCKTHORNE
BUD 74590
BUD 500825
BUDDUG 76727
BUDDY 48358
BUDE Lg Woolwich Town Cl motor. Ex GUCC/BW
BUDGIE 68030
BUFFALO 53229
BUGALUGS 30256
BUGBROOKE 82139 Tug 19'6" BW-OGU

BUGGALUGS II 67775
BUGSIE 45319
BULLDOG G14488 NbST 40' blue. B: 1994 North Shropshire Narrowboat, f/o by owner/ professional joinery. Lister 3 cyl LPWS. Base Pike & Eel marina, R.Great Ouse. 24805
BULLDOG 74078
BULLDOG 74978
BULLDOG 99898
BULLFINCH *Butty. Bl/wh/red*
BULLFINCH 49066
BULLFINCH 73246
BULLFINCH 103501
BULLRUSH Hire. NbC 45' blue/red. Base The Wyvern Shipping Co, Linslade, GU 00448
BULLRUSH 64701
BULLRUSH 69457
BULLRUSH *NbT 60' bl/red*
BULRUSH 46589
BULRUSH 52653 R.R. & W.M. PEMBERTON MILTON KEYNES NbC 45' red/blue. B: 1993 J L Pinder & Son, Bromsgrove. Perkins 3HD20 3cyl. Base Milton Keynes marina. 21335
BULRUSH 54782
BULRUSH 75742
BULWARK 104686 ALVECOTE No. 26 NbT 55' royal blue. B: 1996 Colecraft, fit-out Narrowcraft Ltd, Alvecote. Kingfisher KD26. Base The Boatyard, Robey's La., Alvecote 22487
BUMBLE NbT 50' grn
BUMBLE 70518
BUMBLE 79464
BUMBLE *see RUMBLE*
BUMBLE B 49812 NbC 26' grn/red. B: 1991 Springer, owner f/o. Thornycroft type 33. Base Devizes, K&A canal. One of the last Springer Eng. boats built before name changed to Springer UK Ltd. and delivered after the change over. 22467
BUMBLE B G11444
BUMBLE BEE 101694
BUMBLEBEE 51618
BUMBLECHUGGER 68383
BUMBLEMOUSE 53857
BUNBURY *62523 NbC brown/crm*
BUNDOORA 77825
BUP 45855
BURDE 65079
BURGHFIELD BELLE Barney(30) 1973 32'
BURGHFIELD OWL 076002 (owl/crescent moon motif) NbST 40' blue/crm. B: 1981 - total design self-built. 1.8 BMC - prop and main drive with forward steering connected to out-drive unit under fore deck, with separate tiller steering aft. Oval windows, non-standard bow. Base K&A canal. 21322
BURHOU 46802
BURLAND 500611
BURLAND Tug BW-NW
BURLISSA *NbT 50' mar/blue*
BURMA STAR 97481
BURNHAM 31660
BURNLEY 89615 BW-
BURNT MILL 12m BW-L&S
BURSCOUGH 89616 MV BW-NW

34

BURSLEY 78769
BURSTON 48830
BUSINESS 67228
BUSTER 500471
BUT 'N' BEN 500352 1215 NORTON NbT 50' mar/dk blue.   B: 1995 South West Durham Steelcraft. BMC/Calcutt 1.8. Base Sawley marina. Nice steelwork - no straight lines fore or aft. "Owner designed down to last inch - inside and out". 24777
BUT N BEN 69374
BUTE 52351
BUTTERFLIES 60917
BUTTERMARKET 73686
BUTTERMERE 71574

BUTTERMILK M21065 & 054269 T J & S J DEAN - YALDING   NbT 61' dk grn/red. B: 1986 Sagar Marine, Brighouse, self f/o. Russell Newbery DM2. Continuous cruising. No gunwale on forward part. Cruised Thames estuary from R.Medway and Severn estuary prior to going under new Severn bridge on cruise from Bath to Sharpness. 22404
BUTTERWEED 62330
BUTTON OAK 49300
BWYTHYN DWR 46643
BUXTON 62371 Lg Woolwich Town Cl motor. Ex GUCC/BW/WW
BYFIELD 60491
BYFORD 78513
BZ NEEZ 49637

C

A "Crossroads" star, a down-under connection, cats aboard, a boat with a bow window, some motor racing links, charitable efforts, claims to fame, an elderly and hot Countess and going Wild at Calcutt.

CADDER PRINCESS *Trip boat - Forth & Clyde canal*
CADENZA 64556
CADI 46632
CAELMIRI 49359
CAEN 53033
CAER GLEAW *67926 NbC 40' red/grn*
CAERNARVON 54426
CAERNARVON 71925
CAGGY 61460 Harris, Netherton c1930 Tug
CAIRNGORM Motor vessel BW-NW
CAIUS 103916
CALABRESE 69631 CATTESHALL LOCK Nb 45' grn/red. B: 1974app., believed at Fenny Compton. Yanmar 2 cyl. Base Welford Arm, GUC. 'Canoe' bow. Believed ex-hire boat.   261061
CALADAN 51945
CALAMITY JAYNE 53477
CALDER ROSE 65132
CALDICOT CASTLE Hire. NbC 45' grn/yel. Base Castle Narrowboats, Gilwern.   00213
CALDON 66654
CALDON 75627
CALDON JAY *45721 NbT 60' mar/grn*
CALEDONIA B1205
CALIBAN 53520
CALICO 61907
CALLIOPE 62291
CALLIOPE Barney(1) 1969 45'
CALLISTO 54779
CALLISTO 68099 Sm Woolwich Star Cl motor. Ex GUCC/London Fire Brigade (WW2)/UCC
CALLISTO 77757
CALLY *NbC 35' red/grn*
CALLY HANNA *68957 NbC grn/red*
CALM 83127
CALMAR 50481
CALM CHAOS BO392
CALMORE CHERVIL 61724
CALMORE CHERVIL II 73864 MARGARET & DAVID JAMES SOUTHAMPTON NbC 48' grn/crm. B: 1978(?79) Calcutt Boats. 1500 BMC. Base Calcutt marina (the Pond). Name changed from *Wild Chervil IV* on purchase by present owners from Calcutt hire fleet (Calmore is home village). They also bought the original *Wild Chervil IV* from Calcutt 12 years ago! Recent experience of inadequate winterising involving a full water tank emptying itself into the boat - floor under 4" of water. Hoping dehumidifer will save the day - but still laughing about it!   20162
CALTCOTT Flat 11m BW-LAP
CALYPSO 63250
CALYPSO 65966
CALYPSO 87590
CALYPSO *NbT 60' grn/crm*
CALYPSO ROSE 64666
CAM River Cl butty. Ex BW
CAM 207
CAMARETTE 101719
CAMARILLA 52716
CAMBERWELL BEAUTY 69672
CAMBERWELL BEAUTY 78615
CAMBOURNE Lg Woolwich Town Cl motor. Ex GUCC/BW
CAMBOURNE 80619 BW-
CAMBRIAN 60700
CAMBRIAN 71434
CAMBRIAN Motor vessel Mtce boat BW-NW
CAMELOT 45125
CAMELOT 45458
CAMELOT 045945 Hire. NbC 52' grn/red. BMC 1.8. Base Evesham Marina, R.Avon.   0371031
CAMELOT 46238
CAMELOT 49133
CAMELOT 63526
CAMELOT 68851
CAMELOT 71146
CAMELOT 72003
CAMELOT 93430
CAMEO 48914 C.D & M.L. GAIT KNOWLE HALL WHARF NbT 56' Mauritius blue. B: 1990 Gary Gorton shell, f/o Stephen Goldsbrough Boats. Thornycroft 1.8. Base Napton marina   20195
CAMEO Hire. NbC 58' red/grn. Base Rose Narrowboats, Brinklow, N.Oxford canal.   026705
CAMILE 75607
CAMILLA MAY *NbC Midway 235 23' brown/crm*
CAMILLE 47669
CAMINO 82319
CAMOYS 67311
CAMPBELL 69401
CAMPION 30557
CAMPION 47560
CAMRAY 65893
CANADA GOOSE 52894
CANAKALE 77157
CANAL CREEPER 47419
CANAL EXPLORER 40102
CANAL EXPLORER 53163
CANALETTO 53247
CANALGESIC 75304
CAN CARIAD 76920
CANDIDA II 50762
CANDY 63644
CANDYFLOSS 80293
CANDYTUFT 45637
CANIS No 246 Sm Woolwich Star Cl motor (ex butty).
CANIS MAJOR No 2 79482 Tug
CANNIZARO N6788
CANNOCK *69980 NbC 50' red/grn*
CANNY 50399 K.L. & J. BYE Nb 50' mid grn/ Mercedes red. B: 1991 T.P. Services, formerly of Patricroft (Manchester), owner f/o. Solé based on Mitsubishi 1994cc. Base L&L canal.   23728
CANNY FOX *NbT 60' yel/grn*
CANNY FOX 76994

CANOPUS Motor vessel 15.24m BW-NE
CANOPUS *NbC 30' blue*
CANOPUS 48225
CANTABILE 52486 NbT 50' navy blue/mar. B: 1992 Shotbolt Engineers Ltd., f/o Nene Marine, Whittlesey. Beta BV 1505 /Kubota 4cyl 1.5 L 37hp @ 3,000rpm, Hurth 125 2.5:1 g'box, 17x10 prop. Base Crick marina, GU-Leics. 24794
CANTABLE 64464
CANTERBURY 047638 CLIFTON CRUISERS Hire. NbC 60' grn/crm. B: 1993 Arcrite Fabrications, f/o Clifton Cruisers. BL 1.8. Based Clifton Wharf Rugby 025682
CANTERBURY 50860
CANTERBURY 71047
CANTICLE 48525
CANTLEY 60241
CANUCK 61644
CANUTE 100333
CAPABLE 61622 NbC 55' red/grn. B: 1976 Rugby Boatbuilders on Colecraft shell. Lister SR3 (1975 production). Base Anderton. Originally hire cruiser named *Styx*. 21372
CAPE 50634
CAPELLA 60242
CAPELLA Sm Woolwich Star Cl butty. Ex GUCC/BW/WW/BL
CAPELLA *70230 NbT blue/grey*
CAPERCAILLIE 49481
CAPERCAILLIE 54148
CAPERCAILLIE 75553

CAPI 49950
CAPN KIDD 51014
CAPPRICIO 87716
CAPRICE 62629
CAPRICORN 48959
CAPRICORN 52588
CAPRICORN 62101
CAPRICORN 67393
CAPRICORN 69665
CAPRICORN 74221
CAPRICORN 77274
CAPRICORN 84101
CAPRICORN N6262
CAPRICORN Barney(48) 1975 40'
CAPRICORNS DULCITEDO 50743
CAPSICUM 68368
CAPTAIN 62953
CAPTAIN BARNET 63497
CAPTAIN BARNETT *Nb 70' red/bl*
CAPTAIN COOK 71840
CAPTAIN FLINT 65177
CAPTAIN HARRY *NbC 30'*
CAPTAIN MAGOO 87144
CAPTAIN MORGAN 101351
CAPTAIN SCOTT 500669
CAPTAIN STARKEY 48296
CARA 053862 J & B GLEN PORT DUNDAS NbST 50' dk blue. B: 1994 Derby narrowboats, Littleover. Kubota BV1305. Base Calder & Hebble Navigation. 20136
CARA T 69052
CARACTACUS 71773
CARAMEL 80693
CARAN II 78157
CARAWAY 49500
CARAWAY No 39 *NbT 50' grn/red*
CARBOLATE 62124
CARDINAL 60023 drawing: 4 cardinal points of the compass NbT 45' red. B: 1980 Hancock & Lane. 1.5 BMC (situated on port side) driving a pump which then drives an hydraulic motor on the prop shaft. Base Lyme View marina, Macclesfield canal. 24872
CAREFREE 72606
CAREFREE 101109
CAREITH 53458
CARELA B1158
CAREN 102839
CAREY GINGER 52511
CARIAD 45896
CARIAD 49438
CARIAD 050513 BURGHFIELD NbST 59' British Racing grn/Mercedes red. B: 1991 Colecraft, f/o Rugby Boatbuilders, Hillmorton (Last but one boat built before ceasing to trade). Diesel Engine. Base Burghfield Island Boat Club, K&A canal. 23653
CARIAD 79876
CARIAD B1204
CARIAD FÂCH 054542 BREWOOD NbT 53' blue/dk red. B: 1995 G & J Reeves, f/o Blue Haven Marine. Lister 4 cyl Canal Star. Base Hatherton marina, S&W. One piece foldaway 6' x 4'6" bed. High-tech electrically. 24799

COOLMATIC

12v & 24v DC Fridges & Freezers

- Cabinet sizes from 35 to 215 litres
- Split - systems
- Special-builds available

- **Quality products**
- **Excellent service**
- **Competitive prices**
- **Now available direct**

COOLMATIC - *"The Boat Fridge People"*
38 Maxwell Road, Littlehampton,
West Sussex. BN17 7BW.
Tel / Fax : 01903 723492.
E-mail : coolmatic@aol.com

CARIANNE 49899
CARIBOU 70678
CARIBOU 95527
CARINA Butty.
CARING YO-YO 66933
CARINO 60251
CARINYA 48977
CARLI DAWN 99887
CARLIER 66762
CARLOTI ROSE 71330
CARLTON 84405
CARMARGUE 66942
CARMEN 61408
CARMEN 69516
CARMEN 74041
CARMEN B0133 PRESTON BROOK NbC 38′ grn/red. B: 1975 Black Bull Engineering Bootle, home f/o. SABB 10hp. Base Preston Brook marina. *Carmen's* claims to fame include a Granada Reports TV appearance in March 1995 because the 2 lady owners had gained a Transport Trust Award for restoring a Box Boat; also for towing Nb *Gifford* back to Ellesmere Port Boat Museum after her 1995 restoration at Malcolm Webster's, Malkins Bank, Sandbach. 23721
CARNABY 80640 Motor vessel 13.6m BW-
CAROL ANN B0989
CAROLINE 64720
CAROLINE 74383
CAROLINE 79579
CAROLINE GAYTON 68007
CAROLINE LOUISE 48666
CAROLINE TOO 65139
CAROLYN 46674
CAROLYN B1553
CAROUSEL Hire. NbC 40′ red/grn. Base Rose Narrowboats, Brinklow, N.Oxford canal. 026699
CAROUSEL 60039
CAROUSEL 63853
CAROUSEL 69385
CAROUSEL 69505
CARPE DIEM 45754
CARPETBAGGER 48587
CARRALDO 68108 NbC 40′ grn/red. B: 1975 Hancock & Lane. Lister SR2. Base GU canal at Pitstone Wharf. Original 'Norseman' design. 21212
CARRIBBEAN 47436
CARRICK ROSE 76299
CARRIE 65051
CARRIE LAURA 62082
CARRIE LOFTHOUSE 46354
CARRISBROOKE 69309
CARROBLIA 60255
CARSAIG 61830
CARSON 50516
CARTONIA 53165
CARTREF No 1 70102
CASA BLANCA 47519
CASCADE 52548
CASCADE 63510
CASHFLOW 63510
CASILDA 62234
CASPAR 77211
CASPAR *NbT 60′ blue/grey*

CASPIAN TERN 50155
CASSANDRA 45323
CASSIE MAY 050990 J.A. & A.E. ROWLAND Nb 50′ grn/red. B: 1991 Larose f/o on GT hull. Mitsubishi. Base Llangollen canal. 21370
CASSIEU 67555
CASSIO 82159 Motor vessel 18m BW-
CASSIOPEIA 68925 Sm Woolwich Star Cl motor. Ex GUCC/BW
CASTAWAY 69888
CASTLEFIELD B0010 Trip Boat - 50 seats. Composite Nb conversion 71′6″, b 7′1″ bl/graining. B: circa 1906 Fellows Morton & Clayton Ltd., converted 1981 by Lorenz Bros. Lister HA2 air cooled. Base Castlefield, Manchester. 0351006
CASTLEGOLD 65742
CASTLE HOWARD 53934 NbT 60′ midnight blue/light blue. B: 1994 GT Boatbuilders (no.71), f/o Nimbus Narrowboats, (no.21). Perkins MC42. Continuous cruising. Fitted as a comfortable home for two in early retirement. Name derived from "castle", as in Englishman's home and the owner's surname. 23589
CASTLE ORWELL 69364
CASTLE ROSE 62490
CASTLE WINDOW 78261
CASTOR 68101
CASTOR 71109
CATERINA 88963
CATFLAP 048976 B.A & M.A. RAMAGE & DOG NbT 50′ Royal grn/pale grn. B: 1996 Warble Narrowboats. BMC 1.8. Base Farncombe Boat House moorings, Wey & Godalming navigation. Built for exhibition by the builder at 1996 Braunston show as *Burlesque*. Then bought and, as *Catflap*, exhibited at IWA Dudley Festival coming unofficial runner up in the Lionel Munk trophy. Noted for the cartoon cat painted on the sides and fully tiled, full width walk through shower/toilet. 23579
CATFLAP 53898
CATHERINE 101527
CATHERINE B1140
CATHERINE BESSIE 73526
CATHERINE JAYNE 75933
CATHERINE POWERS 78043
CATHY MILFORD 47774
CATREF 50872 NbST 31′ red/blue. B: 1991 Midland Canal Centre, Stenson. Lister-Petter LPWS2. Base Stenson marina, T&M canal. 23602
CATRINA 51483
CATRINA II 53044
CATS PAW 75680
CATS TOR 64183
CATS WHISKERS 48907
CATTALINA 47251
CAVALIER 46196
CAVALIER 78642
CAVALIER 101384
CAVENDISH *NbT 50′ blue/wh*
CAXTON M21404 Trip Boat. Widebeam Nb 40′, b 9′ red/grn. B: 1980. Perkins 4108 4 cyl. Base Tonbridge, R.Medway. 021496
CA Y EST 62380

38

CECIL 047682 Hire. NbC 63' navy blue/lt blue. B: 1990. Lister LPWS. Base Sally Boats, Bradford on Avon Marina. 013234
CECILE 48331
CECILEO N6651
CECILIA 91537
CECIL JAMES No. 281 *NbT 45' blue/red*
CECIL JAMES 72939
CECYANNE 47069
CEDAR 61276
CEDAR 500390 Unconverted working Nb butty used for commercial carrying. 70'6", b 7', d 3' blue/yel. B: 1935 W.J. Yarwood, Northwich. Built as matching butty to Cypress *(see entry)*. Leased to and working for Ivor Batchelor. 23640
CEDAR Work boat unpowered. Boat Museum
CEDOR CROFT 79293
CELESTE 48330
CELESTE 95941
CELESTIAL STAR 54713
CELESTINE 64918
CELIA 68930
CELIA 93383 CARA CRUISER SWANSEA Grp 15' crm/peacock. B: 1979 Caracruisers Ltd. Brundall, Norfolk. Volvo Penta 9.9hp 4 stroke ob. Trailed. Can also be used as a caravan. 20173
CELIA FENNES 45549
CELTIC EAGLE 54522
CENHINEN BEDR 66781 NbC 49' Donegal grn/Papua red. B: c1979 Arcrite. BL 1.5. Base Fenny Stratford. 23604
CENTAUR Nb. Boat Museum
CENTAURI 500 Sm Woolwich (shortened to 35')
CENTAURI Motor boat 38' BW-OGU
CENTENARY 65246
CENTRE LINE 70743
CENTURION *75431 NbC 60' red/blue*
CEOL NA MARA 75796
CEPHELUS Sm Woolwich Star Cl motor. Ex GUCC
CERAMM 68228
CERES *see M.S.C.Co. WORKS TUG No.2*
CERES 73427
CERES 74898
CERES 76754
CERI 66841
CERTA CITO 71088
CERYS 48205
CESTREFELD 77910
C'EST LA VIE 60235
C'EST LA VIE 68560
CETUS 89848
CHAD III 63797
CHADAWAY *NbT 45' blue*
CHADLEIGH 68238
CHAFFWEED 62264
CHAFFWEED Barney(57) 1976 35'
CHAK CHAK 62222
CHALAND 72203
CHALFONT 66131
CHALFORD 47527
CHALLENGER 46834
CHALLENGER 67101
CHALLENGER 75082
CHALLENGER 78434
CHALLENJA 50436
CHALLONER 45895
CHAMOIX 50871
CHAMP DONNE 51214 BOSTON NbC 52' blue/red. B: 1991 Staniland of Thorne marina. Nanni 1.5 L. Base R.Witham nr Boston. Features owners' paintings of a shire horse's head and of St. Botolphs Church - Boston stump - helps put Boston on the map. 21319
CHANCE ENCOUNTER 72286 PORT-LINCOLN BATES ASTRAL 8.10 Grp 27', b 10' ivory/pale blue. B: 1979 Bates. 1.8 L BMC 48 bhp. Base Lincoln marina. Wood panelled deckhead with 4 flush-fitted brass lights. 22466
CHANELLE Hire. NbC 50' red/grn. Base Rose Narrowboats, Brinklow, N.Oxford canal. 026701
CHANTELA B7317
CHANTELLE 100398
CHANTERELLE 60275
CHANTEUR 30182
CHANTICLAR 78794
CHANTILLY 54500 KENNET & AVON CANAL NbST 46' dk blue/grey. B: 1995 Gary Gorton, f/o J D Boat Services (Gailey). Vetus Mitsubishi 3cyl 22hp. Base Bradford on Avon, K&A. Features small sliding hatch within the large sliding hatch covering the whole of cockpit. 22514
CHANTILLY 65433
CHANTILLY *65769 NbC 50' blue/wh*
CHARENTE 76177
CHARIENE 79561
CHARIOTS OF FIRE 70609
CHARIS 49544
CHARISMA 68017
CHARISMA 76321
CHARISMA *500384 NbT 40' brown/blue*
CHARITY 66802
CHARITY 70381
CHARITY 73857
CHARITY *74991 NbT 35' blue*
CHARITY No 6 46129
CHARLANTA 104280
CHARLIE 50725
CHARLIE 78957
CHARLIE *Trip boat*
CHARLIE B 66553
CHARLIE C G11426
CHARLIE Q 50787
CHARLIES GIRL 73237
CHARLOCK 68537 NbC 45' Oxford blue/crm. B: 1975 app (builder not known). Perkins 4cyl. Base Hatherton marina. Wooden laminated rail at rear. 22472
CHARLOTTE *49584 NbT 50' grn*
CHARLOTTE 52215
CHARLOTTE 54906
CHARLOTTE 66905
CHARLOTTE 69715
CHARLOTTE 75113
CHARLOTTE *NbT 70' red/grn*
CHARLOTTE-B *NbC 45' blue*

Continued on page 50

(l-r) (foreground boats) GU mb (large Northwich), GU mb (large Woolwich), BCN tug, sterns of (set back) Thomas Clayton mb and (nearer) GU mb (large Northwich), GU butty (small Woolwich) [Harry Arnold, Waterway Images

Yet more books would be needed to explain the origins of all the boats included in this one. But it seemed necessary to offer a brief summary of how it all began. So, the chance meeting with David has led to this short introduction to ...

HISTORIC NARROW BOATS
by David Daines
Associated Canal Carriers Limited

Most of our canal system was created some 200 years or so ago for one primary purpose, "Trade". The Duke of Bridgewater had coal which he wished to sell in Manchester and Josiah Wedgwood had pottery which could not withstand the rigours of the existing pack horse transport system. For them both, investing in the new transport system was sound commercial sense. Little detail remains of the earliest boats used, there was nothing glamorous about a coal boat. The passenger packets were more noteworthy, though regrettably short-lived, the coming of the railways cut their reign short.

Few boats then still exist from before the turn of the century, particularly so since the majority were of wooden construction. The oldest survivors are most often examples of the earlier iron or iron composite boats, such as the steamers built by Fellows Morton and Clayton and others, though some older hulls do still exist; hNBOC archives have a record of an ice boat built probably in the 1830s. Practically all the old boats were hot riveted together, notable exceptions to this being those of welded construction built in 1935 for Severn & Canal and the Admiral and River classes built for the nationalised waterways. These days some caution is needed in identifying an 'old' boat by the presence of rivets. Many new boats have had washers welded to them in imitation of the former construction. Whilst many are well done, it is unfortunate that some of the less skilfully boats so modified are more of a 'parody' than a 'faithful copy'. We would also do well to remind ourselves that the motor or engine driven boat is a 'modern invention', "Breaking down the banks and stirring up the mud" as the well known line from the film *Painted Boats* puts it. It is still true to say that the horse and the mule have provided the power for our canals for a longer period than the internal (or external) combustion engine.

Fellows Morton and Clayton

Probably one of the most well known of the major carrying companies, FMC had a large fleet of boats which evolved from the early wooden horse drawn examples, through steam power, to the Bolinder fitted motors of the period between the wars. All the steamers subsequently had Bolinders fitted and many still survive, just a few still sporting the cantankerous, idiosyncratic but indestructible 'Bolinders Patent Crude Oil Engine'. We all admire the elegant shape of the 'Josher' and many present day builders attempt to emulate the classic lines. As you would expect, joshers 'swim' well, most historic boats do, but joshers especially are deep draughted and, with no balance on the rudder blade, are extremely heavy to steer. I can vouch for this having had to use my feet on the tiller when steering *Jaguar*.

Thomas Clayton (Oldbury) Ltd.

The Clayton family were much involved in the canal carrying business. Through the 19th. century their business thrived, but increasingly concentrated on the specialised task of transporting liquids, often associated with town gas production. Eventually in 1889 the general carrying business was merged with Fellows Morton & Co. to form FMC (see above) leaving Thomas Clayton to continue with the carriage of bulk liquids. In 1904 Thomas Clayton (Oldbury) Ltd. was incorporated. (currently owned by Richard Booth, hNBOC Secretary). In the light of the rapid decline in their canal carrying trade just a few years later, it is surprising that the fleet reached its most numerous state as recently as 1952. Practically all the Clayton boats were built of wood, three iron composite boats were tried after the second world war but they were not popular and were soon sold. In view of this it is perhaps surprising that a significant number of the fleet survive today, maybe it has something to do with the preservative nature of the cargoes they carried. Certainly the cargo, and the means sometimes used to liquefy it for easy removal, has often caused the extraordinary measure of 'hogging' which many of the motors display.

Bows (l-r) FMC butty, FMC Steamer (of 1909), Thomas Clayton mb (wooden), FMC mb (of 1913),   [Harry Arnold, Waterway Images

Grand Union Canal Carrying Co.

In 1930 the newly formed Grand Union Canal Co. decided to move back into operating their own carrying fleet. They bought a small concern called Associated Canal Carriers Ltd. (now owned by the author) and started to expand the fleet and its contracts. In 1934 the carrying business was renamed the Grand Union Canal Carrying Co. Ltd. There followed the biggest expansion plan ever seen on our canals. If the trade and, more particularly the crews, had been found for all the boats built, the business would have thrived, unfortunately despite greatly increased trade, it was not a total success. In all some 362 boats were built, mostly by three companies. Walkers of Rickmansworth built wooden boats and Harland & Wolff of Woolwich and W. J. Yarwood & Sons of Northwich built in iron, steel or composite. (Metal sides and elm bottoms.) Apart from the small fleet of the 'ponderous' Royalty class, the main orders commenced with the 'Star' class, 88 pairs of these were built, including an order to Yarwoods for just 8 pairs with deeper holds, rounded chines and steel bottoms. These were followed by large orders, amounting to some 86 pairs, distributed amongst all three yards, for the even deeper Town class boats. As one of the most numerous fleets, many of them built of steel or iron, it is perhaps not surprising that a sizeable number survive in one form or another.

The Erewash Canal Carrying Co. Ltd.

This was not a large fleet, interesting in that the boats were, in all important respects, identical to the GUCC Star class, logical since the Erewash company was a subsidiary of the GU Co. Built by Yarwoods in 1935 and intended to be named after trees, one motor was incorrectly named *Cyprus* instead *Cypress*. Both pairs still exist, though one motor is 'in disguise' as hotel boat *Mallard*. The one significant difference from the rest of the Stars is in the overall length at 70ft. 6ins., 1ft. shorter than the GUCC boats, it made negotiation of a short lock on the River Soar less tedious. (*Cyprus & Cedar*, and the Erewash Canal Carrying Co. are owned by the author.)

Samuel Barlow Coal Co. and S.E. Barlow

'Barlows' was another of the names prominent in the history of canal carrying. Samuel Barlow built up the first business, which bore his name, during the latter half of the last century. As the name implied, they specialised in the carriage of coal, from pits in the Tamworth area, often to far off destinations such as the Huntley & Palmers biscuit factory in Reading. The company prospered. During the first world war the firm was converted into a limited company and the name changed to Samuel Barlow (Tamworth) Ltd. After the war the family progressively lost its controlling interest in the company, though the business continued to thrive until 1926 when matters outside the canal business caused the then controlling interests to go into liquidation. Many of the boats were sold but the company

Bows (l-r) GU butty (small Northwich), BW mb (Admiral class), GU mb (large Woolwich) [Harry Arnold, Waterway Images]

survived, changing its name to the Samuel Barlow Coal Co. Meanwhile, a grandson of the original founder Samuel Barlow established his own carrying business of S.E. Barlow, also specialising in carriage of coal. The two concerns ran in parallel and had an amicable working relationship. In 1957 the S.E. Barlow company was bought by the Samuel Barlow Coal Co. The boats of both fleets were a somewhat heterogeneous collection, some second-hand, many built by Nurser's of Braunston, and predominantly though not exclusively, wooden. In the 1940s the Barlow coal company took over the running of Nurser's yard at Braunston and boats continued to be built there until 1958 when the *Raymond* was launched, the last wholly new wooden working boat to be built. Fortunately a fair number of ex Barlows boats survive though with the increasing difficulty of maintaining wooden boats, their long term future may be problematical.

Cowburn and Cowpar

This firm, based in Manchester used narrow boats to transport liquids, often of an unsavoury or dangerous nature such as hydrogen disulphide. Originally carboys were used to contain the liquids but later boats had tanks fitted. Between 1933 and 1936 eight new motor boats were built by Yarwoods of Northwich, all named after birds with the first letter being 'S'. The first two were of composite construction but the remainder were all steel with an unusual rounded bilge. The fore end shape was similar to that of the boats built by the same company for FMC, but another unusual feature was the somewhat pointed shape of the counter. Gardner single cylinder hot bulb engines were fitted, these were far more manageable than the cantankerous Bolinders fitted to FMC boats having a proper governor and a reverse gearbox. One well known canal person has a water can painted with the inscription, "No, its not a Bolinder, its a Gardner" All eight boats still survive, one of them, *Swan*, was made famous in the well known book by John Liley (*Journeys of the Swan*).

Severn and Canal

This company is a good example of a river based carrying business which operated a number of river tugs and barges in addition to its narrow boats. What is unusual is the degree of co-ordination and common usage achieved between the two classes of craft. The canal boats had substantial towing posts built in to allow long trains of boats to be towed by tug on the river. The most interesting boats built for this company were the class of eight motor narrow boats which were welded together by Charles Hill & Sons of Bristol in 1934 & 5, this at a time when welding techniques were not developed as they now are. Named after trees, several of these boats survive in some form and confound those who would use the presence of rivets to identify an 'old boat'. Previously to this latter class, all the motor boats had numbers only, unlike the named, non-powered boats.

Cadbury's

Many of us remember the large warehouses and unloading sheds alongside the Worcester and Birmingham canal at Bournville, now replaced by a housing estate. Cadbury's developed the site, and with it a fleet of narrow boats, to transport raw materials between the various parts of the chocolate manufacturing process. All the boats were named *Bournville* followed by a number. In 1928 Cadbury's decided to discontinue their own fleet operations and to rely on the SCC Co. (above) in which the Cadbury brothers had financial and management interests.

Wander & Co. (Ovaltine)

The well known Swiss firm of Wander & Co., producers of Ovaltine and other food products, had their own fleet of boats built to deliver coal to the canal-side factory at King's Langley. The boats were built by Walkers of Rickmansworth and probably the most well known surviving example is *Albert* painstakingly restored from an amazingly decrepit hulk into its present superb condition by Chris Collins.

The Salt Boats

There were a number of companies involved in transporting salt from the area of the 'wiches, Northwich, Nantwich, Middlewich mostly to the coast for trans-shipment. These included, The Mersey Weaver Co., The Anderton Co., Henry Seddons and The Salt Union. Many of these boats had a distinctively rounded cross section described as 'barrel sided' which greatly improved the 'swim' though it made them somewhat 'tippy' or 'crank'. Like all wooden boats the long term survival of those still existing is extremely problematical.

British Waterways

After nationalisation in 1948 there was a serious imbalance in the types of boats available to carry the still significant trade, particularly as many wooden boats were 'well out of guarantee'! Several steps were taken; in one extraordinary move two FMC motor boats were converted into butties. Several of the more useful (and elegant) day boats built for the LMS by Yarwoods, were given cabins and named after railway stations. Orders were placed with several companies for new all welded boats of more than usual bluff appearance and incorporating novel 'improvements'. One of these was the remarkable 'outboard' (!!) Harbourmaster engine unit, another was the 'Portacabin' like lift out cabin unit. Of more practical value was the attempt to simplify the method of covering cargoes in the hold. The River class boats built for the SE division used revolutionary blue fibre-glass covers, which had a habit of blowing off if not restrained! The Admiral class boats built in the NW had more conventional canvas covers but stretched over hoops and retained by wooden wedges. None of these boats swam as well as the older, more shapely craft which preceded them, but they could carry a greater tonnage.

Day Boats and 'Joey' Boats

No-one knows how many boats were built, mostly in the Birmingham area, for short distance working between coal mines, iron works, factories, power stations or railway trans-shipment basins. Many were fairly non-descript, practical working hulls but others display a degree of elegance way above that which may be expected. Some of these have become much prized for conversion into new motor boats, there are builders who specialise in such work. There were notable builders whose hulls make this point. Thomas Bantock built boats with a distinctive fore end and at least one other unique feature. When built these hulls were composite, that is iron with an elm bottom, but in addition, the footings, that is the very bottom level of the sides, were an oak plank. Genuine Bantock hulls may be identified, if the knees can be seen, by the 'joggle' needed to accommodate the greater thickness of this oak strake. One notable Bantock hull, motorised and converted for residential use, exists in the Batchworth area and *still has its wooden footings and bottom*, though now over-plated for safety. Another notable class was the 'Railway' boats, built specifically for trans-shipment between the railways of the area. Yarwoods built some of these for the LMS and they were selected by British Waterways after nationalisation, for conversion into butties, with full cabins, and named after railway stations. Of course day boats were not motor driven. Horse power was universal, though in later days motor tugs were used. Several haulage companies created powerful tugs to pull prodigious strings of loaded boats on lock free stretches. One well known such boat, now meticulously preserved, was converted from a war damaged FMC boat, equipped with a massive and magnificent 5 cylinder Gardner engine. Many day boats were double ended, that is the rudder could be hung at either end avoiding the need to wind the

Sterns (l-r) FMC mb (of 1913), Thomas Clayton mb (wooden), FMC Steamer (of 1909) and bow of BCN Joey (day) boat   [Harry Arnold, Waterway Images

Bow of BW 'River' class on left, then (l-r) GU butty (large Woolwich), GU butty (small Woolwich), GU mb (large Northwich), GU butty (small Woolwich)
[Harry Arnold, Waterway Images]

boat. Cabins on day boats were rudimentary, if they existed at all, being just a shelter for the boatman. Perhaps the most remarkable day boats were the 'Ampton (Wolverhampton) boats which were, at about 9′ by 80′ too large to pass the locks in the area, but which could of course carry larger loads on the Wolverhampton level of the BCN.

The No. 1's, and the other companies

I am aware that I have, in this short piece, omitted mention of several important carrying companies and their boats. If the omissions include the particular interest of the reader, I apologise. The canal world was also blessed with a large number of owner boat operators, called 'No 1s', though these were gradually squeezed out by the carrying rate war with the railway companies, nevertheless some survived until the end. In a sense, the present day boat owner is a 'No.1', just remember what a proud tradition you are keeping alive.

Many old boats survive from the commercial origins of the canal system, some of us are dedicated to keeping alive the boats and the traditions of that period. The problems involved in keeping afloat historic *wooden* hulls are indeed daunting! Many of us will talk *very willingly* of our boats and their history, we only ask the present day boater to appreciate the limitations of old engines and deep draughted hulls, we don't always occupy the centre of what channel exists, by choice.

CHARLOTTE DUNDAS 77426
CHARLOTTE EMMA 45105
CHARLOTTE JANE 73356
CHARLOTTE M 75185
CHARLOTTE ROSE 45744
CHARLTON *NbT 50' blue/scumble*
CHARMA ET FILS 48483
CHARMAINE 73435 HEREFORD & WORCESTER PLYNLIMON TRUST Charity hire for elderly, handicapped and disabled people. Nb 70', d 30" grn/red. B: 1986 Manpower Services Commission Camel-Laird apprentices, Monks Ferry Workshop. Perkins 4.108. Base Stourport basin. Accommodates 12 day passengers, 6 sleeping, 2 crew. Features large windows and hydraulic wheelchair lift. The *CHAR* in the name stands for Committee for Hereford Amateur Rafters who organise the annual 100 mile, 3 day R.Wye raft race to provide the funds. Lottery funding recently will greatly assist in maintaining *Charmaine*'s charitable work into the future. 22438
CHARMATE 75644
CHARNWOOD 66988
CHARNWOOD 93130
CHARNWOOD 96508
CHARTLEY 46710
CHASE END 51476
CHASELEY 71695
CHASELEY 74204
CHATTEL 69445
CHEAM Lg Ricky Town Cl butty. Ex GUCC/BW
CHEDDLETON 62007
CHEDDLETON 65472
CHEDDLETON MILL 76902
CHEERS 46563
CHEERS 50395
CHEERS *89672 Grp 18' yel/wh*
CHEERS 4 102060
CHEERS! B0780
CHELMER 47650
CHELONIAN 54114
CHEMAINUS 66311
CHEPSTOW CASTLE Hire. NbC 32'6" grn/yel. Base Castle Narrowboats, Gilwern. 00218
CHERIE 49067
CHÉRIE 51134 E & S NAYLOR & SON STOCKTON NbT 56'6" Mercedes red/dk Royal grn. B: 1991 Graham Edgson Norton Canes, f/o Blue Haven Marine. Lister Alpha 4 40hp. Base Blue Lias marina GU canal. *Chérie* took part in the Belgian Flotilla in 1995. 22432
CHEROKEE 60746
CHERRY 64702
CHERRY 78521
CHERRY 78961 MIDDLEWICH NARROWBOATS No 11 Hire. NbC 50' grn/red. B: Hancock & Lane, f/o Stowe Hill Marine. BMC 1.5. Base Middlewich. Ex Waterway Holidays, Weedon; original name *Altair*. 028739
CHERRY Hire. NbC 45' blue/red. Base The Wyvern Shipping Co, Linslade, GU. 00449
CHERRY B 102275
CHERRY EYE 49519
CHERRY HILL 46960 J & M CULLEN

KENNET & AVON No.5 Hire. NbT 70' red/dk blue. B: 1989 Mike Gration then Steelcraft (Cherry Hill Estate, Old, Northants. - hence name), f/o Paul Homer. Perkins D 3 152, Newage PRM 160 transmission. Base K&A Ladies Bridge 120. Beautifully fitted, solid pine, Victorian tiling in galley & bathroom, quarry tiles on galley floor giving stunning farmhouse/country cottage feel and appearance. 2032
CHERRY LEA 64418
CHERRY LEA see *MACNOON*
CHERRY TREE 45825
CHERUB TOO 46587
CHERWELL 79830
CHERYL 74997
CHES B1722
CHESAMISU 64546
CHESAPEAKE 51814
CHESHIRE CAT 46448
CHESHIRE CAT 73239
CHESHIRE ROSE 500566 D & J SMITH MACCLESFIELD NbC 55' Oxford blue/Spanish gold. B: 1995/96 R&D Fabrications, f/o Malcolm Rhodes, Shardlow. Perkins MC42, 3:1 g'box. Base Adlington, Macclesfield canal. Cabin front is not flat but bow-window style. New low wash stern shape. Roses and buds adorn sides. 24812
CHESTER 46167
CHESTER 53727
CHESTER 70722
CHESTER 78652
CHESTER CASTLE 52026
CHESTNUT RUSH *NbT 50' grn/red*
CHESTNUT RUSH 70670
CHESWOOD GRANGE 76349
CHEVIOT 89571 Motor vessel Mtce boat 38'9" BW-NW
CHEVIOT 77053
CHI 42826
CHIANTI 104126
CHICKSAW 64949
CHICKWEED 62025
CHICKWEED Barney(59) 1976 35' (ex *Badger*)
CHIEF 70193
CHIEFTAIN 76230
CHILKANA 72053
CHILTERN 48236
CHILTERN No 352 Motor. Ex FMC. Boat Museum
CHILTERN Motor vessel Mtce boat 38'9" BW-NW
CHILTERN ROSE 049151 NbST 52' blue. B: 1990 Stowe Hill Marine. Lister LPWS4. Base Thrupp, Oxford canal. 25976
CHILTON CHAFFINCH 70707
CHIMAY 49221
CHINA BAY 63455
CHINA DOLL 85085
CHINA GIRL 49348
CHINA GIRL 100911
CHIP 69564
CHIPP No.4 *NbT 27' bl/wh*
CHIPPY 63657
CHIPPY 71639

CHIPPY 88279
CHIPPY'S DREAM
CHIRK 64132
CHIRK CASTLE 47940
CHIRK CHAFFINCH 76080
CHISWICK Lg Woolwich Town Cl motor. Ex GUCC/BW
CHIIVES 71292
CHLOE 51851
CHOAMIE 66565
CHOICE 500595
CHORLEY GIRL 69270
CHOUGH 47712
CHRISAN II 75839
CHRISMAR 72613
CHRIS'S RHAPSODY 47327
CHRISTA 68296
CHRISTENA B1184
CHRISTINA 45263
CHRISTINA 51733
CHRISTINA 69180
CHRISTINA 75898
CHRISTINA 80033
CHRISTINA 104470
CHRISTINA 500908
CHRISTINA II 69351
CHRISTINA ALICE 72379
CHRISTINA K 49173
CHRISTINE 47720
CHRISTINE 83856
CHRISTINE 103499
CHRISTINE MARGARET 60730
CHRISTINE MARIE 64856
CHRISTOBEL 70306
CHRISTOPHER JAMES Tug. Ex L Leigh & Co.
CHRISTOPHER ROBIN 47336
CHUB 89184 Mtce boat 9.2m BW-
CHUBASCO 60324 CLATTERCOTE WHARF NbT 50' red/grn. B: 1980 Alan Pickford in ex BR works at Swindon. 1.5 BL (1974). Base Crick marina GUC. Won John Player award at 1980 IWA Rally. 23582
CHUBBS NOOK 51752
CHUCKLEBUTTY *52452 NbC 30' red/grn*
CHUG 70668 NbT 29' blue/beige. B: 1981 Eggbridge marina, f/o previous owner. Sabb 760cc single cyl 10hp. Base Fox's marina, March. Previous names *Thunder* and *Thunderballs*. 24871
CHUG-A-LONG 86479
CHUG-A-LUG 92237
CHUGGER *Grp 30' wh*
CHURCH MOUSE 53205
CHURMA SAMAKI *NbT 55' grn/mar*
CHURNET Motor vessel BW-NW
CHURNET 45322
CHYSAWYA 70444
CHY YN DOWR 51004
CHY YN DOWR 70011 JOAN AND DAVID DREDGE NbST 46' grn. B: 1980 originally 30' Peter Nicholls, stretched and f/o Stowe Hill 1985. Leyland 4 cyl 1500cc. Base Staffs & Worcs canal north of bridge 43. Unusually long pointed stern deck of Sheerness pattern. Name means "Home on the Water" in Cornish. 20125
CILGERRAN CASTLE Hire. NbC 36' grn/yel. Base Castle Narrowboats, Gilwern. 00217
CINDERS 76620
CINDY 76034
CINDY 102388
CINNAMON 66512
CIRCUMBENDIBUS 74142
CIRRO STRATUS 60864
CIRRUS 48713
CIRRUS 68206
CIRRUS 73095
CITY Bantam "Pusher" tug, commercial and navigation maintenance 23', b 8'6", d 4' blue/red. B: circa 1950 E C Jones & Sons, Brentford. Lister JP3. Base Mill Wharf, Wyre Piddle, Lower Avon. Ex British Waterways Board stationed until declared "surplus to requirements" in 1963 at Brentford Docks, when purchased by a small consortium of Lower Avon Navigation Trust members to enable restoration of Lower Avon to be completed and then maintained. Subsequently all "shares" were transferred to the Trust by gifts. See Waterways World December 1989. 033907
CITY OF BIRMINGHAM 46355
CITY OF SALFORD B7630
CLAIRE 94758
CLAIRE JUSTINE 50256
CLAIRE LOUISE 45046
CLAIRE LOUISE 53690
CLAIRE MARIE 50763
CLANCY *52173 NbT 60' blue/mar*
CLANFORD 89275 Power boat 18m BW-CATM
CLAN MACDONALD 74596
CLANSMAN 48298
CLANSMAN 68834
CLARA 51141
CLARA 64628
CLARA 68217
CLARA-SU
CLARA SUE 52618
CLARE ELIZABETH 76646
CLARENCE 48925
CLARENCE HENRY 65176
CLAREPOOL 45660
CLARET 68612 SAISONS Hire. NbT 50' mar/grn. B: 1978 Hancock & Lane, f/o Alvechurch Boat Centre. BMC 1.5. Base Welford. 009137
CLARICE ELIZABETH 54750
CLARRIE *45635 NbT 30' red/grn*
CLARRY 45635
CLASSIC 74916
CLAUDIO 500822
CLAY DANCER 47127
CLAYDON 76322
CLAYHANGER 46914
CLAYTON 62562
CLAYTON BLUEBUOY 45632
CLEA 60523
CLEARWATER Weed boat 15' BW-BBC
CLEARWATER 82160 12' BW-LON
CLEE HILL 78048
CLEEVE CASTLE *NbT 30' red/blue*
CLEM 70368

CLEMATIS Yarwoods fleet no. 331. Ex WW. Motor to *GIFFORD*
CLEMENTINE 51269
CLENT 54810
CLENT 61310
CLENT 354 71242 Motor. Ex FMC/BW
CLEO 51663
CLEO 73169
CLEOPATRA 64696 NbC steel hull, wooden top 54' blue. B: 1969 - hull by Graham Parker, no. 13 at Norton Canes; top and f/o for Wyvern Shipping at Leighton Buzzard (was hire boat 1969-81). Lister 2 cyl SR. Base Calcutt marina, GUC. Has a 6" keel the length of the boat. 1996 wooden top steel cladded at Norton Canes. 24756
CLEOPATRA 67488
CLEOPATRA II 79512 V J & M T DRAPER UXBRIDGE WHARF NbC 55' red/grn. B: 1975 Black Bull Engineering Bootle. BMC 1.5 fitted 1984 (prev. SABB 2cyl). Base Uxbridge GUC. Boat named *Askari* until c1986. Regd. in Liverpool No. 21 in 1975 official no. 364400.22446
CLIB CONDOR 72242
CLIFTON 62230
CLIFTON 83749 Power boat 16m BW-CATM
CLINKER 75605
CLIO B1507
CLIO No 4 Motor
CLIPPER 50964
CLIPPER 73950
CLIPSTON 47475
CLITHEROE II Motor vessel BW-NW
CLIVE OF INDIA 80511 BW-
CLOTTED CREAM 99850
CLOUD 69951
CLOUD CUCKOO LAND 79213
CLOUDED VISION 45317
CLOUD NINE 52642
CLOUD NINE 60282
CLOVER 52799
CLOVER 77570
CLOVER Commercial carrying working motor in livery as formerly operated under Captain Cargo Ltd. - red/grn/yel; steel composite construction. B: 1935 for Fellows, Morton & Clayton Ltd. Lister 2HB. Base Coventry & GU canals. 031814
CLOVER NbC 45' grn/red. B: 1978 Colecraft, "but f/o seems to have been carried out by a one-armed, one-eyed chimpanzee". BMC 1.5D/PRM160 g'box. Base Egerton Narrowboats. Short 5' foredeck, long 32'6" cabin. Currently undergoing complete refit for eventual residential use. Unique central heating system involving Squirrel stove up front and an Ellis Heatmaster at back end, both coupled using 28mm pipe and 3 radiators - high quality installation by owner *(ask him about it!)* - 2 winters aboard: never been lower than 26°. 251011
CLOVER Barney(51) 1975 48'
CLOVERLEAF 94229
CLOVERLEY 89250 Maintenance boat 52' BW-BBC
CLUB CENTURION 51762
CLUB CENTURION III 45736

CLUB CLASSIC 51761
CLUB KNIGHT 68197
CLUMBER 65091
CLUTHER 94000
CLYDESDALE 51428
CLYTIE 60288
COALSACKS 65848
COASTER 50485
COBBLERS 66136
COBWEB 53284
COBWEB 74687
COCH Y BONDDU 66572
COCKATOO 47724
COCKLE 102022
COCKLESHELL 91461
COCKLESHELL 104226
COCKNEY REBEL 64165
COCKNEY REBEL Barney(45) 1975 35' *(ex Knotweed)*
COCK ROBIN 076752 THRUPP NbC 59'6" Mercedes red/mid Brunswick grn. B: 1983(?). Lister ST3. Base Thrupp Canal Cruising Club, S.Oxford canal. 20190
COCKY 60768
COCO 74466
COCO-DE-MER 102818
COFFEE CREAM 66174
COFFEE JOHNNY 51886
COG Hopper 21m BW-LAP
COIRE NA CISTA 61006
COLDSTREAM 101911
COLE Motor **boat 11m** BW-LAP
COLEFORD 76324
COLEHURST *NbT 50' mar*
COLEMERE 72659
COLESHILL 064203 FOXTON BOAT SERVICES LTD Nb Large Woolwich motor, unconverted, all steel. 71'6", d 3'6" dk admiralty grey/orange. B: 1930s Harland & Wolff, Woolwich. Lister HA3. Base Foxton bottom lock. Used for carrying, contracting, odd jobs, etc. 0381082
COLIN TOO 79446
COLLEDGE Motor boat 11m BW-LAP
COLLETTE 46936
COLLETTES STAR 100361
COLLIE CROSS 47649
COLLINGWOOD BIRMINGHAM & MIDLAND CANAL CARRYING Co. No.5 "Admiral" class commercial Nb, Camping boat ("Camping Afloat") 70', b 7' coach grn/chrome yel. B: circa 1959 Isaac Pimblott & Co. Ltd, Northwich for British Transport Commission (Waterways). Armstrong-Siddeley AS2 twin cyl 20bhp. Base Birmingham Gas Street basin. Exterior preserves original look. Interior provides sleeping, cooking and living accommodation for up to 12 people "under canvas". Normally cruises BCN and Northern Stratford canal. Operates anywhere on system (inc. M.S.C.) but mainly on long circuits from Birmingham through Midlands. Acted as support boat for St. John Ambulance Brigade charity walk, Birmingham to London 1995. 034993
COLNE Motor vessel BW-NW
COLONEL No 65 Saltley motor. Ex FMC

River Severn passenger vessel *MV Conway Castle* at Upton-on-Severn

COLONEL BOGEY IV 47804
COLONEL BY 70123
COLUMBA 73721 Sm Woolwich Star Cl motor. Ex GUCC
COLUMBA *NbC 25' red/blue*
COLUMBIA B0640
COLUMBINE 31637
COLUMBUS 65227 NCCC HIGH LANE Grp centre cockpit "Buckingham" 25' wh/bl. B: 1970 approx. Leisure Craft, Wolverhampton. Yamaha 10hp petrol ob. Base Macclesfield canal. Adventurous cruising in past few years has included Manchester Ship canal, R.Weaver, R.Dee above weir, Severn estuary Sharpness-Bristol, R.Ouse Selby-Ripon, R.Trent Keadby-Cromwell and Rochdale canal. 20171
COLUMBUS No 1 45374
COMBERMERE 45661
COME ON EILEEN 49134
COMET Sm Woolwich Star Cl motor. Ex GUCC/BW
COMET 87456 Tug BW-NW
COMET 68979
COMET 70140
COMET 75705
COMFORTABLY NUMB
COMFREY 49273
COMFREY 60292
COMFREY No 348 *NbT 60' blue/red*
COMFREY Barney(11) 1971 62'
COMMANCHE 70384
COMMANCHE 71790
COMMANDER 84674
COMMUNICATOR Motor
COMMUNICATOR 51259

COMPROMISE 73096
COMRADE 65911
COMUS 61663 COVENTRY Nb 36' sky blue/wh. B: 1970 Sam Springer. 1500cc Morris 4cyl keel cooled, PRM 100 g'box. Base Wyken Old Pit Basin, Coventry. Original Springer £480 hull + £220 superstructure! 20140
CONCORDE 77389
CONCORDIA *NbT blue/red*
CON DE MAR 75108
CONDER MILLER 76132
CONDOR 61884
CONGER 47686 H G & J A WINTER SAUL JUNCTION NbT 65' grn/crm. B: 1988 R & W Davies & Sons Ltd, Junction Dry Dock, Saul Junction. 1955 Gardner 4LW marine with marine gearbox - rebuilt by owner. Base High House marina, nr Weedon, GUC. 21329
CONINGSBY GODALMING Nb 42' grn/crm. B: 1974 Farncombe Boat House. Lister SR2 MGR2 aircooled. Base Godalming R.Wey. First narrow boat built by Farncombe Boat House with Plaque No. 1. 23670
CONISBROUGH 47622
CONISTON 48015
CONISTON 72960 GREENSLADE & SON DEVIZES Nb 58' red/grn. B: 1981 Liverpool Boatbuilders. Base Devizes marina. "Happy family boat". 24852
CONNAUGHT 65448 BURLAND NbT 40' grn B: 1974 Water Travel, Autherley Junction. Lister. Base near Bunbury, SU. One of earliest purpose built traditional narrowboats for leisure use. Owning family have motor racing connections; boat named after British car that gave a British

driver the first Grand Prix win for Britain in 31 years - at Syracuse in Sicily in 1955. Cratch painted black/white chequerboard design to represent this victory and superstructure is of course British Racing green. 25951
CONNIE 73379
CONQUEST 65147
CONQUEST 102837
CONSALL FORGE 77968
CONSILLO 69760
CONSTANCE NbC 40' red/grn
CONSTANCE 52665 NbC blue
CONSTANCE 69467
CONSTANCE MAY 78775
CONTACT B1042
CONTENT 68385
CONTESSA 65333
CONUNDRUM PYRFORD NbC 43'9" grn/red. B: 1984 Colecraft. BL 1.5. Base Pyrford Marina, R.Wey. 23754
CONWAY 79284
CONWAY No 2 54493
CONWAY CASTLE R.Severn passenger vessel
COOMBES WOOD 78110
COOMESWOOD 49367
CO-OPERATION 78525
COPELIA 90878
COPPERKINS II 52627 NbT 50' grn/crm
CORAL 45657
CORAL Hire. NbC 56' blue/red. Base The Wyvern Shipping Co, Linslade, GU. 00441
CORAL ...(something) see MISSY
CORAL BAY 76855
CORBAR 64066
CORCORAN 46338
CORDELIA 49046
CORDELIA 77198
CORDELIA 101939
CORIANDER 53885
CORIANDER 54110
CORIXA 49262
CORIXA 66810
CORIXA N6812
CORIXA II 073426 S & M ARKLESS & SON HOPWAS NbT 43' Oxford blue/red. B: 1985 Springer. 1.5 BMC. Base Hopwas School Br.20185
CORKSCREW 53419
CORMORANT 61665
CORNCOCKLE 79822 Grp
CORNCRAKE 47715
CORNDOLLY 69786 NbC 35' red/grn. B: 1980 Eggbridge, Newark. Lister SR2. Base Bristol City docks. Cratch fitted. 24829
CORN DOLLY 74691
CORNELIAN 67670
CORNELIAN 500601
CORNMILL NbT crm/blue
CORNWALL Motor vessel BW-NW
CORNWALL 46943
COROLLA Nb Small Woolwich motor - unconverted. All steel (new bottom) undergoing restoration 71'6", d 3'6" rust. B: 193- Harland & Wolff. Lister HA3. Base Foxton bottom lock. Has been Water Wagtail, BW Zoo Bus, Regents Park & Brummagem Fly tripper in Birmingham.0381084
COROMANDEL 63786
CORONA 79685 TREVOR MAGGS RUGBY Nb Working: commercial cargo carrying and pleasure. 72', b 7', d 3' grn/red. B: 1935 Harland & Wolff Ltd, Woolwich for GUCCC. Lister HR2 air cooled 2 cyl fitted 1970. Base Rugby Wharf. Restored to original working condition except no cloths. 21264
CORONATION 070676 BCN 14404 Bantock Butty (motorised and converted to full cabin) 70' red/grn. B: 1895 T. Bantock Ltd., guaged at Tipton, Old Hill, Oldbury on 3rd July 1895. Numbered 24 in the Bantock fleet. Cabin conversion by Ivy Bridge Marine Braunston, f/o by Kelvin White & Jeff Dennison. BMC 1.8 & Volvo hydraulic drive. Base Ansty, br.14 N.Oxford canal. As built this was a long distance Joey but had no name or cabin. Much of working life served in fleet of T&S Elements Ltd. of Birmingham and Oldbury. Passed to BWB in 1947 and subsequently used as part of a floating pontoon landing stage at Newark. Purchased by Willow Wren Kearns Ltd., Middlewich in 1980 and re-sold to Northern Canal Carriers in January 1981 who carried out rebottoming and much other restoration, naming her Coronation. The full history of further restoration to the present is an interesting one and can no doubt be learned by those who see and enjoy the show "They're Coming Back to the Water" by Folkwise for whom the boat is a base. 25983
CORONATION 79685
CORONIS (not a complete vessel) Restored lettering of GUCCCo. Ltd. in 1937 livery Nb butty (part of), rivetted steel hull, wooden bottom 25' (cut down to), b 7' blue/red. B: 1935 Harland & Wolff Ltd., cabin carpentry restored by Tony Forward. Base as Exhibit at London Canal Museum. This is the rear end of ex-GUCCC Small Woolwich butty (1937 fleet no. 259), restored as walk-through indoor exhibit from a derelict hull in 1992-94. Original front 40' is in other ownership, converted as a NbC with same name. 0361013
CORVUS 80220 Motor vessel 21.6m BW-NE
CORYDORAS 63803
COSA NOSTRA 85854

GET SMART
Quality **CANOPIES**, frames,
COVERS, etc. @ sensible prices
INC. fit **NO** VAT
Contact David on **01492 592652**
Also repairs by post
11 Y Bryn, GLAN CONWY LL28 5NJ

COSETTE 46599 RICKMANSWORTH NbT 39' grn/red. B: 1987 Arcrite. Vetus. Base Rickmansworth GUC. 21272
COSTA PACKET 78307
COTESBACH 76783
COTSWOLD 052367 SCC CO. NbTug 44', d 2'10" blue/grn. D: 1992 Simon Wain, Stretton Wharf, SU canal. Lister HRW 2. Base Stretton Wharf. Josher replica. Named after last Josher to be ordered and which was scrapped after construction. 24810
COTSWOLD Motor vessel Mtce boat 38'9" BW-NW
COTSWOLD *NbT 50' mar/grn*
COTSWOLD 76312
COTSWOLD 500575
COUNT see ENTERPRISE No. 1
COUNTESS 49997
COUNTESS 51575
COUNTESS 072897 FELLOWS MORTON & CLAYTON LTD 1396 NbT Iron hull with steel cabin. 60' bl/wh. B: 1897 Saltley, Birmingham. ex FMC steamer - now Lister JP3 vintage diesel. Based Staffs & Worcs. canal. FMC contracted out the steamer to John Dickinsons of Croxley as a "paper dasher". It was painted in their colours for many years. Presently fitted with full length cabin incorporating trad back cabin and engine room by Gilberts of Charity Dock. Historic Narrow Boat Owners' Club Ref 721 22503
COUNTESS 74436
COUNTESS II 50689
COUNTESS 3 66777
COUNTESS OF MOIRA 60398 BCN 18751 NbT riveted iron 50', b 7', d 2'9" grn/red. B: 1890's unknown builder. Turner V twin 12hp (last engine made by Turner Mfg. Co). Base Hinckley Boat Club, Hinckley Arm. Hot Holer built with iron bottom. 24823
COUNTESS OF THE CUT 66775
COUPAR ANGUS 78109
COVERDALE 66158
COWLEY TUNNEL 63722 *NbC 30' mar/crm*
COYPU 67274
COZZEE REMBRANDT 46091
CRACKLIN' ROSIE 100294
CRACKLIN' ROSIE *N5155 NbC 40' red/grey*
CRAGDALE 79231
CRAIGDALE CREEPER 076288 NbC 65' grn/mar. B: 1982 Clubline Cruisers, self f/o complete 1986. 1.8 Thornycroft. Base Old Lea Wharf, Br 42 SU canal. 20206
CRAMOND BRIG 91957
CRANE 43 Motor. Ex FMC/BW
CRANESWATER 46971
CRANFLEET Motor vessel 11.5m BW-NE
CRATES CASTLE 48538
CRAVEN MAID 65312
CRAWFORDS CLAN 78799
CRAYCOMBE COMPANION 77350
CRAYFISH 45932
CRAYFISH 53737
CRAZY FOX *50' blue*

CREAM CRACKER 54067 ROSEMARY & JOHN / JOHN & ROSEMARY WORCESTER Nb 62' crm/ brown. B: 1992/94 Norton Canes Boatbuilders, f/o Warwickshire Narrowboats. Perkins MC42 Base Lowesmoor Wharf, Worcester. Electric piano organ, full air conditioning, permanent double bed swings up to form cabin wall, treatment to give rust-free hull! Name has many connotations including a "code" for MG car owners who will be aware of the team of MG trial and rally cars known as "cream crackers"; the team was so successful that other competitors complained of unfair competition! The cars' cream/brown colour scheme has been repeated on the boat and owners like them as a change from usual nb colour schemes. "She is a Cracker!" 20155
CREAM CRACKER 65466
CREAMCRACKER 54067
CRE-DAL-WOOD 48510 ERIC & DOREEN WOOD WHITTINGTON NbST 50' red/grn. B: 1990 Canal Transport Services Norton Canes, Dennis Cooper. Thornycroft 1.8 LD Ford. Base Br. 80 Coventry canal. 23650
CREEPING JENNY 68033
CREST OF A KNAVE 100745
CRESTED GREBE 68977
CRESTED GREBE 89965
CRESTED LARK 50391
CRETE 48246
CRETE *NbT grn*
CRICKET Mtce boat flat powered BW-NW
CRIMOND 51569
CRIMOND 65914
CRINAN 48651
CRINKLEY BOTTOM 51404 NbC 36' blue/lt blue. B: 1991/92 Springer, diy f/o. BMC 1.5. Base Wheelton, L&L canal. Cruised all L&L incl into Liverpool, Rufford, Preston Dock, Douglas, Ribble. 24811
CRISP 61836
CRISTAL 62415
CROMDALE *75918 NbT 55' crm/grn*
CROMFORD 49249
CROSBY *500726 NbST blue/red*
CROW 74962
CROWFOOT 75756
CROWN 1 74802
CROWN 192 Tug.
CRUACHAN 66645 Nb 44' grn/mar. B: 1974 Fernie hull, f/o by Phil Gardner, Welford Canal Boats. Lister S.T.2. Base GUC. 22443
CRUISE ALONG 60309
CRUSADER *Grp 35' crm/brown*
CRUSADER 45434
CRUSADER 52037
CRUSADER 67932
CRUSADER 73408
CRUSADER II 77002
CRUSOE 64103
CRUSOE TOO 73373
CRYSTAL Hire. NbC 56' blue/red. Base The Wyvern Shipping Co, Linslade, GU 00440
CRYSTAL 47694

CRYSTAL 75542
CUDDINGTON Weaver Packet. Boat Museum
CUDDLY DUCK *NbC 45' crm/red*
CUDDY 53998 NbT 28' grn/red. B: 1993 R&D Fabrications, diy f/o. Nanni. Base R.Soar.   251010
CUIDADO B0251
CULDROSE 78832
CULPIN *Nb 40' wh/bl*
CUMBERLAND 73188
CUMBRIA 73841
CUMBRIAN LASS 72943
CUMUDA 64058
CUMULUS TWO 46032
CUNHELDA 52758
CURDWORTH Flat 12m BW-CATM
CURIOSITY 80884
CURLEW 47144
CURLEW 60213
CURLEW 94058
CURSTAIDH 69240
CUSHY 102905
CUSHIE BUTTERFIELD 061455 Nb orange/ Donegal grn. B: 1972 Braunston Boats Ltd. (Chris Barney(14)). Sabb 8hp. Base Wyken basin, Coventry Canal Society.   203
CUSHY BUTTERFIELD 47719
CUT ABOVE 76175
CUTLASS 51898
CUTLASS 3 66269
CUTTER 73935
CUTTER 78858
CUTTY'S ARK 68862 WHITWORTH TCC STAINFORTH NbC - Springer 26' yel/red. B: 1961-66 Stuart Whitworth, Lister SL1. Base TCC Stainforth basin, nr. Thorne. Renovated from Rust Bucket to CofC May 1996 and admired greatly! Visited by 81 year old Eric, relative of owner from Adelaide, who crewed from Thorne to Selby and Leeds to Stainforth which gave him much needed fillip to LIVE! He had heard about the boat and made models of gypsy caravans to sell to raise his fare for the visit. *Cutty's Ark* now flies copy of R.Murray flag of 1860 and is famous in Adelaide!   23568
CUTTY WREN 70066
CUTTY WREN 76460
CUTY P 79028
CWM TUDU 77626
CYBELE 67868
CYDER APPLE 68490
CYGNET 46633
CYGNET 62479
CYGNET 70881
CYGNET 74913
CYGNET B0637
CYGNET 20 101220
CYGNUS 51295
CYGNUS Sm Woolwich Star Cl butty. Ex GUCC/BW
CYGNUS NOVA *77204 NbT 35' mar/blue*
CYNUS OLOR 69788
CYGNUS OLOR 74284
CYMAR 68388

CYMBELSTERN 75958
CYNBARITU *NbC 50' blue*
CYPRESS Commercial Nb "Tree" class, originally a motor, currently no engine; originally composite (steel sides, elm bottom), now all steel. Commercial contract work. 70', b 7' cabin awaiting further restoration - no decoration at present. B: W J Yarwood & Co Ltd, Northwich for FM & C Ltd. Used as butty, to *Collingwood*, *Yeoford* or other motors. Base Birmingham Gas Street basin. Starred in Cliff Richard's film "Take Me High" c1974 under alias of *Sophie*, while still in normal condition. Also starred regularly in TV "Crossroads" as residence of "Vera Downend", actress. Operates BCN/Midlands.   034994
CYPRINA 51771
CYPRUS 70186 Unconverted working Nb motor used for commercial carrying and pleasure. 70'6", b 7', d 3' blue/yel. B: 1935 W J Yarwood, Northwich, Cheshire. Armstrong Siddley AS2 (originally a Russell Newbery engine). Construction essentially as original (except for engine replacement) including composite, i.e. elm, bottoms. Butty built at same time is *Cedar* (see entry). These were one of two pairs originally ordered for the Erewash Canal Carrying Co. Design chosen was that of GUCCC "Star" class except one foot shorter to make operation through a particularly short lock on R.Soar less of a problem (also helps with passage through BCN, says owner with feeling!). Base Braunston.   23639
CYRALICE 79026
CYREET II 31112
CYRUS LILY 77327

D

Ducks galore, a BCN tug made to fit, UA engineer celebrated, a trip to Jerusalem (partly), a "Magic" boat and many energetic DIY projects.

DABBLER 101373
DABCHICK 60914
DABCHICK 66685
DABCHICK 69304
DABCHICK 79887
DACE 89209 Mtce boat 9.2m BW-
DAEDALUS 77688
DAFFERS 78128
DAFFODIL Hire. NbC 42' blue/red. Base The Wyvern Shipping Co, Linslade, GU.   00454
DAFFODIL 67788
DAFFODIL 77048
DAFFODIL 89139
DAFFODILS 500065
DAFFS 63055
DAFFY MAJOR 92014 Grp Trentcraft 20 6.8m yel/wh. B: 1978 trentcraft, f/o by owner. Ob. Base Osberton, Chesterfield canal. Square windows which had previously been driven to Jerusalem (in

a motor caravan), right hand drive. Craft was not named after a politician who was unknown in 1978. 261076
DAGRO 73578
DAGY 1 30259
DAISEY 65807
DAISY 49223
DAISY 49417
DAISY 49885
DAISY 68062
DAISY 72642
DAISY 86924
DAISY 103123
DAISY ADELE 64306
DAISY ANN 46720
DAISY H 65886
DAISY MAY 049990 Hire. NbST 45' navy blue/lt blue. B: 1991 Brummagem Boats. Base Bradford on Avon marina. 013228
DAISY MAY 52672
DAK HAAN 45850
DAKIMA 78276
DALE 075471 P & D PENIKET AND SONS STOURBRIDGE NbT 47' British racing grn/mar. B: 1986 Delph Marine, self f/o. Petter twin (1947). Base Hawne Basin, Dudley No. 2 canal. 24897
DALESCRAFT 68700
DALES LADY 71424
DALESMAN 64412 Grp 26' wh/blue. B: 1978 Creighton. Yamaha 15hp elec start 2stroke. Base Roberts Farm, Mon & Brec canal. 23575
DALES PIONEER see ORION
DALES VOYAGER see ORION
DALMAH 71801
DAMACENA 51846
DAMARIS 053495 NbT 45' dk blue/mar. B: 1992 Liverpool Boats, self f/o completed 1993. BMC 1.5. Base Hainsworth Boatyard, Bingley. 23643
DAMARKAND 45177
DAMON 89715
DAMSEL 85025 Grp Norman Conquest 20' wh. B: 1979 Norman. Yamaha 9.9 4-str ob. Base Hoe Mill Lock, Chelmer & Blackwater Navigat'n.24869
DAMSELFLY 046641 J.W.F. & J.M. GREEN BRAUNSTON NbT 60' midnight blue/signal red. B: 1989 Colecraft, f/o Rugby Boatbuilders. Russell Newbery DM2. Base Welton Hythe marina. 20188
DAMSON 51244
DAMSON 71630 MIDDLEWICH NARROW-BOATS No.3 Hire. Nb 60' grn/red. B: 1989 Colecraft, f/o IML Anderton, much modified by Middlewich Narrowboats since acquired in 1991. Base Middlewich. Ex IML Anderton marina - original name *Bedale*. 028743
DANBURY 76033
DANCER 30498
DANDELION 49601
DANDELION 60109
DANDELION 064613 NbC 45' grn/red. B: 1974 Rugby. Lister SR2. Base Aylesbury Arm GU.23657
DANDELION 74890
DANDELION *NbT 70' red/grn*
DANDILY 101477

DANE 18 60329 Motor. Ex SCCC/T Clayton
DANE Motor vessel + crane BW-NW
DANGLEBERRY 50798
DANIEL 54561
DANIEL 71367 Motor
DANIEL 54561 CADDICK & CO. TOWAGE & STEERAGE NbT 43' dk grn/ivory. D. 1995 Phil Jones Hatherton Junction, owners f/o 1996, lettering/scrolls by Dave Moseley. Vintage Lister HA2 with Lister g'box. Base R.Soar Loughborough area. Built by BCN specialist to replicate a BCN tug of 1930's era. Length determined precisely by length of owners' garden mooring. Trad boatmans cabin, remainder finished with an 'Edwardian' feel including 'Godin' solid fuel stove of the period. 205
DANIEL *NbTug 50' mar/bl*
DANIEL ADAMSON MSC Tug. Boat Museum
DANIELLA J. 47439
DANIEL OAKLEY 47122
DANIEM 46163
DAN JAN 101247
DANMARK 79633
DAN & MAT 103665
DANNY BOY 47113
DANNY BOY 63972
DANSCIGAR 63580 Nb 40' royal blue. B: c1975 Springer in "Old Sam's time". BMC 1500. Base Pitstone Wharf GU. Apparently a previous owner called Dan smoked long cigars. 2095
DAPHNE 48 Nursers motor. Ex Barlow
DAPHNE 491
DAPHNE 72622
D'ARCY 70196
D'ARCY DANCER 61963
DARK STAR 51051
DARK STAR 52112
DARLEY 135 Large Woolwich Town Cl motor. Ex GUCC/BW/WW
DARLEY 160
DARREN B8107
DARSTAR No 6 49443
DART 53053
D'ARTAGNAN 66692
DARTMIST 77432
DARTMOOR 61960
DART OF GAYTON 71625
DARWEN 80086
DASA B1368
DASH 73166
DASH 75530
DASH 85116
DASHBAR 53979
DASHWOOD 48834
DATLEDO 75023
DAVID HUTCHINGS 064002 NbC 44' wh/dk blue hull. B: 1974 Shropshire Union Boatbuilders, Norbury Junction. 42hp Mercedes-Benz. Base Willowtree Marina GU (Paddington Arm). 'Frobisher' style cruiser top, sliding roof over main cabin. Large aft deck, tiller steering plus alternative hydraulic wheel steering + duplicate instrument console from front cabin. Present at opening of Upper Avon Navigation in 1974 - named after the

57

engineer with his permission. Cruised Anderton lift, Manchester Ship canal, Severn Estuary Sharpness-Avonmouth & tidal Thames   22476
DAVID LEWIS 72108
DAVID LIVINGSTONE *NbC 45' wh/blue*
DAVID "PAPA" THOMAS (hull no. 80485) Passenger Trip Boat Steel hull, timber cabin 36', b 7'6" red/grn. B: 1973, converted to trip boat 1993, builder unknown, f/o and operated by Swansea Canal Society. 20hp petrol ob. Base Swansea canal at Pontardawe.   2010
DAVINEKA 73189
DAVRO N6231
DAVROS 76215
DAVRU 79269
DAV-YVON 62807
DAWDLER 62433
DAWDLERS DREAM 54974
DAWN 77010
DAWN 78554
DAWN 78846
DAWN 82697
DAWN B7584
DAWN ADVENTURE 78208
DAWN-A-LOU 80213
DAWN BREEZE 50621
DAWN CHORUS 50332
DAWN DRIFTER
DAWN LIGHT 30119
DAWN MIST 64486
DAWN MIST 67751
DAWN MIST 75620
DAWN PIPER 53265
DAWN PIPER 74352
DAWN PIPER 77866
DAWN STAR 50194 Hire. NbC 50' blue/yel. B: 1991 John South, f/o Starline Narrowboats. Lister TS3 Hurth HBW 150 g'box. Base Upton marina, R.Severn.   008112
DAWN STAR *NbC 50' blue/crm*
DAWN STAR 70950
DAWN TRADER 50043
DAWN TREADER 46808
DAWN TREADER 52525
DAWN TREADER 60714
DAWNTREADER 62122
DAWN TREADER 64409
DAWN TREADER 64567
DAWN TREADER 92015
DAWNTREADER G14264
DAWN TREADER M21538 KINGFISHER PROJECT Purpose-built day-trip boat for the handicapped. 27', b 10'6" blue. B: 1992 Mike Sivewright, Middlewich. 20hp Vetus. Base Wateringbury, R.Medway   21348
DAYBREAK 63349
DAYDREAM 46976
DAYDREAM 63441
DAYDREAM 65222 Cruiser 11m. B: 1978 Frank Davies. Perkins 4203. Base High Onn. Ferro concrete hull, pine superstructure with sliding canopy all built by same man.   21256
DAYDREAM 66897
DAYDREAM 67759

DAYDREAMER 63063
DAYEQ 50997
DAYJO 64612
DAYLIGHT 64564
DAYLIGHT KATE 77221
DAYS AWAY *NbC grn/red*
DEAD SLOW 52954
DEAL *78409 NbC 35' mar/blue*
DEANBROOK 74033
DEBBIE 51052
DECKWYN 95854
DEE 67693
DEE 79784
DEE 89312 Motor vessel Piling Craft BW-NW
DEE BEE 71254 NbC 35', b 7' grn/red. B: 1982 Springer, diy f/o. BMC 1.5, Hurth g'box. Base Sileby Mill Boatyard.   24866
DEE BEE 98107
DEEBELL 71250
DEE DAY 98669
DEE DEE V 75961
DEEPLY DIPPY 87656
DEEP PURPLE 52448
DEERFIELD 48453
DEE VALLEY 45574
DE HOOP CONCORDIA 719038 (port of London) LONDON Dutch sailing barge (Ooost Zee Tjalk) 21.9m, b 4.95m, d 1.3m Lt brown/burgundy.   B: 1886 Swartsluis, Netherlands; conversion to residential 1953 by Zwolle, Netherlands. 6 cyl Ford 105bhp + single mast gaff/sloop rig sail. Base Shepperton, R.Thames. The only tjalk of its kind in this country (only a few in Holland). Sea-going as well as inland. Used to trade wood from the East sea islands to Holland/North England via the East Sea canal. Iron hull, single piece 50ft spruce mast.   261073
DEIMOS 82 Sm Woolwich Star Cl motor. Ex GUCC/BW
DEINOS 65447
DEJA-VU 74288
DE JA VUE *Grp 18' blue/wh*
DELAMERE 62514
DELAWARE 62032
DEL-BOY 80851
DELFT 54686
DELICIA 49010
DELIGHT 52539
DELILAH 51952
DELILAH 75213
DELILAH 91470
DELLADE'ERA 52241
DELL RITA 104286
DELMAR III 67526
DELOS 67845
DELPH 69493
DELPHI 60091
DELPHI No 1 47840
DELPHI II 51222
DELPHI II 70085
DELPHINIUM 49206
DELPHINIUS 25984 MARKET HARBOROUGH NbT 50' mar/dk blue. B: 1990 M&N Narrowboats. Leyland 1.8. Base Debdale Wharf,

GU-Leics. 25984
DELTA Dredger 14m BW-LAP
DELTA 47443
DELTA DAWN 63269
DELTA LADY II 53082
DELTA STAR 62750
DEMBY ROSE *NbT 35′ red/grn*
DEMELZA 51380
DEMETRIUS 53697
DEMI SEC 100420 Grp - Cleopatra 700 Weekender 23′, b 8′6″ wh/orange freeboard. B: 1973 Essex Yacht Builders Ltd, Vallasea Island. Ford XFlow petrol. Base Fossdyke. 24813
DENBY ROSE 72119
DENDERA 50637
DENEBOLA 12501
DENELZA *51380 NbC 40′ blue/grn*
DE NIJVERHEID 72288
DENMARK 51400
DENMEAD *NbT 50′ grn*
DENMEAD 74249
DENREA 62146
DEOGRENE 61188
DEPHIN 70307
DERBY 49550
DERI II 49857
DEROLA 68998
DERRY MIST 500768
DERVAIG 70912
DERWENT 77805
DERWENT 78050
DERWENT Tug 10m BW-NE
DESDEMONA 69889
DESIDERATA B1196 NO. 2 NbT 60′ bl/wh. B: 1975 Keadby Marine. BMC 3.8hp. Base Walton, Bridgewater canal. Steel, glazed cratch. Originally timber top - steel top fitted 1995. 20122
DESPERADO B0261
DESSIE 79558
DESSY 67657 NbC 51′ red/grn. B: 1978 Sandpiper, f/o Grand Junction Boat Co., Blisworth Arm GU. Lister 2cyl air cooled. Base Barbridge, SU. "Just pure magic! - great charm and character with all mod cons". 22402
DESTARTE 52595 *NbC 50′ blue*
DESTINY 45203
DEUX CHEVAUX 48737
DEUX JEANS 46115
DEVA 61535
DEVA BO957
DEVANNY'S DREAM B1216
DEVON Motor vessel BW-NW
DEVON AYRE 80836 Grp 17′ red. B: 1968 Microplas model 501. Honda 10hp ob. Trailed, generally Ashby canal. 25965
DEVONIA STAR 54926
DEVON MIST 49560
DEVON REX 72171 NbC 50′ grn/red. B: 1987 Delph Marine, Brierley Hill. Perkins 4108. Base Residential - Bonded W'house, Stourbridge 22401
DEVON ROSE 96597
DEWBERRY 76595
DEWDROP 75836
DEWSBURY 64406

DEWSBURY 89752 Motor vessel 14.95m BW-NE
DIADEM 48789
DIAMOND J Chrichton, Saltney butty. Ex Mid & Coast/FMC
DIAMOND Hire. NbC 54′ blue/red. Base The Wyvern Shipping Co, Linslade, GU. 00438
DIAMOND 48185
DIAMOND 73712
DIAMOND 77047
DIAMOND 78305
DIANA 51508
DIANTHUS B 61993
DIDDICOY B0987
DIDI TWO 95409
DIDO 69029
DIDO 102901
DIE FLEDERMAUS 49966
DIESEL & DUST *500120 NbT 70′ grey/blue*
DIESEL DAISY *NbT 40′ mar/bl*
DIGBY 63041
DIGBY TOO 67146
DIGGER 60315
DIGGER 72310
DIGNITY 49283
DIHEDRAL *NbT 55′ blue/red*
DIHEDRAL 500612
DILIGENCE *71028 NbT 30′ grn/red*
DI LIZ 68579
DILKARA 71333
DILLEN 54930
DILLY BROWN 46231 PETE & PAT BROWN OXFORD CANAL Nb 54′ d 30″ brown/crm. B: 1989 complete owner built steel hull and superstructure and f/o including engine and bow thruster. 1939 Lister CE - twin flywheels - originally a stand-by generator, marinised and fitted with PRM 160 g'box driving 22″x18″ prop & 5 KVA generator. Base Oxford canal. Low style hull. Roof extends over well deck to cratch board, scalloped edge to top. 22447
DINARD 61706
DINARD 61707
DINGBAT II 62168 *Cruiser 25′*
DINGY 71442
DINKUM Dredger 15m BW-
DINKY 50070
DIOGENES 52917
DIPPER Sm Woolwich Star Cl butty. Ex GUCC/BW
DIPPER *NbC 40′ mar/lilac*
DIPPER 45594
DIPPER 51882
DIPPER 54486
DIPPER 69921
DIPPER 73704
DIPPER 84209
DIPPER 96378
DIRE STRAITS 45102
DIRE STRAITS 73135
DIRTWATER FOX 77001
DISCOVERY 53187
DISCOVERY 60106
DISSLEDO 64834 NbT - Oak and Elm - 40′

mar/grn. B: 1969 (?) Walton Deepfields Coseley. Air cooled SR11. Base Hawn Basin, Halesowen. Believed started as hire boat (SU Cruisers). 261063
DISTILLATION 52477
DITCH CRAWLER 78428
DITTON Yarwood "Station" open boat ex LMS/BR/BW/Threefellows
DITTON 66217
DIVER-SION II 49962
DIXIE 64505
DIXIE 65409
DIXIE 72764
D'KAP 72614
DOBBIN 49573
DOBERMAN 60551
DODGER 102500
DODI 47911
DODI 101973
DODONA Little Woolwich built in 1935 - shortened later to 50'. Now restored to working condition after conversion. Originally a butty but now has Lister SR3. She was a particular favourite of Susan Woolfitt, as she described in her book "Idle Women". Based GU-Leics. near Watford. Owners have spent 18 months on complete traditional restoration from near dereliction. When complete, livery will be predominantly yellow with blue trim. Original GUCCC fleet no. 269 - paired with *Columba* but later separated before sale to British Waterways, 1948. Currently used for leisure (?retired) *Dodona* may yet be available for lighter carrying duties in the near future. 23747
DOG HOUSE 51287
DOGFOOD 54605
DOLGOCH 79726
DOLICHE 68151
DOLLAR TILLER 53113
DOLLIANNA 53763

Is Your Boat In It?
Is the Entry Accurate?
Please see page 12 to find out how to get included or amended in the next edition

DOLLIANNA 573653 A & J C SHARPE NbST/Tug 50' midnight blue. B: 1994 G & J Reeves, f/o John Milburn Boats, Napton. Perkins. Base Kegworth Marine, R.Soar. 24800
DOLLY 45475
DOLLY 54682
DOLLY 73171
DOLLY BLUE 50418
DOLLY D 73847
DOLLY 'EM' *103364 Grp 20'*
DOLLY GREENE 500842
DOLLY MAE *NbC 40' grn/red*
DOLLY MAE 49591
DOLLY TUB 70900
DOLLY VARDEN 66664
DOLPHIN 60357
DOLPHIN 67629
DOLPHIN B0675
DOLPHIN 294 Yarwood motor. Ex FMC
DOM AELRED B1442

DOMANDA 71811
DOMINION B1467
DOMINO 45022
DOMINO 88939
DONA FILIPA 46275 *NbC 50' grn/red*
DONCASTER Motor vessel + crane 17.85m BW-NE
DONDEL 71516
DONELA *NbC 45' red/grn*
DONNA MAY 75339
DONOVAN B7496
DON'T PANIC! *NbT 50' red/blue*
DON'T PANIC 52902
DORA *NbC 50' blue*
DORA 73099
DORADO 80618 Sm Woolwich Star Cl motor. Ex GUCC/BW
DORAL B1350
DORANDA IV 66349
DOREEN 48700
DOREEN see *SAVILE*
DORELLA 79916
DORIAN B 79684
DORIC 64188
DORIC I 89156
DORIS 070133 Nb 43' fibreglass cabin on steel hull wh/yel. B: 1972 Swan Line, Fradley Junction (for private owner, not hire fleet). Lister air-cooled. Base Hargrave, SU/Chester arm. 22425
DORIS 70382
DORIS 79191
DORIS ALICE 60647 LONDON NbC 48' grn/red. B: 1978 Alvechurch Boats on Colecraft hull, interior refit 1986. Originally for hire as *Mistral*. 1.5 BMC. Name change in memory of owners' respective widowed mothers, Doris and Alice, who made boat ownership possible. 261067
DORMOUSE 72080
DORNE 95529
DOROTHEA 68702
DOROTHY ANN 65969
DOROTHY DEE 70047
DOROTHY GRACE 69934
DOROTHY LOUISA 73396
DOROTHY MARY 47987 NbC 28' mar/grn. B: 1990 builder unknown. Mitsubishi Vetus (7kw). Base Rugby Wharf. 22389
DOROTHY MAUD 51385
DOROTHY MAY 75140
DOROTHY ROSE II 73154
DORPETS DREAM 52269
DORROD 45237
DORSET 61816
DORSET BLUE 104369
DORY Yarwoods motor. Ex FMC/BW (conv to butty)
DOTTIE 75579
DOUBLE HAPPINESS B0990
DOUBLE JOY 71767
DOUBLE VISION 77895
DOUBTING THOMAS 74539
DOUBTING THOMAS II 50412
DOUGAL 72415
DOUGLAS II Crane boat BW-NW

A Spring early morning at Newbold, Rugby with *Dorothy Mary*

DOUGLAS BARWELL Purpose built welded steel hopper barge with removable 20 ton capacity hold. Used for navigation maintenance by Lower Avon Navigation Trust Ltd. 40', b 10', d 9". B: 1991 Watercraft, Worcester. Propulsion by Tug "City" *(see entry)*. Base Mill Wharf, Wyre Piddle. 033911
DOVE 63378
DOVEDALE 48611
DOVE OF BELGRADE 61691
DOVER 072072 CLIFTON CRUISERS Hire. NbC 45' grn/crm. B: 1985 Colecraft, f/o Clifton Cruisers. BL 1.5. Base Clifton Wharf. 025680
DOVETAIL 73318
DOWSABELL 45446
DOZY DORA TWO 52802
DRACK 50600
DRAGON 64983
DRAGON 67390
DRAGON 296 75265 Yarwoods motor. Ex FMC/BW
DRAGON 76489
DRAGONELLE 60705
DRAGONET 96752
DRAGONFLY KENNET AND AVON CANAL TRUST Trip boat - 12 seats. 25' red/grn. Base Pewsey, K&A raising funds for K&A Trust. 030856
DRAGONFLY Mtce boat, flat, dumb 30' BW-NW
DRAGONFLY 45381
DRAGONFLY 50130
DRAGONFLY 62588
DRAGONFLY 63839
DRAGONFLY 65038
DRAGONFLY 66780
DRAGONFLY *69190 Nb unconverted red/grn*
DRAGONFLY 70532
DRAGONFLY 75995
DRAGONFLY 76494
DRAGONFLY 79134
DRAGONFLY 81407
DRAGONFLY 88926
DRAGON LANCE 76597 NbC 49' to be repainted. B: John South. Lister Mark II ST2 air-cooled. Base Braunston marina. 2080
DRAKE Mtce boat, flat, dumb 9.15m BW-NW
DRAWK 67482
DRAWK TWO 51035
DRAYTON DRAGON 62809
DRAYTON MANOR 73895
DREADNOUGHT 47499
DREAMAKER 45682
DREAMFINDER *NbC 35' mar/red*
DREAMLAND TONIGHT 77874
DREAM MAKER 48012
DREAM OF AVALON 53445
DREAM ON 81351
DREAM SONG No 2 72818
DREAM STAR 50371
DREAMTIME 50564
DREAM TUNE B0890
DREEMS 69396
DRESDEN LADY 62943
DREYFUS 62079
DRIFT 2 83827
DRIFTER 63268
DRIFTER 63810
DRIFTER 65917

DRIFTER 73378
DRIFTER 77369
DRIFTER 78956
DRIFTER *500152 NbT 55' grn*
DRIFTER No 2 47856
DRIFTWEED 47606
DRIMBLE II 50236
DROMORE 45464
DRONE Mtce boat, flat, dumb 30' BW-NW
DRUM 73902
DRUM BEAT 67470
DRUMMER 77829
DRUNKEN DUCK 64471
DRYSDALE 45668
DUBGHALI 68630
DUBHE 272 Sm Woolwich Star Cl. Ex GUCC/BW
DUBTUB 45486
DUCHESS 50227
DUCHESS 52043
DUCHESS 52763
DUCHESS 60378
DUCHESS 60816
DUCHESS 65898
DUCHESS II 65010
DUCHESS II 65006
DUCHESS III 65007
DUCK 50507
DUCK 99829
DUCK EM ALL 72574
DUCKETT 65131
DUCKLING 49809
DUCKON 51998
DUCKWEED 63303
DUDLEY CASTLE 49912
DUDLEY CASTLE 61761
DUDLEY CASTLE 72674
DUET 53344
DUET 53504
DUET 85793
DUFFLEPUD 50091
DUGIRIS 66058
DUKE 45058
DUKE 50636
DUKE 54122
DUKE 72884
DUKE 73822
DUKE OF BRIDGEWATER *NbC 55' red/grn*
DUKE OF BRIDGEWATER 66593
DUKE OF BRIDGEWATER 77265
DUKE OF LANCASTER 61652
DUKE OF RUTLAND 73470
DUKERIES POACHER 71184 NbT 45' red/grn. B: 1988 M&N, New Ollerton, diy f/o. Vetus. Base Blisworth Tunnel Boats. Stained glass windows: ducks, fox & kingfisher. 251018
DULCIE DOMUM 48732
DULCIE MAY 046128 WARWICK NbST 12.49m grn/red. B: 1989 Jonathan Wilson, then at Stenson; f/o Kate Boats. Mitsubishi FMK41 Type K4E - sound baffles and exhaust water system for quiet running (has been mistaken for an electric boat). Base Kate Boats. 21331

DULWICH 62869 Nb - Grp top on steel hull 55' wh/grn. B: 1979: Seasteel Gordon's (ex-hire). 2cyl Lister ST2, hydraulic drive. Base Napton marina. One of the last Grp top narrow boats still in original colours - most now repainted to look like steel. 22413
DUN BOATIN 79583
DUNCHURCH 76362
DUNELM 47578
DUNGT 85599
DUNHAM DAWDLER 52240
DUNKLEYS' OF THE FOLLY 52930 HERTFORD (painted on removable magnetic rubber sheet below picture of stag). NbC 45' blue/red. B: 1993 Liverpool Boats, f/o ACH Narrowboats, Deeside, Clwyd. 35hp Kabuta/Beta. Base Stanstead Abbots, R.Lea. 20179
DUNLIN Butty. Ex Cadbury's horse boat
DUNLIN 49944
DUNLIN 63625
DUNMINING 104649
DUNMOW FLITCH *NbT 40' blue*
DUNNIT 54526
DUNNIT 101418 KAREN & DENNIS HOLMES Grp 33', d 2'10" mustard/dk grn. B: 1991/93 Dennis Holmes, Rocester, Staffs. Yanmar YSE 12, Enfield outdrive. Base Chirk marina. Originally started in early 70s as a prototype by firm called "Craft Mouldings"; remained in pieces as empty shell for several years. Bought by owner from Exchange & Mart advert, transported by car/trailer to drive at home by present owner. Unique - only one ever made (moulds destroyed), constructed from 5 vertically flanged sections, panoramic views to saloon seating area, diesel fired central heating, hardwood interior lining. Name derived from owner's loud expression of feeling on completion! 24896
DUNROBIN *Grp 21'*
DUNSOARING 90024
DUNTEE CHIN 48575
DUNVEGAN GLEN PARVA Luxemotor Dutch Barge 48', b 10'6", d 2'9" dk blue/lt blue. B: 1997 French & Peel, f/o by owner. Mercedes; hydraulic wheel steering. Base Glen Parva, GU-Leics. 24853
DUNVEGAN 45710
DUNVEGAN 66761
DUNWICH ROSE 61959
DUORF II 79869
DURHAM 71599
DURHAM GIRL 71079
DURHAM LADY 45442
DUSK 68012
DUSKY LORY 68315
DUSTY 73312
DUSTY 73436 Motor 60' blue/graining
DUSTY 91899
DUSTY MILLER *NbC 35' blue/crm*
DUSTY MILLER 67791
DUTCH 54075
DUTCH N7353
DUTCH OWL 50910
DUTEOUS No 6 60002 Motor

DUTIFUL DUCK 54669 MIKE & MARY ANTCLIFF BATH NbC 42' grn/red. B: 1995 Prestige Boats, Holt nr. Worcester. Lister Canal Star 36. Base Somerset Coal canal, jnc. K&A. Features painted, plastic and fluffy ducks. 22488
DUTY FREE 62741
DUXON 73089
DWAALI 88341
DWR GLAS 91548
DYNAFE 49163

E

Parliamentary matters, a joke leads to a name, a "honeymoon boat", a very muddy engine and a gorgeous shape. Two Dukes featured, as are Castles from India. The most powerful tug on the cut. And the first semi-trad?

EACON 84894
EAGLE No. 5 47000 OMICRON AND COMPANY ADLINGTON MANCHESTER near perfect "Josher" replica bow, full length cabin with authentic and totally trad. boatman's cabin, open engine 'ole, 62', d 32" red/grn. B: 1989-90 (1 man/1 year full time) David Harris - shell built at Burton-on-Trent, f/o at Stone, T&M. Gardner 3LW Hurth 360 1.5:1 Crowther 24"x20" prop. Base Marineville Higher Poynton. Owner proud of the "gorgeous shape" achieved with the 6 steel planks either side to produce the double curvature, GU swim at stern. Loves rivers, e.g. Trent Falls, Greenwich tidal barrier, etc. Idiosyncratic bucket loo and bidet side by side, described as a "serious boater's statement" but considered totally practical for serious cruising! 23564
EAGLES PROVIDENCE 66880 NbT 36', d 30" red/blue. 1968 Harborough Marine hull no. 21 - built with cruiser stern and composite top then new steel top and trad. stern (rare for Harborough Marine boat) in 1987 by Teddesley. F/o by owner. Lister SR2 air cooled 13hp (1969 - never been rebuilt). Base Milton Keynes, GU. 24778
EAGLE 45501
EAGLE 54615
EAGLE 73540
EAGLE 102800
EARL OF DUDLEY 75318
EARL OF EMSWORTH 71400
EARL OF GREYSTOKE 53859
EARLSTON 47989
EARLSWOOD 61733
EARLY GO 75509
EARWIG Mtce boat, flat, dumb 30' BW-NW
EARWIG 89124
EARWIGO 52809
EASDALE 48608
EASTERN STAR 53732 Hire. NbC 45' blue/yel. B: 1994 John South, f/o Starline Narrowboats. Lister TS2 Hurth HBW150. Base Upton marina R.Severn. 008459

EASTERN STAR 53732
EAST HILL 52945
EASY 52871 Nb 26'6" grn/red. B: 1992 Springer. 15hp ob. Base Newbury Boatyard 22475
EASY RIDER 87719
EASYRIDER 500417
E AUSTEN JOHNSON 062744 DUKE OF EDINBURGH'S AWARD and cypher. Steel barge 44', b 10', d 2' grn/bl. B: 1978 Hancock & Lane, f/o Sowerby Bridge, W.Yorks. Perkins. Base South Pennine Boat Club, Battyford. Duke of Edinburgh's Award: disabled young people. Commissioned by HRH Prince Philip at Leeds Lock 26.10.78. Used regularly by schools for disabled and similar groups (maintained solely by donations and collections, always short of funds!). Open plan, electric lift. Large brass portlight from ship sunk during war - presented by Anglesey sub aqua club. *(Contact by potential users welcomed - see page 14).* 20204
EAU ZONE Viking 23 Grp 23' wh. B: 1991 Honda 15 petrol ob. Base Anchor Boat Club, Eaton Hastings, R.Thames 20189
EBBA B1636
EBB TIDE *66718 Grp Nauticus*
EBLEY 70566
EBONY Hire. NbC 56' blue/red. Base The Wyvern Shipping Co, Linslade, GU 00442
EBONY 50151
EBONY 52814
ECLIPSE 45821
ECLIPSE 49121
ECLIPSE 50994
ECLIPSE 54915
EDA OF GAYTON 68886
EDELWEISS *Grp 40' crm/mar*
EDEN *64049 NbC 20' crm/grn*
EDEN HALL 45065
EDEN VALLEY 77958
EDGAR JESSOP 68530
EDGEBASTON 10 102257
EDGECOMBE *NbST 60' blue/red*
EDGECOMBE 67224
EDGE OF LIGHT 47566
EDGEWARE 138 69837 Lg Woolwich Town Cl motor. Ex GUCC/BW/WW
EDINA MONSOON 72264
EDITH 74963
EDITH Boat Museum
EDITH B 48528
EDITH LOUISE 66834
EDITH TYNDALE 48539
EDMUND 49740
EDNA II 50413
EDOR 51336
EDWARD BEAR 64555
EDWARD BEECH 71712
EDWARD THE CONFESSOR 73987
EDWYN 75811
EDZELL 73689
EEL No.911 40044
EFFIE 97721

EFFINGHAM Motor vessel Mtce boat BW-NW
EGGBOX 46488
EGMONT 68084
EIGHTSOME REEL 54617
EILA 83451
EILAGUAL 85148
EIN HAFOD 51194
EIRENE Day launch semi-trad 21', b 5'8" bl/wh. B: 1990 The Steam and Electric Launch Company, Ludham, Norfolk. Electric DC series wound 1.4kw, 48 volts. Base Shepperton, Mddx. Mahogany trim and fore and aft decks. 21258
EIRLYS 077208 Restaurant trip boat. NbT 70' red/grn. B: 1981 Hancock & Lane, f/o by owner. 1.8 Thornycroft. Base The Old Wharf, Trevor, Llangollen canal. 01122
EISVOGEL 47754
EISVOGEL III 73337
EKWU 71995
ELAN 65102
ELANOR 62031
ELBERETH
ELBOW 67609
ELDER No 2 63160
ELDER FLOWER 69700
ELDORADO 74141
ELEANOR 72562
ELEANOR ANNE B1360
ELEANOR CLAIR 47836
ELEANOR CRAWSHAW 46652
ELECTRA 70493
ELECTRA 71070 REG AT RICKMANSWORTH 48 (FLEET No 40 GUCCC) Small Ricky unconverted wooden motor boat 70', b 7', d 3' bl/graining. B: 1935 W H Walker Bros. Lister 3 cyl. Base GU canal. Built with butty *Ethiopia* (could be on Basingstoke canal); part of batch of 12 pairs built for GUCCCo. History being researched *(see page 14)*. See also *Sirius*. 24841
ELECTRA Nb 60'
ELEMENT 62533 LEICESTER NAVIGATION Ex-working Nb believed to be one of - if not the - first 'semi-trad' style conversion 49' blue. First registered 1884, hull by Thomas Bantock of Ettingstall, Wolverhampton. Gardner 4 LK (1955) with heavy flywheel. Base Sileby Mill Boatyard, R.Soar (part of Leicester Navigation). Sold to, and worked for, T & S Element (hence name) under BCN No. 11903 as a cabin butty carrying rubbish around Birmingham. Sunk at Aston locks for many years. Purchased and salvaged 1964 and named *Pensax* (after the tunnel that was never completed); shortened to 45', fitted steel bottom, wooden cabin and 1923 15hp Bolinder. Taken to Halesowen in 1983, lengthened to present length, steel cabin fitted (was this the first semi-trad?) and Gardner engine fitted. 24893
ELEMO II 65629
ELEN 78771
ELERI 64070
ELEUTHERA 61155
ELEVENOAK 66844
ELFIN 100756
ELI 77789

ELICASU 95380
ELIDOR II 91648
ELIJAH 63887
ELIN 45560
ELINOR L'AUTRE FEMME 72926
ELISABETH WALLER 47159
ELISA TOO 65453
ELISE *104038 Grp Romero 30'*
ELISHA 63886
ELISSA 61945
ELITE 103260
ELIXER B0700
ELIZA 72615
ELIZA 87382
ELIZABETH 48041 No. 10 ALVECOTE NbT 58' aircraft blue/crm. B: 1990 R&D hull, Narrowcraft f/o. Ford 1.6 XLD. Base Calder & Hebble. Last f/o for private ownership in Narrowcraft fleet. African parrots painted on side doors. 23553
ELIZABETH 050138 Hire. NbST 50' navy blue/lt blue. B: 1991 Heritage Boat Builders. Lister LPWS. Base Sally Boats, Bradford on Avon Marina. 013231
ELIZABETH 67225
ELIZABETH *70546 NbT 66' wh*
ELIZABETH II 74611
ELIZABETH ALICE *Grp 30' crm*
ELIZABETH ALICE 69106
ELIZABETH ANNE 45937
ELIZABETH AUSTIN 53651
ELIZABETH E 60213
ELIZABETH ETHEL 49650
ELIZABETH JANE 49890
ELIZABETH ROSE 52415 PAT & COLIN HEALEY NbC 57' 2-tone blue. B: 1991/2 Arcrite, self f/o. Lister type 12/2 industrial - twin flywheels - 12hp 2cyl maximum revs 650rpm. The engine was built 1953, exported to S.Africa, probably used on farm to pump water. Found rusted solid and full of mud. Overhauled, shipped to UK and installed. Reconditioned TMP 1:1 g'box, 18"x18" prop. Revs at canal speed about 400rpm. Base Willow Park Marina Stoke Golding. Features sliding decorated wooden shutters. 22414
ELIZABETH SARA 72175
ELIZA DOOLITTLE 46680
ELKAY 73105
ELKHOUND 68643 No. 44 NbT timber cabin on steel hull 44' red/wh. B: 1975 Braunston Boat Co. (Chris Barney(44)). Sabb 2HG 18hp 2cyl. Base Gayton junction GU. 23689
ELLA MAYS 50245
ELLAND Power boat 16m BW-CATM
ELLAN VANNIN 61312
ELLANO 66631
ELLEN 70604
ELLEN 76693
ELLEN GEE 46583
ELLEN JAY *NbC 40'*
ELLEN JEE 72185
ELLEN LOUISE 72829
ELLEN VANNIN B1270
ELLENROSE 73550

ELLESMERE *(hotel boat with Brackley)*
ELLESMERE 47543
ELLESMERE 60167
ELLESMERE 71923
ELLESMERE B0749
ELLIE 31029
ELLIE 50580
ELLINGTON B1222 R & H DUNFORD PRESTON BROOK NbTug for pleasure and as floating showroom for decorated canalware 50', d 33" bl/brown. B: 1988 Les Allen & Sons Oldbury, f/o by owner. Russell Newbery 18hp ex Dagenham. Base Preston Brook, Bridgewater canal. Painted "black brown and beige" - a classic (Duke) Ellington composition. 2085
ELLIS DEE (TUGBOAT No1) Tug
ELM 54795 STENSON NbT 36' blue/crm. B: 1995 Midland Canal Centre, Stenson. Lister Alpha 3, delta g'box. Continuous cruising. 22380
ELMET CASTLE 70236
ELMLEYBROOK 47788
ELNAR 71751
ELOISA 76483
ELOUISE 72131
EL PIRATA 080403 Heavy Grp ex-naval open work boat - yard boat 17'6", b 5'. B: not known. Lister SR2. Base Sileby Mill Boatyard. Rarely seen outside yard. 032890
ELSA 48878
ELSA CLAIRE II 77919
ELSE 66778
ELSEEBELL 52793
ELSIE D 50846

ELSIE MAY 97800 River Rat Gypsy Grp NbC 18'6" grn/yel. B: c1979 Wilderness Boats. Honda 7.5 ob. Base Hallingbury Mill R.Stort. 20183
ELSIE MAY 98098
ELSIE POTTER 72692
ELSIE ROSE 53669
ELSIE ROSE 77533
ELSINORE 64848
ELSINORE Barney(34) 1973 32'
ELSTREE Lg Woolwich Town Cl motor. Ex GUCC/BW/WW
ELSTREE 161
ELTHORNE 74900
ELTON 71284 Lg Ricky Town Cl butty. Ex GUCC/BW/WW
ELVENOAK 066844 Hire. NbC 37' grn/red. BMC 1.5. Base Evesham Marina, R.Avon. 0371032
ELVER 47666
ELVIND 72686
ELVIRA 62182
ELY 76662
ELY D 53710
ELYSIAN FIELDS 68506
ELYSIUM 45185
ELYSIUM 74452
EMELINA 078066 NEWBURY Nb butty stern 40' grn/red. B: late 1970s-80 approx Whittle, Chorley (sold boats with butty style in this period). BMC 1.5. Base K&A canal. Stepped rear cabin. 24922
EMERALD Hire. NbC 54' blue/red. Base The Wyvern Shipping Co, Linslade, GU. 00437
EMERALD Motor vessel BW-NW

EMERALD 54549
EMERALD 60434
EMERALD 64700
EMRALD No 1 68652 Tug
EMERALD 74651
EMERALD 76146
EMERITUS 49036
EMERSON 72328 NbT 55' grn/yel. B: 1985 Colecraft, f/o by M McDonald Market Drayton, refit Graham Booth Wolverley. Lister. Base Whixall, Llangollen canal. 24789
EMILENE 70002
EMILEON II 73406
EMILY *workshop boat blue*
EMILY 45878
EMILY 61606
EMILY 72796
EMILY B0008
EMILY B1510
EMILY ANNE 52884
EMILY BRONTE 63488
EMILY 'C' 47152 NbC 40' grn/red. B: 1989 R&D Fabrications, f/o by Phil Gardner Waterways Services - bridge 29 GUC. Vetus 3 cyl. Base Farncombe Boat House, R.Wey. 23659
EMILY GRAY 74168
EMILY JANE 51070
EMILY ROSE 054021 THORNE NbC 45' blue/burgundy. B: unknown - internal DIY refit 1993. Perkins. Base Sawley marina. 22391
EMLEY 51533
EMMA 48024
EMMA 53023
EMMA 64281
EMMA 73068
EMMA Barney(60) 1976 35' (ex ?-Burinka)
EMMA HAMILTON 73159
EMMA JANE *NbT 50' orange*
EMMA JANE 48295
EMMA JANE 53836
EMMA JANE 62779
EMMA JANE 74457
EMMA JANE 75338
EMMA-JANE II MIKE OWEN, BOAT-WINDOW BOAT SALES, DEWSBURY NbT 50' red/blue. B: 1981 Sagar Marine. BMC 1.5. Base Dewsbury canal basin. *Emma-Jane II* was used as "The Honeymoon Boat" in the TV series "Watching". 2067
EMMA JAY 65507
EMMA LOUISE 72630 Grp cruiser 32' brown/crm. B: 1985 Highbridge Cruisers Ltd. Dudley, W.Mids. 10hp 4 str Yamaha petrol. Base Country Wide Cruisers, Brewood, SU canal. 21222
EMMA LOUISE 100867
EMM-AN-GEE 93787
EMMA RIDGEON 54178 STERLING BANK NbC 45' grn/mar. B: 1993 Liverpool Boats, f/o Bromsgrove Boat Builders. BMC 1.5. Base Wyre Mill, Lower Avon. 25950
EMMI 66256
EMMY OTTENS 2 *96782 Grp wh*
EMPEROR 50302
EMPIRE QUEEN 51077

EMPRESS 50425 *NbT 50' grn*
EMPRESS No 2 46798
EMPRESS OF BRITAIN 64725
EMPRESS OF INDIA 67170
EMRAL 89318
ENA MAY 52242 WINCHAM WHARF NbT 40' grn/red. B: 1991 Liverpool Boats, f/o 1992 Colliery Narrowboat Co. Wincham Wharf. Beta/Kubota 1001cc 3cyl. Base Nantwich & Border Counties Yacht Club. Features Boatman's Cabin (perhaps unusually in 40' boat). Tested in "Canal & Riverboat" Aug 92. 21305
ENCHANTED 045951 Hire. NbC 30' grn/red. BMC 1.5. Base Evesham Marina, R.Avon. 0371052
ENCHANTED FOREST 62999
ENCHANTRESS *52405 NbT 60' grn/red*
ENDEAVOUR 47863
ENDEAVOUR 52273
ENDEAVOUR 53721
ENDEAVOUR 65684
ENDEAVOUR 78584
ENDEAVOUR N6937
ENDEWA 67601
ENDORA XII 65856
ENERGY *NbT grn/red*
ENFIELD 68445
ENFIELD 79997
ENFIELD Hopper No 91 BW-NW
ENFIELD 12m BW-L&S
ENGADINE 90829
ENGLAND 76897
ENGLANDS GLORY 46111
ENID ROSE Barney(28) 1973 35'
ENIGMA *Nb 60' grn/crm*
ENIGMA 71760
ENIGMA 80641
ENIGMATIST 52335
ENNERDALE 68429
ENSEMBLE *NbC 50' grn*
ENSIGN 54676
ENT No 4 52398
ENTERPRISE No. 1 HALES & PARTNERS, WALSALL BHP NbTug ex-working 52', b 7', d 3'+ red/grn. B: 1899 as FMC Steamer *Count* at Saltley with composite hull and powered by FMC steam engine with Danks boiler. In 1925 converted by FMC to motor boat with 15hp Bolinders semidiesel. Carried general cargoes. Damaged by bomb in Birmingham in WW2. 1945 acquisition by Ernest Thomas, Walsall resulted in a powerful 52' manoeuverable tug - *Enterprise No.1*. With a 1931 Gardner 5 cyl L2 engine. Until early 1960s used for towing trains of wharf boats ('hamptons) to Birchills power station. Disposal led to private purchase but decay and sinking led to a 1973 (4-year) extensive restoration at Peter Keay and Son's yard at Pratt's Bridge Dock. Winner of Best Marine Engine award at 1995 Gardner rally. The most powerful surviving narrow beam tug - payload 400 tons. Has the largest prop on the cut - 35". 261068
ENTERPRISE 49784 DMBC Grp centre cockpit cruiser with stern deck 29' wh/blue. B: 1963 Creighton, Colne, Lancashire. BMC 1.5 L. Base

Derby Motor Boat Club, Sawley Cut. 23577
ENTERPRISE 60408 NbT Wooden top on steel hull 55' grn. B: 1973 Springer. Lister SR2. Residential BCN. 22408
ENTERPRISE 69394
ENTERPRISE 78865
ENTERPRISE 104640
ENTERPRYZE 70911
ENVOY 70345
ENWAY ENDEAVOUR 78837
EOS 65247
EPANDOR II 70794
EPERNAY 74613
EPERNAY *914613 Grp wh/blue*
EPHESUS CRUSADER 48728
EPSILON 68806
EPSILON 68952
EPSOM Lg Woolwich Town Cl motor. Ex GUCC
EQUANIMITY *NbT 70' mar/grn*
EQUANIMITY 68962
EQUINOX 73965
EQUINOX 76943
EQUUS 66699
ERACHT 76310
ERASMUS 50631
ERIC BLOODAXE 74665
ERIC OF LINCOLN Tug 9.55m BW-NE
ERITH 47581
ERMINE 71673
ERNEST GRACE 46714
ERNESTINE 46797 *NbT 50' red*
ERNEST THOMAS II 73368
ERODA 49313
ERRIGAL 49524
ERSKINE MAY 079675 NbC 37'11" red/grn. B: 1978 Colecraft, f/o by Rugby Boatbuilders. BL 4cyl 30bhp 3000rpm from 1.489 L. Base Wheelton Boat Club, L&L. The name *Erskine May* appears on the cabin sides over a portcullis - boat was originally built for Sir Richard Borlas, Recorder in the House of Commons; hence the name because Erskine May was author of "Parliamentary Procedure", frequently referred to in "Today" programme. 21323
ERYCINUS 054581 BRAUNSTON NbT 50' midnight blue/red. B: 1995 Colecraft, f/o Utopia Unlimited Braunston. Perkins MC42 PRM Delta g'box 2.83:1 reduction to 19"x12" prop. Base Braunston Marina. *Erycinus* is the telegraphic address of C E Heath Plc - the word signifies 'heath'; mention made of it by Antony Brown in his biography "Cuthbert Heath, Maker of the Modern Lloyd's of London". A friend of the Heaths drew a sketch of a ficticious ship, the *Erycinus* jokingly owned by Cuthbert Heath & Co. and given a 100 A1 classification at Lloyd's. The present vessel's owner worked for 40 years for the firm and, now in retirement, it seems appropriate to adopt the name for a leisure craft as a reminder of the good days with the many friends and colleagues of those years. 2093
ERZANMINE 51650
ESCALUS 101709

ESCAPADE Hire. NbC 52' red/grn. Base Rose Narrowboats, Brinklow, N.Oxford canal. 026704
ESCAPE 48986
ESCAPE 79577

Using the *Listing*
A "how to use" guide is on pages 13-14
Frequent abbreviations inside front cover
Full list of abbreviations included in
Location Glossary at end of book

ESME 46475
ESME 74167
ESME OWL 78123
ESMERALDA 65353
ESMERALDA 78118
ESMERALDA 78984
ESOX LUCIU 101417
ESPERANCE 48984
ESQUE 74612
ESQUIRE 63648
ESSEX 53728
ESSINGTON Mtce boat 41' BW-BBC
ESSINGTON SWAN 63469
ESTELLA 47262
ESTHER 62525 No. 2 J.B. SAMUEL & CO. GUNTHORPE NbST 60' red/grn. B: 1973 Denis Cooper, Canal Transport Services Norton Canes. 1.8 Thornycroft water cooled. Base Colwick Marina, R.Trent. Lengthened from 48' in 1976 and steel cladding added to original wood superstructure, all by original builder. Distinctive horse's head on cratch. Unique interior. 21257
ESTHER 66949
ESTHER 76845
ESTHER AMELIA 51160
ESTON GRANGE 46389
ESTO PERPETUA 64218 *Grp 25'*
ESTORIL 69901
ESTRELLA 64033
ESTRELLA N4046
ESTRELLE *Grp 35' blue/wh*
ETHELBERT 61905
ETHELDOLIDOOTOO 54390 JE & SF HODGKINSON KINGSWINFORD NO 1 NbTug 60' blue/ gold. B: 1995 Orion Narrowboats, f/o Ivan J Baker. Lister Alpha 4 cyl water cooled. Base Canal Cottage, Hinksford, S&W. 8' front decking, half boatmans cabin, British Waterways Transport colours. 24875
ETHEL JEAN B1147
ETHIOPIA *see ELECTRA*
ETHNA 500969 BARLOW NbC 58' marine blue. B: 1996 Jonathan Wilson Rotherham, f/o by Mitchell & Sons Stanley Ferry Marina. Vetus PH7. Base Fradley junction/extended cruising. 24767
ETTA No 3 54880
EUEQUE 77144
EUGENE 90341
EUPHRATES Trip boat 74' BW-BBC
EUROPE 69340
EURWOOD LADY 66376
EVA *NbT 40' grn*

EVELYN 78198
EVELYN BROADBENT 78084
EVELYN GEORGE 75317
EVENING CLOUD 45802
EVENING LADY 64728
EVENING STAR 54798 Hire. NbST 60' blue/yel. B: 1995 John South, f/o Starline Narrowboats. Lister TS3. Base Upton Marina, R.Severn. 008108
EVENING STAR *NbC 60' grn/wh*
EVENING STAR *B1596 NbT 45' grn*
EVENLODE 69660
EVENSONG 48458
EVE OF SPRING *Nb 57'*
EVE OF SPRING 48853
EVERGREEN 53004
EVESHAM 65020
EVIVA BRODY 62498
EVLAN 500839
EVROS 69525
EXCALIBUR *NbC 60' blue*
EXCALIBUR 46208
EXCALIBUR 61850
EXCALIBUR 62361
EXCALIBUR 62951
EXCALIBUR 74816
EXCALIBUR Barney(6) 1970 48'
EX DENTIBUS 63933
EXE 67960
EXELBEE 53756
EXELBEE 75717
EXETER 48247
EX IML 70804

EXMOOR 47984
EXODUS B0376
EXODUS II 64895
EXPERIENCE *66809 NbC 20' grn*
EXPLORER 48167
EXPLORER 100595
EXTON *47321 NbC 35' red/grn*
EXTON 54705 NbC 40' midnight blue/turquoise. B: 1995 CT & P Fox, March. 1.8L Ford XLD. Base Crick, Northants. Stern door panels hand-decorated with traditional daisies; castle scenes are of Jagmandir Palace on a lake in Rajasthan, India, showing the Maharana's State Barge. 22516
EXVALE 69694
EYE BEE 60978
EZICK 61607

Evesham Marina Holidays Ltd
Kings Road, Evesham, Worcestershire, WR11 5BU.

Cruise Shakespeare's picturesque River Avon and canals aboard a comfortable narrowboat from our base at Evesham.
'Do' the Avon Ring via the Upper Avon, Stratford Canals (including aqueducts), Worcester and Birmingham Canal (including Tardebigge Flight and Tunnel), the River Severn and the Lower Avon. Places of interest to visit include Stratford Upon Avon, Warwick (via Hatton Flight), Worcester, Stourport, Tewkesbury and Gloucester.
We are a family owned and run business set in the beautiful Heart of England. Boats of 2-12 berths available at competitive prices. Please phone for a brochure.

Tel (01386) 48906 or Fax (01386) 442827

Qualify for your Inland Waterwaficate, aboard our certified craft or yours, with friendly experienced instructors in the beautiful cruising area of the Vale of Evesham. Qualification easily upgraded to International Certificate for continental cruising. Enjoy a weekend with us including overnight accommodation ashore or buy your loved one a voucher for the ultimate gift!

Long & Short Term Moorings
Craneage & Slip Facilities
Repairs and Servicing

RYA RECOGNISED TEACHING ESTABLISHMENT

F

Tales of tooth-pulling, a "lucky" successor, a 70 foot boat from a kit(!), pussy passengers, a long and fascinating "wooden" life, radio control, a saintly craft and "the best purchase we ever made!"

FABIAN STEADMAN 68914
FABIS 67619
FABULOUS 47513
FAELTE E Barney(32) 1973 48' *(ex Trelawney)*
FAGINS FOLLY
FAIR CUMULUS III 71429
FAIR LADY 63840
FAIR LADY 102262
FAIR LADY II 31337
FAIRLAND 60423
FAIR ROSAMUND 46317
FAIR ROSAMUND 74966 NbT 45' blue/crm. B: 1988 R&D Fabrications, f/o Narrowcraft Ltd. BMC. Base Harefield marina, GU   23613
FAIRWATER No.2 *NbT 40' blue/red*
FAIRWATERS 31863
FAIR WINDS B0471
FAIRWINDS G6654 D & R BARBER MARCH NbT 49' blue/beige. B: 1980 CT & P Fox, March at 38' and lengthened 1994. BMC 1.5 30hp. Base Fox's marina. Typical "Fox" construction to suit guillotine locks on R.Great Ouse and Nene.   24870
FAIR WYN 85287
FAITH 47794
FAITH 61064
FAITH 70530
FAITH 74842 P & S TUCKER PINCHBECK NbT 55'2.1/2" dk grn/red. B: 1976 West Riding Boat Co Ltd., first owner f/o complete 1978. Lister SR2W, 2:1 reduction. Base Bill Fen Marina, Ramsey. Unusual feature is rudder contained within contour of hull, supported on skeg 4" wide x 1.1/4" thick. Only a small button fender therefore required.   21328
FAITH *Nb 50' red/grn*
FAITH *B0537 NbT 55' grey/red*
FAITH *NbT 55' blue*
FAITH, HOPE AND CHARITY 52506 BRAMWITH BRIDGE NbST 57', d 2'10" Donegal grn/Buckingham grn. B: 1992 Eastwood Eng., Owston Ferry, DIY f/o almost complete! Perkins MC42. Base Bramwith Bridge. The name is the same as that given to 3 flights of steps at the former Royal Naval Establishment of HMS Ganges (now a police training centre). The steps led up to what was then the dental surgery and known as the "Toothwright's Shop". Later it became the owner's temporary home. (Any connection with "Wisdom, Strength and Beauty" is also valid!).   20167
FALCON Butty. Ex E.Thomas
FALCON 19 Yarwoods motor. Ex FMC
FALCON *Grp 25' wh*
FALCON 46752
FALCON 52376
FALCON 61394
FALCON 63293
FALCON 68860
FALCON 75696
FALCON 76827
FALCONBROOK 10.67m BW-L&S
FALCONDALE 72813
FALLING SANDS 52656
FALMARI 054766 NbT 30' mid brown/deep red. B: 1990 Water-craft, Maesycwmmer, owner f/o. Yanmar 2GMF20 18hp. Base Aynho Wharf. Proper narrowboat shape (round stern, full cants, trad cabin) in most compact dimension.   20207
FALSTAFF 51170
FAME 77905
FAMILY AFFAIR 50832
FAMOUS GROUSE 76531
FANCY FREE 45568
FANCY THAT II 65042
FANFARE Hire. NbC 56' red/grn. Base Rose Narrowboats, Brinklow, N.Oxford canal.   026710
FANGHORN 45578
FANNY 102797
FANNY ADAMS 74039 RUTLAND NbT 60' grn/blue. B: 1988 Colecraft, f/o John Woollard, Wharfside Boatfitters Old Wolverton. Russell Newbery DM2. Base Shardlow marina. Full size boatmans cabin, 6' engine room, 18' lounge, 250 gal water tank.   24859
FANNY SUMMERS 049369 BRISTOL PAT & KEITH HULBERT NbST 53' burgundy/dk blue. B: 1990 Steelcraft, Norton Junction, f/o Weltonfield Narrowboats. Lister LPWS3, PRM Delta 30 g'box, 20" x 12'½" Crowther high efficiency propeller. Base Bradford on Avon marina. Two extra berths possible under cratch cover - opens fully for summer cruising. Name from owner's grandmother who was a mill girl in the cotton mill on the side of the feeder canal at Barton Hill Bristol at the end of 19th C.   24830
FANSHAWS BOUNTY 48709
FANTASIA 100707
FANTASY 67090
FARLEIGH *52004 NbT 60' grn*
FARNABY 61676
FARNHILL Motor vessel BW-NW
FAR NIENTE 76990
FARRADAWN 046729 Hire. NbC 45' grn/red. BMC 1.5. Base Evesham Marina, R.Avon. 0371036
FASGADH 66221
FATAL ATTRACTION 54643
FATHOM 49484
FAULKNOR 52173 KE & JM SHARPE & H HUNT STOKE GOLDING NbT 60' dk blue/mar. B: 1992 Midland Canal Centre, f/o by first owner. Beta BD3 Tug. Base Ashby canal. The oldest regular crew member served on *HMS Faulknor* - WWII destroyer - seeing service on Atlantic and Arctic convoys and in the Mediterranean - "a lucky ship!"   25987
FAVERSHAM 046683 Hire. NbC 64' grn/crm. B: 1990 Acecape Fabrications of Old, Northants, f/o by Oxfordshire Narrowboats, Lower Heyford. Lister LPW3 Alpha. Base Clifton Wharf, Rugby. Until 1994 boat was *Queen Anne* in Oxfordshire

Narrowboats fleet. 025684
FAWN 49688
FAWN *NbT 55' mar/bl*
FAX 73140
FAY B1714
FAYE LOUISE
FAY IRENE 100868
FAYRE EXCHANGE 78076
FAZELEY Commercial carrying working butty - forecabin boat in livery as formerly operated under Captain Cargo Ltd. - red/grn/yel; iron composite construction. B: 1921 for Fellows, Morton & Clayton Ltd. Base Coventry & GU canals. 031821
FAZELEY Power boat 15m BW-CATM
FELICITY 51528
FELICITY ANN 81541
FELICITY MAY 51373
FELIS CATUS II 49272
FELIX 66689 NbT 40' grn/red. B: 1974 Albert Watson, Macclesfield canal. Lister SR3. Base Golden Nook Farm, Hargrave, Cheshire. Original owner Ken Goodwin (of the IWA). Lovely lines and William Morris interior. Chimney on the "wrong" side. Displays many early rally badges. *Felix* was one of Mrs. Goodwin's nicknames and is also that of a saint. Felix was bishop of Felixtowe in the 7th C. Boat has a fine icon of him by Sr. Gillian Mary of the Anglican Community of the Sacred Passion (she takes the boat for a trip every year). Engine room doors decorated with George Bodley's design from the font cover at Worcester Cathedral. 21350
FELIX 62234 NbC 42' grn/blue. B: 1978 Harborough Marine (Build no HM1037, regd. in HM Classic Boat Club). Lister ST2. Base Golden Nook, SU canal. 25949
FELIX B0204
FELLOWSHIP NbC wooden superstructure on steel hull 40', b 6'5" crm/brown. B: 1978 R.Nene. BMC 1.5. Base Orchard marina Northwich. Built by a company on R.Nene which diversified from trawlers and other sea-going vessels for 5-6 years to produce about 12 narrow boats all of narrower than standard beam. 22412
FELLOWSHIP 61924
FELLOWSHIP 71503
FELLOWSHIP 72890
FELLOWSHIP 73789
FELSPAR 47790
FEMERAINE 54632
FENDERS 69866
FENNEDUC 49535
FENNISC-OWL 46869
FENNY 141 Lg Woolwich Town Cl. Ex GUCC/BW
FENNY DRAYTON 63384
FENNY WREN 76338
FENRIS *NbC 40' yel/bl*
FENRUNNER G9950 BUILDERS NO. 18 NbST 40', b 7'6" burgundy/navy blue. B: 1974-5 Fox's Boatyard, March. Original f/o unknown but now being refitted. BMC 2.2 4 cyl. Residential Fox's marina. 23585
FEN SWALLOW 66799

FENTON 62138
FERDINAND 60408
FERN 68022 Yarwoods motor. Ex FMC/BW
FERN 68793
FERN 72802 JOHN AND KARIN THOROGOOD HAWKESBURY NbC 40', b 6' 2-tone grn/wh. B: 1980 Hancock & Lane. 1.5 BMC. Base Hawkesbury Junc. Ex hire boat (Castle boats, Evesham), converted to private use approx 1986. "The Best Purchase We Ever Made!" 21336
FERN 77021 NbC 33' red/grn. B: 1981 Harborough Marine. Bukh DV10ME single cyl. Base Napton marina. Originally Anglo Welsh hire boat at Trevor, Wootton Wawen, until 1986. 25925
FERNDALE 73627 RUGELEY NbC 44' blue/grn. B: 1986 John North, f/o Ian Cundy of Starline Narrowboats, Upton-on-Severn. Lister TS2. Base Rugeley, T&M canal. Livery is that of W Gash & Sons, a Newark bus company, now defunct but which employed owner's son-in-law. 20156
FERRET 066948 FELLOWS, MORTON & CLAYTON No 58 Working Nb Motor, iron hull wooden bottom 70', d 3' grn/red. B: 1926 Yarwoods, Northwich, f/o by FMC Saltley; converted to houseboat circa1967; re-converted and restored by M E Braine 1980. Bolinder type BM 15hp semi-diesel. Base as exhibit at Canal Museum wharf, Nottingham. Much of time spent on northern canals. History incomplete but known to be full of variety. See information available at museum which has restored *Ferret* to very much original state, the engine rebuilt and put into good order by Ken Ward. See *Ilkeston*. 020458
FERROXY LADY 51884
FERRUM VITEA 67579
FERRY QUEEN *Trip boat - Forth & Clyde canal*
FERROUS 66669 EDWIN W FASHAM BIRMINGHAM River tug design - modified for narrow canals. Cabin semi-trad; hull welded steel, cabin composite steel/wood/aluminium. 50', b 7'0.1/2" British racing grn/wh. B: Porter & Haylett, Wroxham, Norfolk. Design, engineering, cabin & f/o by Edwin W Fasham, Birmingham. Gardner 4LK (marine version) 3.8 L 4 cyl, 40bhp @ 1500rpm; self-changing gears, 2 to 1 reduction, 24"x19" prop. Base Coombeswood Canal Trust, Hawne Basin. Very unusual hull shape based on river/sea tug design with all curves and profiles modified to conform to narrow beam, including well-rounded chine. Semi-trad deck raised 10" above gunwale level giving good view and accommodation below. Radio control from lockside possible via electrically operated gear change set up. 22499
FESTINA LENTE 49800
FESTINA LENTE 71981
FESTINA LENTE 500157
FESTINA LENTE 64349
FESTIVAL 77615
FETTLER 73830
FFION 068178 Restaurant boat. NbT 70' red/grn. B: 1980 Hancock & Lane kit, built and f/o by owner. Marinised Massey Ferguson (1950's). Base

70

The Old Wharf, Trevor, Llangollen canal. 01121
FIDDLER 53162
FIDDLER 68663
FIDDLERS FANCY 74716
FIDDLERS GREEN 79821
FIGARO 66713
FIGHT OF FANCY 76821 Grp Bourne hull, wooden superstructure 28' dk brown/stone. B: 1966 Dobsons, complete internal/external refit 1989 at Braunston marina. Lister SL2 inboard/Honda 15 ob. Base Harefield marina, GU. 24920
FIGMENT 102957
FILIPA 65165
FINGOLFIN 45579
FINHAM III NbC 35' grn/red
FINI 75118
FINLANDIA 73826
FINLANDIA 79194
FINLANDIA NbC 40' red/grn
FINN McCOOL 79837
FIONA 64361
FIONA MAY 102068
FIONLA 65949
FIR 61839 NbTug 55', b 7'0.1/4", d 2.9'. burgundy/trad red (lead). B: 1935 Charles Hill, Bristol. Lister HR2 air cooled. Base Sydney Wharf, K&A. Built as one of set of 8 boats - the first steel welded narrow boats, all named after trees. 7 believed to remain (*Oak* at Nat. Waterways Museum Gloucester). *Fir* worked on R.Severn probably for Cadbury carrying crumb and chocolate waste until 1960. Then bought by Wyvern Shipping Company. Shortened from 72' and steel bottom added to original composite hull. Sold in 1970 and again in 1990 to Duncan R Knapp who did a superb f/o and added rest of cabin to make residential boat; he also added the HR2 (original power would have been a 9hp petrol engine). 23671
FIRBOB 52428
FIRCOMBE HALL 53510
FIR COTTAGE 95565
FIRECREST 45399
FIRECREST 74906
FIRE ESCAPE B7370
FIREFLY 45666
FIREFLY 60983
FIREFLY 79794
FIREFLY 73333 *Steam*
FIREFLY Flat 12m BW-CATM
FIREFOX 54428
FIRST ATTEMPT 73993
FIRST ATTEMPT B1616
FIRST EDITION 51917
FIRST LADY 67834
FISH 52791
FISHER 60443
FISHERMAN 100061
FITZ HENRY 049993 Hire. NbST 69', b 7' navy blue/lt blue. B: 1991. Lister LPWS. Base Sally Boats, Bradford on Avon marina. 013240
FIVE HANDS 64509
FIVE MATES 76734

FJORD COUNTESS 71732
FJORD DUCHESS 65153
FJORD EMPEROR 74336
FJORD MONARCH 49788
FJORD PRINCE 52771
FJORD PRINCESS 65154
FJORD PRINCESS 72712
FLAMINGO 544
FLAMINGO 48270
FLAMINGO 74639
FLAMINGO 78757
FLANEUSE 46330
FLAT BOTTOM GIRL 500131
FLATCAP 52724
FLATTERY NbT 60' grn/graining
FLAX 74484
FLEA Mtce boat, flat, dumb 30' BW-NW
FLECKNOE 76587
FLEDGLING 62677
FLETCHER LYND NbT 60' blue/mar
FLETCHERS WYND 74346
FLEUR D'EAU 67518 (a registered British ship - Official No. 333966 with a "British Tonnage Certificate" issued 25th August 1969) PORT OF REGISTRY GRIMSBY, HIGH LANE MACCLESFIELD CANAL. Grp/wood cruiser 23.9', b 6.51', d 2.75' wh hull/varnished topsides. B: 1968 Dobsons of Shardlow. Stuart Turner ST4 MRE 12 hp petrol. Base High Lane Arm, Macclesfield canal. Was builder's exhibit at 1969 Earls Court Intn'l Boat Show. First boat fitted with above engine. Maintained in original condition and extensively cruised by owners for last 26 years. Only a few boats on inland waterways, mostly constructed in 1960s have retained full British Registry. The certificate is a title deed and absolute guarantee of ownership; the name cannot be used by any other British registered vessel. 20203
FLEUR DE LYS 54490
FLEURY 31294
FLIGHT OF FANCY 76821
FLIGHT OF FREEDOM 63847 NbC 45' blue. B: 1974 Fernie, self f/o. BMC 1500. Base S.Oxford canal. 23542
FLIMBY 61978
FLIPPER 62545
FLIPPER 66227
FLIPPER 75805
FLIRTY GIRTY 54541
FLO 65691
FLOATING BEAR II J.V.H HAMBLEDEN Nb 32' red/grn. B: 1981 Galadriel Manchester, f/o by previous owner. Angle mounted engine. Base Hambleden, R.Thames. Pictures of Winnie the Pooh on his honey pot (Floating Bear) either side of bow. 23619
FLOATING FOX 31456
FLORA 50744
FLORA Nb blue
FLORENCE NbC 45' blue
FLORENCE 30177
FLORENCE 50965
FLORENCE 53878
FLORENCE 66590

71

BOATWIFE'S LAMENT
by A M Buxton

(Taken from *A Human Face* - a collection of poems written by County Councillors for Leicestershire Year of the Arts '96, attempting to demonstrate that politicians are human after all. First published in *Rutland Review* in 1976)

You can't get in the hall. In fact
you can't get past the door.
There's bits and pieces everywhere
A-littering up the floor.
It's starting to resemble now
Some run-down chandlers' store!
'Cos me husband's been and bought a bloody boat.

It's no use trying to clean a house
All lumbered up with gear,
And if he smiles placatingly:
"I'll clear it up, my dear"
And you believe him, then you're mad -
'Twill still be there next year
If your husband's been and bought a bloody boat.

Resign yourself. (You may as well
Give up, or run away),
"If you can't beat 'em, join 'em"
As my mother used to say.
Just leave the washing AND the house
Then YOU can sail all day
In your husband's rotten, leaky, bloody boat!

FLORENCE EDITH 48345
FLORENCE JAMES 75567
FLORENCE MAY 50957
FLORENCE MAY 52137
FLORENCE MAY 53149   JR & EA BLAKE THURMASTON NbT 63' grn/red. B: 1993 GT Boatbuilders, f/o Nimbus Narrowboats. 1949 Kelvin J2 (petrol start). Base The Boatyard, Thurmaston. Traditional boatmans cabin, vintage engine/engine room.   25969
FLORENS 72461
FLORENTIA 53542
FLORIAN 53338
FLORIANA 49469
FLORRIE 69443
FLORRIE 71638
FLORRIE KENDAL 64052
FLORRIE KENDALL *NbT 61'*
FLOSS 70401
FLOSSIE 45902
FLOSSIE III 50298
FLOSSIE WILLIAM 78492
FLOWER 65478
FLOWER 68035
FLOWER OF COLWICH   64098   NbC 50' wh/beige
FLOWIN 53908
FLUKE 51267
FLUKE 79617
FLUTTERBYE 52305
FLY 54309
FLY II NbT 50' cobalt blue/lemon. B: 1997 John White, f/o Triton and homebuild. Lombardini 4 cyl 33 1/2hp. Base John Goode marina, GU. Name from owners' children, Fiona, Lawton, Yvette.   25927
FLYCATCHER 79066
FLYING ANGEL 92980
FLYING DUTCHMAN B1771
FLYING EAGLE 52239
FLYING FOX 77686
FLYING FOX 91609
FLYING FOX 102761
FLYING HAGGIS 66642
FLYING KIPPER 83644
FOLKESTONE (under construction in 1996) Hire. NbST 54' grn/crm. B: 1996/7 South West Durham Steelcraft, f/o Clifton Cruisers. Base Clifton Wharf.   025687
FOLLOW THE DREAM 50052
FOLLY 86258
FOOTLOOSE 86669
FOOTY 51604
FORD GARTH 70819
FORD OF WINDSOR 65568
FORELLE 65750
FORESAIL 73676
FOREST 90974
FORESTER 67535
FOREST OF ARDEN 50205
FOREST OF DEAN 70508
FOREVER CUT 51680
FOREWARD 75867
FORGET-ME-NOT 53439
FORGETMENOT 54128

FORGET ME NOT 68424 *Hotel*
FORGET ME NOT 73363 H GRANTHAM Wooden Motor Nb used for carrying - mostly materials for recycling or re-use - 71'6", b 7', d 2'8" (empty) grn/oak scumble. B: 1927 Lees & Atkins Polesworth for Number One boatman Henry Grantham. Perkins 4108 driving through 3:1 reduction box and 23" Crowther high efficiency prop. Base Ashton under Lyne Portland Basin Industrial Heritage Centre. Carefully restored by the Wooden Canal Craft Trust, *Forget Me Not* has had a long and fascinating life, for the first 2 years carrying coal as a horse drawn boat from the Coventry coalfield to Dickensons paper mills near Hemel Hempstead. In 1929 fitted with a Bolinder semi-diesel engine at Nursers boatyard, Braunston. Re-named *Sarah* in 1941 on acquisition by Samuel Barlow Coal Company. The full history is contained in a leaflet obtainable from the Trust at 33 Beauchamp Street, Ashton under Lyne OL6 8LF who would welcome a donation for it towards their work.   0019
FORMALHAUT 43 Small Ricky Star Cl motor. Ex GUCC/BW. Boat Museum
FORTUNE 65033
FORTUNE 69763
FORTYTWO 75208
FORTY WINKS 52007 SHIPLEY WEST RIDING NbC 50' blue/crm. B: 1992 John White, f/o North West Narrowboats Riley Green. Kubota 4cyl 35hp. Base Spring Branch, Skipton, L&L. The front well is enclosed as integral part of superstructure forming dinette with large front and side windows.   24798
FORWARD 74845
FORWARD *NbST grn*
FOSSE 68516
FOUR BIKESON 70056
FOUR JAYS 65703
FOUR NO TRUMPS
FOUR OF CLUBS 72139
FOUR SEASONS 46272
FOUR SEASONS 63437
FOUR SEASONS 68971
FOUR SEASONS 74961
FOUR SEASONS 75376
FOUR SEASONS 78919
FOUR SEASONS *NbT 40' grn/red*
FOUR WINDS 68404
FOUR WINDS 75666 CHOLMONDESTON NbC 50' Oxford blue. B: 1988 Liverpool Boats. Thornycroft/Mitsubishi ACYL 33hp. Base Venetian Marine, Nantwich, SU canal   21339
FOUR WINDS 78851
FOWALUA 65183
FOWALUA B0085 DAVE & KAREN WRAY NbC steel with grp top 40'. b 6'6" lt blue/dk blue. B: 1978 approx The Canal & Riverboat Company, Sowerby Bridge. Lister SR2. Base SA Marina, Grappenhall, Bridgewater canal. Previously hire boat with Clare Cruisers, then Wharfage Boat Company.   22502
FOX 72538 SHARDLOW NbC 35' crm/brown. B: 1986 Mike Haywood, f/o by Stephen

Goldsbrough at Shardlow (the first boat he fitted out commercially). May sometimes be seen with a dog and 6 cats on the passenger list (featured in "Your Cat" magazine). 21337
FOXDALE 66150
FOXEARTH 50182
FOXGLOVE 47450
FOXGLOVE 357 69500 Yarwoods motor. Ex FMC/BW
FOX-GLOVE 64224 NbST 40' grn/red. B: 1976 Mkt. Harborough. Lister. Base Debdale Wharf, GU-Leics. Hoping to make it all knotted pine internally. 25979
FOXGLOVE Hire. NbC 48' blue/red. Base The Wyvern Shipping Co, Linslade, GU 00451
FOXGLOVE 79431
FOXHOUND 61592 FOXTON BOAT SERVICES LTD Hire. NbST all steel (now) 45' rotavator orange/dk admiralty grey. B: 1975 Fernie Steel, re-fit by Foxton Boat Services/Harborough Boats. Lister SR2. Base Foxton bottom lock. 0381077
FOXHUNTER IV 51429
FOXTAIL 064202 FOXTON BOAT SERVICES LTD Hire. NbST all steel (now) 36' rotavator orange/dk admiralty grey. B: 1969 Harborough Marine, re-fitted twice by Foxton Boat Services/ Harborough Boats. Lister SR2. Base Foxton bottom lock. 0381079
FOXTROT 50500
FOXY *72450 Grp crm*
FOXY LADY 30784
FOXY LADY 47338
FOXY LADY 47708
FOXY LADY 49496 NbC 58'6" blue. B: 1990 Tayburg, f/o Monarch. Mitsubishi 4cyl. Base Hinckley Boat Club, Ashby canal. 23727
FOXY LADY 52032
FOXY LADY 52776
FOXY LADY 70198
FOXY LADY 70822
FOXY LADY TWO 79990
FRADLEY 63053
FRADLEY SWAN 74183
FRAGIL 52704
FRAN 66423
FRANCEEN 77396
FRANCES 50209
FRANCES 75577
FRANCES No 1 74512
FRANCES ANN 53649
FRANCES ANN 103415
FRANCES ANNE 73818
FRANCHISE 64519
FRANCIS EGERTON 64077
FRANILL 77212
FRANK 048056 Hire. NbC 63' navy blue/lt blue. B: 1990. Lister LPWS. Base Sally Boats, Bradford on Avon marina. 013236
FRANLENE 51931
FRASISCO 77104
FRATERNITY 49897
FRED 54092
FREDA 51850

FREDA 73342
FREDA B 77271
FREDERICK 047834 Hire. NbC 69' navy blue/lt blue. B: 1990. Lister LPWS. Base Sally Boats, Bradford on Avon marina. 013238
FREDERICK II 51273
FREDERICK WHITTINGHAM Tug
FREDERICK WILLIAM 52010
FREEBOOTER 67742
FREEDOM 53607
FREEDOM 63929
FREEDOM 65903
FREEDOM 67993
FREEDOM 70407
FREEDOM 71260
FREEDOM 73361
FREEDOM 73478
FREEDOM 75878
FREEDOM 78089
FREEDOM 78544
FREEDOM 80439
FREEDOM 96125
FREEDOM 103972
FREEDOM 104393
FREEDOM B7751
FREEDOM 4 68772
FREEDOM FIRST 050862 BRAUNSTON N & P HALLARD & FAMILY NbT 58' dk blue/grey. B: 1991 Trent Marine, f/o Pat Lee. 1.8 BMC. Base Braunston marina, GU. Believed to be unique shape - tapered and very pointed bow and tapered stern. 22462
FREEMAN 75157
FREESIA 75564
FREE SPIRIT *NbC 50' grn/red*
FREE SPIRIT *Grp wh*
FREE SPIRIT 46251
FREE SPIRIT 50360
FREE SPIRIT *(in Welsh)* 54753
FREE SPIRIT 54838
FREE SPIRIT 76269
FREE SPIRIT 76394
FREE SPIRIT 78398
FREE SPIRIT N6156
FREETH 81838 BW-
FREE THYME 50303
FREETIME 70736
FREE TIME 70088
FREEWHEELER 51445
FREEWHEELER *NbC 45' blue*
FREJYA 67519
FRENCH LEAVE 64709
FRENCH LEAVE 72239
FRENCH PEEL 45992
FRENCHLANDS 69240
FRESH FIELDS 94447
FRESNO 62432
FREYA 47077
FREYA 48386
FREYA 64632
FREYA 66506
FREYA 80812
FRIAR TUCK Tug 12.19m BW-NE
FRIENDSHIP 49665

FRIENDSHIP Butty. Ex J Skinner No.1. Boat Museum
FRIENDSHIP 49762 NbC 45′ grn/red. B: 1991 John White, Liverpool, f/o Mike Carter, Wirral. Thornycroft 60I - one of the last true Thornycroft K3D. Base Stoke Hall, Middlewich Branch. Named after Joe Skinner's *Friendship*. 21268
FRINGILLIDAE 67496
FRISBY 51392
FRODISHER No.123 01464
FRODSHAM 74384
FROG 80106
FROG No.1 52468
FROG *Short tunnel boat with lifting gear*
FROGMORE II 73336
FROG PRINCE 30045
FROTH 103802
FRUGAL 46521
FRUIT & NUT 76216
FULBOURNE 142 73167 Lg Woolwich Town Cl motor. Ex GUCC/BW
FULLMONTY *62592 20′ grey/wh*
FULMAR 45591
FUMBLE 99335 Day hire. Nb-style purpose built 22′6″, b 6′ red/grn. B: 1970ish, believed by Kingfisher Hire at Hoo Mill; lengthened Sileby Mill 1991/92. Originally powered by Stewart Turner petrol engine, now by small 2 cyl diesel. Base Sileby Mill Boatyard, Soar Nav. Further information - see *Rumble*. 032888
FUNHAM III 72752
FUNKLE 77174

FURNESS 67141
FURNESS 72392
FUSILIER 65025
FUSSY KATE *Grp 25′*
FU-URTHER 79201
FUZZ-E-BEAR II 74348
FYNE LADYE 46624

G

A boat in a puzzle, unique design, a TV star, a Grp first at a bargain price, a coal fired steamer, into the Wilderness and lots at Guildford

GABBIT 61749
GADWALL 51685
GADWALL 67306 & B1001 NbC 35′ red/grn. B: 1981 Hancock & Lane Norseman hull. Yanmar YSE 12G single cyl. Base Lyme View marina, Macclesfield canal. Retains distinctive original hopper type windows. 20106
GAEN 73234
GAFFER 71350
GAIA 53158
GAIA 54181
GAIA 71060
GAILEY 80156 BW-
GAILEY RANGER 62470

GAINSBOROUGH 71895 Lg Woolwich Town Cl motor. Ex GUCC/BW
GAINSBOROUGH see **NIMROD**
GALADRIEL 53268
GALADRIEL 53313
GALADRIEL 70693
GALAPAGOS No.27 *NbT 60' blue/wh*
GALATEA 54964 NbT 52' blue/yel. B: 1995 Bridgewater Boatbuilders, Worsley. Lister Canal Star 4 cyl. Base K&A canal. 24838
GALERIE 67936
GALFRIUS 71251
GALILEO 47130
GALILEO 64575
GALLIARD *45793 NbT 60' grey/red*
GALLIARD 68964
GALLUM 71529
GALLY'S DAWN 64436
GAL ON THE CUT 76560
GALTON 71888
GALTON 81840
GAMBA 66000
GAMBIA *Nb red/grn*
GAMBLER 68057
GAMBLER *76175 NbC 50' blue/wh*
GAMEBIRD PYRFORD MARINA RIVER WEY. Grp cruiser crm/red. B: 1987 Shetland. Ob. Base Pyrford marina, R.Wey 21347
GAMECOCK B7905
GAMEKEEPER 67395
GANDALF 51425
GANDALF 75214
GANDELFE 48772
GANDER 60078
GANGES 72512
GANNET 46280
GANNET *NbC 40' grn/red*
GANNYMEDE 66821
GARALDI 75514
GARAN No.5 74559
GARANCE 51025
GARDENIA 63833
GARDER 72653
GARTH 78258
GARTH *NbT 70' bl*
GAVANTINA B1433
GAVOTTE Hire. NbC 34' red/grn. Base Rose Narrowboats, Brinklow, N.Oxford canal. 026697
GAVOTTE 60880
GAWBURN 82748 Motor vessel + crane 17.4m BW-NE
GAWKSWORTH 65492
GAYDREAM 92008
GAYEDAWN 64939
GAYO 64974
GAYTON 82059 Motor boat 52'6" BW-OGU
GAYTON GREBE 63704
GAZEBO 53536
GAZEBO *NbST 50' red/grn*
G.B. 31977
GEARANOOK 048042 CHIRK MARINA Nb 30' peacock blue. B: 1991 Mick Sivewright. Volvo 2000. Base Chirk marina, Llangollen canal. 21252

GECKO 67381
GEEDEE 64926
GEFFA 101288
GEFION 47583
GEISHA GIRL 102229
GELDY 79023
GELFLING 066845 Hire. NbC 34' grn/red. BMC 1.5. Base Evesham Marina, R.Avon. 0371028
GELTON 72390
GEM 45392
GEM 2 92969
GEM II 64597
GEMAIRE 51069
GEMERIS 53057
GEMI II 76041
GEMINI 46735
GEMINI 46735
GEMINI 53825
GEMINI 60067
GEMINI 66029
GEMINI 74739
GEMINI 82715
GEMINI G11727
GEMINI I 65586
GEMINI III B1506
GEMINI Barney(52) 1975 28' *(ex Girl Molly II)*
GEMINI DREAM 73148
GEMINI LADY 52033
GEMINO 60476
GEMMA 70079
GEMMA LOUISE 78269 Marine ply cruiser 26' wh/blue. B: 1968 Carr & West, Norfolk. Inboard converted Ford 105E petrol, Z drive. Base Heritage marina, Scholar Green, Macclesfield Canal. Includes 4 berths, central heating, shower. 23569
GENESIS 49445
GENESIS *49921 NbT 40' grn*
GENESIS 53761
GENESIS 54352
GENESIS 61610
GENESIS 75451
GENESIS 75707
GENEVIEVE 62379
GENEVRE Steam launch with canopy, cold moulded /ply, brass stanchions for canopy 19'6", b 5'6", d 2' dk blue hull. B: 1990 Glyn Lancaster Jones, Port Dinorwic. Coal fired, boiler Blackstaffe type 3 drum vertical water tube. Engine: compound 2" + 3.1/4" x 2" both built Precision Steam, Tavistock. Base Bushnells Boat Yard, Wargrave on Thames. Has classic steam launch lines. 21292
GENIE 91971
GENII 70748
GENISTA No.3 72635 NbC 43' lt grn. B: 1985 Simolda Ltd. Nantwich. Lister ST2 air cooled. Base Hatherton marina, S&W canal. Originally built as hire boat for Simolda Ltd. as *Queen Valerie.* 24808
GENTILY 72429
GENTLE GIANT 79475
GENTLE GYPSY 49654
GEORDIE 102884
GEORDIE GIRL 45901

GEORGE Work boat unpowered. Boat Museum
GEORGE *48137 NbST 50' blue/red*
GEORGE 051431 Hire. NbST 69' navy blue/lt blue. B: 1992. Lister LPWS. Base Sally Boats, Bradford on Avon marina. 013241
GEORGE 53302
GEORGE 65838
GEORGE 75474
GEORGE No.4 72127
GEORGE AND THE DRAGON 79933
GEORGE ELIZABETH 70726
GEORGE PAGE 60448
GEORGE SMITH 78011
GEORGIE GALL 68253
GEORGIE GIRL 78020
GEORGIE GIRL 90413
GEORGINA 72520
GEORGINA II 49679
GEORGINA V 46296
GERALD 61438
GERALDINE 75479
GERANIUM 73360
GERANIUM 79090
GERTIE 79790
GERTRUDE 70266 Butty
GETAWAY *Grp 20' blue/wh*
GIDDY KIPPER 66815
GIDEON 74459
GIFFORD 60 Nurser butty. Ex T Clayton. Boat Museum
GILDA ROSE 78864
GILLENA 76850
GILLIE 51572
GILL ROY II 83910
GILL THORN 74009 M G & M DRURY SKIPTON NbT - sheeted 55' dk grn/bl (sheet) B: 1989 South West Durham Steelcraft. Ruston & Hornsby VSO 15hp 1000rpm (1943) 2:1 g'box, Crowther prop 22x20; 4mph @ 650rpm. Base Skipton, L&L. Replica loaded working boat, half sheeted advertising boat builder. Originally a 37' tug. With a 35' butty featured in "Pieces of Parkin" (Yorkshire TV) ascending Bingley 5 rise locks. Also part of feature onthe L&L and Aire & Calder in "Women & Home". Since sold butty and 16'6" put in *Gill Thorn* to make today's replica. 24858
GILLY BEAN 78530
GILLYS 46377
GILWERN LADY 54520 Hire. NbC 32' yel/brown. B: 1995 Evans & Son, Hixon, f/o Road House Narrowboats. BMC 1.5, Delta box to 16x 10 prop. Base Gilwern, Mon & Brec canal. 014259
GILWERN PRINCESS 53919 Hire. NbC 36' yel/brown. B: 1994 Springer to Road House design, f/o Road House Narrowboats. BMC 1.5, Delta box to 17x12 prop. Base Gilwern, Mon & Brec. 016261
GILWERN QUEEN 51413 Hire. NbC 36' yel/brown. B: 1992 Arcrite Fabrications, f/o Road House Narrowboats. Lister LPW2, Delta box to 17x12 prop. Base Gilwern, Mon & Brec canal. 015260
GIMLI 85831
GINA 71802

GINALLY 45973 STOKE GOLDING NbC 45' mar/Oxford blue. 1976 Bingley Marine (16th boat built in 1976). Lister SR2 air cooled. Base Ashby Canal Centre. 24825
GINETTE 46302
GINGER 52667
GINGER B 49254
GINO WATKINS 48609
GIPSY ROSE 65107
GIRL JEANNI 500907
GLADIATOR 87178
GLADLY *62428 Grp 30'*
GLADSTONE 74081
GLADYS 53248 THE REDFERN HOTEL CLEOBURY MORTIMER NbST 45' grn/red. B: 1993 Heritage Boat Builders, Evesham. 1500cc Beta. Base Staffs & Worcs canal. 22427
GLADYS LILLIAN *Gravel barge - R.Trent*
GLAIN 53151
GLAMIS 64605
GLASCOTE 67536
GLASLYN 45894 Grp cruiser 27' wh/blue. B: circa 1980 Norman Cruisers Ltd. Honda 9.9hp ob. Base Savile Town Basin, Dewsbury. Named after Afon Glaslyn - a river in Snowdonia. 23608
GLAS Y DOKIN 74156
GLAS-Y-DORLAN 74356
GLAVIA 45325
GLEANER 53553 NANTWICH NbC 36' dk blue/wh. B: 1993 Stoke on Trent Boat Building Co. Ltd., Longport Wharf. Beta/Kubota BV1305. Base Nantwich & Border Counties Yacht Club, SU canal. Large living area with gas fired Squirrel stove. Name derived from a family working boat which operated in the late 1800s and early 1900s on the Huddersfield Narrow canal and which was recovered from the canal at Marsden Tunnel End, it having sunk sometime earlier. Also the Royal Navy's smallest boat is also a "Gleaner" - a fibreglass survey boat. 20165
GLENCOE 50960
GLENDALE 71565
GLENDALE 73174
GLENELG 64427
GLENFIELD No.2 71635 A.W. BROOKES & CO. OLDBURY NbT 60', d 2'6" grn/red. B: 1984 L Allen & Sons, Oldbury, f/o by owner. Russell Newbery DM2. Base Bonded Warehouse, Stourbridge canal. 26 foot cabin, remainder sheeted as a working boat looks. Featured on "The Boat Rally" jigsaw by Lockmaster Crafts. 20192
GLENGARRY 52683
GLEN MARLIN 65157
GLENMORE 45624
GLENMORE 64835
GLENMORE 74835
GLENRICH 47832
GLENRICH II *NbC 25' grn/red*
GLEN USK 51340
GLOBE TROTTER 46775
GLORY 54503
GLORY No.1 *NbT 70' grn/red*
GLORY BE 63312

GLOSTER ROSE 60872 No. 1 OLDBURY NbT 39'11" red/grn. B: 1966 Halmo Engineering Ltd. Halesowen; machinery/topsides Les Allen & Sons Oldbury; f/o Newbridge Boats, Wolverhampton. Lister SR3 air cooled. Base Wyre Mill Club, Warwickshire Avon. Prototype hull to design of Cyril Taplin & Partners of Quinton, Birmingham. Subsequently produced as the "Lionheart" hull for Malcolm Braine. 24906
GLOUCESTER 70914
GLYN 50122
GLYN GARTH 50375
GNOMES 77571
GODNOSE TOO 48714
GOING PLACES 60791
GOLBOURNE 078672 Restaurant/Trip boat. NbT 70' red/grn. B: 1981 Colliery Narrowboats, Northwich. Electric power. Base The Old Wharf, Trevor, Llangollen canal. 01124
GOLDBERRY 48795
GOLDBERRY 52816
GOLDBERRY 62453
GOLDBERRY 80631
GOLDBERRY II 70783
GOLDCLIFFE GREENFINCH 70708
GOLDCREST 70825
GOLDEN DOVE 72650
GOLDEN EAGLE 62314
GOLDEN EAGLE 64568
GOLDENEYE Tug 19'6" BW-OGU
GOLDENEYE 91395
GOLDEN FALCON 60100
GOLDEN FALLS 46677
GOLDEN GIRL 50754
GOLDEN HARMONY 75537
GOLDEN HAWK 60634
GOLDEN LINNET 73611
GOLDEN MERLIN 75973
GOLDEN ORIOLE 61725
GOLDEN ORIOLE 64478
GOLDEN PHEASANT 61726
GOLDEN PLOVER 51473
GOLDEN SPRAY *Workboat*
GOLDEN VALE III 60150 Grp Nb Wilderness Beaver 23' mustard/grn. B: 1979 Wilderness Boats. Yamaha 10hp ob. Base Pewsey Wharf, K&A canal. Classic example of well maintained 'Beaver'. 24771
GOLDEN ZEPHYR
GOLDFINCH 71876
GOLDSTONE 78232
GOLDSTONE *see THESEUS*
GOLDSWORTH 47356
GOLIATH Tug - work boat used on canal restoration and maintenance 24', b 8' grn/bl. B: circa 1950 - builder not known but boat purchased for use by Cotswold Canals Trust from Wessex Water in 1981 (previous use on Bristol R.Avon). Lister HA3 3 cyl 36hp air cooled. Base Eastington, Stroudwater Navigation. See also *Leviathan* 027724
GOLIATH 51610
GOLLUM 60185

GOLLUM 68878
GOLONDRINA 74901
GONDOLIERS MOON 46639
GONE ROAMING 75531
GON FISHIN 65804
GONGOOZLER 66022
GONZALO 68590
GONZO 76259
GOOD BUDDY 102336
GOODENOUGH 49803
GOOD LIFE 72254
GOOD LIFE 72435
GOOD TIMES 77436
GOODY TWO SHOES N5781
GOOGLY 75914
GOOSANDER Hire. NbC 40' blue/crm. B: 1980 Godalming Narrowboats on Colecraft hull. BMC 1.5. Base Farncombe Boat House, R.Wey. 00378
GOOSANDER 48613
GOOSANDER 65324
GOOSANDER 67118
GOOSANDER 4 48629
GOOSEFAIR 47011
GOOSEMOOR *48162 NbT 50' grey/wh/bl*
GOOSENOIR 48162
GOPHER 80031 Dredger (hydraulic) 45' BW-NW
GO PLACIDLY 78275
GORDALE 73454
GORDANN 49616
GORDON BENNETT *65764 55'NbC beige/blue*
GORRIT 48578
GORSE 240 62200 Yarwoods ice breaker. Ex FMC/BW
GORT NbT 70' grn/graining. Samuel Barlow Coal Co. Ltd.
GOSHAWK 47714
GOSWIN B1413
GOT IT 48025
GOTRIK 72652
GOWER No.2 77775
GOWKER LILY 49747
GOWY 89245 Motor vessel BW-NW
GRACE No.12 *NbT blue*
GRACE 50185
GRACE 50464
GRACE 65768
GRACE 75330
GRACE 75406
GRACE No.1 65870
GRACE DIEU 61892
GRAFTON MANOR 75490
GRAINNE MHAOL 45378
GRALYN 74724
GRAMPA'S LADY *NbC 50' blue*
GRAMPIAN 47623
GRAMPUS 54329 P.D. CARLILE AND SON BANBURY NbTug 56'6", d 30" dk blue/red/wh. B: 1994 Steve Hudson Boatbuilders, Glascote Basin. Lister FR2. Base Hurrans Wharf, Banbury. 20175
GRANBEA 51489
GRANBY 45756
GRAND ARKWRIGHT 46498

GRAND DUCHY 47417
GRANDEE 45032
GRAND MARNIER 77547
GRANDMA SCRUFF *52111 NbST 45' blue*
GRAND PRIX 85414
GRAND SLAM 88851
GRANGE No.261 *NbT 71' blue/red*
GRANGE 51455
GRANGEWOOD GIRL 50174
GRANITA 47522
GRANNY WYTCH 76974
GRASMERE 60887
GRASMERE 67475
GRASSHOPPER 82113
GRAYDON G10186 Nb 49'6" crm/mar. B: 1986 Springer. Base Fox Marina, March. 22470
GRAYL 53753
GRAYLING *KACHINA*
GRAYLING 51760
GRAYLING 53409 BW-
GRAYLING 89233 Motor vessel BW-NW
GREAT SKUA 52171
GREAT WESTERN 75739
GREAT WESTERN *NbC 40' grn*
GREBE 61341
GREBE 61453
GREBE 65664
GREBE 66752
GREBE 67360
GREBE 72661
GREBE 76144
GREBE *see ANTELOPE*
GREEBO 77745
GREEN ANARCHIST 74912
GREENDALE 71685
GREENFIELD 60202
GREEN GODDESS 64854 NbC 40' grn/red. B: 1976 Fisher Caithbeam. 1.5 BMC. Base Great Northern Basin, Langley Mill. Boat Safety Certificate issued Sept '96. 21250
GREEN HOWARD 50216
GREEN HOWARD 63386
GREEN JOEY 60461
GREENMAN Tug
GREEN MAN 52703

GREEN MAN 71544
GREEN MAN 74434
GREENOCK 144 Lg Woolwich Town Cl motor. Ex GUCC/BW/WW
GREENPEACE 71444 Centre cockpit cruiser, wood/grp superstructure on steel hull 30' wh/orange. B: 1981-84 Reg Goodall, Newark. Bukh 10hp coupled to outdrive leg, 2:1 reduction. Base Derby Motor Boat Club. A one off home designed and built with hollow keel, or inverted top hat section, unballasted; unique bow shape. 21327
GREENPEACE 73557
GREENSLEEVES 62408
GREEN TARA 500499
GRENADIER Hire. NbC 56' blue. B: 1980 Godalming Narrowboats on Colecraft hull. Lister ST3. Base Farncombe Boat House, R.Wey. 00373
GRENVILLE 80080 Motor vessel BW-NW
GRESHAM *see OTTER*
GREYBACK 45569
GREYBACK 62049
GREYCOAT 53566
GREY DOVE 70899 DEWSBURY Grp cruiser, wood above gunnels 28' grey. Commissioned 1953, launched 1958, Ripleys of Ripon. Lister 7hp twin. Base Dewsbury basin. Originally built for Wash and canals and rivers but spent a lot of time on Norfolk Broads. Believed to be one of the first Grp hulls to be built; the fully fitted price was £1,200. 23609
GREY HERON 61670
GREY HERON 67909
GREYHOUND Nb Commercial carrying working motor livery as formerly operated under Captain Cargo Ltd. - red/grn/yel; iron composite construction. B: 1926 for Fellows, Morton & Clayton Ltd. Single Bolinder (direct reversing). Base Coventry & GU canals. 031815
GREYHOUND 72300
GREYLAG 70884
GREY OWL III M21875 Beaver Cub trailable Grp cruiser 17'6" laurel grn/brown. B: 1993 Wilderness Boats, f/o Mick Sivewright, Barbridge. 9.9hp Yamaha ob. Base Medway Wharf marina, Wateringbury, Kent. Very complete little boat with

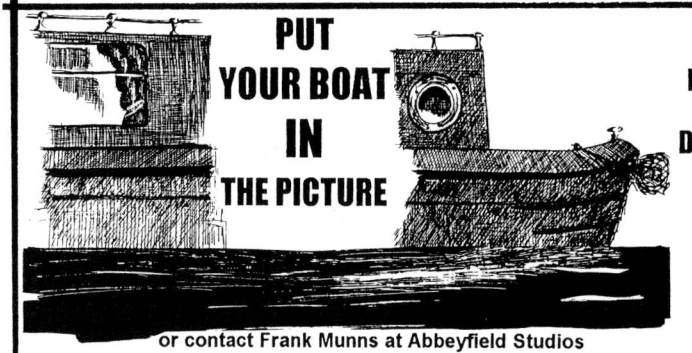

PUT YOUR BOAT IN THE PICTURE

Commission FRANK MUNNS to DRAW OR PAINT YOUR BOAT from your own photographs

0116 : 284 9596
0116 : 286 2538

or contact Frank Munns at Abbeyfield Studios
The Mews Gallery, 22A Coventry Road, Narborough, Leicester LE9 5GB

ALL the mod cons of a caravan, inc central heating. 21304
GREY PARTRIDGE 53904
GREY POPLAR see WALNUT
GREYSLUG 66535
GREY WAGTAIL 51474
GREYWELL TUNNEL 46897
GRIDDLEBONE 60157
GRIFFIN 60911
GRIFFIN B0181
GRIZEDALE 54547
G ROSE 64876
GROWLTIGER 61865
GROWLTIGER 77625
GRUMBLEWEED NbC 35' wh
GRUMBUSKIN 68370
GRUSHKA 72844
GUANABARA 66589 Grp 20' wh
GUCCI 45339
GUELDER ROSE 72396
GUELROSE 46576 NbT 60' grn/red
GUILDFORD AMBASSADOR GUILDFORD BOAT HOUSE Hire. Nb 65' grn/crm. B: 1988 Alvechurch. Base Guildford Boat House, R.Wey. 024636
GUILDFORD BARONESS GUILDFORD BOAT HOUSE Hire. Nb 40' grn/crm. B: not known. Base Guildford Boat House, R.Wey.024621
GUILDFORD CASTLE GUILDFORD BOAT HOUSE Hire. Nb 55' grn/crm. B: 1990 Alvechurch. Base Guildford Boat House, R.Wey. 024632
GUILDFORD CONSORT GUILDFORD BOAT HOUSE Hire. Nb 53' grn/crm. B: 1988 Aivechurch. Base Guildford Boat House, R.Wey.024630
GUILDFORD COUNTESS GUILDFORD BOAT HOUSE Hire. Nb 50' grn/crm. B: 1990 Alvechurch. Base Guildford Boat House, R.Wey. 024624
GUILDFORD DRAGON GUILDFORD BOAT HOUSE Hire. Nb 50' grn/crm. B: 1977 Colecraft/Farncombe Boat House. Base Guildford Boat House, R.Wey. 024628
GUILDFORD DUCHESS GUILDFORD BOAT HOUSE Hire. Nb 50' grn/crm. B: 1988 Alvechurch. Base Guildford Boat House, R.Wey. 024627
GUILDFORD DUKE GUILDFORD BOAT HOUSE Hire. Nb 55' grn/crm. B: 1987 Alvechurch. Base Guildford Boat House, R.Wey.024631
GUILDFORD GRYPHON 48396
GUILDFORD KNIGHT GUILDFORD BOAT HOUSE Hire. Nb 40' grn/crm. B: 1988 Alvechurch. Base Guildford Boat House, R.Wey.024622
GUILDFORD LADY GUILDFORD BOAT HOUSE Hire. Nb 50' grn/crm. B: 1988 Alvechurch. Base Guildford Boat House, R.Wey.024625
GUILDFORD MARQUIS GUILDFORD BOAT HOUSE Hire. Nb 65' grn/crm. B: 1990 Alvechurch. Base Guildford Boat House, R.Wey.024635
GUILDFORD MONARCH GUILDFORD BOAT HOUSE Hire. Nb 69' grn/crm. B: 1987 Alvechurch. Base Guildford Boat House, R.Wey. 024637

GUILDFORD PRINCESS GUILDFORD BOAT HOUSE Hire. Nb 63' grn/crm. B: 1990 Alvechurch. Base Guildford Boat House, R.Wey.024634
GUILDFORD QUEEN GUILDFORD BOAT HOUSE Hire. Nb 50' grn/crm. B: 1988 Alvechurch. Base Guildford Boat House, R.Wey.024626
GUILDFORD REGENT GUILDFORD BOAT HOUSE Hire. Nb 60' grn/crm. B: 1993 Alvechurch. Base Guildford Boat House, R.Wey.024633
GUILDFORD VISCOUNT GUILDFORD BOAT HOUSE Hire. Nb 53' grn/crm. B: 1989 Alvechurch. Base Guildford Boat House, R.Wey. 024629
GUILLEMOT 45656
GUILLEMOT 74956
GUILLEMOT II 48868
GUINESS 47534
GUINEVERE 46077
GUINEVERE 47430
GUINEVERE 60525
GUINEVERE 66406
GUINN'S 47018
GULLIGAN 71727
GULLION 62327
GULLIVER 47605
GULLIVER 78167
GULLIVER No.2 NbT 55' grn/red
GULLS CRY 50006
GULLY J 46337
GUMBO 70343
GUNNER 64232
GUPPY 68284
GWENDOLEN 72578
GWENDOLINE 46848
GWENDOLINE 52262
GWEN EREWI 62667
G-WHIZZ 72100
GWYNNETH ANN 97351
GYMMN LADD 64799
GYPSEY ROSE 61445
GYPSY 47098
GYPSY 71487
GYPSY Grp 18'
GYPSY LOU 52249
GYPSY PRINCESS Trip boat - Forth & Clyde canal
GYPSY QUEEN 63198
GYPSY ROSE 61145
GYPSY ROSE 69714
GYRFALCON 49145
GYRFALCON 66932

H

Going Dutch in a big way, a powerful engine takes us weir-leaping, happiness is a good layout, a significant Royal occasion, a tribute to a Broads sailing fleet and a memorial to a generous navigator.

HADLEY 52266
HADLEYBROOK 51477
HADLEY RAIL Lg Woolwich Town Cl motor. Ex GUCC/WW
HAFAM CIL 74586
HAGAR 76022
HAGAR 74212
HAIDA 49132
HAJ + TWO B0415
HAKINA MATATA 54480
HAKUNA MATATA 75929
HALCYON 47907
HALCYON 54464
HALCYON 60187
HALCYON 65809
HALCYON 68761
HALCYON 68761
HALCYON No 183 101901
HALCYON DAZE 68694
HALCYON DAZE 102031
HALCYON LADY II 66351
HALCYON ROSE 465662
HALE & HEARTY 49395
HALE LADY 48009
HALF A PAIR 52695
HALF-A-SIXPENCE *71198 NbT 40' grn*
HALF PINT 48201
HALF PINT 75911
HALF PINT *NbT 25' red/grn*
HALIA II 102792
HALIFAX 71266
HALLAM 75152
HALLOWEEN 50729
HALSALL 62577 Lg Woolwich Town Cl motor. Ex GUCC/BW/WW
HALTON CASTLE 48969
HALTON EXPLORER B1240
HAMBA GHASHLE 73559
HAMILTON 63578
HAMILTON 74972
HAMLET 53422 BOURNE END NbT 50' red/blue. B: 1990 Bill Nyer (BWB), f/o Nicolas Stainer. BMC 1.5. Base Weybridge, R.Thames 22410
HAMMIE 63696
HAMPSHIRE 49098
HAMPSHIRE ROSE 51228
HAMPTON Butty
HAMSELL MEAD STREETHAY WHARF Nb 62' grn/crm B: 1981 Les Allen, Oldbury, f/o by Ray Bowern & Phil Gameson in Brazilian mahogany and ash; Back cabin, etc. Gardner 4LK 45-60hp (as used in midget subs and buses). Base Streethay Wharf. Classic BCN private Nb which has cruised many unusual places - R.Humber to Hull, Beverley Beck, R.Ancholme, etc., The Wash, Thames Estuary, R.Wey, R.Severn to Portishead. But the major feat was to follow the Severn Bore from Sharpness up the Severn, over Mazemore Weir at Gloucester and back into the docks, Autumn 1991. 261066
HAMSTER Dredger 16.7m BW-
HANBURY DAWN 500531
HANDY 102913
HANDYMAN 73746
HANLEY 64480
HANNAH 46556
HANNAH 47458
HANNAH 50993
HANNAH 51304
HANNAH 51307
HANNAH 051446 Hire by Bruce Trust to groups of disabled, disadvantaged, elderly people. Wide ST 61'8", b 10'9" dk grn/red. B: 1992 Greentour, Welton Hythe. Lister. Base Great Bedwyn, K&A. High standard f/o with facilities for disabled people. 00560
HANNAH 69828
HANNAH 101027
HANNAH B0884
HANNAH CLAIR 73865
HANNAH OF BROGDEN 500610 BARLICK (local name for Barnoldswick) NbC 55' blue. B: 1995/96 Tunnel Marine, Foulridge; f/o and paint E J Lyon, Dick Nuttall and friends. Nanni Kubota 4 cyl. Base L&L. Wheel steered from rear collapsible wheelhouse, front door half width of front cabin, lounge floor raised 7'/₂", all steps into front and rear cabins shallow rise. 24862
HAPPY DATE B0015
HAPPY DAZE 53144 NbC 30', b 6'8" Oxford blue/Monarch red. B: 1989 Springer. Thornycroft 60D 3 cyl. Base Zouch Mill, R.Soar. Typical V-bottom Springer hull but not typical Springer f/o; this done to first owner's specific wishes by Springer, with galley & toilet/shower in central area, saloon/double berth forward and dinette/double berth aft. "Good layout!" 251020
HAPPY GO LUCKY *NbT 40' mar/grn*
HAPPY OURS *75133 Grp Dalescraft wh/bl*
HAPPY TALK 80050
HAPPY UNION 46627
HAPPY WANDERER 95361
HARE Grab dredger 13.11m BW-NE
HAREBELL 48214
HAREBELL *Nb bl/wh*
HARECASTLE Motor vessel BW-NW
HARECASTLE TUNNEL 71865
HARGREAVES 65314
HARLECH 74946
HARLECH CASTLE Hire. NbC 41'6" grn/yel. Electric propulsion. Base Castle Narrowboats, Gilwern. 00214
HARLEQUIN 48179
HARLEQUIN 051518 BATH HOTELBOAT COMPANY Hotelboat -wide beam 70', b 12'6" dk grn/red. B: 1992 Colecraft. 2.7L 4 cyl. Base Sydney Wharf, Bath, K&A canal. 6.5k diesel generator. Traditional style external appearance,

internally takes advantage of the wide beam for comfort. 251019
HARLEQUIN 53184
HARLEQUIN 63216
HARLEQUIN 75207
HARLIN B1775
HARMONY 48124 R&J GLYNN & SONS STOWE HILL WHARF NbT 47'3" dk grn/yel. B: 1990 Mr. Hill, Stowe Hill Boatyard. Vetus 4.4. Base Whilton marina, GU. 23664
HARMONY 54460
HARMONY 66116
HARMONY B0539
HARMONY B0746
HARMONY B0830
HARMONY *NbT 25' red/grn*
HARMONY *NbT brown*
HARNSER 75496
HAROLD 76271
HARPEG 74771
HARPEN 77266
HARPO 70125
HARPOON No 1 54226 *NbTug grn/mar 50'*
HARRIET 45113
HARRIET 52804
HARRIET 69852
HARRIET 73477
HARRIET No 12 76966
HARRIET ANN 53523
HARRIETT 49158 NbC 33' brown/ lt yel. B: 1989 Brummagem Boats - original + later 8' extension, f/o N J Iliohan and helpers (original and extension and present engine). Beta BD1005 3 cyl (1991 replacing original Vetus). Base Welford Boat Station, R.Avon. 20191
HARRY 48950
HARRY 71788
HARRY 73929
HARRY 75284
HARRY STEVENS Trip boat - open sided 56', b 13' grn. B: 1972. Base Guildford, R.Wey. Named after last proprietor of R.Wey navigation before donation to National Trust. 016333
HART *(see Hind and Hart - hotel boat pair)*
HARTHILL Motor vessel 12.5m BW-NE
HARTSHILL Flat 9m BW-CATM
HARTWELL 45079
HARVESTER *NbC 36' red/wh*
HARVEST MOON 053570 MONSAL 35 NbT 35' blue. B: 1993 M&N Narrowboats, Ollerton, Notts. 3 cyl Beta Kabota. Base Warings Green, North Stratford canal. 24828
HARVEY 49793
HARVEY FREDERICK 52513
HASTY 67747
HATHERLEIGH *NbC 30' grn/red*
HATHOR WROXHAM Charter. Wherry Yacht 56', b 14'3", d 4' bl. B: 1905 Daniel Hall, Reedham. Sail. Base Wroxham, Norfolk Broads. Only 6 wherries capable of sailing now -this is one of fleet of 3 (see also *Norada, Olive*). 01226
HATTAFORT 75587
HATTS 45330
HATUNA PESA SASA 046590 TRISH & MIKE NbDutch Barge type. 65', d 30" crm/blue. B: 1990 K&A Boat Builders. Perkins 4018. Base Hilperton marina. To owners' knowledge this is the only one of its type with all steel cabin on back and access to front. 20121
HAVEN *68150 Grp 20' blue/wh*
HAVOC II 51411
HAWK 50551
HAWK 72883
HAWK 76225
HAWK 92276
HAWK 104556
HAWK *Grp 20' blue/wh*
HAWKE 68056
HAWKESBURY 67345 Lg Woolwich Town Cl motor. Ex GUCC/BW
HAWKEYE N5584
HAWKSWORTH 51893
HAWKWIND 52214
HAWTHORN Hire. NbC 50' grn/yel. B: 1980 Godalming Narrowboats on Colecraft hull. BMC 1.5. Base Farncombe Boat House, R.Wey. 00374
HAYGILLEU 74726
HAYSTACKS 70789
HAYTON Motor vessel 10.97m BW-NE
HAYWAIN 67995
HAYWOOD 77872
HAZEL Ex Bridgewater
HAZEL 60160 MIDDLEWICH NARROWBOATS No.10 Hire. NbC 56' grn/red. B: (date not known) Mindon, re-fit 1990. Lister SR3. Base Middlewich. Ex Rose Narrowboats, originally called *Pascali*. 028737
HAZEL 65564
HAZEL 100168
HAZELHURST 54528
HAZEL JONES 63896
HAZELL NUT *NbT 50' blue/red*
HAZEL NUTT 65777
HAZLEMERE 64179
H.D. No 14 Grab dredger 13.11m BW-NE
HEART OF GOLD 52903
HEART OF GOLD 65124
HEART OF OAK 77721
HEARTSEASE 52579
HEATHCLIFFE *52307 NbC brown/graining*
HEATHER 50078
HEATHER 44221
HEATHERBELL *54614 NbT 60' blue/red*
HEATHER BELLE 60836
HEATHER T 75378
HEBBLE 47196 ex Working boat conversion - rivetted iron hull, steel superstructure 50', b 12'7", d 3' blue/red. B: 1907 as workboat for the Aire & Calder Canal Co. at Bottom Boat, Stanley Ferry. Lister HB2. Base Apollo Canal Cruises, Shipley. Originally used as a maintenance boat on Aire & Calder. Later fitted with engine (not yet identified). Later used as the stonemason's boat on L&L canal and had the HB2 at that time. Retired in late 1980s and sold to Apollo Canal Cruises where it had new cabin and used as restaurant boat. Purchased by present owner 1995 and converted for private use "Never seen another boat quite like it!" 22437

HEBE 65232 O. & E. BAILEY BLABY BRIDGE NbC 40'5" red/lime grn. B: 1977 Colecraft, f/o Clubline (lengthened by Sawley Marina). BL 1.5. Base GU-Leics. near Blaby Bridge. 20205
HECLA 50445
HECTOR 052191 BRAYFORD POOL LINCOLN NbTug 57' dk blue/red. B: 1992 started by Charles Cox Narrowboats, completed by John Pinder & Son. 1961 Ruston Hornsby 2YD powering multi-variable pump driving hydraulic motor (no prop shaft allows full head-room in boatmans cabin). Base Brayford Pool. 22454
HEDGEHOG No.3 45207 NbT 70'
HEDGEHOG 67653
HEDGEPIG 75653
HEDGE ROSE 61676
HEDGE SPARROW 45592
HEDGE SPARROW 49837
HEINECAN B0091
HELAIRE 48134
HELEN NbT 50'
HELENA No.1 NbT 55' blue
HELENA KNOWSLEY 74155
HELENE 49829

Using the *Listing*
A *"how to use"* guide is on pages 13-14
Frequent abbreviations inside front cover
Full list of abbreviations included in
Location Glossary at end of book

HELENE 80662
HELENE OF TROY 47766
HELENE OF TROY Workshop Nb red/blue
HELEN MARY 61742
HELGA B0626
HELGA ELLEN 76717
HELGE 78668
HELIANETH 103077
HELIOS 77256
HELIX 47111 ALEX JENNY & LUCIEN NbT 45' grn/red. B: 1990 Springer. Ruggerini twin 26/18, Hurth gearbox, Aquadrive. Base St. Pancras Cruising Club, Regents canal. Extra long foredeck easily seats 8. *Helix* was one of only two narrow boats which took part in August 1995 VJ Day Parade on the Thames to accompany The Queen from Lambeth Pier to HMS *Britannia*. 24851
HELLEBORUS 74038 CALCUTT NbST 42' grn/ red. B: 1987 Stowe Hill Marine. Vetus type M4.14. Base Calcutt Marina. One of the first semi-trad narrowboats; featured in Waterways World Aug 1987 because of this distinction. 21280
HELLEBORUS No 2 45149
HEMLOCK 68211
HEMLOCK 74793
HEMMINGWAY 75297
HENGIST 51785
HENOPA 50408
HENRY II 62130
HENRY HUDSON 72810
HEORTFORDIA 78148

HERBAL SECOND BOAT 77408 STAFFORD BOAT CLUB NbT 40' dk grn/red. B: 1978 C T Fox, March. BMC 1.5L. Base Stafford Boat Club, S&W canal. The log of this extensively cruised boat (average 800 miles per year) shows 318 different crew members (including 158 children) in 16 years, while the female owner (whose surname is "herbal") often cruises single-handed. 22435
HERBIE 46736
HERBIE 65032
HERBIE II NbT 60' mar/grn
HERCULES 61532
HERCULES 76079
HERCULES 80042 BW-
HEREFORD Station Cl butty. Ex BW
HEREFORD 78843
HEREFORD 500577
HEREWARD 52523
HERITAGE Mtce boat 41' BW-BBC
HERMES 67853
HERMIONE 500881
HERMITAGE 54602
HERNANDEZ-CORTEZ 69874
HERNE 048158 CLIFTON CRUISERS Hire. NbC 36' grn/crm. B: 1989 Arcrite Fabrications, f/o Clifton Cruisers. BL 1.5. Base Clifton Wharf, Rugby. 025677
HERO 45029
HERO 52085 Nb 60', d 3'3" mar/gold. B: 1990 Colecraft shell, boatmans cabin builder not known. Lister JP2 (1934 - ex hospital standby gen-set engine), PRM 160 g'box. Base Thurmaston. Sheeted hold. Built as working boat in 1990 for diesel and coal sales and mobile workshop for original owner. 25996
HERO 78953
HERON Butty
HERON 47408
HERON 49155
HERON 50033
HERON 50249
HERON 53406 Tug 20' BW-NW
HERON 61681
HERON 61983
HERON 62328
HERON 62513
HERON 63403 JANE AND ERIC CROSS NbC 50' mar/navy blue. B: 1985 Black Prince - Fernie pattern. Lister ST3. Base Grebe Canal Cruises, Pitstone Wharf. 25985
HERON 66554
HERON 67051
HERON 68214
HERON 68467
HERON 68975
HERON 69435
HERON 77407 Grp cruiser 23' wh/blue. B: 1974 approx - Norman. Yamaha 15 PE 2-str ob, electric start (1982 approx). Base Sileby Mill Marina, R.Soar. Internal f/o still as original. 21298
HERON 79237
HERON 95930 Grp Norman 20' wh
HERON 101414
HERON N5856

83

HERON *NbC 40' grn*
HESKETH 73825
HESKETH *NbC 35' blue*
HESPERUS No 1 77578 Sm Ricky Star Cl motor. Ex GUCC
HESTER 51260
HETTY 51686
HEULWEN 45977
HEYFORD 65237 Motor
HEYFORDIAN 051642 FURNACE WHARF NbST 50' dk blue/red. B: 1992 Delph Marine, f/o by previous owner. BMC 1.8. Base Whilton marina, GU canal. 25945
HEYHO 103681
HEZIPBAH 52675
HIDE A WAY 65760
HIDE-A-WAY B1304
HIDEAWAY 45835
HIDEAWAY 77515
HIGGLER 47661
HIGHAM 52309
HIGHAM TUNNEL 71974
HIGH CALYPSO 48284
HIGHDALE B1402
HIGH JUMP 500903 CHURT Nb trailable, aluminium 23' olive grn/lt grn. B: 1996 Sea Otter Work Boats Ltd. Inboard Beta 13.5hp. 21277
HIGH KELLING 52433
HIGH LADY 74464
HIGHLAND 46021
HIGHLANDER 67554
HIGHLANDER 68401
HIGHLANDER 82353
HIGHLAND LADY B0838
HIGHLAND MIST 53427
HILBILLY 94480
HILBRE 63599
HILDA ELLEN *see LOUISA MAY*
HILDA HELEN No 2 77666
HILDEGARD 45205
HILLMORTON 77100
HILTON 60557
HILTON B1171
HIND 500624 and **HART** 500625 *(inseparable hotel boat pair)* H & H NARROWBOAT HOTELS NbT 70' grn/mar. B: 1996 Harborough Boats, Mkt Harborough. BMC 1.8, Volvo ARS hydraulic drive. Base Crick marina. Glazed observation lounge on *Hind*; unique tunnel linkage when breasted; stepped stern. Newest pair of hotel narrowboats on inland waterways *(Aug 1996).*2069
HINDERTON 61361
HINDLEY BLUE 71539
HINE TE AWA
HINKSFORD 46353
HINKSFORD 81712 BW-
HINKSTORD Mtce boat 16.9m BW-
HI NOON 100360
HINTON Mtce boat 41' BW-BBC
HIRONDELLE 47508
HIRONDELLE 51538
HIRONDELLE *Grp 20' wh/red*
HIS N' HERS 103753
HIS 'N' HERS *Grp broad beam 25'*

HISPANIOLA 45701
HISPANIOLA 65173
HOBBIT 76361
HOBBIT 92624
HOBBIT B1227
HOBBY 45597
HOBO 52476
HOBO *Nb 62'*
HOHER RIFFLER 50750 Dutch Barge (Luxemotor) 70', b 12'10", d 4' blue/crm. B: circ1924 original builder unknown, f/o by S M Hudson for personal use. Bolinders 4cyl, approx 5L, 3:1 reduction box, 46bhp (at prop) @ 1500 revs, 4-str. Base Sileby Mill Boatyard. Typical Luxemotor barge with original back cabin, folding wheelhouse and fully converted forward. 23723
HO-HUM 45859
HOLIDAY SPIRIT 51791
HOLLAND 73456
HOLLEMY 53095
HOLLIE 73614
HOLLY 65189
HOLLY 71705
HOLLY 72632 MIDDLEWICH NARROWBOATS No.8 Hire. NbTug 47' grn/red. B: 1985 Mike Heywood, Hoo Mill; f/o Mike Heywood/ Middlewich Narrowboats. Lister SR3. Base Middlewich. Well known hire boat - subject of water colour by Gordon Miles - has Boatmans cabin, trad engine room, long cockpit, cratch, top plank and covers. 028740
HOLLY 73573
HOLLY *Nb 50'*
HOLLY *see WALNUT*
HOLLY No 8 72632
HOLLY B *NbST 50' red/grn*
HOLLY BLUE 74671
HOLLY LASS GUILDFORD BOAT HOUSE Hire. Nb 43' grn/crm. Base Guildford Boat House, R.Wey 024623
HOLLYOWL 45840
HOLLYOWL II 53516
HOLOISE 47596
HOLYSTONED 51396
HOME MAID 77206
HOMER No 5 46960
HOME SWEET HOME 49224
HONDA 100651
HONEST 074146 No. 1 AYLESBURY NbT 60' navy blue/terracotta. B: 1987 Roger Farington, Ivybridge Marine, Braunston. Lister TL3 flat top. Base Aylesbury. 22384
HONEY 64868
HONEY BEE 74238
HONEY BUZZARD 52795
HONEY DEW 1000275
HONEYDEW 70886
HONEYSUCKLE 65951
HONEYSUCKLE 73953
HONEYSUCKLE 78689
HONOURMEAD 63423
HOOP DOET LEVEN SSR 43263 C BOUT Luxemotor rivetted steel Dutch Barge 21.3m, b 3.8m, d 1.4m lt blue/wh. B: 1926 Pelbeyer te

Oude of Wetering, Holland. Ford BD6 naturally aspirated 128hp mod 2725 6 cyl. Base R.Thames. C. Bout was original owner. Built specially for a small section of waterway in Holland. Exceptional condition for age. Red, white, blue livery over a black hull. In 1994 travelled to rally in France on Canal Du Nivernais, Vincelles organised by Friends of the canal; Won cup for the competitor who travelled furthest to get to rally some 1850Kms total, 392 locks. Also father of owner's wife won cup for oldest crew member (79yrs). Has only been owned by one previous family - 1926 to 1991 - four generations of this family were reared on board, hence her condition. 24865

HOOP OF WELVAART 49382
HOO'S HOO 66541
HOOT *10431 Grp 20'*
HOOTENANNY 54827
HOPCOTT 72199
HOPE 66323
HOPERIDGE 45347
HOPGROVE 60632
HOPPY 101096
HORACE *45397 NbT red/grn*
HORNBEAM 63358
HORNBEAM *NbC 60' red/blue*
HORNBEAM *see WALNUT*
HORN BLOWER II 63519
HORNET 63048
HORNET 74146
HORNET Mtce boat, flat, dumb 30' BW-NW
HORSELEY 52069
HORUS 45700
HOTCHIWICHI 50741 No.2 - KING & CO. - NASH MILLS NbT 60' mid coach grn/mar. B: 1991 Colecraft, f/o by Rugby Boatbuilders. Lister Alpha 4. Base Gayton marina, GU canal. 21361
HOTSPIN 85077
HOUDINI 46213
HOUSE MARTIN 47713
HOUSE SPARROW 49839
HOWARD 68107
HOW MUCH? 60891
HRJ 48854
HUBBERHOLME 70062
HUCKLEBERRY 51742
HUDSON 48695
HUFFLER No. 3 75648 A & M MERRIDALE NbT 55'6", d 2'9" dk grn/red. B: 1989 Dave Thomas (Boatman cabin & rear doors painted by Ron Hough). Gardner 2L2 (1933 or 1929) with Type 2 gearbox (engine found in road roller and gearbox from Trinity light ship). Base Braunston. It is understood that "Huffler" is a northern word meaning somebody who works on boats but lives in a house on land. 20199
HUGGY 101126
HUGH EVANS 103873
HULBE II 76891
HUMBER 78720
HUMBER Tug 9.15m BW-NE
HUMBUG 79656

Home from Home

85

HUNSBURY 71882
HUNTER *NbT 60' grn*
HUNTERS MOON 45026
HUNTERS MOON 53993
HUNTERS MOON 75103
HUNTONS ARK 61339
HUNTRESS 80858
HUNTS ROGER 71617
HURDY-GURDY 500366
HURLESTON 76924
HURLY 52508
HURON Barney(18) 1972 32'
HUSTLER 74118
HUSTLER No. 6 49026 A & C SEWARD GUNS MOUTH NbTug 40' grey/mar. B: 1990 Colecraft hull. Perkins D3. Base R.Wey. The name *Hustler* is a tribute to the securing of the future of the last traditional Broads sailing fleet originally set up by Percy Hunter at Ludham; there are 5 Hustlers - excellent 2 berth yachts often sailed by this boat's owners - hence the present "No.6". For "Guns Mouth" see Glossary 22518
HYACINTH 79756
HYDE 48920
HYDRA 47797
HYDRANGEA 72468
HYPERION 514
HYPERION 78996 Sm Woolwich Star Cl motor. Ex GUCC
HYPOTENUSE 76846 5113 NAUTICUS 27 Grp cruiser 27' blue/wh. B: 1972 Malcolm Thomas Plastics, Uxbridge Keel No. 112. 1600cc Gulf diesel. Base Bristol floating harbour. Cruises extensively from Bristol including Bristol Channel, R.Severn, Sharpness, R.Avon, BCN, Bristol Avon, K&A. 21307
HYSSOP 47941
HYTHE 73221
HYTHE 78514

I

More steam, lazy days, island dreams, candy stripes and recognising the "idle women".

IANDE 68173
IAPETUS 71140
IASIYN 78144
IBEX Yarwoods motor. Ex FMC/BW/UCC
IBIS 62783
IBIS 70662
IBIS 102203
ICARES 49784
ICARUS 70322
ICEENA 79872
ICHABOD 76983
ICHTHUS 47815
ICHTHUS 54859
ICHTHUS 68822
ICHTHUS 51891

ICTUS 500956 FAVERSHAM British Ship Registration 726541 Steam Launch 55', b 7', d 30" varnished teak/dk blue hull. B: 1989 Bay Class Yachts Conyer Teynham, Kent. Steam Lifu engine (built by Alex Ritchie, Wrabness), compound condensing paraffin fired, Yarrow type boiler. Base Rugby Wharf. Traditional steam launch with open deck and engine forward; glass cabin amidships, deck at stern. Cruised from Faversham - where built - up the Swale and Thames sea-way to the canal system. 21340
IDASYD *NbT 50' red/grn*
IDLENESS 48211 IDLE CRUISING CO. BOURNE END NbTug (very low in water) 60', d 2'9" Mercedes red/regency crm. B: 1989 Mike Heywood, f/o by first owner. Lister JP3 (1943 ex Humber Keel) top end re-built 1993, beds 1996. Base GU South. Normally to be seen with a garden bench on front deck. 23570
IDLEWILD 62098 NbC 44' mar/crm. B: 1977 Hancock & Lane Norseman, f/o Western Cruisers (for hire fleet - *Western Sun* - till 1987); extended 1993 by David Thomas, Braunston, front end refitted by Merlin Narrowboats. BL 1500, PRM 160. Base Braunston marina. 20147
IDLEWILD 65076
IDLE WOMAN 48985
IDLE WOMEN port side: GRATWICK & STEVENS MACCLESFIELD stbd side: JOHN & PAULINE RUSH LITTLETHORPE NbC 42' grn/red. B: 1996/97 Liverpool Boats, f/o Phill Barton, Barton Boat Services / Jantex of Congleton (soft furnishings). 1.5 BMC. Base Macclesfield. Named in recognition of group of women who worked the inland waterways during WWII - a small brass plaque will explain this fact. 24921
IDRIS 49537
IGUANA 31822
IGUASSI 72076
IKAN BESAR 54450
IKKI MARU B1302
IKOYI 98233
ILA 94482
ILEX 68487
ILFORD Butty. Ex FMC
ILKESTON 066057 FELLOWS, MORTON & CLAYTON No 210 Working Nb Butty, composite iron hull wooden bottom 72' wh/bl. B: one of batch of 12 built between 1911-1913 by Braithwaite & Kirk, West Bromwich for FMC, registered Birmingham 1273. Base as exhibit at Canal Museum wharf, Nottingham. Originally horse drawn or towed by FMC steam powered narrowboat, later a motor narrowboat. Carried general cargoes. One of 4 boats sold in 1945 to the Manchester Ship Canal Company - used as mud boat on dredging operations on their Bridgewater Canal (re-named *Mudboat No 3*). In 1975 sold into private ownership and used as a home, first at Bull's Bridge basin, then Nottingham. Later purchased by Nottingham Canal Museum and restored to original condition. 020459
ILLUSIONS 49314 NbT 70' blue/mar. B: 1991 Pat Buckle. Vintage Lister HRW3 44hp (restored

1951). Base Welton Hythe, GU-Leics. 24895
ILLUSTRIOUS 74104
IMAGINE 61608
IMAGINE 72690
IMAGINE 74938
I'M CRACKERS II 47201
IMEERINI 72924
IMER-DA 62134
IMJO 71030
IMLADRIS *40916 NbT 50' grn*
IMOGEN ROSE 66708
IMP 74093
IMPALA 60484
IMPALA 95964
IMPELLER 64735
IMPNEY 1 49826
IMPNEY 2 51479
IMPROMPTU *NbT 30' grn/bl*
IMPULSE 50532
IMPULSE 52485
IMPULSIVE 73295
INACHIS IO 50941
INAMINIT 65060 OF CARDIFF Grp cruiser 22' wh/blue. B: 1958 approx - Loftus Bennett; complete interior redesign and refit 1979. 9.9 Johnson (high thrust) ob. Base Sharpness marina. 21274
INCA WARRIOR G12838
INCOGNITO 47552
INDALO 91491
INDEPENDENCE 71277
INDIA *NbTug 70' mar*
INDIA 52288
INDIAN CHIEF 72833
INDIGO 72527
INDULGENCE 46190
INGA 46057
INGEMAR 77067
INGLETON 69451
INGLEWOOD 49039
INHERITANCE 65386 NbC 36' grn. B: 1978 Springer Engineering, owner f/o. Lister SR2. Base Lowesmoor Wharf, Worcester. 2087
INNESFREE 45939
INSAYN JAYN 45538
INSPIRATION 47175
INSPIRATION 48123
INSULATION 76309
INTALOK 61077
INTEGRITY 46762
INTENTION 75506
INTERLUDE 51584 J K & D E ADAMS BRAUNSTON NbST 60' midnight blue. B: 1991 Billington Dewhurst Ltd., West Houghton, Lancs., f/o North West Narrowboats, Blackburn. Perkins MC42. Base Braunston marina. Rear port holes etched with names and compass points. 21255
INTERLUDE 62305
INTERLUDE 70299
INTERMEZZO 050602 NbST 56' mar. B: 1991 GT Boatbuilders, Stafford. Lister Alpha LPWS4 Canal Star 40hp. Base Little Hallingbury. 22441
INTERVAL 61544
INTERVAL 76650
INTREPID 68246

INVICTA 69170
INVICTA 74473
INVIDIOUS 75205
INVINCIBLE 053362 No 21 ALVECOTE NbC 57' dk grn. B: 1993 Narrowcraft (Alvecote) on Colecraft shell. Ford 1.8 XLD. Base Alvecote (almost exactly half-way between the joint owners' homes in Surrey and Lancashire!). 21270
INVANGA 50526
IOANA 77931
IOLA 48241 *Steam*
IOLANTHE 62647
IONA 12543 GODALMING PACKETBOAT COMPANY Horse drawn trip boat. Nb butty, steel with elm bottom 72', b 7', 1'8" mar/grn. B: 1935 Harland & Wolff. Base Godalming bridge, R.Wey. Started life as *Bellerophon* for GUCCC. Used in film "The Bargee" in 1960. Name changed in 1960 when replacing old *Iona* as a trip boat at Norbury Junction. Been on R.Wey as trip boat since 1984. 261085
IONA 49724
IONA 53643
IONA 54120
IONA 67624
IONA 74728 NbT 50' dk grn/lt grn. B: 1987 Davidson Bros, Sawley Marina. Volvo Penta 28hp. Base Weltonfield, GU. 22429
IONA 78246
IONA HEBDEN BRIDGE Nb 40' Delph blue/crn. B: 1994 Pickwell and Arnold as "sailaway", remainder f/o by owner. BMC 1.8 by AMC Diesel, Preston. Base Mayroyd Moorings, Hebden Bridge. Owners' wedding blessing took place on front of boat with full wedding and morning dress - photo on cover of "Manchester Packet" IWA magazine. 207
IPPI 64712
IPSI 77715
IRENE 50085 ASHBY CANAL NbT 41' grn. B: 1991 Peter Nicholls, Napton Brickworks. Boatserve Mitsubishi 4cyl. Base Willow Park, Ashby canal. 23615
IRENE ADLER 48557
IRENIC 101545
IRIANNE *see RACHEL*
IRIS 68271
IRISH ROSE 76522
IRISON 500637 A.J. STANIFORTH NbST 56' burgundy/blue. B: 1995 Marque Narrowboats, Ecclesall, f/o Navigation Narrowboat Co., Nantwich. Beta. Base Lyme View marina, Macclesfield canal. First Marque customer's boat to have candy striped boarding rails at bow between gunwhale and cabin top; others have since taken up the idea. 24809
IROKA 63562
IRONBRIDGE 71394
IRON DUKE 61813
IRON DUKE 68525
IRON GOOSE 64318
IRON-HENRY 54251
IRONIS 54182
IRON LADY 51517

IRONSTONE 79018
IRON MAIDEN 51959
IROQUOIS 500840
ISAAC NEWTON 53230
ISAAC ROBERTS 63873
ISABELLA 103467
ISAMBARD 75913
ISIS 63368
ISIS 65068
ISIS 68279
ISIS 69124
ISIS 69483
ISIS 72807
ISIS *NbC 40′ bl/red*
ISLAND PRINCESS 79076
ISLE OF ARRAN 71592
ISLE OF IONA *94503 Grp wh*
ISLE OF PENDER 103100 Beaver Cub trail boat 17'6", d 11" olive grn. B: 1995 Wilderness Boats. Yamaha 9.9hp 4-str. Base Bath, K&A canal. Was the original demonstration Beaver Cub. 21283
ISOBEL MARIE 74519
ISOLDA 73834
ISTANA 53630
ITCHEN 81753 Motor vessel 16m BW-NE

ITESHALE 75671
IT'LL DO 76708
ITSA BITSA 103359
ITZOURS 67521
IVANHOE 73364
IVANMEE 90752
IVAR 72654
IVER DREAM 54999
IVORY Hire. NbC 56′ blue/red. Base The Wyvern Shipping Co, Linslade, GU. 00443
IVORY 47693
IVORY QUEEN 49959
IVY 63381
IVY 70210
IVY 71642
IVY 78673
IVY B0200
IVY MAY 51793
IVY ROSE 65434
IVY ROSE II 73877
IVYLEE 72177
IVY WILLS 76086 THE ASHBY TRIP S&B JEFFERY NbT - Brum tug with cabin extension 32′ grn/burgundy. B: 1985(?) Brummagem Boats. Farymann 2cyl. Base Sutton Cheney. 015288

J

Jubilee boats, the Flanders Flotilla, a loveable boat, de-weeding made simple, Glennifer sought, a Welsh connection, fairground expertise, a powerful job and "Nothing exciting, but it's ours!"

JABALLEN 79795
JABEZ 66382
JABIRU 50721
JABRIYAH 53610
JABRIYAH *NbC 50' grn*
JACAB 76283
JACABELL 60417
JACANA 73108
JACANAMIST 500209
JACANNAITH 61965
JACARANDA *Nb 60' red/grn*
JACARANDA II 7007
JACARANDA III 74998
JACARANDI II 94342
JACK 61989
JACKAL Yarwoods motor, Ex FMC
JACK DEMPSEY 61335
JACKIE B *46503 NbT 35' blue*
JACKIE DEE 62558
JACK MON 72705
JACK OF DIAMONDS 74853
JACK THE LAD 78533
JACKAL 62151
JACKDAW 47716
JACKDAW 74374
JACMAR 63073
JAC-MAR 30893
JACNANDRA II 68847
JACOB 48769
JACOB 78617
JACQUALAN 76903
JACQUELINE III 53817 JACQUI & TED MILSOM CRIGGLESTONE NbT 50' navy blue/mar. B: 1994 Mike Heywood - Evans & Co. Hixon, owner f/o. Kubota-Beta 1505 35bhp 4 cyl. Base BW Wharf Doncaster, SSY Navigation. Individualist signwriting and roses/scrolls as the retired signwriter who did the work usually decorates fairground equipment. 24873
JADE *46274 NbT dk grn 56'*
JADE 62757
JADE 68196
JADE B1684
JADE Hire. NbC 56' blue/red. Base The Wyvern Shipping Co, Linslade, GU. 00444
JADE MARIE 049931 WELTON HYTHE NbT 45' dark/mar. B: 1989 North Shropshire Boatbuilders. Perkins M4108. Base Welton Hythe. 21215
JADE STAR 53206
JAEGAN *NbC 35' red/grn*
JAEMS 61527
JAGO LADY B8051
JAGUAR Nb Commercial carrying working motor in livery as formerly operated under Captain Cargo Ltd. - red/grn/yel; steel composite construction. B: 1927 for Fellows, Morton & Clayton Ltd. Single Bolinder (gearbox). Base Coventry & GU canals. 031816
JAGUAR No 195 69274
J'AI VECU 71035
JAKANOMA 65865
JAKARA 69613
JAKE 52690
JAKE 68620 I & K HARRISON STAINFORTH NbT 60', d 30" dk grn/mar. B: 1976 Hancock & Lane, f/o by owner (whilst living abroad with wife and baby!). Glennifer DB2 (1936 - from ships lifeboat, plus 2 spare engines) 24hp twin with original air start. Engine weighs over 1 ton. (*Owner would be interested to discover any other craft with the same make of engine - see page 14*). Base Rose Cottage moorings, Lapworth. 24848
JAKE 96922
JAKE 100818 Grp trail boat - Marina 'Cadet' - Marina Boat Co. Solihull. Volvo Penta 99 ob. 2089
JAKI 63003
JAKOMENA *Grp 21'*
JAMAICA 060053 STOCKTON RUGBY NbC steel hull/grp cabin 36' royal blue/yel. B: 1975 Dartline. Lister SR2. Base The "Paddocks" Stockton, GU. Named after *HMS Jamaica*, an 8,000 ton cruiser of 39-46 war on which owner served. 25973
JAMAICAN CHARLIE 61398
JAMAN QUEEN 67880
JAMARA 50114
JAMBALAYA 2 *Grp broad beam wh/grey*
JAMBO 50448
JAMES II 72856
JAMES ARNOLD 61366
JAMES BRINDLEY 69101
JAMES BRINDLEY 69995
JAMES CLIFTON 48213
JAMES ERNEST B0823
JAMES LOADER No 8 67459 Tug
JAMES MALTBY *Nb 50'*
JAMIE 48688
JAMIE 49100
JAM-NEE-JAR 52343 AMPTHILL NbC 40' Oxford blue/yel. B: 1992, original by Narrow Boat Sales, Leigh nr Manchester; re-f/o by Bestcraft, Milton Keynes Marina, GU. Kingfisher KD-14-1. Base Milton Keynes marina. Specially shaped cratch with initials - JNJ - in copper plated brass on front. 23649
JAMOUEL TIGGER 63435
JAM TODAY 72439
JAN 68904 Nb 42' grn/crm. B: 1974 Springer. Lister SR2. Base Watford. Early Springer still going strong; recently fitted self draining aft deck and only one known to owner with wooden window surrounds. 23566
JAN 73960 CHOLMONDESTON Grp 30' blue/wh. B: 1975(?) Dawncraft. Ob. Interior layout modified to increase space; original fibre roof replaced by hood. 24835
JANAQUA 63537
JANCIS 50533 Grp cruiser 23'10" wh/blue. B: 1986 Viking Mouldings, owner f/o of bare hull.

Honda ob. Base Bridgewater & Taunton canal or on trailer at home in Winter. Car alternator fitted to back of outboard engine to supply power to fridge; separate starting and cabin batteries. Other modifications by owner include walkway with handrail at back and special engine mounting frame to help tilting to de-weed. 22530
JANCLIFF 52622
JANE 71580 Butty
JANE LOUISE B7743
JANE REDFERN 46724
JANELL 50316
JANEL ALISON 69628
JANET MARY 77485
JANICE - LIKE PHIDASH 78340
JANICK 48444
JANIE DIDDLE NbC 40' red/grn
JANINE 45738
JANORGO 72733
JANSU 74844
JANUS 71593 NbT 60' grn/red
JAQUAMANDA 60247
JAQUELINE 66604
JAQUELINE 69625
JAQUELINE 101786
JAQUELINE ELLEN 48559
JARA 52155
JARALANDA 48141
JAROWISH 65707
JASE 73384
JASMARA 52253
JASMIN 45410
JASMINDA 81244
JASMINE 62900
JASMINE 103273
JASON 68237
JASON 75411
JASON 89223 Motor vessel Piling craft BW-NW
JASON Trip boat - Regents canal
JASPER 60259
JASPER 63274
JASPER 70118 ATKINSON-WALKER (SAWS) LTD NbST 11.88m grn/red. B: 1979 privately. Coventry Climax (1951 - originally fork truck engine) approx 15hp. Base L&L canal. 21338
JAVA 45348
JAVA 78790
JAVE 49202 NbST 62' blue. B: 1989 Mike Heywood, Hoo Mill, f/o J R Fisher. Daimler-Benz 2.4L. Base Debdale Wharf. 24827
JAY 49846
JAY 52208
JAY 61738
JAY 72557
JAY 77318
JAY 500479
JAY B0895
JAY B1672
JAY I 68059
JAY No 1 B0101
JAY II 77464
JAYBEEDEE 76123
JAYBIRD 49618
JAY FIFE Thames Slipper Launch 26', b 5' varnished deck, grn hull. B: 1989 M Dennett, Laleham. Petrol engine. Base R.Thames. Copy of Andrews Slipper Launch previously owned; shown at Wooden Boat Show, Greenwich. 23548
JAYFREE Nb 52' blue/wh. B: 1981 Hancock & Lane. Base R.Thames. Probably one of the last boats built by Hancock & Lane - owned since new. 23547
JAY JAY 31218
JAYNAR 47812
JAYNE 65570
JAZE B0430
JEAN 96885
JEAN GENIE 92166
JEAN GILMORE 49856
JEANNE MARIE 74427
JEANNIE 63085
JEANNIE 77399
JEANNIE LEE 72356
JEANNIE LEITH 47807
JEBUS 53563 REGISTERED AT STROUD No. 7 NbC 35' blue. B: 1993 Peter Else, Tom Pudding Narrow Boats, Avon Dassett, Oxford canal. Beta BD 1005. Base Saul Junction. Tom Pudding design hull with false "Jebus" bow. 21326
JED B1746
JEEVES 68855
JEGS 63446
JELAINE 72909
JELLICLE MOON 73352
JELLICOE Mtce boat, dumb BW-NW
JEMARU 74753

Is Your Boat In It?
Is the Entry Accurate?
Please see page 12 to find out how to get included or amended in the next edition

---

JEMIMA 30142
JEMIMA 50950
JEMIMA 54470
JEMIMA 60601 REGD. STROUD No. 16 River/canal cruiser in Bruynzeel plywood 33'9" bl/wh hull, varnish sides, buff deck. B: 1965 by the late H E Abbott, Canal Pleasurecraft (Stourport) Ltd. Volvo MD11C (successor to original MD2). Base Saul Junction. Large stern cockpit, high bow. Jemima in brass letters on cabin sides, also motif depicting Welsh lady in national costume against background of 2 French ships at anchor, with date MDCCXCVII. Named after Jemima Nicholas of Fishguard. Made many tideway passages including R.Severn Bristol - Sharpness 44 times (featured Waterways World Sep '90 with photographs). 20169
JEMIMA 049187 NbC 42' grn/red. B: Stan MacNaughton, Liverpool Boats. Isuzu 997cc. Base Uxbridge. 23616
JEMIMA 73018
JEMIMA D 65029

90

JEMIMA PUDDLEDUCK 64198 NbC fibreglass (Swedish) foam sandwiched, 23', d 14" pale orange/wh/blue. B: 1973/4 Jack Carlisle, North Hykeham, Lincoln. Yanmar YSE 12, belt drive from manual g'box. Base Monmouth Brecon & Abergavenny canal. This boat has extensive cruising history - starting as home-build project in Lincolnshire, remains in excellent condition since. Many awards at boat rallies for best boat/best amateur built boat, etc. Profile models of Jemima Puddleduck - from the Beatrix Potter stories - appear on sides (though these are replicas of the original builder's carvings in applewood). Children love her. Features bluff bow, headlights moulded into hull, tiller plus forward inside steering position. 22505
JEM JEN H247 Grp 24', b 8'6" wh/burgundy. B: 1982 Eastwood. Ford Watermotor petrol. Base Dilham, R.Ant. Long unmullioned windows. 22517
JEMLKA G III 100670
JEMMA 47103
JEMMA 63641
JEMMA 64116
JEMMA EVE 48626
JEMORA 53525
JENALA 48865
JENAND B1367
JENICKA No 2 74003
JENNA 46722
JENNAH 46772
JENNALI 68170
JENNIA 52986
JENNIE 48847
JENNIE No 5 53228
JENNIE J 48847
JENNIE MAY 46552
JENNIFER E 62026
JENNIFER ECCLES 100555
JENNIFER ECCLES II NbT 50' mar/blue
JENNY GEDDES NbC 45' mar/bl
JENNIFER JAMES 53238
JENNY 49527
JENNY 74258
JENNY 92935
JENNY DARLING 47100
JENNY GLEN 4 77437
JENNY JONES 78274
JENNY LEE 47131
JENNY M 92903
JENNY MAY 52086
JENNY MAY 70762
JENNY MAY NbT 50' red/grn
JENNY O II 100726
JENNY WREN 46394
JENNY WREN 49672
JENNY WREN 52478
JENNY WREN 66093
JENNY WREN 66500
JENNY WREN 67152
JENNY WREN 70832
JENNY WREN 80488
JENNY WREN II 51169
JENNY WREN Grp Burland wh
JENNY WREN OF FULWOOD 65847

JENSEN 70414
JENSEN 74130
JEREMY FISHER Hire. NbC 47' B: 1980 Godalming Narrowboats on Colecraft hull. BMC 1.5. Base Farncombe Boat House, R.Wey. 00376
JEREMY FISHER 50502
JEREMY FISHER 52921
JEREMY FISHER 73354
JERICHO 63939
JERICHO Trip boat 70' BW-BBC
JEROME 48459
JERSEY GIRL 49030
JERSEY LILLIE 500661 UPTON-UPON-SEVERN NbST 52' ambassador blue. B: 1996 Starline Narrowboats on a John South shell, Upton-upon-Severn. Perkins MC42 4cyl. Base Upton-upon-Severn marina. 7hp electric bowthruster. Rear folding pram cover (illustrated in WW July 1996 p78). 22489
JESMOND 60610
JESS 83915
JESSAMINE II 52053
JESS & DOLL 53875
JESSEL 54363
JESSICA 52943 NbC
JESSICA 76637
JESSICA 78131
JESSICA 79546
JESSICA 96992
JESSICA WHETTY 50548
JESSIE 45497
JESSIE 51039
JESSIE 53987
JESSIE 101526
JESSO 62261 Grp 30' wh
JESSOP 63054
JESSWIN 71913
JESTER 45469
JESTER 52749
JESTER 78031 S.G. SCHOLES HUDDERSFIELD NbC 34' grn/red. B: 1978 Black Bull Engineering Liverpool. BMC1.5. Base South Pennine Boat Club, Battyeford, Calder & Hebble Navigation. Painting of Jester's head on each side. 23665
JESTER SONG 74920
JET 73591
JE T'AIME 103128
JEZEBEL 73567
JIDLER 500833 NbC 35' British Racing grn/poppy red. B: 1996 Liverpool boat; f/o to lined sailaway by Gloucester Narrowboats, design & f/o by owners. 1.8 Westerbeke. Base Hilperton marina, K&A. "Nothing exciting, but it's ours!!" 22507

JIGSAW 74919
JILECO 71954
JILL 50402
JILL 54644
JILL NbC 40' red/blue
JILLIAN 47859
JILLY 86355
JIMBO 54472
JIM & BO 77945

CAMPAIGNING BEGAN HERE

The first National rally of boats, organised by the embryo Inland Waterways Association took place at Market Harborough in 1950 and put the canal preservation and restoration movement firmly on the map.

In the IWA's Jubilee Year 1996 the Leicestershire IWA Section and the Old Union Canals Society re-created the Rally, opened by Sonia Rolt and attended by about 50 boats. The original 1950 banner was dusted off and can be seen (the long one) on the old warehouse. VIPs are arriving on board *Vanguard* (see entry). The Rally provided the impetus for a restoration of the basin area.

JIM HAWKINS 79143
JIMINY CRICKET 76999
JIMISADA 85191 WEY C.C. Dolphin marine ply cabin cruiser 20′ mahogany/blue/wh hull. B: 1962 Brooklands Aviation, Northampton. 15hp Honda 4-str ob. Trailed from home, Guildford. Unusual in that she still exists, unchanged, as built. 22406
JIMSONWEED 74893
JIPSY 72082
JO 500924
JOADIE PIE 103181
JOAN 73861
JOAN B II 53938
JOANNA 047744 J.M.B. CANNEY & CO. NEWBURY NbT 59′6″ Mercedes red/Atlantic blue. B: 1989 Norton Canes, f/o Blue Haven Marine. Russell Newbery DM2. Base Blue Lias marina, Stockton, GU. 20178
JOANNA 81819
JOANNA B 65148
JOANNA CHRISTINE 66331
JOANNE 52833 NbC 60′ mar/grn
JOANNE 60940
JOANNE 62610
JOANNE 71256
JO BRADLY 76104
JOBUZZ II 85959
JOBY 54125
JOCARA TWO 75536
JOCASTA 62617 NbT 30′ grn/red
JODEN 88379
JODOR 79484
JODY 67556
JOE 74856
JOEFISS 53442
JOEL No 9 65963 Motor. Ex L&NER Eng. Dept.
JOEY Hire. NbC 58′ red/grn. Base Rose Narrowboats, Brinklow, N.Oxford canal. 026706
JOEY 45603
JOHANNA 65521
JOHNATHAN 52714
JOHNATHAN LIVINGSTONE 73137
JOHN B 80202
JOHN BARLEYCORN 67884
JOHN CABOT 48745
JOHN CABOT 69677
JOHN E DEE 45784
JOHN G BROWN Dudley tunnel tug
JOHN GRAY Butty
JOHN OF HAMPDEN 70268
JOHN RUSKIN 70606
JOHNSON 88668
JOHNSTONE 62515
JOHN THOMAS 64369
JOHNTY B 74213
JOHN WILKINSON 49678
JOHREEN B0921
JOHRIS 78359
JOINT VENTURE 52848
JOINT VENTURE 66290
JOINT VENTURE 74220
JOINT VENTURE 99113
JO JO 50888
JOKA II 51633 NbT 65′ grn/red

JOKER 63277
JOKER 64741
JOKERS WILD III 73741
JOLA OF THORNE 62646
JOLAIN 50698
JOLEEN 82372
JOLEEN 3 76440
JOLLY JOHN 45864
JOLLY ROGER Nb 39′ red/crm. B: 1974; new steel top & refit 1989. Lister SR2. Base Hallingbury Mill, R.Stort. 22461
JOLLY ROGER 63615
JOLLY TAR 60627
JOLLY TODGER 46660
JOLYJO 96805
JOLYN 45981
JOMATOMSA 68425
JOMOSA 65111
JONATHAN II Grp Microplus 600 yel/wh
JONKRIS 49073
JONOME 61909
J'ORDEAN 104358
JORENE 80826
JORVIK 87876
JORVIK ONE 72770
JOSALADE 49505
JOSALARA 64777
JOSANDA 76372
JOSANICA 54708
JOSEL 46169 NbST 56′ crm/red. B: 1989 Arcrite Fabrications, self f/o. Vetus 414. Continuous cruising. Originally cruiser style but converted to semi-trad - fitted with a 7′ x 3′9″ hatch cover on roller bearings. Extensively cruised incl. tidal Thames through Barrier. Josel was one of the 31 narrowboats on the Flanders Flotilla 1995 in Belgium. 23617
JOSEPH 047683 Hire. NbC 63′ navy blue/lt blue. B: 1990. Lister LPWS. Base Sally Boats, Bradford on Avon marina. 013235
JOSEPH HENSON 50180
JOSEPHINE 54287 Nb grn/red/graining
JOSEPHINE 67856
JOSEPHINE 90533
JOSEPHINE III 62740
JOSEPHINE ANNE 70023
JOSEPH WRIGHT 52316
JOSH 53147
JOSH 79979
JOSHMIEL 70653
JOSHUA 49606
JOSIAH 54479 NbT 62′, d 30″ bl/red/wh. B: 1974 Five Towns (Roger Fuller), f/o Lofthouse & Wilson. Josher replica in FMC colours. 24845
JO'S MAPLE LEAF 64573
JOSS No 1 74096
JOURNEYMAN 45716
JOURNEYMAN 52607
JOURNEYMAN 52711
JOURNEYMAN 62805
JOURNEYMAN No.1 NbT 60′ grn
JOWEN 76137 NbC 30′ grn/wh. B: 1982 Eggbridge Marina, Waverton, Chester. Petter Mini Twin. Base Venetian marina, SU canal. 20166

JOY 52990
JOYBELLE II 065338 L.C.B.C. - ACE Grp 26', b 8'6" wh/blue. B: 1973 Freeman. Ford Watermota petrol. Base Bridge House marina, Garstang, Lancaster canal. Davitts fitted. 24860
JOYCE 78854 C.D. SHARPE, JERICHO Nb dk blue/grn. B: 1981 Colecraft; refitted 1989 by College Cruisers, Oxford. BL 1.5. Base College Cruisers, Combe Road Wharf, Jericho, Oxford. 21290
J.R. 85995
JUANITA II 48699
JUBILATE DEO 104174
JUBILEE 45445
JUBILEE 60070
JUBILEE 67080 REGD - AUTHERLEY No 22 R G DOBBS & CO - HALESOWEN NbT 60', d 32" grn/red. B: 1977 Water Travel Ltd. Wolverhampton Petter PJ3 (1977). Base Hawne Basin. Fully fitted boatmans cabin. *Jubilee* was moved for the first time on Silver Jubilee Day 1977, hence the name. 22448
JUBILEE 46257 Nb 10m blue. B: 1977-1989 (due to owner's relocation and house restoration), shell by Somers Engineering, Gainsborough, f/o G Foster, Boston, Lincs. 1.5 BL; Parsons Marinomatic gearbox with 2:1 reduction (Parsons gearboxes usually in seagoing vessels - have advantage of retaining forward drive in event of failure). 'V' bottom following barge skippers' advice that flat bottom unsuitable on tidal part of R.Trent. Owner does not regret that decision. Base Ashby Canal. 22500
JUBILEE KENNET AND AVON CANAL TRUST Trip boat - 35 seats. Nb 65' red/grn. Base Bath, K&A raising funds for K&A Trust. 030803
JUBILEE 1946-1996 NbST 59' blue (*IWA Jubilee boat*)
JUBILEE 69848
JUBILEE MOND B0364
JUBILEE VENTURE 64522
JUBONNIE III 75444
JUDY *NbTug 25' blue/crm/red*
JUDY No 2 69366
JUGANI *49421 NbC 30' red/blue*
JUGGLER 67566
JUKARDA 100242
JULIA 63673
JULIA 78286
JULIA M 47517
JULIANA 48027
JULIANA 50632
JULIANA 69378
JULIE 48803
JULIE ANN 48304
JULIE ANN 48378
JULIE ANN 74812
JULIEANNE 68456
JULIE ANNE 77948 MERSEY MOTOR BOAT CLUB Wooden cruiser, mahogany on oak 30', b 9' red/wh. B: 1960ish Taylors of Chester. Yanmar single 12hp, 3:1 reduction, 17"x13" prop - engine in bows. Base Lydiate near Ormskirk, L&L. Originally "one-off" as *Lady Beatrice II* with Stuart Turner 8hp (Original *Lady Beatrice* went searching for monster on Loch Ness but was wrecked). Built to a shortened Dunphy design. Spent time on R.Dee, R.Weaver, Lake Windermere and cruised Preston Dock, Ship Canal. 21371
JULIET 61770
JULIET 78664
JUMA *68552 Grp Norman blue/wh*
JUMBLE 99332 Day Hire. Nb-style purpose built 17'6", b 6' red/grn. B: 1970ish, believed by Kingfisher Hire at Hoo Mill. Originally powered by Stewart Turner petrol engine - now by small 2 cyl diesel. Base Sileby Mill Boatyard, Soar Nav. (Additional information - see *Rumble*). 032889
JUMBO 76369
JUNA 68552
JUNE II B0578
JUNE ROSE 31008
JUNE ROSE 75088
JUNE ROSE 80085
JUNIC II 48514
JUNIPER 50270
JUNIPER 53361 No. 7 I.C. BAILEY / OLDHAM CANAL CARRIERS & STEERAGE Working Nb - fitted under cloths 70', d 32" red/grn. B: 1978 Braunston Boats Ltd (believed), wooden boatmans cabin f/o not known, hold f/o 1995-96 by owners. Lister JP3 (1952 - believed in fishing boat at Hull till 1978), 26"x25" prop. Base Willow Park marina, Stoke Golding. Base plate to gunwale is 5 feet. 22409
JUNIPER 52911 MIDDLEWICH NARROWBOATS No.12 Hire. NbST 54' grn/red. B: 1993 Liverpool Boats, f/o Mancunian Narrowboats, Manchester. BMC 1.5. Base Middlewich. 028741
JUNIPER 75697
JUNIPER see *WALNUT*
JUNIPER HILL 65092
JUNO 49314
JUNO 62057
JUNO 295 69098 Sm Woolwich Star Cl motor. Ex GUCC/BW
JUNO II 73142
JUNO 75042
JUNO 79295 C.J. TERRY FOXHANGERS NbC 50' burgundy red/sharkskin grey. B: 1979 Hancock & Lane, f/o Weltonfield Narrowboats. Lister SR3. Base Dee Basin, Chester. Ex hire craft - first hire boat to be fitted out by Weltonfield. Originally 42', stretched in 1982 and Lister ST2 replaced with SR3. 24781
JUNOR 75741
JUNTOS 49166
JUPETER 77671
JUPITER 100260 S P B C Grp sports cruiser 21'8", b 8' wh/blue. B: 1986 Picton. Mariner 100hp ob (runs on 2 cylinders only when cruising on canals). Base South Pennine Boat Club, Battyeford, Calder & Hebble Navigation. 23666
JUPITER 53177 A D & S R CLARKE, STOKE GOLDING NbT 61'6", d 31" grey/bl. B: 1993 S M Hudson, Glascote. Lister JP2. Base Glascote Basin Boatyard. 1993 winner Lionel Munk Trophy. 23719
JUPITER 67765

JUPITER *NbT 50' brown*
JUSTANIA 61582 NbT 40'4" poppy red/racing grn. B: 1980 Coles Marine, Rugby. Bukhs 20hp. Base Mountsorrel, R.Soar. 251002
JUST CRUISIN' 82902 Grp 20'3" wh. B: 1970-80 Norman. Honda 10hp ob. Base Tewkesbury marina. 23578
JUS TODAY 54992
JUST CALL ME ANGEL 69670
JUST CRUISIN
JUST ELSIE 54396
JUSTINE 77032
JUST PATIENCE NbST 60' blue/yel. B: 1991 Harborough Marine. BMC 1.8. Base Wraysbury, R.Thames. Many features incl. bow prop, high internal specification incl. designer galley by 'Stoneham'; external paintings - and circular flower arrangements. 23567
JUST PERFECT *68574 Grp 30' blue/wh*
JUST PERFICK 53029
JUST US III 73308
JUST WILLIAM 87066

Where Is It?
Look it up in the Location Glossary

K

In which we meet some real horse power and a recycled gas holder (a big one!), an inspiration, a Monty veteran, oodles of teddies, different steering positions, a Rochdale first and a much loved Mother-in-Law

KACHINA 50520 KINGSTON Replica Edwardian Inspection Launch, Nb dimensions 54' crm/grn/mar. B: 1991 David Forth, Millington, York. Ford XLD 1.8 L 4-cyl. Base GU & R.Thames. *Kachina* is the generic term for the spirit gods of the North American Hopi and Navaho indians. Formerly *Grayling*. Wood-lined steel canopy/roof continuation over forward open well deck; extended open rear deck with tapered, rounded, overhung Edwardian 'motor boat' stern and wheel steering; second wheel steering position in forward cabin. 24797
KADUNA 77029
KAFUPI 75377
KAJAKAS 91942
KALAFRANA 68797 Grp centre cockpit 32' wh. B: 1972 Creighton, Nelson, Lancs. Renault 4 cyl. Base Mayors Boatyard, Tarleton, Rufford Branch, L & L canal. 20208
KALISPELL 54492
KALKARA 69225
KALLISTA 77107
KALMIA 47150

KAMI 75802
KANAWANA 48480
KANDA *72988 Nb Dutch barge style 50'*
KANGANGI 500052
KANGAROO Nb Commercial carrying working motor in livery as formerly operated under Captain Cargo Ltd. - red/grn/yel; iron composite construction. B: 1928 for Fellows, Morton & Clayton Ltd. Single Bolinder (direct reversing). Base Coventry & GU canals. 031817
KAOS 47342
KAOS 62699
KARADESA II 104087
KARAND 70901
KARELIA 63571
KAREN 73125
KAREN B 104447
KAREN KAWA 64001
KARENSA 47697
KARI 78641
KARIBOU 500829
KARIBU 61714
KAR-I-MAR 78141
KARINGAL 47496
KARISMA *Grp Nauticus 25'*
KARIZMA 74649
KARKEN 64124 N2267
KARMEL B1381
KARROO 45681
KASABA 30913
KASHGON 49781 Narrow beam Dutch Barge 45' crm/brown. B: 1991 Starcraft, Ilkeston. Perkins MC42 3:1 g'box, 20x15 prop. Base Macclesfield canal. "Exploits" include being escorted across The Wash in a Force 6 after National Festival at Peterborough in 1992; through Thames tidal barrier to Woolwich; first boat not based on Rochdale canal to reach summit (1996) since Tuel Lane blocked. 20135
KASHMIR 67403
KASIM *NbTug 50' blue*
KASTEAN 72549
KATANNE 54267
KATE 30019
KATE 30445
KATE 61219
KATE JANE 50572
KATE OF HARGRAVE 62580
KATH II GUILDFORD BOAT HOUSE. Hire. Nb 30' grn/crm. B: 1980 Colecraft / Farncombe Boat House. Base Guildford Boat House, R.Wey. 024620
KATHARINA 87820
KATHERINE 45608
KATHERINE 64316
KATHERINE No 9 46738
KATHLEEN 64740 BRAUNSTON NbC 45' grn/red. B: 1977 Hancock & Lane, f/o Western Cruisers, Stratford-on-Avon. 1.5 L BMC. Base Braunston marina. Previously *Traveler Peace*. 2081
KATHLEEN 047681 Hire. NbC 54' navy blue/lt blue. B: 1990. Lister LPWS. Base Sally Boats, Bradford on Avon marina. 013233
KATHLEEN 93487

KATHLEEN 98534
KATHLEEN ALICE 46780
KATHLEEN LOUISE 79134 NbC 40' burgundy/dk grn. B: 1981 Hancock & Lane, f/o by unknown hire boat operator, refit by present owner. Lister ST2 20hp. Base BCN main line. Originally 6 berth hire boat, now refitted to comfortable cruising/residential accommodation for 2. Re-engined 1991 Much-loved mother-in-law provided name. 22452
KATHLEEN MARIE 51203
KATHLEEN MARY 53652
KATHY 64342
KATHY 66070
KATHY D 61791
KATHY SUE 65907
KATIE 500128
KATIE II 82138
KATIE B 31097
KATIE JAMES 49361

KATRINA 102466
KATRINA 500341
KATY IV N5613
KATY LOU 98808
KATY MAY 063891 N D & M F PANZETTA No.2 NbT 30' dk grn/old gold. B: 1974 Barrington Wright, Dobsons Boat Yard. BL 1.5. Base Braunston. Hull made from 1/2" galvanised plate from a Victorian gas holder which was bought by Shardlow Co. from the Lichfield Lane Gas Works. *Katy May* is one of 3 boats so made (+ *Credalwood* and one unknown). 23612
KAYA 62569
KAYA MANTZI B0854
KAYLEIGH 47316
KAYOSS 60186
KAYSMAN 81520
KAZI MINGI 53843
KEAH 67709
KEARPAWNI 47549

Katie Louise at Sileby Mill Boatyard on the Soar Navigaton

KATIE LOUISE 54377 FENNY COMPTON NbT 48' mid grn/dk grn. B: 1994 Evans & Son, Hixon, Staffs, f/o J&D Pendred, Thrapston, Northants. Beta Marine Kubota 1505 1.5L keel cooled. Base Sileby Mill Boatyard, Soar Nav. "Josher" style with distinctive flared bows and rivets. 22513
KATIE MARIE 68791
KATIE MAY 63891
KATIE ROSE 47786
KATIE ROSE 103770
KATIES DREAM TOO 49670
KATISHA 47653
KATOHA 61891
KATRIN 53682
KATRINA 63624
KATRINA 82893

KEATS 61078 NbST 42' dk grn/red. B: 1970 Harbour Marine (HM 1002) / David Scott, Tunnel Marine, Foulridge, Lancs. Steel top replacing wood top in 1994. Lister air cooled LR2 (original). Base Wanless Bridge (Barrowford), L&L canal. HM Classic Boat. 21253
KEBA 77009
KEBEC 50364
KEELY 47672
KEEPING UP 51257
KEEPING UP 53526
KELANIE 61589
KEL-DOR B1614
KELLEN 46550 NEWLAY BRIDGE WEST RIDING NbC 55' bottle grn/mar. B: 1989 TT Marine, Thorne, d-i-y f/o. BMC 1.8. Base Fallwood marina, Bramley, Leeds. Rear deck enclosed by collapsable wheelhouse. 24854

KELLS 48209 NbC 50' grn/red. B: 1987 Liverpool Boats. BMC 1800 4 cyl, keel cooled. Base Cowroast marina, GU. 21276
KELLY JEAN 85189
KELLY MARIE 51872
KELPIE 46604
KELPIE 103146
KENAL 79230
KENAL D1659
KENCO 54972
KENCO 79560
KENDOR 53750
KENDOR 2 67798
KEN KEAY GRAZEBROOK & CO WOLVERLEY NbTug - hull of oak/larch, steel cabin - 50' navy blue/blue. B: hull 1979 Peter Keay & Son, Walsall; cabin 1990 Canal Transport Services, Norton Canes. Perkins HD3. Base Wolverley. Replica BCN tug hull, intended to be first of a production run, but Keay went out of business; completed Canal Transport Services who had to develop technique to fit steel cabin. 22431
KENLIS 48338
KENMARIE 61919
KENNET 50193
KENNET CLOVER
KENNET GREBE
KENNET VALLEY KENNET BOAT COMPANY HORSEBOATS NEWBURY Wide beam horsedrawn trad trip boat 67', b 10' grn/red. B: 1976 Willoughby Fabrications, Southam, Warks. Cross-shire heavy horses: HANNAH, 15 years and BONCELLA, 9 years, daughter of Hannah who was discovered to be in foal after purchase. Boncella is the Zulu word for "unexpected gift or bonus". Base Kintbury near Hungerford. Particularly bright and well decorated side panels painted by the late Ian Lewendon of Newbury, in traditional roses and castle design. 019456
KENT 77054
KENTINGS II 49850
KENTISH ROSE N4324 NbC 36' red/grn. B: 1980 Springer. Perkins 4108. Base Northampton Boat Club, Weston Favell. 2094
KENTS 61078
KEPPAL Mtce boat, dumb BW-NW
KEPPEL Yarwoods Admiral Cl butty. Ex BW
KEROLIK 77264
KERRIDGE 50801
KERRY DAN 72243
KERRY DAN II B1400 W.C.C. Grp centre cockpit 32' (34' with outdrive) blue/crm. B: 1978 Norman. 1000cc Mitsubishi 3 cyl inboard. Base The Olde No.3 between Bollington & Agden, Bridgewater canal. Steering from centre cockpit as standard Norman but also tiller aft, making steering much easier. History not known, except previous name was *Musi-o-Tunta* (Swahili for clouds that thunder, meaning the Victoria Falls in Africa). Many trophies won for best decorated/illuminated boat at various rallies. 261022
KERRY LEIGH 53240
KES 49188
KES B7876
KES NbT 45' grn/crm
KESHO BOURNES WHARF NORTHIAM NbT trailable 24'6" blue/red. B: 1994 South West Durham Steel, owner f/o at home. Kingfisher single cyl horizontal 330cc. 2.5 tons 'V' hull. Fit-out ongoing (hence no reg. no. yet), proposed maiden voyage: R.Rother, Rye. 21324
KESHAN 60132
KESTREL 45988
KESTREL 46328 Butty
KESTREL 54657
KESTREL 61488
KESTREL 63525
KESTREL 202 65104 Yarwoods motor. Ex FMC/BW
KESTREL 65308
KESTREL 68980
KESTREL 71833
KESTREL 73903
KESTREL 76023
KESTREL *78787 Grp blue*
KESTREL 85139
KESTREL B0776
KESTREL B1606
KESTREL III 73223
KESTREL No.7 NbT 55' grn
KETTLEWELL 69461
KEW 60664
KEY LARGO NbT 45' red/grn
KEYMER 74717 NbC 35' red/grn
KEYNOTE B1687
KEZHIAH 45552
KHAYA 74776
KHAYYAM 74928
KHWAI 74940
KIDLINGTON MAY 75443
KILDARE No. 274 Registered at Birmingham 1287 FELLOWS MORTON CLAYTON LTD 1396 (Watermans Hall) 12009 GJC Guaging 21743 BCN Guaging. Rivetted iron bottomed Josher with wrought iron sides 72', b 7', d 2' bl/crm/red. B: 1913 Braithwaite & Kirk, West Bromwich. Butty to *President (see entry)*. Floating museum exhibit, Black Country Museum, Dudley. Bombed in 1940, rebuilt, sold to E Thomas 1948. In 1957 bought by Willow Wren (re-named *Snipe*). Changed hands twice - eventually with Warwickshire Fly Boat where she reverted to *Kildare*. Bought by Black Country Museum in Sept 1991 and there extensively renovated to original FMC appearance - maiden voyage 17.4.92 Accompanies *President* and provides crew accommodation. 261075
KILLARA 50489
KILLERTON 70048
KILNSEY 69462
KILSBY NbC 40' blue/red
KILSOANAS 75253
KILWORTH 74942
KIM 72612
KIMBERLEY 70096
KIMBERLEY Saltley motor. Ex FMC/BW
KIMBERLEY JIM 53930

KIMBRIMAR 77858
KIMRIC 48281
KINDER SCOUT 65474
KINDLY LIGHT 70651
KINDLY LIGHTS 67989
KINFARE 65855
KING 60833
KING ARTHUR 45889
KING ARTHURS PILOT 75755
KING COAL 50125
KINGDOM 48588
KING ELLA 80397
KINGFISHER 45555
KINGFISHER 46966
KINGFISHER 47054
KINGFISHER 49595
KINGFISHER 49980
KINGFISHER 50455
KINGFISHER *53160 NbT grn*
KINGFISHER 54521
KINGFISHER 54603
KINGFISHER 62547
KINGFISHER 63323
KINGFISHER 63350
KINGFISHER 66954
KINGFISHER 67018
KINGFISHER 67316
KINGFISHER 069316 (regd. as British ship in 1960 - no. 301094 - as B.W. *Kingfisher*) Inspection launch (ex. GJCC) 54', d 3'3" mahogany superstructure/wh painted teak hull. B: 1928 J. Samuel White, Cowes, I.O.W., f/o Bushell Bros., Tring. Kelvin P4R (1964) - originally Ailsa Craig petrol engine. Base Yardley Gobion, GU. Last inspection launch to be built in UK (only 4 or 5 survive); transferred to GUCC in 1929 and ultimately British (Transport) Waterways and BW. Private ownership in 1974. Extensive overhaul and Kelvin diesel installed. Much the same as original with addition of shower and 240v circuit. Many original fittings and running gear still on board, incl. set of bone china crockery with "British (Transport) Waterways" logo - from Sir Reginald Kerr's time when, as Waterways Manager, he cruised many of the waterways on *Kingfisher*. She was at the first IWA "National" at Market Harborough in 1950 with the then Waterways Manager, Sir Reginald Hill, on Board. 21357
KINGFISHER 097572 Grp 20' wh. B: 1976 Headline 20. 15hp Yamaha 2-str ob. Trailed from Midlands. 21303
KINGFISHER KENNET AND AVON CANAL TRUST Trip boat -12 seats. 20' red/grn. Base Bradford-on-Avon raising funds for K&A Trust. 030857
KINGFISHER *69329 NbC 45'*
KINGFISHER 70231
KINGFISHER 71747
KINGFISHER 72640
KINGFISHER 73511
KINGFISHER 76799
KINGFISHER 77227
KINGFISHER 77335
KINGFISHER B0152

KINGFISHER B0841
KINGFISHER B1041
KINGFISHER Tug 5.9m BW-NE
KINGFISHER II 61864
KINGFISHER II 76680
KINGFISHER III 48513
KINGFISHER III *Trip boat wh/red*
KINGFISHER No 14 72819
KINGFISHER OF BRAY 49452
KING OF CLUBS 72702
KING OF MADAGASCAR 77164
KINGSCLERE TOO 75184 Grp 23' wh/blue. B: 1973 by owner - total re-fit 1988/89. Yamaha 9.9hp ob electric start. Base GU canal south. 2088
KINGS RANSOME 45083
KING'S RANSOM 45493 M & R KING DERBY NbT 55' dk grn/mar. B: 1989 as 45' by Gary Gorton, stretched 1995 Marque Narrowboats, f/os by Stephen Goldsbrough. Thornycroft 80 /Mitsubishi. Base Warings Green Wharf, North Stratford canal. Calor trophy for best galley and runner-up for Marion Munk trophy (best boat) at IWA National at Waltham Abbey in 1989. 24884
KINGS RANSOME 74834
KINGS ROVER 62374
KINGSWOOD 65617
KINTYRE MIST 50034
KINVER 46143
KIOMI 77808
KIONI 103281 NbST 44' burgundy/grn. B: 1996 Prestige Boat Builders (Holt), owner f/o. BMC Argos 1.5 L, PRM Delta g'box. Base Victoria Basin, Gloucester Docks. 20134
KIPLING 64189
KIPPER NbST 60' red/blue. B: 1978 Hancock & Lane. VW Golf. Base Evesham marina. 22411
KIPPER II 86447
KIRR'EE B1322
KIRSTY 98725
KIRSTY *Grp 25' wh/blue*
KISKADEE 61047
KISKADEE 64310
KISKADEE 74542 No 2 NbTug 42' mar/grn. B: 1988 Mike Heywood, private f/o. Russell Newbery 2 cyl. Base BW Kinver moorings. Boatman's cabin, trad. style centre engine room, rod engine controls. 25947
KISMET *76270 NbC 30'*
KISMET 78071
KISMET 84298
KIT 45287
KIT KAT 64512
KITTIWAKE 61922
KITTY 69891 NO 194 PETER J WARD (*starboard side*) PETER A COCUP (*port side*) NbST 47' Amazon grn/Bounty (mar) & scumble. B: 1971 Harborough Marine (their 194th). Lister SR3. Base Uxbridge, GU. Original Grp cruiser super-structure replaced 1989 with steel semi-trad style. Known locally for 60+ teddy bears in crew, despite name! 23561
KITTY 71807
KITTY 74642
KITTY *NbT 60' grn/red*

KITTY FISHER 47880
KIWI 68915
KIWI 500490
KIWI I 67124
KIWI SCOTT B0292
KJELDAHL 67015
KLEEN SWEEP 72663
KNACKERD 67042
KNAPWEED 60876
KNAVE OF CLUBS 72339
KNIGHT 48412
KNIGHTS AMOUR 54764
KNOBSTICKS 65439 B1209
KNOT 49841
KNOT 060318 Nb 36' royal blue/wh. B: 1976 Hancock & Lane. Lister 2 cyl. Base Hordern Rd, Wolverhampton, Staffs & Worcs. 6' open stern with upholstered seating for 4; 5' open bow seating 4. The name relates to the emblem of the county - the Staffordshire knot (from Lord Stafford's family). 24765
KNOTTY 53712
KNOWLE KINGFISHER 47625 No 33 NAPTON ANN & TERRY MAGGS NbC 50' dk blue/grey. B: 1990 Mike Gration, f/o Stephen Goldsbrough, Knowle (his 33rd - first for a hire fleet, Napton Narrowboats). 1.8 BMC Thornycroft. Base Napton Marina, GU. Private ownership from 1993. 21376
KNOWLE KITTEWAKE 49777
KNOWLTON B1700
KNUT 77064
KOBI 90560
KODOK 69991
KODRAN 47580
KOINONIA *NbTug 60' grn*
KONG SVERRE 73769
KONTIKI 71837
KOOKABURRA 52330
KOOKABURRA 66319 NbC red/grn
KOOKABURRA 76985

KOPPA 77365 Grp narrow cruiser 32' brown/crm. B: 1981 Highbridge Crusader, Highbridge Cruisers, Dudley. Yamaha 9.9hp ob. Base Welford on Avon marina. Was first Highbridge in the Northwest - supplied by Venetian Marine. 21284
KORORA *NbT 30' red/grn*
KOTA BHARU 71015
KOTTINGHAM NbT 40' blue/grn. B: 1984/5 Colecraft, f/o Chris Lloyd, 2 cyl Petter PHW. Base L&L canal. Commissioned and fitted out to form the basis of the "Waterways World Narrowboat Builders Book" *(Reading this book and visiting the part-completed Kottingham at the IWA National at Hawkesbury certainly provided this book's compiler with the idea that he should perhaps "have a go"! It took another "WW" book and Rome (see entry) to finally convince him! Good to see Kottingham here in the Listing).* 23574
KOYUKA 79836
KOWHAI 85682
KOWKA *54723 NbT 55' mar/blue*
KRACKAS II 66614
KRAKATOA 101422
KRIAN OF CHESTER 66214
KRISTABELLE 63811
KRISUE 47639
KRISZTINA 47806
KRYSTINE 46666
K-SIRRAH 62255
KT 88243
KUDOS 91733
KULANAKI 60639
KYLE 76697 *NbTug 60' mar*
KYME 97614 Grp 17'6" blue/wh. B: 1989(?) Seasafe. Ob. Base Welshpool, Montgomery canal. Owners distinguished by involvement in the Montgomery canal restoration for more than 30 years (founder member of Trust). 251012
KYRENIA 75855
KYRONIA 77906
KYTRA 46181

L

A "She Wolf!" but Lots of Lovely Ladies too. The first FMC motor, an elegant history and an early Bolinder, but the youngest owner, no roses - just lillies and the end of the lines

LABADI 62065
LA BAMBA 73668
LA BELLE-DAME 73491
LABOUR OF LOVE 1895 see MAJICA
LA CACHETTE 31493
LACE LADY 50940
LACERTA Sm Northwich tug. Ex GUCC/BW
LA CREME 47065
LADRHA 62211
LADY 52775
LADY 86999
LADY B0596
LADY ACHILL 61698
LADY ANN 73571
LADY ANN B7574
LADY ANNE 52299
LADY ANNE 70561
LADY ANNE 72593
LADY ANNE 78501
LADY ANNE 79501 NbC 35' grn
LADY ANNE 83278
LADY BARBARA II 68750
LADY BARINGS 74827
LADY BEATRICE see JULIE ANNE
LADY BEATRICE II see JULIE ANNE
LADY BEE 51218
LADY BEE 66793 NbC 30' blue
LADY BESS 73680
LADYBIRD 65295
LADYBIRD 74227
LADYBIRD B0194
LADYBIRD Motor vessel Flat 30' BW-NW
LADY BLATHERWICK G11425
LADYBOWER 73553
LADY CAPEL 45451
LADY CARINA Grp 20' Bl/wh
LADY CAROL 66108
LADY CATHERINE 52195
LADY CATHERINE 65851
LADY CATHERINE 85855
LADY CHRISTINA 62720
LADY CHRISTINE 61129
LADY CLAIRE 87513
LADY CLARE 49161
LADY CLARE 69877
LADY CLESHA 100485
LADY CROYSDALE 49761
LADY DAWN IV 45785
LADY DI 50520
LADY DI III 45647
LADY DIANE 68380
LADY DINAH B1533
LADY DOREEN 96998
LADY DOROTHY III B1040
LADY EARLSTON 50475
LADY EDNA 53560

LADYE ELLEN NbT 45' red/grn
LADYE ELLEN 66944
LADY EILEEN B1559
LADY ELEANOR 77592
LADY ELEANOR 77627
LADY ELGAR 52424 DARIUS ARTS - LONDON NbT 60' bl/brown. B: 1993 Limekiln Narrowboats Compton, owner f/o. Perkins 3 HD46. Base GU, Slough Arm.   21278
LADY ELIZABETH 45631
LADY ELIZABETH 64681 NbC 52' grn. B: 1976 Tolladine. 2.2 BMC. Base GU Midlands. Board which joins cratch to cabin is wide with curved sides and folds back giving flat surface and open well deck.   23592
LADY ELIZABETH 72745
LADY ELLEN 65421 SSR 48849 NbC 50' blue/mar
LADY ELLEN 69944
LADY ELLEN LOUISE 52611
LADY EMMA B1566
LADY EMMA JEAN 46741
LADY ESPHA 51260 NbT 40' red/grn
LADY ESTELLE 53296
LADY FRANCES 31132
LADY FRANCES 76143
LADY FRANCES NbC 70' blue
LADY GALADRIEL 46527
LADY GEORGIAN 100557
LADY GERMAINE 77606 Grp 26', b 8'6" wh/blue. B: 1972 Freeman. Perkins 4107. Base Tom Trevithick's Boat Yard, Canal Wharf, Old Lenton, Nottingham.   20193
LADY GODIVA Nb 70' red - adapted trip boat
LADY GRACE 75843
LADY GWENDOLYN 78624
LADY HANNAH 45711
LADY HATHERTON - 1898 70067 Inspection launch 70' wh/royal blue lining. B: 1898 - "as instructed by the Board of the Staffordshire and Worcestershire Canal Company". Lister SR3 (originally horse-drawn). Base Teddesley Boat Co., Park Gate Lock, Staffs & Worcs canal. The extensive history of this boat is comprehensively told in no less than 7 pages in the November 1992 "Waterways World". As the Committee Boat she left her moorings only rarely during her first 50 years, as the Company's minute books show. After nationalisation, used in North West and made inspection trip (still horsedrawn) to Horseshoe Falls, beyond Llangollen and back without difficulty as she drew only 2'9"! Still in official ownership she was regularly moored at Canal Turn at Aintree for the Grand National and borrowed for the day on 19th July 1958 by the Railway and Canal Historical Society to celebrate the centenary of the opening of Netherton Tunnel. In a half sunk state in Bradley Yard in 1960 she was advertised for sale. Despite her rotten hull she began a new life in a succession of private ownerships and gradual restoration. She was re-hulled with the last wooden hull built by Les Allen in 1966. Currently retains much of the original including, for example, extensive cut glass

The elegant lines of historic *Lady Hatherton* with shutters closed. Spotted at Teddesley, Staffordshire & Worcestershire Canal

windows with Canal Company logo, original ventilator for letting out cigar smoke and hitches for horses, etc. Centenary in 1998!! The fuller history is well worth reading. 23560
LADYHAWKE 54473 K & S HARPHAM LINCOLN NbTug 18m mid grn/post office red. B: 1994/95 Mel Davis Boatbuilder, Tuxford, f/o K & S Marine Services. Ruston & Hornsby (India) CD2 2 cyl 30bhp - max 45bhp @ 2200rpm; with a 20x24 prop this pushes along very nicely at about 600-700rpm (an engine with "roots" in Lincoln), David Brown M200 2:1 red gearbox - twin clutch drive allows forward and reverse to be in constant mesh: very reliable. Base Fradley junc, T&M. This engine was on display at 1994 NEC Boat Show and featured in subsequent Waterways World Article. 25933
LADY HELEN 100069
LADY HELEN II 83742
LADY HOLLAND 79956
LADY IN RED 69194
LADY IRENE 84789
LADY IRVINE 60666
LADY ISABELLA 74416
LADY JANE 75555
LADY JANE 84872
LADY JANE III 75907
LADY JANE *NbC 45' crm/grn*
LADY JANELL 52001
LADY JAYNE 062145 A.B.C.C Grp 21' wh/blue. B: circa 1968-70 Norman. Yamaha 9.9 ob. Base Acton Bridge Cruising Club, R.Weaver. 24901
LADY JANINA 48154
LADY JEAN-PIERRE 86608
LADY JENNY 62287
LADY JETINA 68635
LADY JO *50528 NbC 40' mar/blue*
LADY JOSEPHINE 67991
LADY JOYCE II 77885
LADY JUNE B1220 NbC 59' red/grn. B: 1978/79

Hucker Marine. Lister ST3. Base Preston Brook marina. Originally built for Premier Narrowboats of Acton Bridge, then taken over by Black Prince. Originally *William Gladstone*. Privately owned since 1987. 25982
LADY KARENZA 53277
LADY KATE 45230
LADY KATE 66698
LADY KATE *Grp 40'*
LADY KATELYN 71197
LADY KAY 78259
LADY KERR *Trent gravel barge*
LADY LAVINIA 100834
LADY LETITIA 77058
LADY LINDA 102798
LADY LOCKER 70406
LADY LORNA 73858
LADY LOUISE 45096
LADY LOUISE 66491
LADY LOVELACE 73728
LADY LUCK 50366
LADY LUCK 54888
LADY LUCK 76916
LADY MAGDALYN 77985 NbC 61' red/grn. B: 1981 T and J Engineering, Derby. BMC 1.5. Base Lower Shugborough, GU/Oxford. Electric bow thruster; alternative forward steering position. Has cruised R.Humber to Grimsby and back twice and Boston-Wash-R.Great Ouse/Nene. 23726
LADY MARFA II 61181
LADY MARGARET 50916
LADY MARGARET 53551
LADY MARGARET B0123
LADY MARGARET B1449
LADY MAY 52757
LADY MAY 76212
LADY MCKENNA 52306
LADY MELINDA 63209
LADY MELINDA *NbC 30' blue*
LADY NIA *79898 NbC 45' red/blue*

101

LADY NINA 70876
LADY OF HAY NbT 45' blue
LADY OF HERN 61974
LADY OLIVE 62274
LADY PAT 75822
LADY PATRICIA II 60209
LADY PHILLIPPA 49969
LADY "R" 63077 NbC Grp top on steel hull 40' yel/brown. B: 1975 Teddesley, owner f/o. SR2. Base L&L canal. 24784
LADY ROANDY 77519
LADY ROSE 61303
LADY ROSE 73482
LADY RUTH 72922
LADY RUTH NbC 50' grn/red
LADY SABRINA WORCESTERSHIRE CANAL CRUISES DROITWICH Trip boat. Droitwich Barge 68', b 9'6" blue/crm. B: 1980 originally Springer, modified 1996 J L Pinder & Son. Base Droitwich Barge Canal. 23695
LADY SABRINA 50061
LADY SAM 76872
LADY SAPPHIRE 500382
LADY SARAH WINCHAM WHARF Nb 40' grn/red. B: 1992 Wincham Wharf Boatbuilders, Lostock Gralam, Northwich. Kubota BV1205. Base Wincham Wharf. 21354
LADY SARAH 3750 Grp day boat
LADY SARAH 52297
LADY SARAH 65450
LADY SARAH III 67089
LADY SARAH 103750
LADY SHEBA 99497
LADY SUE 86457
LADY SUE 104160
LADY TEASEL 31775
LADY TESS 50657
LADY THALLASA 73299
LADY VAL 60659
LADY VEE B1535
LADY VICTORIA 69637
LADY VICTORIA 71205
LADY VIOLET 69335
LADY VIOLET NbC 40' red/grn
LADYWOOD KENNET AND AVON CANAL TRUST Trip boat - 40 seats. Nb 70' red/grn. Base Bradford-on-Avon raising funds for K&A Trust. 030801
LADY WREN 70486
LAETITIA 61290 NbC Grp top on steel hull 38' red/blue. B: 1972 Tony Gregory, GM Engineering, amateur (?) f/o. Lister SR2. Base Ashby Canal Centre, Stoke Golding. Very bluff bow; ingenious f/o with many one-off features. e.g. vast one piece grp moulding for shower. 24831
LAGAVULIN 54457 NbT 70' grn/crm. B: 1995 GT Boatbuilders, Stafford, f/o Whisky Boat Fitters, Ashby canal. Base Sutton Cheney Wharf, Ashby canal. Bow cabin. 21425
LAINY 75310
LAIRD 69523
LAKIN 61259
LAKME 60354
LA MAÎTRESSE NbC 50' blue/red. B: 1983

Hesford Marine, Lymm, f/o by previous owner. BMC 1.5. Base Sowerby Bridge, Calder & Hebble Navigation. 22457
LA MARGUERITE 69255
LAMBERHEAD LADY 101819
LA MOUETTE 47564
LA MOUETTE 60706
LAMOUETTE 94028
L'AMOUR FOU 61381 NbST 40' navy blue/claret. B: 1970 Swan Line. Lister SR2. Base Jalsea marina, Weaver Navigation, Northwich. Recent purchase - now undergoing thorough restoration. 24760
LAMPREY 316 Yarwoods motor. Ex FMC/BW/WW
LAMPREY Grp 20'
LANAC 72069 NbT 46' grn/red
LANCASHIRE ENTERPRISE 47854
LANCASHIRE LASS 50247
LANCASHIRE LEPRECHAUN 49520
LANCASHIRE UNION 65299
LANCASTER 69689
LANCASTER 71589
LANCASTER PACKET Restaurant boat grn/red
LANCELOT 069960 Hire. NbC 50' grn/red. BMC 1.8. Base Evesham Marina, R.Avon. 0371051
LANDRUTH 71329
LANDSEER 63794
LANGDALE 50859
LANGDALE 54132
LANGDON 46880
LANGHAM 70701
LANGLEY 81775 Power boat 15m BW-CATM
LANGTON 63415
LA NORA BLANCHE 49375 NbC 10.97m, b 2.02m Oxford blue. B: 1990 Springer. Thornycroft/Mitsubishi 3 cyl. Base Festival Park marina, Stoke, T&M canal. 20118
LANSETT 72862
LANTERN Ex R.Ouse Sugar Beet Barge of 35 tons capacity 54', b 12', d 6" unladen bl. B: 1939, builder unknown. Propulsion by tug City (see entry). Base Mill Wharf, Wyre Piddle. Purchased in 1961 from British Sugar Corporation, Ely, by Lower Avon Navigation Trust and used by them for navigation maintenance. These craft have been subject of a Waterways World article. 033909
LA PENICHE 63542
LA PENICHE 64588
LAPLANDER Ice breaker. BCN
LAPLANDER 60704
LA PLEINE LUNE 64914
LA POULE D'EAU SSR 63391 - NRA 009476 ROYAL CRUISING CLUB Grp Broads type cruiser 40', b 12' wh/blue. B: 1993 Porter & Haylett, Wroxham. Nanni, hydraulic drive. Base Wargrave on Thames. Adaptation of Connoisseur Broads hire cruiser; very low air draft, spacious accommodation. 22453
LAPWING NbT 40' blue/crm/red
LAPWING 45609
LAPWING 62988
LAPWORTH 71691
LAPWORTH B0413

LAPWORTH Barney(43) 1975 50'
LARA *Grp 30' mar/yel*
LARA JANE 72561
LARCH 69284
LARCH 69910 MIDDLEWICH NARROW-BOATS No5 Hire. NbT steel hull with traditionally built wooden cabin 50' grn/red. B: Hancock & Lane, cabin by Willow Wren, Rugby. Lister SR3. Base Middlewich. Classic Willow Wren style hire boat. 028736
LARGO 93303
LARK 46308
LARK PRINCESS 71587
LARKRISE 73641
LARKRISE 85944
LARK RISE 87689
LARKSPUR 47586
LAROY II 66113
LAS ROSAS 94629
LASS 64913
LASTAN BLUE 47246
LAST COMMAND 103096 NbC 45' New Brunswick grn/leaf grn. B: 1995/6 Colecraft, f/o Calcutt Boats, Ltd. BMC 1.8 +PRM; 1.5kw invertor + 240volt. Base Thrupp Canal Cruising Club, S.Oxford canal. Built with distinctive Calcutt style "Hector" square stern to hire boat *Wild Mint class* specification. Owner shortly to retire as Captain of large container ship, hence name. 251001
LAST FARTHING B1777
LAST LOVE 80066
LAST ONE 51072 LITTLE GEM NbC 31' beige/blue. B: 1991 Midland Canal Centre, Stenson. Lister Alpha 2cyl 18hp. Base Wyre Mill, Pershore, Lower Avon Nav. Previously Freeman owners, now retired, this demonstration boat called *Aston* was going to be the owners' last. So, by the addition of an 'L' at the beginning and an 'E' at the end is derived *Last One!* 23645
LAST ORDERS 51568
LATHLEY KYLO 65168
LATIN LADY II 69214
LATIN LADY III 67357
LATONA 76102
LAUGHING PLACE 51859
LAUGHING TAM B1427
LAUGHING WATER II B1102
LAUGHTON 70254 Motor. UCC
LAURA *NbT 40' red*
LAURA 64164 B1671
LAURA 73468
LAURA 76286
LAURA 80689
LAURA N6257
LAURA J 60271
LAURA JEAN 54525
LAURA KYLIE 62172
LAURA MAY *78262 Grp crm/brown*
LAURANDY JO 85566
LAUREL No. 45 A.T. SMITH & COMPANY NETHERTON WORCS 'Josher' motor 70', b 7'0½", d 2'9" grn/red. B: 1913 Saltley, Birmingham (FMC) - wrought iron sides, elm bottom (still), d-i-y conversion with 40' cabin added in 1965. Lister FR3 24hp (1957). Base BCN main line at Netherton. Shaped cabin throughout length as hull varies from 6'5" - 7'0½" swept up at front; open well at fore end. Was designed for steam engine but had the 2nd or 3rd Bolinder engine ever fitted. 24758
LAUREL 48429
LAUREL 69049 MIDDLEWICH NARROW-BOATS No 7 Hire Nb Grp top on steel hull 40' grn/red. B: Teddesley Narrowboats, Penkridge. Lister SR2. Base Middlewich. 028742
LAUREMMA 52031
LAVANT 79314
LAVENDER LEE 45389
LAVENDER LEE 48163
LA VIE EN ROSE 52322 NbC 40'6" blue/pink. B: 1992 TT Marine, f/o by owners. Beta BV1205. Base NCCC High Lane Arm. Bow thruster, chine hull concealed fold away double berth to owner's design. 25940
LAYFIELD *NbT 25' grn*
LAYLA 47961
LAYLA 71041
LAZY BEE 68267
LAZYBONES 60364
LAZYBONES 66916 B1088
LAZY BONES 100983
LAZY DAISY *NbC 60' burgundy/grn*
LAZY DAY 48076
LAZY DAY 48776
LAZY DAY 91035
LAZY DAYS SLOW & EAZY HIRE BOAT Hire. NbT 48'6" lt grey/burgundy. B: 1990 and f/o by owner. BMC 1800. Base Mill Lane, Moston, Sandbach, T&M. Good interior headroom; deep forward well to help outside table assembly. 20139
LAZY DAYS 50738
LAZY DAYS 70924
LAZY DAYS 104262
LAZY DAZE 30168
LAZY DAZE 53144
LAZY DAZE 75780
LAZYDAZE 78156
LAZY DAZE 79388
LAZY DAZE 81513
LAZY DEVIL 66040
LAZY JAN V 65854
LAZY LADY 53642 NbT 56', d 30" lt blue/dk blue. B: 1984 Stoke on Trent Boat Building Co. National Twin "in good nick" - taken from Mikron's *Tyseley* during a re-fit 24 v starting. 24846
LAZY LADY 103088
LAZY OTTER 47615
LAZY OTTERS HOLT 54366
LAZY RYTHM 52370
LEA Mtce boat 41' BW-BBC
LEADED LIGHTS 69474
LEAD US 74632
LEAH 49808
LEAH 85350
LEAL LUCY Nb 27' grn. B: 1991 Gary Gorton. ST1 10bhp. Base - hardstanding. *Leal* means faithful, i.e. to her death; *Lucy* refers to *Lucitania*, resurrected in name at least. 24769

LEAM Motor boat BW-LAP
LEAMINGTON LAPWING 79372
LEANDER 66487
LEANN 63445
LEANNE 71547
LEANNE B1512
L'EAU-T CUISINE 49336
L'EAU-T CUISINE 2 71403
LEA VALLEY 61674
LEAWOOD Power boat 16m BW-CATM
LE CANARD 84952
LEDA 060735 NbC 35′ yel/bl. B: Castle Cruisers, Warwick. 1500cc BMC. Base Rowington, GU. 22494
LEDA 91861
LEE ANN 64497
LEFTWITCH 79131
LEGEND 64380
LEGEND 75563
LEGEND 101718
LEICESTER Nb blue/red
LEIGH 67312
LEIGH LADY 52124
LEIGHTON 82183 Wide flat 11m BW-
LEIGHTON LADY 66400
LEIGUEGILA 68636
LEISEL 62282
LE-MAR 102684
LEMMING Dredger (hydraulic) 45′ BW-NW
LEMOODE 67665
LEMUEL 61240

LENANDI 74215
LENAURA 50899
LENDOUS AFIVER Grp 19′ off-wh. B: 1983 Viking Mouldings. Suzuki 16hp 2-str ob. Base Stoke Lock, Guildford, R.Wey 21246
LENGTHSMAN 45790 NbT 50′ blue/grey
LENGTHY AFFAIR 49765
LENNY FROM MANCHESTER 99363
LENTE 69409
LENTEN ROSE 53711
LEN WILSON 65171
LEO Sm Northwich Star Cl butty. Ex GUCC/BW
LEO 48743
LEO 68989
LEO 79613
LEO II Motor vessel Mtce boat 45′ BW-NW
LEOLADY 51456
LEONA 52404
LEONARD 48811
LEONELLA 50083
LEONIDS 69376 Mid Northwich Star Cl butty. Ex GUCC
LEONORA 50272
LEONORA 101433
LEONORE 75672
LEOPARD No 37 Saltley motor. Ex FMC/BW
LEPIDUS 65695
LEPUS 49848
LEPUS Sm Northwich butty. Ex GUCC
LESCARGOT 63171
L'ESCARGOT 67276

Top Lock Services

Supply, Installation and Maintenance of Narrowboat Engines, Electrics, Plumbing, Gas and Heating, Corgi Registered

also
Boat Safety Scheme Examiner

6 ASTON LANE, ASTON FLAMVILLE, LEICS. LE10 3AA
Tel: 01455 250601 - 24 hr answering.   Mobile 0860 687890

L'ESCARGOT 68413
L'ESCARGOT 69361 R E GIBSON RUGBY Nb 60' red/yel. B: 1973 Rugby Boatbuilders. Lister SR3. Base Hillmorton Wharf. 24868
LESLEY ANN 52717
LESLYN 94175
LESUVIC 46447
LETTICE KNOLLYS NbC 50' blue/red. B: 1990 Richard Gill, Blisworth Tunnel Boats. Vetus. Base stoke Druerne area. Internal space includes "The Glory Hole", which has several uses ...
"Lettice Knollys ... born in 1540 at the time of the accession of Mary I, she was a second cousin to Queen Elizabeth and grand daughter to Mary Boleyn - sister of the ill-fated Anne. Christened Laetitia, shortened to Lettice, she became a lady of the Queen's Bed-chamber. Her portraits, both when a young wife and in her elderly years, show an extraordinary degree of sexual magnetism and the expression of a woman who knows she is attractive to men and who regards her equals with grudging respect and her inferiors with scornful contempt. She married three times: to Walter Devereux, Earl of Essex; to Robert Dudley, Earl of Leicester and to Sir Walter Blount. Her secret marriage in 1576 to Robert Dudley outraged the Queen who banished Lettice from the Court and branded her: "That She Wolf!" Yet her son Robert, Earl of Essex became another ill fated favourite of the Queen. Lettice outlived them all, dying at the age of ninety-four, a peaceful benefactor to her village but, above all, a survivor". 22392
LETTICE KNOLLYS 72120
LETTUCE KNOLLYS 47809
LEVELLER 67411
LEVIATHAN Open hold 'Joey' day boat, double ended, metal construction 72' bl/yel. B: c1930. Originally probably horsedrawn, used by Stuart and Lloyds on BCN, subsequently on Upper Avon as maintenance craft. Arrived on Stroudwater in 1995 and operated by Cotswold Canals Trust. See also *Goliath*. 027725
LEVIATHAN 62802
LEVITHIAN 54361
LEVICK *NbTug 50' grey*
LEWIS R JENKINS *see PATIENCE*
LEYKIN 80882
LIABILITY 72463
LIANNE 30251
LIBERATOR 48905
LIBERATOR 51343
LIBERATOR 60710
LIBERTY 49013
LIBERTY 50549
LIBERTY 53272
LIBERTY 53311
LIBERTY 053506 BEVERLEY, YORKSHIRE NbT 50' red/grn. B: 1993 Stanilands of Thorne (last but one built by AF Budge), owner f/o in 10 months. Kingfisher KD26. Base Shobnall Basin. 23752
LIBERTY 53729
LIBERTY 71618 ROSE AND CO BURSLEDON NAPTON NbT 42' rhapsody

blue/crm. B: 1984-6 Colecraft, f/o AJ & AC Rose and sons. BUkh DV2OME 20hp. Base Engine Arm, Napton. The inside rear doors are ex full length work boat doors (age unknown but very old), fitted to the boat's doors. 261054
LIBERTY 74848
LIBERTY BELLE 50140
LIBRA V 70605
LIBRA 73455
LIBRA 76391
LICHFIELD Butty
LICHFIELD 62238
LICHFIELD LAPWING 79371
LIESL JAY 60435
LIFEBOAT 65935
LIFEBOAT 67218
LIFE ENABLER 63534
LIFE O'REILLY 70957 BREWOOD NbC 37' dk blue/burgundy. B: 1985 Colecraft, f/o Peter Worrall, Wheaton Aston, Staffs. 1.5L Thornycroft BMC. Base Brewood SU canal. Beautiful f/o in oak and pine; gold plated bathroom fittings. 25931
LIFE OF REILLY 77983
LIKE WOT 102661
LI'LE OOSTON 48375
LILIAN 83718
LILIAN BEATRICE *NbC 50' blue/red*
LILIAN ROSE 79093
LILIBETH *52613 NbT 40' mar/blue*
LILITH 79392 Joey. Ex S&L
LILLIAN 77507
LILLIAN *Grp 30'*
LILLIAN MAY N7564 Nb 38' red/grn/bl. B: 1987 Springer (Samson). Mitsubishi 3-cyl water cooled. Base Fox's Boatyard, March. No bow door, only large window. Extensively cruised, including a sinking at Little Wellingborough Lock on the way to the 1993 Peterborough Rally. 20123
LILLIAN ROSE 79093 STONE NbC 31' Oxford blue. B: 1981 Harborough Marine. Bukh DV10ME. Base Stone, T&M but can be found anywhere on system between Easter and January. 21282
LILLIPUT 46941
LILLY LOU 75773
LILY 52211
LILY 52745
LILY 67387
LILY 77512
LILY Barney(50) 1975 35'
LILY Boat Museum
LILY BEE 79602
LILY ELIZA 63466
LILY PAD 52560 I R & C M McDONALD NbC 45' dk grn/dk red. B: 1992 GT Narrowboats, Stafford, f/o Nimbus Narrowboats, Thurmaston, external painting Steve Radford. Beta Marine BV1305. Base Thurmaston, R.Soar. Particularly plush interior - she doesn't have roses - she has lillies! 201
LILY PASCAL 63532
LIMBRICK 71740
LIMEHOUSE 82112 BW-LON
LIMITED 73750

LIMITED EDITION *NbT 45'*
LIMPIT 50286
LINCOLN 48610
LINCOLN BCN butty. Ex BW/FMC
LINCOLN IMP *NbT 45' bl/red*
LINDA 61380 LINDA CRUISING COMPANY No. 260 Trip boat. Nb - iron composite 70'6", d 3'3" (static) Dk grn/oak grain. B: 1912 Fellows, Morton & Clayton Ltd., Saltley Dock. Passenger conversion 1954-56. Lister HR2 2-cyl air-cooled. Base Cosgrove Wharf, GU. Original working boat hull with half cabin and canopy. First FMC motor boat - original engine 15hp Bolinder. Worked with FMC to 1948, tug on BCN to 1954, trip boat since then. Carried HM The Queen Mother at re-opening of Stratford Canal July 1964. 23688
LINDA BEA 51066
LINDA JANE G6407
LINDEN ROSE 54229
LINDIAN 68862
LINDISFARNE 46889
LINDISFARNE 76039
LINDOLA 52566
LINDSAY 70257 Yarwoods Admiral Cl motor. Ex BW/WW
LINDSAY Motor vessel Mtce boat BW-NW
LINDSAY JANE 65249
LINDSAY JO CLARK 49368
LINDY HELEN 65207 Mahogany cruiser 33', b 6' mahogany varnished/blue topping. B: 1963 J H Taylor & Son, Chester. Lister SR11 heavy oil. Base High Lane, Cheshire. 23662
LINDY LOU 89234
LINDY LOU B8039 Grp 17'6" wh/red. B: 1976 Callumcraft. Ob. Base Oldfield Quays, Bridge-water canal. Owned by probably youngest owner on the Bridgewater since age 12 (now 15). 24913
LINDYS 72700
LINFORD 71582
LING 80421 Traditional maintenance boat 21.8m BW-
LINGUIST 65896
LINNET 50157
LINTON 87128 Grp - Dawncraft Dandy 19' grn/wh. B: 1975 Dawncraft, Kinver, Staffs. Ob. Godalming Wharf, R.Wey. Named after church in which owner married and lock on R.Ouse (both Yorkshire). 21281
LION 62856
LION 66715
LION 69998
LION 72038
LION 74101
LIONESS 60080
LIONHEART 45606
LION OF JUDAH 77180
LIQUIDATOR 94408
LISA 67166
LISA 80205
LISA *Grp 30' crm/brown*
LISA JANE 72062
LISA MARIE 51186
LISA MARIE *Grp 20' wh*
LITES 103747

LITTLE ANGELINE 67268
LITTLE BLUE 104423
LITTLE DUCHESS B1154
LITTLE EASTERN *see VAGABOND*
LITTLE GEM 52790
LITTLE GEM Hire. NbC 34' red/grn. Base Rose Narrowboats, Brinklow, N.Oxford canal. 026698
LITTLE GEM B1872
LITTLE GYPSY 49526
LITTLE IMP 70418
LITTLE IMP 94801
LITTLE JOHN Tug 6.26m BW-NE
LITTLE LADY 82718
LITTLE LADY B0045
LITTLE LEAH 79975
LITTLE MARVEL 66276 *NbT 30' grn/red*
LITTLE MARVEL Barney(38) 1974 32' *(ex Runnymede Manor)*
LITTLE MO 50163
LITTLE MO B7169
LITTLE MO *NbC 35' red/blue*
LITTLE OTTER 52416
LITTLE OWL 49783
LITTLE OWL 51890
LITTLE OWL 72519
LITTLE PEGASUS 80814
LITTLE POE
LITTLE PRUT 84077
LITTLE SCAMP *30423 NbT short*
LITTLE STINT 46294
LITTLE THEO 54417
LITTLE TRAWLER 54429
LITTLE TWYE 75455
LITTLE VIOLET 45334
LITTLE WILLOW 103549
LITTLE WOL 45897
LIVER BIRD 74634
LIVERPOOL 89633 BW-
LIZ 80395
LIZ FOUR 49021
LIZ GRACE 72343
LIZANNE 65762
LIZARAH 77807
LIZARD 75476
LIZZIE 73297
LIZZIE B1481
LIZZIE ANNE 51756
LIZZIE ANNE II 76972
LIZZIE DRIPPING 88908
LIZZIE JANE 60072
LJUBA 500457
LLAMADOS 45307
LLAMEDOS No.2 46873 NbTug 36', d 2'8" grn/red. B: 1988 (hull) Eddishaw & Jenkins, Markham Moor, f/o 1992 inc sterngear/engine installation by owner. Vetus M4.14 fully soundproofed. Base Newbury Boat Co., Kennet & Avon canal. Shortest tug to Barry Jenkins distinctive design ever constructed. 23749
LLAMEDOS 49592
LOAD OF MISCHIEF 61491
LOCH MAREE 51145
LOCHNOCHER 51246
LOCKHELM 74429

LOCOMOTION 69053
LODS MILL 74882
LODUN 72373
LOFTY B B0297
LOFTY R B0237
LOGRES 50265
LOGSON 52293
LOLLIPOP II *Launch*
LUNA II 76549
LONATOO 85404
LONDON PRIDE 85374
LONDONWEED 48307
LONELY SPUD 51394
LONGFELLOW 68209
LONG JOHN SILVER 73916
LONGTON Motor vessel BW-NW
LONSDALE 66157
LOOP DE LOO 82448
LORD ARTHUR 66099
LORD BENSHAM 53056
LORD BYRON'S MAGGOT 70383
LORD HARRY B1647
LORD JOHN 73976
LORD NELSON 74702 FRADLEY NbT 40′ dk grn/ red. B: 1987 Mike Heywood Hoo Mill, private f/o by K Cookson during following 2 years. Mitsubishi/Thornycroft. Base Whittington, Coventry canal. 24903
LORD RAWDON 61340
LORELEI 64411
LORETTO STRASSE 73562
LORIEN 79048
LORIEN 95842
LORMARBER 48759
LORNA 68984
LORNA ANN 53757
LORNA-ANN *NbT 55′*
LOS BRAVOS 68501
LOTHBURY LADY 51645
LOTHLONEN 53064
LOTHLORIEN No.6 *54310 NbT 72′ red/grn*
LOTTIE VICTORIA 049992 Hire. NbST 50′ navy blue/lt blue. B: 1991 Heritage Boat Builders. Lister LPWS. Base Sally Boats, Bradford on Avon marina. 013230
LOTUS 70237
LOUIE 50879
LOUISA MAY 77666 NbTug 45′, d 30″ red/grn. B: 1981/82 Dennis Cooper, Norton Canes. Kelvin P4, engine no. 35948 P4R. Base Rugby Wharf. Boatmans cabin and central engine room. Formerly *Hilda Ellen*. 21447
LOUISE 45769 STOWE HILL WHARF A.W & R.S. BRIDGES NbT 64′ mar/blue. B: 1988 Stowe Hill Marine, Weedon. 30hp Lister STW3. Base Stowe Hill, GU. 22479
LOUISE 48328 NbST 62′ mar/dk grn. B: 1990/91 Black Prince Holidays Ltd. Stoke Prior. Ford 1.6 XLD. Base Stoke-on-Trent Festival Marina. Originally hire boat, now much modified (improved). 22479
LOUISE 61356
LOUISE 61903
LOUISE 68858

LOUISE II 84174
LOUISE 85234
LOUISE 96418
LOUISE 104829
LOUISE B7248
LOUISE *Mini Luxe grn/wh*
LOUISE *NbT 55′ bl/mar*
LOU LOU 65588
LOULOURA 64609
LOUTH 72293
LOVEBUG 77917
LOVE IS II *65099 NbT 45′ mar/grn*
LOVEJOYS 45957
LOVELY LADY 69291
LOVELY LADY 91849
LOVES DREAM 54419
LOWENA 53791
LOWER GREEN 72511
LOWRI 45724
LOXLEY 74306
LUCILLE 82752
LUCINDA 46767
LUCIUS 74474
LUCKY 64685
LUCKY B 77915
LUCKY DUCK 79063
LUCKY GEM B0253
LUCKY LADY 46393
LUCKY LASS 72616
LUCKY PRESTON 79844
LUCKY TOUCH 51065
LUCY Butty
LUCY 46153
LUCY 63037
LUCY 68514 NbC Grp top on steel hull 11.88m grn/red. B: 1965 approx Dalescraft, Apperley Bridge. Lister SR2. Base L&L canal. Was converted by a previous owner to tow a "butty" - used to carry a Reliant van. Although butty since disposed of the towbars are still on the boat. 20157
LUCY 84672
LUCY ANN 75349
LUCY ANNE 73549
LUCY ELIZABETH 77724
LUCY ELLIS 80165
LUCY GINGER 48364
LUCY ROSE 77101
LUCY TOO B1142
LUCY WITH DIAMONDS 50171
LUDSTONE 61768
LUDWIG 68443
LULU BELLE *46320 NbC 30′ grn/red*
LULWORTH CASTLE 73463
LUNDY 102915
LUNE 68431
LUNE *Leeds & Liverpool short boat brown/wh*
LUPIN 62769 Saltley motor. Ex FMC/BW
LUTINE BELLE 60670
LUVVLY JUBBLY
LYDIA 60752
LYDIA 62801
LYDIA 75404
LYDIA 75948
LYDIA No.2 *NbTug*

Inland Waterways BOAT LISTING

compiler: Douglas Maas
ISBN 09530034 0 X

Copies of this book are available through any bookseller by quoting the above details

Appointed *Listing* Stockists at the time of going to press include:

BATTERDALE BOOKS
10 Batterdale, Hatfield, Herts

CANAL MUSEUM
Stoke Bruerne, Northants

COWROAST MARINA
Fenny Compton, Warwicks

FOXTON BOAT SERVICES
Foxton, Mkt. Harborough, Leics

MIDDLEWICH NARROW BOATS
Canal Terr, Middlewich, Cheshire

NANTWICH CANAL CENTRE
Chester Rd., Nantwich, Cheshire

SILEBY MILL BOATYARD
Sileby, Leics

VISITOR & TOURIST INFORMATION CENTRE
Aldermaston Wharf, Berks

In case of difficulty please contact the publisher:

Inland Waterways Books
8 Clover Close
Narborough
Leicester LE9 5FT

Telephone 0116-2750746

LYDIATE Motor vessel BW-NW
LYFORD CAY 66450
LYMM 75963
LYN 66592
LYNDALL 72165
LYNDA MARIE 72271
LYNDEN LEA 63352
LYNDON'S LAIR
LYNDY LOU 31995
LYNETTE 47503
LYNNROSE II 53894
LYNTON 71168
LYNTON LINNET 64094 *NbC 40' mar/blue*
LYNX 50057
LYNX 50071
LYNX 062732 ASSOCIATED CANAL CARRIERS LTD LONDON & TRING Unconverted working Nb 70', b 7', d 3' 2-tone grn. B: 1935 W J Yarwood, Northwich. Lister HR2. Base GU South. Licensed and used for commercial carrying. Belongs to GUCCC 'Star' class. Construction of wrought iron plates rivetted together; the original elm bottom was replaced with steel in the 1960s. Engine is more modern than the boat. Carrying is done when possible, though opportunities are limited. *Lynx* has carried 'Supplies for Bosnia' to Little Venice as part of the 'Serious Boat Trip' in 1994. In May 1991 delivered a 'token load' of coal to the steam dredger *Perseverance* on the Basingstoke Canal following that waterway's opening celebrations. 23638
LYNX No 39 66999 Saltley motor. Ex FMC/BW
LYNX 70492
LYNX 79009
LYNX END 69564
LYRA 50116
LYRA Sm Northwich Star Cl butty. Ex GUCC/BW
LYSANDER 53580
LYSANDRA 64932

M

A unique craft or two, some questions to ask of Missy, bricks before pleasure, Uncle Joe's sweet connections, a first in black, the working boat people's favourite instrument, Mole's from a kit, a massage with G & S, peace and quiet and a labour of love

M 63123
MAALBA 71711
MABEL 52434
MABEL 68423 Hotel boat
MABEL II 64392
MABRUK 52354
MABS 62763
MAC 74575
MACCS MAID 54194
MACH 1 60575
MACH 1 72109

MACHIAVELLI 67717
MACNOON 46297 SANDIACRE NbC 50′ Atlantic blue/mar. B: 1989/90 R&D Fabrications to Davison 'cutwater' design, owner f/o. BMC 1.5 driving hydraulic pump. Base Sandiacre, Erewash canal. Engine mounted crossways in front cockpit ; the arrangement of steel pipes supplying hydraulic fluid to a vane motor through a spool valve for forward and reverse results in peace and quiet on the rear deck. Owner believes there to be only one other boat with this arrangement - a 40 footer which he built earlier, now called *Cherry Lea*.20153
MADALA 79053
MADAM GEORGE 67864
MADAM MING 104075
MA DARLIN 52872
MADEHLE III 77714
MADELEY WOOD 500137 NbTug 42′ grn/plum. B: 1995 Midland Canal Centre, Stenson, self f/o. Lister Alpha 3. Base Retford & Worksop Boat Club, Chesterfield canal. 22483
MADHATTER 51275
MADHATTER 69614
MAD HATTER 77373
MAD HATTER IV 45905
MADLEY WOOD 68344
MAD MAN MOON 52308
MADRIGAL 67922
MAELSTROM 50633
MAESTERMYN QUEEN 64257
MAGADOR 72934
MAGARETE 68076
MAGERUCLUINE 67898
MAGGIE II 47281
MAGGIE 47942
MAGGIE 90700
MAGGIE BLOGGS 53369
MAGGIE LYNCH 60182
MAGGIE MAE 47017
MAGGIE MARLOWE 90907
MAGGIE ROSE 63968
MAGIC 88331 Cruiser 18′ wh/blue. B: 1976 Marina Sport. Mariner 4 ob. Base Sileby Boatyard, Soar Navigation. 23731
MAGIC 96692
MAGIC DRAGON 73377
MAGIC LADY 74785
MAGIC PENNY 48859
MAGISTRALIS *see NATTAJACK*
MAGNUM OPUS B0530
MAGNUS IV 52948
MAGPIE 72011
MAGPIE Tug 18′ BW-BBC
MAGPIE II 45019
MAGRATHEA 74600
MAGWITCH 64889
MAGWYN 66950
MAHALA 61452
MAHDI 73405
MAIA 54038 NbT 60′6″ navy blue/mar. B: 1995 Roger Farrington, Braunston, f/o by Rex Wain and Peter Borshik. Kelvin P4R (1965). Base Willowtree Marina, GU Paddington. 22399
MAIDENS RETREAT 76548

MAID IN ENGLAND 71603 N0. 1 BUZ & SAM COLLINS FOLK ARTISTS AND MUSICIANS NbT 57′ grey/bl. B: 1985 R&D Fabrications, Ollerton, f/o 1995 by owner while living on board. Kirloskar 3 pot diesel - old air cooled tractor unit built in India. Continuous cruising entire network - base for gigs in canalside pubs, festivals, inc IWA '96 Dudley. Immortalised in song by owners, appeared twice on telly. 24796
MAID MARIAN 74310
MAID MARION 51860
MAID MARION B0848
MAID MARION III 46773 SSR 68373 Grp twin outdrive power cruiser 30′, b 10′6″ wh/red. B: 1970 Marine Projects of Plymouth. Twin Volvo 130 petrol engines. Base Beeston marina, Nottingham, R.Trent. Hard top and large canopy fitted to cockpit; originally would have been pram canopy only. 22394
MAID MARTON 62073
MAID OF KENT N7615
MAID OF KENT NbC 40′ red/grn
MAID OF STEEL 68811
MAID OF STEEL 72713
MAID OF THE MIST 500399 NbT 50′ Oxford blue/yel. B: 1991 Bridgewater Boatbuilders. Vetus/ Mitsubishi 4.14. Base Crooke, L&L. Took part in "The Narrows Flotilla" to Flanders, Belgium, in 1995 following craning out and overland transport between Manchester and Ramsgate. 21362
MAID OF THE MIST B1410
MAIDSTONE 077811 CLIFTON CRUISERS Hire. NbC 47′ grn/crm. B: 1981 Harborough Marine, f/o Clifton Cruisers, re-fitted 1993. BL 1.5. Base Clifton Wharf, Rugby. Unusually, all steel superstructure - most Harboroughs of this age had grp cabin tops. 025681
MAITRESSE 50983
MAJASA B1425
MAJESSA 52392
MAJESTIC 50309
MAJICA 063646 Iron Nb 40′, b 7′1″, d 3′ blue. B: 1895 ex - Bantock butty cut in half. 6hp single cylinder Enfield, hand start. Base Hatton, GU. Iron hull, brand new wooden top, steel counter. Sank 1995 on its 100th Birthday!!! Currently refitting - then to be re-named *Labour of Love 1895* (people keep telling owner that is what it is). 25970
MAKALU 87943
MAKE A WISH 90698
MALACHITE 51524
MALAHAT 53912
MALAM B1384
MALAT 67695
MALAYA 60763
MALAYA *Launch 40′ wh*
MALERISK 73039
MALIA 76641
MALIBU 70089
MALIKA 73304
MALIN 54544
MALISE 51494
MALISE No.2 *NbT 50′ blue*
MALLARD 45966

MALLARD 49107
MALLARD 49328
MALLARD 50086
MALLARD 52957 NbT 60' grn/red oxide. B: 1993 Jonathan Wilson. Beta BD3 tug engine. Base Shardlow area. Internal garage at rear for motorcycle. 22403
MALLARD 53316
MALLARD No.4 *64938 NbT 50' grn/red*
MALLARD 66025
MALLARD 66437
MALLARD 66519
MALLARD 75245
MALLARD 79667
MALLARD *92208 Grp blue/wh*
MALLARD 96701
MALLARD B0381
MALLARD B1780
MALLARD B1799
MALLARD II 63958
MALLARD Motor vessel 17.07m BW-NE
MALLORY 52811
MALMO 71406
MALMO *NbC 40' grn*
MALOUNE Barney(27) 1973 44'
MALPAS 47155
MALSUREE B1542
MALTA Motor. Ex Barlows. Boat Museum
MALTBY MAID 76809
MALTEAZER *Nb operating printing business*
MALUS 80632 21m BW-LAP
MALVERN 47624
MALVERN 53393 Yarwoods Hill Cl motor Ex FMC BW-NW
MALVERN 54952
MALVERN *63057 NbC 45' wh/blue*
MALVERN HILL 78051
MANANA 51138
MANATEE 85263
MANCHESTER Little packet. Boat Museum
MANCUNIAN 40070
MANDARIN 46883
MANDARIN 48554
MANDARIN 50287
MANDARIN 70171 NbC 35' Danube blue/ Venetian red. B: 1980(?) R&D Fabrications, Ollerton. Lister SR2 air-cooled (ex ship's lifeboat engine). Base Lionhearts C.C., Milton Keynes, GU. Owner says: " Nothing special except it's ours". 24788
MANDARIN 75430
MANDRAKI 84895
MANDY B1465
MANDY B 71924
MANDY D 47200
MANIPUR 70208
MANJU 70325
MANOMET B7088
MANTIS Mtce boat, flat, dumb 30' BW-NW
MANTY KIY 77147
MANX MAID 83717
MANX MOUSE 60878
MANX SHEARWATER 45595
MAPLE 71970 MIDDLEWICH NARROW-BOATS No.2 Hire. NbT 60' grn/red. B: 1981 Malkins Bank Canal Services, Sandbach, f/o 1983 Middlewich Narrowboats. Lister SR3. Boatmans cabin; traditional engine room / controls; "Little Woolwich" style hull. Much travelled hire boat, inc Lincoln, London, Fens, etc. 028735
MAPLE 74984
MAPLE LEAF 50035
MAPLE *see* **WALNUT**
MARACAS BAY B265 an 'E' in arrow design Grp Eastwood 24 - 24', b 8'6" wh/blue. B: 1975 The Eastwood Yacht Company, Walton-on-Thames. Renault 1300cc petrol marinised by DTN in the 1970's. Base Town Reach, Beccles, R.Waveney. One of several hundred of these still popular boats produced, with modern appearance having a reverse sheer. All vary slightly according to owners' requirements - *Maracas Bay* was Medway based and used in the Thames Estuary and accordingly now suits the tidal conditions of the Broads. Due to the lack of information on the class, magazines are interested in researching it. Subject of article in Practical Boat Owner in 1960s, "A Quart in a Pint Pot". 21377
MARAI *Grp 30'*
MARALA *NbT 30' bl*
MARALINGA 64209
MARANATHA 45976
MARAPILI 71948
MARAUDER *see* **STELLERN**
MARBURY Ice boat. Boat Museum
MARBURY LADY 53767 ANDERTON Nb 32' dk grn/red. B: 1994 Jonathan Wilson, f/o Venetian Marine, Nantwich. Lister LPW/S 2 cyl 18hp. Base Anderton Marina. 22492
MARCEAU 69839
MARCEL 52825
MARCELLA 46014
MARCELLUS 66031 REG BRENTFORD 561 FLEET NO. 308 motorised butty (new motor stern) 69'9", b 7', d 34" navy blue/red. B: 1935 Harland & Wolff, conversion 1994 Ian Clifton. Petter PJ3 air cooled. Base Llangollen canal. 01125
MARCH HARE 45121
MARCH MOLE 46200
MARCO POLO 72670
MARCUS ANTONIUS 52748
MARDI J 65829
MARENGH 66546
MARFORD 66302 Grp 22' wh/blue. B: 1968 Teal. 950 3 cyl Kubota Z drive. Base Wheelton, L&L. Name from MARgery & CliffORD. Owner has inlaid teak cabin door with beech and walnut diamonds. 24902
MARGANNE B0012
MARGANTO 79478
MARGARET 46912
MARGARET No.192 *54404 NbT 50' blue*
MARGARET 60873
MARGARET 72631
MARGARET 75726
MARGARET MARY 68551
MARGARETHA 49582
MARGARETTA 71119

110

MARGARITA 52630
MARGARITA *73497 NbC 50' grn*
MARGATE 61010 N7720 NbC 44' grn/red. B: 1980 Colecraft, f/o Calcutt, Stockton. BMC 1500 4 cyl, PRM gearbox. Base R.Nene. Calcutt Square Frigate stern. Hire boat until 1994. 20196
MARGAUX 50675
MARGE THE BARGE 76863
MARGO 75114
MARGUARITE 48646
MARGUARITE 74653
MARIA Nb 35' grn/grey. B: 1972 Braunston Boats - "Barney Boat". Sabb 8/10 hp single cyl. Base Dunstable & District Boat Club, Cooks Wharf, GU. 22481
MARIA 50630
MARIA 66838
MARIA 72158
MARIA *Horse-drawn passenger boat*
MARIA Barney(23) 1972 35'
MARIA CONSULATA 70233
MARIANNA 54642
MARIANNE 98556
MARIANNE 99014
MARIANNE I 65827
MARIANNE III 93876
MARIC 48548
MARICHY 52230
MARIE 48237
MARIE 060653 Hire. NbC 40' red/grn. B: 1970 (?) Dobsons of Shardlow. BL 1.5. Base Sileby Mill Boatyard. 032892
MARIE II 95064
MARIE LOUISE 50517
MARIE LOUISE 67752
MARIE LOUISE IV 48852
MARIE STELLA 74333
MARIGOLD 53217
MARIGOLD 69799
MARIGOLD 79992
MARIGOLD 90176
MARIGOLD Hire. NbC 42' blue/red. Base The Wyvern Shipping Co, Linslade, GU 00455
MARIGOLD Barney(22) 1972 32'6"
MARIKA 73028
MARINDA 64274
MARINE LEGEND 104695
MARINER 103509
MARINKA 70944
MARIPOSA 72826
MARIPOSA 74755
MARIS 075381 NbTug 35' red/grn. B: 1975 David Piper. BMC 1.5. Base Welton Hythe marina. 25928
MARJAM 101475
MARJILO 45158
MARJORIE 54652 ROY & PAT ELLIS COVENTRY NbC "WYSIWYG" 43' red/grn. B: 1995 Club Line Cruisers, Coventry, f/o part by builder, part by owner. 1.8 Ford. Base Coventry. 21302
MARJORIE A 48045
MARJORIE MILLICHOPE 50454

MARK II Cruiser 27', 6'6" wh/bl/blue. B: 1958-62 approx, builder unknown. 1.5 BMC & Z drive. Base Clayton-le-Moors, Lancs. River/canal cruiser, single chine. Fitted aft cabin 1974; distinctive shape; possibly one of two ever built, owner never seen another. 23556
MARK ANTHONY 68263
MARK ANTHONY 49270
MARKEN 46164
MARLI 71382
MARLIN 31817
MARLIN 66453
MARLIN 69580
MARLIN 75428
MARLOW IV 48900
MARLYN 98927
MARLYN Light craft. Boat Museum
MARMADUKE 74182
MARNA B 46449
MARNE II 50989
MARONA 67308
MARPESIA 49528
MARPLE 72643
MARPLE 72644
MARPLE 2 77066
MARQUIS No.3 45151 *NbT 60' grn/red*
MARRAKESH 51016
MARRANDUS 052829 NbTug 50' navy blue/gold. B: 1993 Black Country Narrowboats, Stourbridge. Nanni 35hp keel cooled. Base marina, GU, Northampton. Tug style with cruiser stern. 22534
MARRIC 101784
MARRICK 51136
MARROW 71126
MARSDEN Boat Museum
MARSHA 65437
MARSHAG II 068245 Cruiser - single diagonal carvel, larch on oak 24'10" wh/blue. B: 1965 Harborough Marine. Ob. Base North Cheshire Cruising Club, High Lane, Cheshire. First boat built as new by Harborough Marine. 2083
MARSH HARRIER 51359
MARSH WARBLER 48797
MARSHWIGGLE 49916
MARSHWIGGLE II 68049
MARS TIPTON B1094
MARSTON 51912
MARSTON No 7
MARSTON Power boat 16m BW-CATM
MARSTON MAGPIE 76670
MARTEN 53995 NbT 42' Atlantic blue/grey. B: 1994 Midland Canal Centre, Stenson. Lister LPWS 3. Base North Oxford canal. Exhibited by MCC at 1994 Nottingham & Braunston boat shows. 21369
MARTHA ALICE 50055
MARTHA ANNA 54317
MARTHA GUNN 49060
MARTHA GUNN 72542
MARTIA 77870
MARTIN 93204
MARTIN E *NbC 40' red/grn*
MARTLET 72190

MARTLET 74813
MARY 51444
MARY ALICE 45211
MARY ALICE 500770
MARY ANN 48021
MARY ANNE 67343
MARY ANNE 67994
MARY ANNE 71157
MARYBET 47348
MARYBUNN 49152
MARY DOLAN 76523
MARYELENMAY 54466
MARY ELLEN 45282
MARY ELLEN 66445
MARY JANE 51840 D&PE HARTLEY No.1 BAMBER BRIDGE NbST 45' dk blue/bright red. B: 1991 Jack Sumner, f/o by owner. Isuzu. Base L&L at Adlington. According to the owner, the special feature of *Mary Jane* is a "nut with a beard usually stood on the back sometimes wearing a bowler hat". *(Uncannily similar to this book compiler's boat's special feature!).* 24795
MARY JANE 65270
MARY JANE 66111
MARY JANE 69783
MARY KATE 67037
MARY LOIS 99309
MARY MAY 101608
MARY NANETTE 68373
MARY POPPINS VII
MARY REDDEN 62984
MARY ROSE 50496
MARY ROSE II 45183
MARYS 75626
MARY TAY 66173
MASQUERADE 51108
MASQUERADE Hire. NbC 50' red/grn. Base Rose Narrowboats, Brinklow. 026702
MATADOR Hire. NbC 53' red/grn. Base Rose Narrowboats, Brinklow, N.Oxford canal. 026709
MATADOR 70659
MATAMBA B0651
MATTABOOBOO NbT 60' claret red/jade mist grn. B: 1996 Evans & Son, Hixon, d.i.y f/o in Southampton. Beta 37.5bhp. Base K&A canal. Rayburn No.1 cooker - more than 40 years old. 23618
MATTHEW BOULTON NO.2 78267 NbT 50' grn/bl/blue
MATTIOLA 76396
MATTI RICHARDS 46015
MAUBAR 62764
MAUDELAYNE TYNE OLDBURY 66675 NbT 62' dk blue/pale blue. B: 1971 Les Allen & Sons, Oldbury, f/o Tony Pelayo, Aylesbury. Lister SR3. Base Hanbury Wharf, Droitwich. First owner, Capt. Kirk, commissioned building. Registered with British Register of Shipping No. 341496. Blue Book has been kept up to date. Present owner, as schoolboy, decided if he ever owned a boat she would be called *Maudelayne* after the Shipmans barge in Chaucer's Prologue. The Allen brothers were not happy with proposal to change name of *Tyne Oldbury* so the three were added together and Blue Book altered. Original wood cabin was rotten so Allen Bros have welded steel skin on to it. Original side hatch with window panels retained and addn'l hatch added to left side. 22477
MAUDESLEY 48857
MAUREEN 60790
MAVERICK 46483 NbT 50' dk red. B: 1989 Delph Marine. Ruggerini 2 cyl. Base Braunston area. 208
MAVIS 31577
MAVIS 62348
MAVRON 62404
MAXEY 97208
MAXIMUS 52105
MAY Dayboat Ex LMS
MAY 51953
MAY 67750
MAYA 68417
MAY B 62655
MAYBARA 52116
MAYBE 48765
MAYBEE N4486
MAYBEL 31079
MAYBIRDS 74727
MAYBLOBS 66803
MAYBUG 49322
MAYBUG NbC 18' red/blue
MAYFAIR 53050
MAYFIELD 68352
MAYFIELD ROSE 68222
MAYFLOWER 46947
MAYFLOWER 47497
MAYFLOWER 54757
MAYFLOWER III 54777 NbC 40' grn/red. B: 1970 Harborough Marine; steel roof & cabin 1995 by Harborough Boats. Lister SR2. Base Oxford canal. One of the very few boats to have navigated the tidal doors from the Old Bedford River (Middle Level) to the Great Ouse (Waterways World May 92 + more recent correspondence). 25980
MAYFLOWER IV 79254
MAYFLY 69929
MAYFLY 76667
MAYFLY 79619
MAYFLY 87039
MAYFLY 87450
MAYFLY N6965
MAYFLY II 76471
MAYFLY Unpowered flat 6.7m BW-
MAY LADY *64112 NbC 305 mar/blue*
MAY ONE 69004
MAY QUEEN 60796
MAY QUEEN 62326
MAYTHORN 52458
MAYTIME 53931
MAZAPATEL 100700
McBUCK 47906
McCREADY 47194
McGINTY 51980
MDINA BAT 100828
MEADOW BLOOM *77007 NbC 45' bl/red*
MEADOW PIPIT 49838

MEADOW SWEET 49753
MEADOWSWEET 63780
MEADOW WATERS 65015 Nb 42' blue. B: 1975 Harborough Marine. Lister SR2. Base Hunts Lock, T&M canal. Former Anglo-Welsh hire boat. 21242
MEAFORD 78390
MEANDA 51349
MEANDER 46035
MEANDER 47561
MEANDER 47613
MEANDER 52016
MEANDER 72875
MEANDER 74342
MEANDER B1508
MEANDER AGAIN 72144
MEANDERER 50771
MECCA 50318
MECCA No.50 61844 *NbTug*
MEDDLE 67679
MEDIEVAL KNIGHT *Grp 35' wh/blue*
MEDINA 73592
MEDITROX 100455
MEDUSA 77799
MEECE 89306 Motor vessel BW-NW
MEG 77165
MEGAN 48757
MEGAN 54354
MEGAN 73911
MEGAN *NbC 70' grn*
MEGAN No 3 51335
MEGAN ELIZABETH 47861
MEGA PIPIT Steel cruiser 35', b 9' blue/wh. B: 1996 (still being completed) Shotbolt Engineering, Ramsey, Cambs. 36hp Lister 4 cyl. Base Shotbolts, Ramsey. One of 3 small steel craft with a distinctive appearance designed by owner - see also *Puddleduck* and *Pipit*. 00792
MEG MERRILIES 45630

MEGS 47707 *NbT 60' grn/blue*
MEINZAPINT *NbT 30' mar*
MEJAK 65077
MELACHELLE 30561
MELANIE 64514
MELANIE ANN Barney(31) 1973 35'
MELANIE ANNE 69774
MELISSA CHERLOTTE 90088
MELLOW 51862
MELLOW MIST 45778
MELLYN 71033
MELMAR 78718 G12747 Grp cabin on steel hull - ex Dart Line Shackleton class Shropshire Union cruiser 49' wh/blue. B: 1976 Dart Line. Lister SR3, LH150 g'box. Base GU canal. This and similar craft represent early examples of hire fleets' efforts to design hire boats for canal use; clear influence from Thames and Broads hire craft. 22445
MELODEON HURLEY NbT 40' grn/red/wh. B: 1983 Colecraft (Sam and Don), f/o Len Beauchamp, paintwork Ron Hough; owner notes that all these craftsmen took pride in their work. Thornycroft 1.5. Base Hambleden, R.Thames. F/o in solid timber - parana roof lining, Brazilian mahogany beams/side panels, American white oak floor (caulked). Name is a reminder of the favourite instument of working boat people. 20172
MELODY 46432
MELODY 62247 SSYN NbT 36' deep grn/red. B: 1977, builder not known - information would be appreciated *(see page 14)*. Lister SR2 air-cooled, Lister LH150 hydraulic reversing gear unit and reduction gear 2:1 -3:1. Base Sheffield & South Yorkshire Nav. 23647
MELODY 62902
MELODY 73617
MELODY 73722
MELODY *Nb 20' bl/wh/red*
MELODY *NbC 35'*

113

MELODY FAIR 90598
MELROSE 085519 WELSHPOOL Grp 19' wh.
B: 197-? Dawncraft. Honda ob. Base Montgomery
canal. 25999
MEMETTE 76364
MEMORY 50410
MENAGERIE 74545
MENDHAM MAID 62775
MENDIP Yarwoods motor. Ex FMC/BW/WW.
Boat Museum
MENENIUS 93181
MENTOR No 2 72767
MERAK 69830
MERAK Sm Ricky Star Cl butty Ex GUCC. Boat
Museum
MERAK *NbT 50' red/bl*
MERCHANT 48485
MERCHANT OF VENICE 61232
MERCHANT OF VENICE 67202 NbST 50'
grn/red. B: 1979 Kevin Hancock, f/o by owners in
1992. Perkins 4:108 diesel and Ross electric
propulsion. Base Lower Heyford, S.Oxford canal.
  21346
MERCHANT TAYLOR 51384
MERCURY 78719
MERCURY 80072
MERCURY 80241 BW-
MERCURY 80250 BW-
MERCURY Butty. Ex Midland & Coast
MERCUTIO 73506
MERCY 52906
MERE 89174 Motor vessel BW-NW
MERE DETAIL 47695
MEREDITH ROSE 73753
MERGANSER II 036595 SSR 1383 Hotel
cruises. Dutch Barge 24.3m, b 4.1m grn/wh.
B: 1931 Noordhorn, Rotterdam. Daf DT615. Base
R.Thames. Distinctive white canopy gives sun
shade to over half upper deck. 2031
MERGANSER 52257
MERGANSER 73050
MERIDEN 77395
MERIDIAN 45144
MERIDIAN 51443
MERIEL 49017
MERLIN 45590
MERLIN 045962 Hire. NbC 62' grn/red. BMC
1.8. Base Evesham Marina, R.Avon 0371035
MERLIN 47035
MERLIN 47128
MERLIN 50271
MERLIN 50981
MERLIN 51128
MERLIN 52504
MERLIN 61774
MERLIN 61986
MERLIN 62570
MERLIN 68220
MERLIN 71887
MERLIN 73784
MERLIN 74422
MERLIN 74982
MERLIN 75978
MERLIN B1000

MERLIN B7320
MERLIN B7437
MERLIN II 97327
MERLIN Tug 6m BW-CATM
MERLIN *NbT 60' bl/wh/red*
MERLIN SIGH 101264
MERLOT 49362
MERMAID 85742
MEROPE Sm Ricky Star Cl motor. Ex GUCC.
Boat Museum
MERRIE ENGLAND 46125
MERRIE PIPER 72876
MERRIMINT 62362
MERRY 69758
MERRYGOLD 61009
MERRYWEATHER LEWIS 71794
METEOR 75423 Sm Woolwich Star Cl butty.
Ex GUCC/BW
METEOR 87452
METEOR No 2 47247
MFUPI 072990 NbC 32' red/grn. B: 1985
Colecraft f/o Medley Boat Station. BMC 1.8. Base
Greenham Lock, Newbury. Name Swahili for
"short one". 22442
MIAMI MICE 104492
MIBOYCLIVE 45725
MICHAEL 71288
MICHELA 50453
MICHELA JANE II 78973
MICHELLE 64495
MICHELLE 73922
MICHELLE 77670
MICHELLE Hire. NbC 50' red/grn. Base Rose
Narrowboats, Brinklow, N.Oxford canal. 026707
MICKEY MOUSE 65431
MIDAS 85074
MIDDLETON MOONRAKER 53466
MIDDLEWICH *see* POPLAR
MIDNIGHT NbC 54' bl. B: 1989 Fenmatch Ltd,
Evesham, self f/o 1989-95. Calcutt BL 1.8. Base
Allington Marina, R.Medway. Intends permanent
cruising from 1997. Name on brass/mahogany
plaques hanging from stern rail. Appearance is a
striking combination of black/mahogany/brass;
perhaps the first all black pleasure nb - inspired
many others as Fenmatch used her in promotional
posters. 22471
MIDNIGHT *NbT 60' blue/wh*
MIDNIGHT 48419
MIDNIGHT DIAMOND 49627 NbST 45' blue/
red. B: 1990 TT Marine Ltd, Thorne. Lister
LPWS3. Base Fenny marina, Fenny Compton,
S.Oxford canal. 23572
MIDNIGHT LADY *NbT 50' bl*
MIDNIGHT MOTH 67917
MIDNIGHT RAMBLER 74430
MIDSUMMER DREAM 66213
MIDSUMMER NIGHTS DREAM 74566
MIDUCK 64491
MIJO Grp Dawncraft Dandy 19' blue. B: 1979
Dawncraft, Stourport. Honda 4-str 15hp. Base
Weir Stream, R.Thames, Oxford. 20124
MIKADO 64749
MIKADO 103310

114

MIKALIND B0709
MILFORD 67294
MILFORD 73871
MILFORD STAR 89924
MILFORD STAR NbT 70' trip boat
MILKON 86797
MILLBURY 77347 NbT 65' grey
MILLENIUM 54279
MILLICENT 72832
MILLIE No 7 51736
MILLPOND 51696
MILLPOOL Hire. Nb 39' grn/red. B: 1984 hull by L.R. Harris of Leicester. F/o to very high standard by original owner, believed to be an architect. Base Sileby Mill Boatyard. 25966

> **Is Your Boat In It?**
> **Is the Entry Accurate?**
> Please see page 12 to find out how to get included or amended in the next edition

MILL REEF 81847
MILLSTONE 70036
MILLSTONE GRIT 79238
MILLSTREAM 075769 Hire. NbT 62' grn/red. B: 1988-? Rugby Boatbuilders. BL 1.8L. Base Sileby Mill Boatyard. Built originally for Bank of England and called *Watermark*. 032891
MILL VALE II 75081
MILL WHARF 101213
MILLY MOLLY MANDY 50248
MILTON No 5 46765
MILTON MAID The last modern type work boat, built for moving china ware on the Caldon Canal for Johnson Potteries which ceased trading in 1995 - powered by mini engine. Based at Streethay Wharf.
MIMAS Motor. Ex Ovaltine
MIMRAM 60353
MIMULUS 53973
MINCHIATE 72599
MINDEN ROSE 76393
MINERVA 31769
MINERVA 47482
MINERVA 52715
MINERVA 60467
MINGUS B0680 Grp 23' wh. B: 1992(approx) Norman Cruisers, Shaw, Oldham. 1.5 Leyland, Transa drive Z LE9. Base Worsley Cruising Club, Patricroft, Bridgewater canal. 24849
MINIHAVEN 64265 NbC wooden top on steel hull 38' wh/red. B: 1973 as 30' brick carrier; bought 1975 - Willow Wren cabin fitted, owner f/o; 1979 lengthened by Braunston Boat Services to 38'. BMC 1500. Base Willow Wren Wharf, Rugby. Constructed by Roy Willoughby and used by his associate, Roger Preen, to carry bricks when constructing the Calcutt hire cruiser base on the GU. Has cruised extensively - 80% of system covered including national and local IWA rallies, etc. for fundraising. A "quart into a pint pot" - numerous ingenious gadgets. 21306

MINILASS 90725
MINKY B1366
MINKY II *Grp*
MINNOW Yarwoods Fish Cl. Ex FMC/BW
MINNOW Nb 24'
MINORITY 52897
MINOS 68699
MINSTREL 54534
MINSTREL 64490
MINSTREL 66418
MINSTREL 67447
MINSTREL 73691 NbC 25' mar/crm
MINTBALL 72984 M S N & S ATTY, BRAUNSTON, WIGAN & CHELTENHAM NbC 52' blue/red. B: 1986 Ron Tinker, Middleton, Manchester, f/o Foster & Day, Rochdale and by owners. BMC 1.5. Base Braunston marina. "Atty's Mintballs" were the fore-runners of the famous "Uncle Joe's Mintballs" now manufactured by William Santus of Wigan. 21317
MINUET 51093
MINX 64172
MIPPERTY 79408
MIRACLE 46628
MIRAGE 70090
MIRAGE 100391
MIRAGE 102101
MIRAND 66172
MIRANDA 103787
MIRANDA *Grp 16'*
MIRANDA JAYNE 52610
MIRFIELD 89747 Motor vessel 14.95m BW-NE
MIRGAES 50046
MIRKWOOD 49357
MISBOURNE 47089
MISCHIEF 45867
MISCHIEF NbC 35' grn
MISCHIEF Grp 30' wh
MISS ACTIVITY see *MISSY*
MISS CHIEF 70807
MISS ELISABETH 95296
MISS ELKIE "B" 74865
MISS GEORGE 71077
MISS GILLIAN 66378
MISS HELIOTROPE 54385
MISS HOLLY B1438
MISSING LINK 67534
MISS JAY 72368
MISS KELLY 47550
MISS LAURA 68657
MISS MAGIC 95575
MISS MATTY 500127 NbT 60' dk grn/red. B: 1995 Peter Nicholls, Napton. Base Iver, GU Slough Arm. 25998
MISS PIP 48231
MISS PUSS 63867
MISS PUSSY 45898
MISS SAIGON 61835
MISSUS MOUSE 71290
MISS WORTHINGTON 73300
MISSY OU53 Motor cruiser, carvel built mahogany on mahogany 28', b 9'6" silvery grey/lt blue. B: 1960 (probably) possibly by Coral Craft, then of Horning. BMC 2.2. Base Wroxham,

115

Norfolk. Foredeck winch. 7' air draught makes her sit high! Previous name *Miss Activity* ("ugh!"); originally possibly *Coral* ... something. Owner would like to find someone who knew her previously *(see page 14)*. 24885
MISTA JAY 71053
MISTER B 53689
MISTER BAGGINS 75165
MISTER C III 51048
MISTER CHRISTIAN 101577
MISTER FRED 52865
MISTER MOUSE 78061
MISTER PICKWICK 48863
MISTER SOFTEE *102063 Grp 20' wh*
MISTER T *NbT 60' blue*
MISTERTON Motor vessel 16m BW-NE
MISTLETHRUSH 49642
MISTRAL 50924
MISTRAL 61757
MISTRAL 63051
MISTRAL 67688 BURLAND Grp 26' wh/red. B: 1979 Stone Boat Builders (Burland). 15hp Honda 4-str ob. Base Meadow Farm marina, Barrow upon Soar. Very distinctive paintwork. Owner claims first boat on R.Soar to have Certificate of Compliance. 23751
MISTRAL 45715 NbT 60' midnight blue. B: 1989 Roger Farrington, Ivy Bridge, Braunston - No. 9. Russell Newbery 2 cyl DM (believed built 1942 - probably used as wartime generator). Base Cosgrove, GU. 24762
MISTRAL 88234
MISTRAL *see DORIS ALICE*
MISTRESS 63398
MISTRESS BECCY 97593
MISTRESS FORD 104712
MISTRESS PAGE 104035
MISTRIS 75650
MISTRY 88909
MISTWEAVE 46857
MISTWEAVE 48059
MIST WEAVE No.8 *NbTug 55' red/grn*
MISTY 045942 Hire. NbC 65' grn/red. BMC 1.8. Base Evesham Marina, R.Avon 0371029
MISTY 47982
MISTY 50947
MISTY 52839
MISTY 66911
MISTY 75655
MISTY 77222
MISTY 85707
MISTY 99388
MISTY II 70028
MISTY BLUE 31224
MISTY BLUE 50582
MISTY BLUE 74189
MISTY GEM 94982
MISTY J 77325
MISTY LADY 52271
MISTY LADY 54607
MISTY LADY 71957
MISTY MOON 90640
MISTY MOON *Grp Norman*
MISTY MORN 51507

MISTY MORN II 68629
MISTY WATERS 52039
MITCHELS FOLD 74715
MITHRANDIR 60841
MITHRANDIR 66709
MITHRIL 48120
MITHRIL 48424
MITHRIL THREE 50117
MITZI 64199
MITZI 78548
MIZAR 2 45437
MIZPAH 47881
MIZPAH 52349
MIZPAH 2 76969
M'KEG 67196
MOANNA ROA 92709
MOBLEE 90126
MOBY DICK 89159
MOBY DUCK 45050
MOCHYN DU 62215
MODERN MISS 84673
MOESIE TWO 71454
MOHAWK 50773
MOI-MOI *63849 NbC 35' red/grn*
MOINTEACH 48915
MOIRA 73334 NbC 42' red/blue. B: 1986 Arcrite hull, f/o Nigel Smith. Lister. Base Stoke Golding, Ashby canal. Side double doors feature. Stolen and repainted while on hire in 1994 - found in London and identified. 22469
MOLE 054679 MONTGOMERY Nb 30' dk grn/ bright red. B: 1978 Hancock & Lane, re-fit by owners. BL 1.5, PRM Delta gearbox. Base Whixall marina. Shape of hull cross section is more like a "normal" boat, not the near rectangular box of a narrowboat. 261024
MOLE 54843
MOLE 70960
MOLE 74296
MOLE *500955 Inspection launch crm/blue*
MOLE Push tug. UCC
MOLE Dredger 18m BW-CATM
MOLE'S BOAT 087226 Grp canal boat, ply cabin sides 18'6" grn/coffee. B: 1974 Wilderness Boats. Ruggerini diesel ob. Base Pewsey Wharf, K&A. Boat is an early Water Rat; was used as hire boat on the Thames; thought to have been built from a kit. 23539
MOLL FLANDERS B0146
MOLLY 49675
MOLLY 51935
MOLLY 72917
MOLLY MOG 47140
MONACO 500400
MONA G 91106
MON AMI 52378
MON AMI 73845
MON-AMI 70150
MON-AMIE II 50956
MON AMOUR 50967
MON AMOUR II 45669
MONARCH 156 FELLOWS MORTON CLAYTON NbT 62' (was originally full length, 70', but shortened by previous owner for use on

L&L canal - it is intended to restore to full length) bl/wh. B: 1908 as one of original FMC steamers at their yard in Saltley, Birmingham at a cost of £600. Put back in steam in 1992. Built of rivetted iron, typical Josher hull, distinctive large black funnel, cargo area under cloth. *Monarch* steamed 800 miles in 1996. 22463
MONDAY 047512 SUTTON CHENEY NbT 50' grn/ red. B: 1989/90 J Wilson, f/o Phoenix, Coventry (their first). Mitsubishi K4D. Base Sutton Cheney, Ashby canal. 23720
MONDAYS CHILD 75617
MONET 73855
MONI 93422
MONIQUE 73584
MONITOR 61373
MONKEY BUSINESS 76126
MONKS HAVEN 70820
MONKSHAVEN Barney(3) 1970 40'
MONSALVAT 501481 JC & GM BEECH WELTON HYTHE Nb 42' burgundy/blue. B: 1996 Greentour/ Weltonfield. Lister LPWS3 Canal Star. Base Welton Hythe. 251017
MONTROSE 53784 B0839
MONTY 54665
MONYCOM 75360
MOOCHER 45478
MOOCHER 84587
MOOD INDIGO *NbC red/grn*
MOODY BLUE 73258
MOODY BLUES 45363

MIDDLEWICH NARROWBOATS

Relaxing canal holidays in comfortable character boats from the centre of the N.W. England canal system. Good tuition given
Send for brochure

ALL CANALSIDE SERVICES
including shop, laundry (when available), dry dock, Calor gas, diesel, pump out, disposal
BETWEEN BRIDGE 169 AND 3 LOCKS TRENT & MERSEY CANAL, MIDDLEWICH
44 CANAL TERRACE,
MIDDLEWICH, CHESHIRE CW10 9BD
TEL 01606 832460

MOOLOOKABA 75374
MOOMIN 69114
MOON 77685
MOON 70248 Sm Woolwich Star Cl butty. Ex GUCC/BW/WW
MOONBEAM *60159 NbC 50' grn*
MOONFLEET 67816
MOONFLEET 79489 Grp motor sailer 21', b 7'8" wh/navy blue. B: 1973 Smallcraft, Portsmouth. BMC 1.8 L Barnes marine conversion. Base Mon & Brecon canal. Built as a motor sailer with bilge keels for estuary work; believed to be unique specimen on inland waterways system. 21321
MOONFLOWER 052663 A M and M J WYATT NbST 45' Brit. Racing grn. B: 1992/93 Gary Gorton, f/o J.D. Boat Services, Gailey. Perkins Perama M.30. Base Burghfield, K&A canal.261059
MOONGLOW 61153
MOONGLOW *NbT 50' blue/wh*
MOONGLOW *NbC 40' mar/blue*
MOONHUNTER 51234
MOONLIGHT LADY 50044
MOONLIGHT SHADOW 74110
MOONPENNY 45054
MOONPENNY No.7 *NbT 60' grn/red*
MOONRAKER 49624 Grp 43'. B: 1974app. Morgan Giles, Teignmouth, Devon. 1.5 BMC Thornycroft, hydraulic pump driving motor mounted on drive leg. Base Mersey Motor Boat Club, Lydiate, L&L canal. 24833
MOONRAKER 50551
MOONRAKER *60071 NbC mar/blue*
MOONRAKER 62934
MOONRAKER B1131
MOONRAKER B1563
MOON RIVER 54375
MOON RIVER *NbC 50' grn/red*
MOONSHADOW 48786
MOONSHADOW 75738
MOON SHADOW 73103
MOONSHINE 45242
MOONSHINE 500136
MOONSPINNER 69646
MOONSPINNERS 45016
MOONSTONE 49031
MOONSTONE 60268
MOONSTONE 76404
MOONWIND 70716
MOONWIND II *71786 Grp 20' wh/blue*
MOORE HALL 47803 B1625
MOORGLEN 63706
MOORHEN 54346
MOORHEN 62818
MOORHEN 71787
MOORHEN Tug 6m BW-CATM
MOORHEN *NbC 40' red/grn*
MOORLANDER 51864
MOPON 52688
MOPONBLUE 47603
MOPPINS 53620
MORDEN 51212
MORDEN No 2 48322
MORDRED 46209
MORFE LADY 73972

117

MORGAM Mtce boat 8.9m BW-
MORGAN 72295
MORGANS PRIDE 102992
MORLAS 89260 Motor vessel BW-NW
MORLEY 80509
MORNING CLOUD 66702
MORNING FLATULENCE 65331
MORNING GLORY 71996
MORNING MIST 52946
MORNING MIST 53781
MORNING MIST 63072
MORNING MIST 74823
MORNING STAR 47028
MORNING STAR 48565 Hire. NbC 50′ blue/yel. B: 1990 John South, f/o Starline Narrowboats. Lister TS3, Hurth HBW 150. Base Starline Narrowboats, Upton Marina. 008111
MORNINGSIDE 77130
MORPH 53227
MORVENA 48867
MORWENNA 65004
MORWENNA see *TOADFLAX*
MOSS 71541
MOSSDALE Work boat, unpowered. Boat Museum
MOSTLY FORWARD 77842
MOTH 47651
MOTH Flat 12m BW-CATM
MOTH see *WASP*
MOUETTE 77420
MOUNTBATTEN 66297 Yarwoods Admiral Cl motor. Ex BW/WW
MOUNTBATTEN 68807
MOUNTBATTEN CRUSADER Adapted trip boat
MOUSE Short tunnel boat
MOUSTIQUE 99141
MOYA 66388
MOYNA 73422
MOZARK 45826
MR BADGER 61658
MR BADGER 77629
MR BENN 77848
MR BLEU DEUX 51293
MR BOWJANGLES 98636
MR CRUSTY 74134
MR ED 62704
MR E OWL 49448
MR HUMBY 75573
MR JAKE 63690
MR LONGERBOTTOM 66991
MR MICAWBER No. 269 70671 NbT 40′ bl
MR MISTOFFELEES 76547
MR MOLE TOO 52294
MR NODDY 95068
MR PERKINS 75020
MR PIP 52015
MR PRICKLES No.7 Nb 60′ blue/mar
MR PUNCH 500780 SHEPPERTON NbC 30′ blue/ red. B: 1984 Peter Nicholls, Napton. Kubota Z751-B. Base Shepperton, R.Thames. Features various "Mr. Punch" paraphenalia. 22493
MR PUNCH NbC 60′ wh/blue
MR TOAD II 88018

MR TOD 72679
MR TOD NbC 40′ grn/red
MRS TIGGYWINKLE 61604
M.S.C. CO. WORKS TUG Nº2 BWB 045569; GU GAUGE NO 12727 (BRENTFORD) Unconverted Nb Motor - rivetted iron hull and superstructure 71′6″, b 7′0½″, d 3′3″ grey/grn. B: 1935 Harland & Wolff, Woolwich; restored by Ian Kemp, Stour-bridge. Lister HA2 (National Twin 1935-62). Base Stourbridge. Unconverted Little Woolwich motor, first registered 25/9/35 Brentford as GUCCC fleet no 27 *Ceres*. Sold to MSC Co Bridgewater Depot in 1947 as maintenance boat. Sold to present owner in 1989 and used occasionally for carrying/towing. 25934
MUCKLE WALLA 78256
MUDBOAT No 3 see *ILKESTON*
MUDLARK 69420
MUDLARK B0137
MUDLARK 89370 BW-
MUDLARK II B1106
MUDPUPPY 054412 NbT blue/grey
MUFFIN No.3 75624 D M & A SMITH & FAMILY NbT 50′ grn/mar. B: 1988 R&D, self f/o. BL 1.8 L Thornycroft. Base L&L canal. 24840
MUFFIN TOO 65653
MULBERRY 48476
MULLYMUSH B0983
MUMBLE see *RUMBLE*
MUMBLE PACKET 85889
MUMBLES 77628
MUNCHIE 83803
MURINDA II 73572
MURMANSK 75658
MURMANSK NbC 40′ red
MURRILLO II 89500 Mtce boat 40′6″ BW-NW
MUSCADET 51058
MUSICMAKER 51808
MUSIC MAN 50528
MUSIC MAN 68845
MUSI-O-TUNTA see *KERRY DAN II*
MUSKETEER 65054 NbC 54′ grn/red. B: 1988 Springer, extended from 42′ tug with cruiser stern by D Thomas, Braunston in 1992. Thornycroft 80D. Base South Yorkshire. 24916
MUSKRAT 70001
MUSKRAT RAMBLE 71262
MUTHAIGA 45130
MUTTLEBURY 45728
MUTTLEY 63515
MUTTLEY 73049
MUTTON SONG 77384
MUZZY 50607
MYAN MIST Grp 31′, b 10′ crm/brown. B: 1982 Birchwood Boats. Twin Volvo Petrol engines. Base Thames & Kennet marina. 20168
MY BLUE HEAVEN 50039
MY DREAM 49988
MY FAIR LADY 51579
MY FAIR LADY 61802
MY FAIR LADY NbT 50′ mar
MYFANWY 52956
MYFANWY 73685
MYFANWY Adapted trip boat

MY GIRL 68248
MYGWEN 84093
MY JAY 53666
MYKRIS IV 70226
MY LADY 93928
MYLES AWAY 96398
MYONA PRINCE 77612
MYRDDIN 63299
MYRDDIN 75153
MYRIAD 49260
MYRTLE TOO 53038 NO. 2 SILEBY MILL NbST 50′ grn/red. B: 1991 Graham Edgson, Norton Canes Boat Builders, f/o J Pegg completed 1993. Lister Alpha 3. Base Sileby Mill, R.Soar.
2099
MYSTERY 72907
MYSTIC III 54654
MYSTIC DANCER 045944 Hire. NbC 57′ grn/red. BMC 1.5. Base Evesham Marina. 0371030
MYSTIC LADY 73966
MYSTIC LADY 500644 CHADWICK BROWN - LIVERPOOL NbC 70′ mauve pink (salmon?)/blue. B: 1995/6 Liverpool Boats. Beta Marine tug engine, hydraulic transmission. Permanent cruising. Walk-through engine room usually only in traditional style boats. Fully equipped for massage therapy. No gas on board - all diesel + solid fuel fire. The decorative panel on sides depicts "Mystic Lady" from Gilbert and Sullivan's HMS Pinafore, with "G & S" over proscenium arch. Theatrical masks adorn bows and rear doors. 23693
MYSTIC SINGER 045943 Hire. NbC 57′ grn/red. BMC 1.5. Base Evesham Marina. 0371043
MYSTIC WATERS 62571
MYSTIC WATERS 500583
MYSTRALE 92842
MY SWEET LADY 53558
MYTH B1585
MYWAY 48160
MYWAY 49605
MYWAY 66161
MY WAY 68798
MY WAY 72720

In ice on the Caldon canal

NAMES FOR BOATS
by Douglas Maas

Remarkably, when the time comes to name a baby, it is possible to buy a book listing potential names. I suppose this *Listing* might serve the same purpose when wishing to name or re-name a boat. The familiarity with boat names which comes with the process of typing in around 10,000 of them, far exceeds - I assure you - that which comes from idle observation when cruising by. Two facts became fairly clear. Firstly that almost any combination of the 26 letters of the alphabet could quite readily form a boat name. Secondly that a goodly amount of time must have been taken in thinking up many of them. Or is that the case, in fact?

Well known are the many proud names of the historic working boats. Their names often have that clear and timeless quality which requires no explanation. *Australia, India, Dane, Sultan, Monarch, President, Brighton, Chiltern, Cyprus, Comet, Pegasus, Phoebe, Betelgeuse, Wye, Hyperion, Oak, Swan, Sunny Valley, Spey, Zodiac*. And so many more. Most fall into categories - or classes - Town, River, Tree, Star, Station - which the history books and some of the entries will amply explain. Other names sometimes instantly place a craft on a particular waterway, not necessarily canals.

So the owner wanting to name a new boat - or having a desire to re-name - can be at perfect liberty to choose such a name with confidence. Adding *No.2* or *II* perhaps. But in fact I suspect there is a reluctance to do so, possibly out of a kind of reverence for those old respected names.

It is clear that many boats are named positively out of respect for a person - living or dead - who will thereby be remembered. *Robert Aickman, David Hutchings, Alfred Leroy, Sir Francis Drake* .... That theme of course continues with personal commemorations - so many names of people, male and female (as well as pets maybe), live on in the names of boats, possibly bought with the aid of the generosity or will of a relative. *Dorothy Mary* is one such that I happen to know. There is, I think, a preponderance of female names but maybe not so pronounced as might be found with seagoing vessels. Most are straightforward but the idea of using people's names is sometimes interestingly extended. What about *Marge the Barge* and *Lord Byron's Maggot*?

Speaking for themselves are the endless numbers of boats named, quite simply, after birds, plants, animals, rivers and places. *Bracken, Dragonfly, Sea Hawk, Ruddy Duck, Powys, Oakwood* and the numerous *Bluebell, Merlin, Swallow* and *Kestrel*. I like to think that those names actually reflect an interest or experience, at home or abroad, currently or previously enjoyed by the boats' owners. Others, more mysterious, seem to use foreign language or some secret mysticism to do the same - *Aiyoni, J'ai Vecu, Kafupi, Ric-Sher-Marda, Y'Genni, Zingaro*.

But then of course some mysterious names appear as well, as a result of combining people's names into new words. Think of your own!

A very large category of names are those which might be considered frivolous but nevertheless bring a smile to the face of all but the dedicated purist. Many carry very clear messages or descriptions. I like the contortions of *Phiphtyphut*. The honesty of *Struggle, Poverty Street, Shambles, Nervous Wreck, Costa Packet, Obsession* and *Nomad Rush*. The idea of possession is a common theme - *At Last, Erzanmine, Our Choice, Our Humble Abode, Our Retreat, Ourouse, Ours II, Just Us III, My Dream, My Way, This Is It* and the expensive-sounding *Hilton*. The exuberance of simply *Luvvly Jubbly* and *Pure Genius* plus of course *Shangri-La*. Rather less easy to classify are *Flying Kipper, Giddy Kipper, Flying Haggis* and *Blue Ice Cream*. Then there's the frankness of *Undecided*. But the prizes for the greatest contradiction in terms go to *White Elephant* and *Swansong No 1*.

I think my own favourite from this general category, for its nice simplicity, while still getting a satisfying message across, is *Tiller Girl*.

Many of the main entries in the *Listing* give explanations about names - interesting, I'm sure, for many readers. But the brief entries (most of those above) do not. Maybe the owners of those boats would like to explain - by sending in a full entry for a future edition.

The name of a boat is usually there for some considerable time. Whatever it is I'm sure it must satisfy the owners. Or how often do boat names change? Possibly following a change of ownership. There are plenty of name changes recorded in the *Listing* cross-references. Some say it's unlucky to change a boat name. Don't ask me - I've no idea.

I NAME THIS SHIP ...
by David Daines

Through the 200 years or so that boats have been built to work on our canals, there have been a number of instances of the name sign-written on the boat not being quite that which the owner intended. Given the lack of literary ability, known to be widespread amongst the canal folk, it was perhaps not too remarkable that mistakes occurred, once the boat was launched it was too late, terribly bad luck to re-name a boat in the water! I think the oldest example of this, I know of, is an ice boat originally built in the 1830s for the BCN and named *Antartic* (Antarctic) The well known booklet on the Grand Union Canal Carrying Co., *The George and The Mary*, tells of two examples in their fleet. The boat *Glaxy* should have been *Galaxy* and the *Triagulum* should probably have been *Triangulum*. I have a strong interest in this matter since one of the boats I own, built for the Erewash Canal Carrying Co. in 1935 as part of a small fleet all named after <u>trees</u> was launched as *Cyprus*, the name of the Mediterranean island. Present day sign-writers are not immune, Aylesbury basin was once host to a boat which bore the legend 'Registered at Watiford'!

(Compiler's note: Antartic is listed here: "mystery solved!" Also see Avion)

N

Here's a friendly and approachable owner (!), heavenly sagas, preserving a canal in a name, a rare Norwegian on the Avon, radical design departures, a near tragedy leads to a Heart of Gold and long trips intended one day!

NAB 69834
NAB III 73210
NABURN Motor vessel 17.25m BW-NE
NACKERED NAVVY 51566
NAESBY 61333
NAGA QUEEN 45655
NAGLESS 73306
NAIAD 49377
NAIAD 49876
NAIAD 51162
NAIAD 68226
NAIAD 68386
NAIAD 69295
NAIAD 76315
NAILER 50523
NAIRDWOOD LADY 74728
NAJORK No 1 50644
NAMASTE 46522
NAMASTE 78479
NAMNI CONWY 65354
NAMUR 54733
NANAIMO II 53734
NANCY 68545
NANCY ANNE 67275
NANCY BELL 73531
NANCY BELL NbT grn/yel
NAN HORAN 76768
NANSEN Yarwood tug. Ex BCN
NAN'S GAMP 49523
NANSHE 51738
NANSHEE 68402
NAN TOO 74017
NAOMI 47998
NAOMI 84167
NAOMI 102625
NAOMI II 89495
NAPIER 76742
NAPTON 51940
NAPTON 79054
NAPTON LASS 72913
NARKOS 54434 HIGH LODE RAMSEY NbT 59'3" dk blue/red. B: 1993-4 Shotbolt Engineering, Ramsey. 35hp Nannishire. Base Southern canals - near Northampton for Winter. 20151
NARKY 79859
NARNIA 61562
NARPIN 69148
NARROWAY 50229
NARROW ESCAPE 49542
NARROW ESCAPE 50314
NARROW ESCAPE 60124
NARROW ESCAPE 67842
NARROW ESCAPE 69975
NARROW ESCAPE 75545 REACH OUT PROJECTS Hire (groups with young people inc. disabled/ disadvantaged and others in community). Nb 65' blue/bl. B: 1986 Steelcraft. Lister TS3. Base Nash Mills, GU. Facilities incl. 12 berths, wheelchair access. 029744
NARROW WHACKER 62155
NARWHAL 71528
NASEBY Tug BW-LON
NASEBY NbC 45' red/grn
NATALIE JOY 75591
NATTAJACK 46767
Grp Seamaster 30 9.14m, b 3.50m, d 0.83m wh/dk blue. B: 1974 Seamaster Ltd., Great Dunmow Essex, f/o by unknown Broads yard. Single screw Perkins 4.237 inboard 80hp. Base R.Severn. Non-standard high quality f/o and layout. Single engine unusual - usually have 2. Originally based on the Broads, then R.Trent, Fossdyke and at Pwllheli, N. Wales before R.Severn. Original name: *Magistralis*, then *Seruwa III*. Owner is "friendly and approachable" and flies the defaced Blue Ensign of the Cruising Association, also flags of the Royal Yachting Association, RNLI and the Seamaster Club. 21243
NATTERJACK 49506
NATTERJACK 70645 NbC 40' grn/mar. B: 1984 Colecraft. 1.5 BMC. Base Braunston marina. 22520
NAVADA 079139 NbC 45' Mercedes red/blue. B: 1981 Hancock & Lane. VW Golf 1.4L. Base Milford Hall Farm marina, Stafford. Originally in Whale hire fleet (till sold in 1988), Cowroast marina, Tring, GU. Complete re-fit 1991 by Phil Gardner, Waterways Services near Weedon. 21251
NATTERJACK 75186
NATTERJACK NbT 60' blue
NAUTI LADY 46040
NAUTILUS Charter boat
NAUTI MAC 49331
NAVARA 83289
NAVICULA 64216
NAVIGARE 52979
NAVIGATOR G9327 67783 Nb - aluminium construction, centre steering 35' grey/blue. B: 1974 Allday Aluminium Ltd. / Custom Marine, Isle of Wight. Lister. Base R.Nene. Refer "Narrowboat Builders Book" page 8. 22439
NAVY BLUE 53970
NAVY DANCER 54656 SHARPNESS T&B GOUGH NbT/ST 50' Dominion blue/mid grey. B: 1993 Delph Marine, f/o 1994 G Priest Stourbridge. Volvo Penta 2003 3 cyl. Base Sharpness Marine, Gloucester & Sharpness canal. Almost full width rear hatch; when open effectively makes boat semi-trad but with the inherent security of a trad. Inheritance from parents enabled purchase; father was in Royal Navy and mother a dancer thus name is nice way of remembering them. 21344
NE 67001
NEARLY 102489

Navy Dancer showing wide slide arrangement

NEBULAE 070880 GU12414 (REG AT BRENTFORD 545) 317 GRAND UNION CANAL CARRYING CO. LTD. PHONE CITY 4755 20 BUCKLERSBURY LONDON EC4 Nb 21.95m red/wh/blue (GUCCC Ltd Jubilee colours). B: 1935 Harland & Wolff, Woolwich; restored Balliol Fowden, Braunston Canal Services Ltd. Perkins 4108 installed to one side of the hold in sound-deadened steel compartment; hydraulic transmission to conventional shaft and stern tube housed in normal swim section built under original butty stern hatches. Base Little Venice, Regents canal. Originally built as part of initial batch of 24 pairs of Type D 'Star' class narrowboats for GUCCC for their ambitious expansion scheme; paired with motor *Planet*. Carrying career limited due to crew shortages and probably spent much of first 10 years laid up. Sold 1946 to LMS then passed to British Transport Waterways (then to BWB) on nationalisation in 1948. Since then used on maintenance duties in the Northwich area. Became derelict and sunken but sold in 1980 to Braunston Canal Services who carried out full restoration (but substituted steel for elm bottom, steel for timber cabin, etc.). Then unusual conversion by present owner to provide luxurious accommodation while retaining traditional external appearance. 25986
NEBULAE 75019
NECESSITY 73023
NEDDIE III 61717
NEDD LUDD 48742
NED KELLY 73369
NED LUD 73043 NbT 40' grn
NEDOS 48110
NEIL GUY 51580
NELLIE 74801
NELLIE GRAY 67669 THE GRIDLEY FAMILY - KERRIDGE NbST 46' grn/red. B: 1978 Coles Morton Marine, Whaley Bridge, internals by Ray Gridley. 20 hp Bukh. Base Kerridge Dry Dock, Macclesfield canal. 21301
NELLIE ROSE B1691
NELSON 65436
NELSON 89645 BW-
NEMESIS 72603
NEMO 67794
NEMO II 30892
NEMUS 66757
NENDA ZAKO 72209 NbT 55' bl/red
NENE DREAM N6789
NENE QUEEN 500053
NENE VALLEY 71376
NEPTUNE 47929
NEPTUNE 500496 Steel barge 49'6", b 11'6", d 2'9" yel/grn. B: circa 1960 believed by R Dunstans of Hessle for British Waterways; converted to pleasure use 1996 by Lorenz & Co. Gardner 3LW 3 cyl. Base East Marton, L&L canal. Built as powered mud hopper as part of an order for 9 boats (7 planets + sun + moon). Purchased by present owner as a sunken derelict, refurbished for carrying then finally for pleasure. 0351008
NERIED 48423
NEROLI 48457
NERVOUS WRECK 67198
NERYS 73670
NERYS 95859
NESSENDORMA 52499
NESSIE 65003
NETHERFIELDS 73348
NETTA 73532
NETTLE 73898
NEV 52419
NEVADA 79139
NEVADA NbC 45' mar/blue
NEVANDO 76635
NEVASSA II 80915
NEWARK 78712
NEWARK Motor vessel 10.97m BW-NE
NEWBOLD 71699
NEWBOLD TUNNEL 68959

NEW BUFOONERY 53007
NEWBURY 79761 Motor
NEWCASTLE 74822
NEW DAWN 5567 Vintage cruiser 19′ dk blue/wh. B: 1960(app) Dolphin Cruisers; re-built above hull in 1991 by owner and friend. Old Penta 5hp ob with controls in wheelhouse. Base Bristol Docks, the Heritage Centre Pontoon. 23541
NEWDIGATE
NEW GENERATION 54080
NEW NAVIGATION 54998
NEWPORT 64991
NEW PROSPECT 65909
NEWT 45704
NEWT 51095
NEWT 54781
NEWTONMERE 45664
NEW WORLD 77801
NIADEO 500222
NICE ITEM 54117
NICE 'N' EASY 53490
NICKY B 52110
NIC-NAC 72526 No. 3 NbT 51′6″ grn/red. B: 1986 as 35′ boat, Braunston Narrowboat Builders; lengthened in 1989. Bukh. Base Whilton Marina, GU. 22397
NICOLA 60850
NICOLA 75043
NICOLA 76603
NICOLANDA 30444
NICOLA OF KENT 74218
NICOLE 47593
NIFTY BEAVER 46703
NIFTY FIFTY 048161 IRENE AND PETER ANDREWS BRAUNSTON NbT 45′ dk blue/lt blue/grey. B: 1990 TT Marine. Lister Alpha LPWS3. Base Braunston. Wind turbine + solar panel. 22512
NIFTY FIFTY II 50770
NIGHT OWL 49878
NIGHT OWL II 49983
NIGHTJAR 70282
NIGHTJAR 72504
NIGHTJAR 78292
NIGHTJAR 500972
NIGHTJAR II 102327
NIKE FOUR 66434
NIKI 99306
NIKIDI II 78944
NIKITA 70008
NIKITA 70168
NIK-NOK 85630
NIMBUS 68212
NIMBUS 92809
NIMBUS IV 71838
NIMBUS IX KRISTENHALM Grp 25′, b 8′6″ wh/blue. B: 1972 Albin, Sweden. Volvo Penta 25hp. Base Wyre Mill Club, Lower Avon. Optional sail/rigging. Believed ex-hire boat on Caledonian Canal. 25938
NIMITZ 75270
NIMITZ 87783
NIMROD 45516
NIMROD 62360

NIMROD 67180 Nb 44′ mar/grn. B: 1975 Canal & Rivercraft. Petter PH2WM. Base Lichfield Cruising Club, Huddlesford. "Waterways World" Boat Test Apr 1976 as *Gainsborough*. 22529
NIMROD 78319
NIMUE 46760
NIMUE 66928
NINDENELLA 72061
NINE DIAMONDS 50792
NING 49805
NING 3 *51188 NbC 25′ crm/blue*
NIPPER 63042
NIPPER 101529
NIPPER TOO S1552 Nb 26′ dk grn/pale grn. B: 1991 TT Marine, Thorne. Kubota Beta Marine 17.5hp. Base Brayford Pool, Lincoln. Ex hire. 22501
NIPPIN 61666
NIPS 76327
NIREE 102991
NIRVANA Grp 25′, b 10′ wh. B: 1981 Birchwood Boats Ltd. Watermota Sea Tiger petrol. Base Wyre Mill Club, Lower Avon. 25956
NIRVANA 050932 ROY & SANDRA NbST 53′ blue/grey. B: 1991 GT Boats (Stafford) Ltd., amateur f/o. BL 1.8, PRM Delta gearbox. Base Longwood Boat Club, Rushall canal, BCN. Vetus 4hp bow thruster. 21352
NIRVANA 81706 BW-
NIRVANA II 73795
NISHA 53202
NISPERO 76051
NIVAMA 48749
NIX *66930 NbC 25′ grn/red*
NOAH 48698
NOASSLE 63796
NOBBY 50824
NOBLE STAR 045968 Hire. NbC 63′ grn/red. BMC 1.8. Base Evesham Marina, R.Avon. 0371039
NOCTURNE 79145
NOD 79532
NO FIXED ABODE 51207
NOGGIN 46965
NOGGIN 77461
NOGGINS 52132
NOMAD 500921 KEGWORTH NbT 47′ mar/orange. B: 1996 R&D, f/o a mix! 1.6 twin. Base Kegworth - Jim Forster. 4′6″ foot wide "flip-up" permanent double bed in fore cabin. Long trips intended one day. 22444
NOMADA 67979
NOMAD OF EREHWON 050208 NbC 42′ grn/red. B: 1990 Liverpool Boats, f/o not known. BMC 1.5 (AMC Argos). Base Ham Manor Basin, Newbury, K&A canal. Originally *Everglade*; now try reading *Erehwon* backwards. 23555
NOMAD RUSH 52333
NOMADS BADGER 75847
NOMIS 61732
NONA Cruiser - timber ply, pine scantlings, Iroka furniture. 7m, b 2.9m sand yel/dk grn. B: 1991 George Payne and Eric Homewood. Honda 9.9hp ob. Base Bridgwater and Taunton canal. Designed by George Payne from first principles to overcome

faults taken for granted in other canal cruisers and has many radical new features. Extremely stable hull with minimum roll characteristics; can be moored to bank without grounding. No side decks provide maximum space and comfort for two with visibility and protection for helmsman provided by innovative rising cover to wheelhouse plus entire rising cabin roof. 24790
NON REA 53212
NOOKIE BARE 13542 (Thames licence) NbC 40' dk blue/crm. B 1995/6 Liverpool Boats, owner f/o. Kingfisher KD14/18. Base Eynsham, Oxford, R.Thames. 23600
NO PROBLEM 46952
NO PROBLEM 65963
NO PROBLEM 67278
NORADA B155 WROXHAM Charter. Wherry Yacht 53', b 12', d 3'9" wh. B: 1912 Ernest Collins, Wroxham. BMC Vedette/sail. Base Wroxham, Norfolk Broads. Only 6 wherries capable of sailing now - this is one of fleet of 3 (see also *Hathor* and *Olive*). 01228
NORATRACE 74178
NORBEN 45279
NORD FJORD 47637
NORDEN BELLE 54809
NORDICA 104595
NORDIC LADY NIDELV 26 Grp 26', b 9', d 3' wh. B: 1990 (build no. 438) Nidelv AS, Norway. Volvo TAMD 31. Base Wyre Mill Club, Lower Avon. Clinker design, rounded stern and semi-displacement hull allows speeds of up to 17 knots at sea (mainly Bristol Channel). H/C shower on bathing platform. This boat is only one of 3 known to be in England. 25943
NO REGRETS 79978 *NbT 30' blue*
NOREX 1 82526
NORFOLK 49749
NORFOLK 53214
NORLANDO 61722
NORLEEN II 63847
NORMAN 62828
NORMAN 66636
NORMAN 80398
NORMAN 92790
NORMAN ALMOND EYES 100613
NORMA ST. CLAIR 53906
NORNIC FLIGHT 49960
NORSEMAN 49509
NORSMAN Day hire. NbTug 40'. B: 1980 Godalming Narrowboats on Colecraft hull. BMC 1.5. Base Farncombe Boat House, R.Wey. 00371
NORTHERN ECHO 72482 *NbC 35' grn*
NORTHERN LIGHTS 47471
NORTHERN PRIDE 46575
NORTHERN STAR 73476
NORTHERN STAR 77928
NORTHLAND 71687
NORTHOLT 73625
NORTHOLT see *SUNNY VALLEY*
NORTHRIDING 65915
NORTH STAR 50542
NORTH STAR 60487
NORTH STAR *NbC 50' blue*

NORTHUMBERLAND 053969 A & B PERCY NbTug 58' grn. B: 1994 Colecraft, incl part lining - remainder owner f/o. BMC 1.8. Base Harefield marina. Features large windows, not portholes.2033
NORTHUMBERLAND 79640
NORTHUMBRIAN *48054 NbC 50' mar/grn*
NORTHUMBRIAN ADVENTURER 79873 STOURPORT NbC 50' grn/red. B: 1979 Bingley Marine, Yorkshire. Lister 2 cyl. Base Stourport Basin. Boat featured on BBC "Hearts of Gold" programme, March 1995 following owner slipping on deck and drowning in Stourport Basin, April 1994. At Kidderminster hospital given 10% chance of survival - air lifted to Glenfield Hospital, Leicester and became first "drowned" person to survive on pioneering ECMO machine provided by funds from Heartlink Charity. *(So pleased that this entry for the Listing was possible).* 20141
NORTHWICH Butty. Ex FMC/BW
NORTON 77564
NORVIC 69974
NORWICH 71734
NORWOOD 60001
NORWOOD B1540
NOSAM 66122 *NbC 35' grn/red*
NOSTALGIA 54284
NOTONECTA 45892
NOTONECTA 68156
NOTONECTA 69512
NOTTINGHAM 61324 WHIMSTER FAMILY NbC 52' red/dk blue. B: 1975 Godalming Narrowboats, refit 1983 by Shire Cruisers (Britannia Narrowboats). BMC 1.8. Base Just Boats, Crick, GU-Leics. 20126
NOTTINGHAM 500301 Crane boat 21.34m BW-NE
NOVA 79326
NOVA CASTRIA 78088
NOVA TEAL 99116
NOVA TWO 45808
NOVA TWO *NbT 40' blue/mar*
NOZOMI 72806
NUMEROUS 63529
NUNEATON Large Northwich Working Nb Motor crm/burgundy. B: 1936 Yarwoods Northwich. Petter PD2. Base R.Thames. Motor to *Brighton* (see entry, also for general information and history). Originally fitted with a National diesel engine and total cost was £900. Original pairing with the Large Ricky butty *Nunhead*. Around 1970 bought by tender by the newly formed Narrowboat Trust. By this time she was derelict and engine scrap. Since undergone extensive restoration and now in excellent condition, regularly carrying 20 ton loads of domestic coal. 022521
NUNHEAD see *NUNEATON*
NUPHAR LUTEA 61789
NUTBROOK 70434 J.L.P. and M.P. LANGLEY MILL NbTug 55' deep crimson/mid grn. B: 1980 as 40' tug and lengthened to 55' by Les Allen, Oldbury. Lengthening and refit by owner 1992/96. Russell Newbery DM2 18bhp. Base Erewash/Cromford canal, Langley Mill. Flush

fore-deck, trad aft cabin. Name from derelict canal branch of Erewash canal. 22474
NUTCRACKER 51464
NUTCRACKER 51722
NUTCRACKER 92022
NUTCRACKER SUITE 47701
NUTFIELD 61882 Butty
NUTMEG 50064
NUTMEG 52233
NUTMEG 54162
NUTSHELL 47498
NUTTY NOAH 72304 *NbC 40' red/grn*
NYCTICORAX 70189
NYM 67680
NYZARK 75201

O

The very first "shared ownership" boat, connections with a Hudson Bay pioneer, a unique shoveler with a good swim, a Springer (?) and busy bees, one to call up, a pig with a curly handrail and quite a bit of info wanted here

OAK Ex Severn & Canal CC
OAK 69907 No. 1 MIDDLEWICH NARROWBOATS Hire. NbT steel hull, wooden cabin traditionally built 70' grn/red. B: Hull 1972 Pinder, cabin by Willow Wren Rugby, rebottomed 1994/95; new boatmans cabin 1980, refitted 1995/96 by Middlewich Narrowboats (little of original boat left!). 12 berths, Trad engine room. Lister SR3. Base Middlewich. 028732

OAK APPLE 063416 NORM & DEE WHERE EVER NbC 57' coral/grn. B: early 1970s Harborough Marine. Lister 3 cyl. Base L&L canal. Began life as hire boat. Sank in lock about 1985. After several owners and name change to *Artichoke*, bought by present owner 1996, changed name back to original, refit started. 24878
OAKLEAF 53811
OAKLEY 61573
OAKLEY 65244
OAKS 66064
OAKWELL 78714
OAKWOOD 67303
OASIS 45796
OASIS *50842 NbST 50' blue*
OATES 64802
OAWR 49565
OBERON 45947
OBSESSION 53478
OBSESSION B1273
OBSESSION B1472
OCCEATHEUS 50874
OCEAN BLUE Motor vessel BW-NE
OCEAN GYPSY 073786 FENNY STRATFORD Grp Thames cruiser 30', b 10'6", d 2'9" wh/red. B: 1960app. Information about builder, date, which hire fleet, when sold to private owner, etc. still being traced - information needed *(see page 14)*. Believed to be part of a hire fleet - one of 7 on Thames named *R.Princess*. 4 cyl Perkins. Base Fenny Stratford, GU. 261026
OCEAN LADY 65440
OCKER 52282
OCTAVIA 46918
OCTAVIA 47658
OCTAVIA 62607
OCTOBER MORN 53463 *NbC 30' Mar/blue*
OCTOPUS 45309

Nona: Radical design from first principles

ODDBALL B1511
ODDMEDOD 62249
ODDNYDOD 47409
ODDYDOD 74026
ODDY Motor vessel BW-NW
ODDYSSEY 62136
ODIN 76045
ODIN II 50234
ODIN No 3 49698
ODINS RAVEN 96265
ODYSSEUS 49817
ODYSSEUS 75902 NbT 50' dk grn/red. B: 1988 by The Wolverhampton Narrowboat & Canal Carrying Company Limited, first owner f/o. Gardner L2. Base Braunston marina. 2068
ODYSSEY 54076
ODYSSEY 65889
ODYSSEY 101533
ODYSSEY *NbC 50' grn/crm*
OGWR 049565 No. 370 H and P A BROWNING HAZELSTRINE NbST 50' grn/crm. B: 1990/93 David Piper, Kidsgrove + owners. Mitsubishi/Vetus. Base Stafford Boat Club, S&W canal. Named after R.Ogmore in Glamorgan. 24867
OHTORI CURLE & COMPANY SUNDERLAND NbC 45' maple grn/red. B: 1990 P M Buckle, Stibbington, owner f/o. Calcutt 1.8 BL. Base Snaygill marina. 23587c
OKEFENOKEE 102728
OKI DOKI 72559
OLAV 77042
OLDBURY MAIDEN 62471
OLD CASTLE 65019
OLD ELM TREE 30723
OLDENBURG 102071
OLD FORD 12m BW-L&S
OLD HUSHWING 54532 *NbT 62' brown/blue*
OLD JOEY 60813
OLD MR. PLOD 63682
OLD MYSTIC B1583
OLD PECULIAR *45633 NbC 30' red/grn*
OLD SEADOG 60899
OLD SMOKEY 62886
OLD SMOKEY 70190
OLD SMOKEY 70673
OLD SMOKY NbC 45' red/grn/yel. B: 1976 Willoughby Fabrications. Yanmar. Base Regents canal. 24774
OLD SPOT 500800 NbST 61' grn/mid brown. B: 1996 Navigation Narrowboat Co. on Marque Narrowboat shell. Beta Marine Kabota 1903. Base Crick marina, GU-Leics. Picture of Old Spot pig at stern panel, barley twist handrails at bow end of cabin mirrored on plant boxes on roof. 21263
OLD STRIPE DEREK & PENNY HACKETT NbT 58'6" grn/red. B: 1996/97 Nimbus Narrowboats, on GT Boats hull. Beta Marine on Kubota 43hp. Base Thurmaston, R.Soar. Named from badger featured in "Deep Wood" by Elleston Trevor. Fully fitted for extended cruising. Derek is licensed radio amateur - call sign G Ø G B V active on 144mhz & 432mhz. 21300

OLDUN 68053
OLIAS 72219
OLIAS *NbT 60' red/grn*
OLIMAR 85632
OLIVE WROXHAM Charter. Wherry Yacht 56', b 13'9'", d 3'6" wh. B: 1909 Ernest Collins, Wroxham. 3hp electric/sail. Base Wroxham, Norfolk Broads. Only 6 wherries capable of sailing now - this is one of fleet of 3 (see also *Hathor & Norada*). 01227
OLIVE 63535
OLIVE 500169
OLIVE MYRTLE 69699
OLIVER CROMWELL 66279
OLIVER CROMWELL Barney(15) 1972 32'
OLIVE ROSE 49002 ALVECOTE No 11 Nb 62' aircraft blue/crm. B: 1990 R&D Fabrications, Nottingham, f/o Narrowcraft Alvecote. Thornycroft (Ford) XLD 1800. Base Crick, GU - Leics. Believed to be the very first of the 'current' generation of shared ownership boats in the country, a concept pioneered by Peter Pratt of Narrowcraft Ltd. Launched Stourport, R.Severn August 1990 after display at Gloucester IWA National Rally. 21313
OLIVERS DREAM 53567
OLIVER T 89885
OLLIE 66559
OLLIE OWL 47160
OLLY 77499
OLTON Tug BW-LON
OLYMPIC 60973
OLYMPUS 79903
OMAR KHAYAN
OMEGA 51588 NbC Midway 295 29'6" blue/mar. B: 1992 Liverpool hull, f/o Mancunian Narrowboats. Beta Kubota 3 cyl BD 1005 25bhp. Base White Bear marina, Adlington, Chorley. After 3 previous boats, *Omega* bought after retirement and considered to be the last, hence name. 20163
OMEGA 47470
OMEGA 47706
OMEGA 51588
OMEGA 52285
OMEGA 53657
OMEGA 67059
OMEGA 67164
OMEGA 67812

Where Is It?
Look it up in the Location Glossary

OMEGA 69836
OMEGA 76446
OMEGA 78252
OMEGA *NbC 40' grn/wh*
OMEGA *Grp Norman 25' wh*
OMMADAWN 67165
OMMADAWN 71750
OMNIBUS 98131
OM SHANTI 48949

ONCE AGAIN 50382
ONDINE 74445
ONE DAY B0909
ONEIDA 79261
ONE OFF B0260
ONESIMUS 45510
ONION BARGEE 50121
ON TICK *48285 NbC 40' red/grn*
ONWARD 54709
ONWARD 64855
ONWARD N6441
ONYX 52326
ONYX 500775
OPAL 52140   Nb 42' grn/red/yel.   B: 1992 Mancunian Boat Co. (their 19th). Vetus. Base Lyme View marina, Adlington, Cheshire. Features on sides: Mancunian Coat of Arms (with busy bees from cotton trade) - Mancunian Boats XIX at base plus rainbow in full colour encompassing "OPAL". 25939
OPAL CROWN 500775
OPATO 63245
OPHELIA 52682
OPHELIA 74489
OPHIUCHUS 68349
OPIUM 102126
OPPORTUNITY 65342
OPRA N7739 NbST 45' midnight blue/mar. B: 1994 Klondyke Boatbuilding. BL 1500cc. Base Woodford Riverside marina, R.Nene. 21267
OPTION TOO 73690
OPUS 75008
OPUS No 1 76238
OPUS IV 77652
ORA 76245
ORA No 2 48390
ORCADIAN 102565
ORCAELLA 52936
ORCHARD LADY 50492
ORCHID 52493
ORCHID 80373 BW-
ORCHID Tug 5.1m BW-
ORDRIS 65686
OREGON 71396
ORENKA 63221
ORFORD 78515
ORIANA 77088
ORION 45198
ORION 49090
ORION 53853
ORION 66683
ORION 69210 Wide beam cruiser - steel hull, grp cabin, wood wheelhouse 40' b 11'6" blue/red. B: 1966 Dalescraft, Bradford Boat Services, Apperley Bridge, Bradford. Lister SR3. Base Apollo Canal Cruises, Shipley. Originally *Dales Pioneer*, built as one of two - the other *Dales Voyager* - to carry hirers' touring caravans for boating holidays. Later fitted with typical Dalescraft style grp cabin, used as hire boat for several years. Then, in private hands, fitted with wheel steering in distinctive wheelhouse. Unusually hull is "shovel fronted" and swims very well. Cruised most northern wide waterways.

Original twin became a trip boat, now at Ferrybridge, which makes *Orion* unique in present state! 22436
ORION 066833 Hire. NbC 50' grn/red. BMC 1.5. Base Evesham Marina, R.Avon   0371048
ORION 78241
ORION XIV 65574
ORION *NbT 45' blue/crm/red*
ORION DAWN 50035
ORLESTONE 46727 M & J DUNK No 1 Registered NORTON CANES 1012 NbT 59'6" dk blue/dk red.   B: 1989 Graham Edgson, Norton Canes Boatbuilder, diy f/o. Thornycroft 1.8. Base Stone, T&M. 20159
ORMISTON No 4   45384   W[M], K & C FRANKLIN IVER NbT 60' grn/red B: 1989-9 Colecraft, f/o Adrian Wagstaff, Valley Cruises, Atherstone, Back cabin Barry Smith, Blue Haven Marine. Lister FR3 (1959) in centre engine 'ole. Base HLY Iver, GU Slough Arm. 22450
ORSUM 31634
ORTON LADY N5306
ORWELL 79330
OSCAR 50776
OSCAR 52042
OSIRIS 52325
OSLO FJORD 47636
OSPREY 50841
OSPREY 52467
OSPREY 61448
OSPREY 63742
OSPREY 64060
OSPREY 64425
OSPREY 66306
OSPREY 69659
OSPREY *72891 NbC 35' orange/blue*
OSPREY 74589
OSPREY 92416
OSPREY 91250 Grp 20', b 8'10½" forest grn/wh. B: 1976 Dawncraft. Evinrude 9.9hp ob. Base Amington, Coventry canal. 20170
OSPREY No 1 75646
OSPREY X 31422 BRIDGEMARSH Grp 23' wh/ blue canopy.   B: 1982 Islander cruiser. Inboard petrol engine. Base Lea & Stort Cruisers Ltd. *(Owner is trying to discover information about builder, etc. - see page 14).* 21211
OSSIE ROUSE 77702
OSTRICH 72490
OSWESTRIAN 47317
OTHER HALF A PAIR 52696
OTLEY 61437 Lg Woolwich Town Cl motor. Ex GUCC/BW/WW
OTTAR 47582
OTTER 45423
OTTER 47121
OTTER 49918
OTTER 51450
OTTER 52604
OTTER 61703
OTTER 61925
OTTER 67558
OTTER 68215
OTTER 70846

OTTER 72773
OTTER 073047 NbST 10.66m grn/red. B: 1976 R&N Fabrications, f/o by first owner and named *Gresham*. Sabb 2 cyl. Base Weltonfields, GU-Leics. *Otter* named after owner's great grandfather's boat - he was employed by the Hudson Bay Company and traded on West coast of British Columbia, bringing furs and fish to Victoria for shipment to England. 20174
OTTER 54860 MATTHEWS VALENCIA WHARF NbTug 30' grn/red. B: 1984 Springer; rebuilt by Les Allen & Sons 1993-95. Mitsubishi K3D, Hurth HBW50 g'box. Base Wyre Mill Club, Wyre Piddle, R.Avon. Prototype Springer, totally tug type with portholes (Doesn't look like a Springer). 24905
OTTER *NbST 50' blue*
OTTER II 50865
OTTERS WAY 50929
OTTER'S WAY G6292 BEDFORD Grp 28', b 9'6" lt crm. B: 1972 Freeman. Perkins 4.108. Base Bedford. Windscreen converted to folding type. 21289
OUR BABE 87390
OUR BOAT 70799 *NbC 25' yel/crm*
OUR CHOICE 63955
OUR HUMBLE ABODE 53949
OUR RETREAT 68483
OUR SUSIE 83234
OUR TREASURE 77024
OUR WINNIE 76801
OUROUSE 67293
OURS II 79125
OUTHOUSE MOUSE 31728
OUTLAW 64691
OUTLAW 70764

OVEN 67380
OVERDRAFT 96164
OWD WHITT 068344 NbC steel with grp cabin 33' grn/red. B: late 1960's or early 1970's *(trying to find out - see page 14)* Shropshire Union Cruisers Norbury junction (Dartline). Lister SR2. Base RWBC Clayworth Wharf, Chesterfield canal. Ex hire boat run by two companies at least. 23590
OWL 46754
OWL 50293
OWL 68550
OWL 71959
OWL 74339
OWL No 11 50737
OWL No 14 47091
OWL No 211 Yarwoods. Ex FMC
OWL WEY & ARUN Crystal 170 - grp cruiser/trail boat 5.1m, b 1.7 wh/blue. B: 1989 Crystal Marine, London (?). Honda 8 ob. Base Pyrford marina, R.Wey. 21273
OWL A PLENTY *47468 NbC 20' grn*
OWLDATDO 73736
OWL DOULENE 51288
OWLER 47553
OWLET 79192 P G AND A J MARKS RED BULL BASIN NbT 38'6" grn/red. B: 1980 David Piper, Red Bull Basin (build no. 240). BMC 1.5. Base Red Bull, T&M canal. 22525
OWL'S NEST B1650
OWL & THE PUSSYCAT 47050
OXFORD 53950
OXFORD 80374 Motor boat 52'6" BW-OGU
OXFORD 1 *Nb 42'*
OXFORD COUNTESS *NbC 48' red/crm*
OXLIP Tug 5.1m BW-
OZY MANDIAS 63337

For a change - wide boats (l) Old style Leeds & Liverpool horse-drawn boat and (r) later Leeds & Liverpool motor boat [Harry Arnold, Waterway Images

P

Look here for several slow and peaceful boats, a training vessel, a much loved steamer, lots of Pride, musical lunches, another first "shared ownership" contender, electric trips, caravan afloat, a Yangtse connection, the ultimate boat's not for sale, a one poster bed and dog kennel and "Don't Panic!"

PACE 48643
PACIFIC SWIFT 52794
PADDINGTON 50733 Grp centre cockpit, steel and timber frame 40' grn/wh. B: shell/engine 1974 Dawncraft, f/o 1974-84. GT marine 40hp 4 cyl Enfield outdrive 1:1.68 reduction, fuel 35src gas oil, prop 13x10$^1/_2$" for canals, 13x8 for deep water. Base GU, Northampton. Designed as long life, low maintenance, good speed, manouverable, weather protected - the "ultimate best boat on the cut". This followed previous high cost, high maintenance, slow boats. *Paddington* offers high comfort full specification with little time wasted on maintenance and "she's not for sale". 20113
PADDINGTON 67522
PADDINGTON *NbT 30' blue*
PADDINGTON II 65933
PADDINGTON BEAR 71634
PADDLEWHEEL 68754
PADGE 104185
PADGE G4463
PADOVA 52008
PAGE II 49118
PAINTED LADY 054328 GRAND UNION NbST 12.19m blue/bl. B: 1994 R&D Fabrications, recent f/o by owners following fire in which boat was completely gutted. Nanni 3 cyl 23hp. Base Maple Lodge canal basin. 24785
PAINTED LADY B1051
PAIRUS 64493
PAJANT 53319 N7364 P & J R STRUDWICK & SONS NbT 51', d 30" blue/yel. B: 1993 Shotbolt Engineers Ramsey, f/o Nene Marine Whittlesey. Kubota Beta marine. Base Rickmansworth, GU. Low air draft for Middle Level bridges. 21368
PAKIAT 78676
PAL 50206
PALADIN 54190
PALJOY B1068
PALLAS 72584 Sm Woolwich Star Cl motor (ex butty). Ex GUCC/BW
PALLISER 77655
PAMADU IV 45735
PAMANDY 51452
PAMELA 101340
PANACEA 53071
PANAGA 51708
PANDIM 73981 *Grp 35' wh*
PANDORA 51930
PANDORA 63199
PANDORA 71061
PANDORA II 63130

PANDORA II 69158
PANDORA II 75639 Nb 48' dk blue/red. B: 1988 Delph Marine. 2 cyl Bukh. Base Bugbrooke marina, GU. 24772
PANDORA No 3 49459
PandQ 101523
PANEMAR 62589 NbST 58' red/bl. B: 1972 Harborough. Lister SR2. Base Robinsons Boatyard, Dewsbury. 23607
PANEMAR N7221
PA'NIK 65459
PANKINA 73149
PANTHER Motor
PANTHER *53530 Workboat 50' bl/wh*
PANTHER 66707
PANTHER 74552
PANTHER No. 2 *NbT 60' bl/graining*
PAPAGENA 63119
PAPANEEK 103646 Grp 32' wh/navy (canopy sides). B: 1993 Creighton Boatbuilders Cheshire, f/o 1993-95. 3 cyl 22hp Nanni, Hurth gearbox 2:1. Base Portavon marina Keynsham Bristol. Built as "one-off" with cabin of 27' craft mounted on 32' giving total 9' centre cockpit. Owners spent 2 years fitting out from scratch including much unfinished basic work left by builders when they went into receivership. *Papaneek* is a corruption of the French for "no panic" - "pas panique", as one of the owners has been known to do just that! 22510
PAPILLON 68905
PAPILLON *73619 NbT 60' blue*
PAPILLON 73707
PAPILLON 102248
PAPILLON 500947
PAPILLON B1332
PARADISE 97895 GALGATE Dawncraft Dandy 19' crm/brown. B: not known. Yamaha 9.9 ob. Base Galgate marina. 25971
PARAGON 79196
PARAGON Station Cl
PARBELLA B1219 British Registered Ship 184853 Bridgewater canal motor barge used for pleasure/office space 70'3", b 14'9", d variable red coamings/grn hatches. B: 1951 Pimblotts of Northwich, refurbished Lorenz & Co. Gardner L3 5 cyl - replaced original 4L3 when craft towed larger lighters. Base Castlefield, Manchester. This was last Bridgewater motor barge, trading until 1986. The Bridgewater barge fleet carried all of the maize for Kelloggs Cornflakes from docks to the Barton factory. They were the largest craft able to pass Hulme locks. The motor barges could carry 80 tons, the dumb barges 100 tons. Built to Lloyds spec. and regularly traded on Mersey estuary, Manchester Ship canal, R.Weaver, R.Dee, etc. *Parbella* was refurbished to original condition externally and is still used on the Bridgewater canal when conditions allow. 0351004
PARCASTLE II B1753
PARDOW B1589
PARFAIT AMOUR 48739
PARKLAND VENTURE 74685
PARNI VARDO 99819
PARRSBORO B0105

131

PARRY Iceboat. Boat Museum
PARSLEY 52190
PARTOUT 77388
PARVA 60751
PARYS 49764
PASADENA 52569
PASCADELL 71755
PASCAL NbT 60' blue
PASCALI see HAZEL
PASERO 67078
PASSIM 31508
PASTA II 77185
PAST CARING 52409
PASTI II 52876
PASTURES NEW 49391
PAT 75235
PATERNOSTER 72897
PATHFINDER 47237
PATHFINDER 68665
PATHFINDER Ex BW
PATIENCE 66364 NbC 60' blue. B: 1974 Humber St. Andrews Engineering Co Ltd, St. Andrews Dock, Hull, f/o Coverglade, Hull. Lister SR3. Base Thorne Cruising Club, Stainforth marina. Built for the Duke of Edinburgh Award Scheme and - as *Lewis R Jenkins* - was handed to the Duke in 1974 at Bingley 5 Rise. Bought by present owner in 1995: still available at no cost for instructing children and community groups. 21365
PATIENCE 47237
PATIENCE 76030
PATIENCE 76168
PATIENSE 46220
PATRIARCH 60877
PATRICIA 48819
PATRICIA 53494
PATRICIA 72383
PATRICIA 95405
PATRICIA Spud leg dredger 45' BW-NW
PATRICIA ANN 45824
PATRICIA ANN 74011
PATRICIA ANN NbT blue
PATRICIA ANNE 63414
PATRICIA M 46695
PATRICIAN JADE B7829
PATSY ANNE 77312
PATSY LOW G9525
PATTY PLOW 72250
PAUHANA 61559
PAULA 84503
PAULA 2 B1145
PAULA DAWN 74229
PAULA ELAINE 84198
PAULINE B1251
PAULINE 80944 BW-
PAUL MARY 62074
PAUPERS PRIDE B1126
PAVANE N7318 P M BUCKLE NARROWBOATS STIBBINGTON Nb 70' mar. B: 1993 P M Buckle Stibbington. BMC 1.8 Calcutt Marine. Base Yarwell Mill, R.Nene. A modern shell/interior re-creation of an "early" Pat Buckle design. 20132
PAWNEE 67336

PAWPRINTS *73926 NbT 50' mar/grn*
PAWS 72195
PAX 53596 NbC 23'6" grn/mar. B: 1994 Mick Sivewright for Midway Boats, Nantwich. Honda 9.9hp ob. Base Page & Hewitts, Tottenham, Lee Navigation. Early model of the "Midway" range of smaller narrowboats. *Pax* is Latin for "peace".21360
PAX 66972
PAX 76829
PAX 82491
PAX B0173
PAY-OUT 53863
PEACE P & O MAKOWER BANBURY Nb 52' royal blue/red. B: 1971/72 Peter Jones, Banbury. Lister SR16 - marinised from bus engine. Base Wargrave R.Thames. Won "Best Amateur Made Boat" 1972(?). Steel hull/wood superstructure magnificently painted by Bob Bush of Aylesbury (son of Binky Bush - Commander, RN -

Flashback to 1974 HRH the Duke of Edinburgh aboard *Lewis R Jenkins*, now *Patience*

a famous waterways character in 60/70s) and still lovingly kept up. Maintained at Tooleys Yard, Banbury. 22421
PEACE 63088
PEACE 70395
PEACE 77636
PEACE 79140
PEACE B1369
PEACE NbC 45' grn
PEACOCK 60892 Saltley motor. Ex FMC
PEACOCK 62923
PEACOCK 070803 Hire. NbT blue/red. BMC 1.5. Base Evesham Marina, R.Avon. 0371041
PEARL Hire. NbC 56' blue/red. Base The Wyvern Shipping Co, Linslade, GU 00445
PEARL 32020
PEARL 45904
PEARL 74255

PEARL 100800
PEARL No 81 60622
PEARL FISHER 48913
PEARL OF PENSETT 49657
PEARLY 100224
PEBBLES 94225
PEBBLES 100375
PEBLEY 69591
PEDIGREE *54444 NbT 50' blue/graining*
PEDLER BEN 68221
PEDLEY Motor vessel BW-NW
PEE JAY 76562
PEEJAY 94511
PEELS WHARF 61710
PEERESS 66853
PEERESS 72729 NbC 42' navy blue/bright red. B: 1985(?). Bukh 2 cyl. Base Hilperton marina, K&A canal. 21295
PEER GYNT 69573
PEGARY 78203
PEGARY 3 46141
PEGASUS 502
PEGASUS 47349
PEGASUS 52411
PEGASUS 53820
PEGASUS 64277
PEGASUS 66067
PEGASUS 66372
PEGASUS 67631
PEGASUS 69238
PEGASUS 73303
PEGASUS B1056 NbC 36' wh/red. B: 1979 Springer, refit Harry Wright. 2.2 L BMC. Base Worsley Cruising Club, Leigh, Bridgewater canal. Refit by Harry Wright, a cabinet maker with 30 years experience of owning and fitting out touring caravans. He accepted challenge of fitting out this 36' Springer having been heard poking fun at the interior designs of narrow boats. The result is a luxuriously fitted caravan within a narrow boat and a view that "caravan designers have much to teach canal boat fitters". Full description of f/o in Canal & Riverboat, Nov 1990. Also note distinctive cratch with scalloped sun canopy and zip on side covers and red deck planks, edged with polished aluminium *(see picture, front cover)*. 23722
PEGASUS N5619
PEGASUS 69 Sm Woolwich Star Cl motor. Ex GUCC/BW
PEGGOTTY 52096
PEGGOTTY 61241
PEGGOTTY JAI 60896
PEGGOTTY *NbC 40' red/grn*
PEGGY 61677
PEGGY 70757
PEGGY ANN *53092 NbC 70' blue*
PEGGY MAY 71244
PEGGY O'NEIL 103207
PEGGY O'NEIL *Nb 30' grn*
PEGOLA 65127
PEGOLGA II 72605
PEGOTTY 76444
PEGOTTY 77125
PEGS 51629

PEG'Y'DON 52920
PEKING No.1 *53947 NbT 50' grn*
PELICAN 53517
PELICAN 64258
PELICAN Crane barge. Boat Museum
PELISTRY 70586 CONGLETON Nb 45' mar/dk blue. B: 1983 Stoke-on-Trent Boat Building Co. Ltd. Lister Canal Star 3 air cooled. Base Macclesfield canal. Hot air ducted from engine to saloon for background heating. A favourite sandy beach in the Isles of Scilly inspired the name. 20115
PELYDRYN 52847
PELYDRYN 64470
PEMA II 78804
PEMBRIDGE 70439
PEMBROKE 51300
PEMBROKE 104285
PENDINE 73705
PENDING 65211
PENDLE 64886
PENDLE 67865
PENDLE B0317
PENDLE B1152
PENDLE DIPPER 51352
PENDLE MAGIC 49490
PENDLE MIST 47004
PENDLEWYTCH 71127
PENDRAGON 47182
PENDRAGON 48080
PENDRAGON 61837
PENDRAGON 68460
PENDRAGON 73307
PENDRAGON 77162
PENELOPE 66143
PENELOPE 102755
PENFOLD 54237
PENGUIN 68265
PENLAN 30673
PENLYN 68055
PENMON 46285
PENNBROOK 47791
PENNIES-MOR 71678
PENNINE 46123
PENNINE 500663
PENNINE Mtce boat BW-NW
PENNY 50079
PENNY 104638
PENNY N5919
PENNY *NbT 45' grn/red*
PENNY II 52657
PENNY JENNY 54681
PENNYMORE 74910
PENNY PEACE *50473 NbC 40' blue/crm*
PENNY WISE 69069
PENNY WISE Barney(21) 1972 35' *(ex Natwester II)*
PENNYWISE II *Grp*
PENSAX 74591
PENSAX *see ELEMENT*
PENSGOOD 46441
PENSHALA 61942
PENSHAM MIST 73101
PENSYLVANIA YANKEE *see STRAW BEAR*
PENTLAND 89574 Motor vess'l 11.81m BW-NE

133

PEN-Y-LES-TOO 73236
PEPPA 50942
PEPPERCORN 53411
PEPPERCORN *NbST 55' mar/blue*
PEPPER POT 31012
PEPPERTREE 53321
PEPPERTREE 62935
PERARDUA 53890
PERCH 62624
PERCH 89180
PERCH Motor vessel 11.8m BW-NW
PERCH No 4 68362
PERCH ROCK 45581
PERCY 49644 R A & G A REDSHAW NEWBOLD VERDON NbT 60', d 30" mar/bl. B: 1990 Tony Redshaw (steelwork and f/o). Gardner 2L2 1942 hydraulic drive. Base Ashby canal. Colour scheme as Cowburn & Cowpar, Manchester (old trading boats). 24763
PERCY VEERE 78649
PEREGRIN 74929
PEREGRIN B8010
PEREGRINATOR II 53589
PEREGRINE 52264
PEREGRINE *NbT 60' grn/red*
PERERIN 45515
PERFECT LADY B1602
PERFICK B1541
PERFIDA 51887
PERI 60433
PE RICO 79718
PERIDOT 64708
PERISILAS 61137
PERIWINKLE 48516
PERMANENTLY CUT III 73376
PERNOTOO 68580
PEROSI 75238
PERPETUAL 72864
PERSEPHONE 76760
PERSEUS 71648
PERSEVERANCE 48192
PERSEVERANCE 48764 B. K. D. & C. J. WHITWORTH BRAUNSTON NbT 57' claret/blue. B: 1990 R&D Fabrications, Ollerton; f/o 1990-96 B Wells & B Whitworth. Perkins 4.108. Base Braunston marina. (F/o period not a mis-print!). 21366
PERSEVERANCE Dredger. Boat Museum
PERSHORE 79166
PERSIA *79697 NbC 40' blue/mar*
PERSOPHONE 75412
PERSUASION 61118
PERSUASION 78112
PERSUASION No. 923 *NbT 60' blue*
PERTAMA G10990
PERTH 66459
PERTH 500725
PERTH Barney(46) 1975 35' *(ex Melanie Jane)*
PERVAGOR 49564
PETAGIN 70725 Steam
PETAL No 2 50201
PETARA 500898
PETER DUCK 79642
PETER DUCK Barney(13) 1972 44'

PETEREL 054089 NbC 36' burgundy/blue. B: 1994 Club Line Cruisers Coventry, diy f/o 1995/96. Ford 1.8. Base R.Stort. *Peterel* is old English spelling of the seabird petrel; the name of a Royal Navy gunboat in which owner's father served on the Yangtze river. 20198
PETER FRIAR 74375
PETER JACK III 66666
PETER LEIGH 69669
PETER MICHAEL 71899
PETER PAN 52348
PETER PAN 52498
PETER PAN 72086
PETERS PRIDE 104489
PETRA Dredger 37'11" BW-OGU
PETREL 1320
PETREL No 81 70247 Saltley motor. Ex FMC/BW
PETRONELLA 78245
PETRONELLA No.1 *NbTug 60' mar*
PETUNIA 54612
PETUNIAS 73430
P FOR POPSIE B0331
PHALAROPE No 8 NbT 49' red/blue. B: 1987 M&N Boatbuilders. Base Wyre Mill Club, Lower Avon. "Well loved". 25978
PHANTOM 49333
PHANTOM 80832
PHEASANT 49302
PHEDORA 500154
PHICKLE PUMPKIN 62356 NbC 50', d 31" wh/bl/blue. B: 1972 - originally Colecraft / Rugby Boatbuilders (their 3rd boat), 1994 rebuild at Newbury Boat Co. - involving 80% of hull and complete cabin, original top plank (curved) remains. "Fitting out will take forever". Standard 1969 SR3 (abused and left alone and very faithful and reliable). Base Reading, K&A canal. Huge settee within - the cabin was built round it. Sank twice in first year - design fault. Awarded six Silver Swords in the 70s. 24776
PHIDASH 78740
PHILIA 52055
PHILOMEL 67735
PHILS FOLLY 52494
PHIPHTYPHUT 52104
PHOEBE 51924
PHOEBE 63307
PHOEBE 68591 Sm Ricky Star Cl butty. Ex GUCC. Boat Museum
PHOEBE 75922
PHOEBE 79677
PHOEBE 80938 Dredger 15m BW-CATM
PHOEBE MAY *NbT 50' red*
PHOENICIAN NbC 32' darkish red/wh. Hull lengthened and refurbished after fire, owners f/o - ongoing. Cub horizontally opposed twin hydraulic drive. Named from old pupils association of grammar school owners attended - Badge was a phoenix which will eventually appear on the side (Owners think they are the only *Phoenician* - but have seen lots of *Phoenix!*). 24877
PHOENIX 45133
PHOENIX 48683

PHOENIX 60656
PHOENIX 68638
PHOENIX 69297
PHOENIX 71847
PHOENIX 72104 NbT 50' grey/crm. B: 1983 Colecraft. Lister SW2M. Base residential mooring Highline Yachting, Slough Arm, GU. 21262
PHOENIX 73528
PHOENIX 77470
PHOENIX 79132
PHOENIX B1601
PHOENIX Tug BW-NW
PHOENIX *Trip boat - electric*
PHOENIX V 54432
PHROLIC 76109
PHYLLIS MAY 47746
PICA 71922 Motor
PICA PICA 83412
PICARE 65198

Using the *Listing*
A *"how to use"* guide is on pages 13-14
Frequent abbreviations inside front cover
Full list of abbreviations included in
Location Glossary at end of book

PICCANINI 46985
PICES 76382
PICES No 73 65578
PICKETTY WITCH 074891 Grp 24' crm. B: 1988 Atlanta 24. Marina 20 ob. Base Rodley, Leeds. 20182
PICTOR 40122
PICTOR 332 62713 Sm Woolwich Star Cl butty. Ex GUCC/BW
PIDDLEBROOK 74524
PIE 81573
PIECES OF EIGHT 53920
PIECES OF EIGHT 67986
PIECES OF EIGHT NbT 50' grn/red
PIED PIPER 53104
PIED PIPER 54884
PIED WAGTAIL 51461
PIG 54619
PIGLET 62180
PIKE LOCK BOAT Grp 15'6" wh/blue. B: 1979 Caracruise, Norwich. Ob (various). Base Eastington, Stroudwater canal. 24782
PILAR 62883
PILGRIM SOUL 46933
PILI-PALA 65577
PILOT 49153
PILOT III 64321 SEND RIVER WEY SEA RANGERS Training/pleasure Nb 50' lt blue. B: 1976 Seasteel, Nassington. 1.5 BMC. Base Send, R.Wey. Purpose built open plan for training Sea Rangers, sleeping 10 and officers. 24917
PILOT KING 53936
PIMPERNEL 53648
PIMPERNEL 68476
PIMPERNEL 73899
PINE Severner. Motor. Ex Severn & Canal CC

PINE Tug 6m 81801 BW-CATM
PINEWOOD Dayboat
PINK APPLE 76441
PINK LADY B1476
PINK PANTHER 79336
PINNER 62063
PINNER 80634 Motor boat 21m BW-LAP
PINNY 50131
PINTAIL 81642 Tug 19'6" BW-OGU
PINT POT 61790
PINTO 66460
PINVIN 50565
PIONEER 75665
PIONEER Barney(42) 1975 70'
PIONEER No 6 Tug
PIPE DREAM 73913
PIPEDREAM II 51249
PIP-EMMA 72402
PIPER 61617
PIPER 87770
PIPER'S PRIDE NbT 55' bl/red
PIPISTRELLE Barney(17) 1972 32'
PIPIT G14215 Steel day/weekend boat 17' blue/wh. B: 1994 Shotbolt Engineering, Ramsey, Cambs. 8hp Honda 4-str ob. One of 3 small steel craft with a distinctive appearance and numerous features designed by owner - see also *Puddleduck* and *Mega Pipit*. 00791
PIPIT 81656 Tug 6m BW-CATM
PIPIT V 73943
PIPNICK 69469
PIPPA NbT 45' blue
PIPPIN 49612
PIPPIN 49884 ROWDY BOAT CO. LONDON Nb 60' red/grn. B: 1989 Springer. Thornycroft. Base Willowtree Marina, Paddington Arm, GU. Interior re-fit to high standard of accommodation. 21254
PIPPIN 67307
PIPPIRI 49062
PIPPIT II 76127
PIRAAT 500207 BARBRIDGE Dutch barge style Nb 39', b 7' mar/blue. B: 1995 Mick Sivewright, Middlewich. Vetus 3-cyl 979cc. Base Barbridge marina. As *Bobby Owler*, featured in Waterways World Jan 1996. 22451
PIRATE 67801
PISCEAN LADY 53945
PISCES 49744
PISCES 54714
PISCES 73269
PISCES 78358
PISCES 88947
PISCES No 14 NbTug 30'
PISCES No 73 Sm Northwich Star Cl motor. Ex GUCC/BW
PISTLE 31633
PITCAIRN 60883
PIXY 64506
PLAIN FAYRE 71960
PLANET 61305 Sm Woolwich Star Cl motor. Ex GUCC. See *NEBULAE*
PLANKS 66033

135

PLANORBIS 72384 BOLLINGTON NbC wooden cabin on steel hull 45′ grn/red. B: 1979 Peter Nichols, f/o Roy Scott, Peterborough. BMC 1.5. Base Bollington, Macclesfield canal. Cabin has little tumblehome. Boat's name is Latin for the common water snail which is depicted on her sides. 23565
PLANXTY FREDERICK 70270
PLATYPUS 47506
PLATYPUS 64054
PLEIADES 72560
PLOD 48866
PLOVER 53407 BW-
PLOVER 68686 Saltley motor. Ex FMC/BW
PLOVER Tug 20′ BW-NW
PLUM 65136
PLUPERFECT 69253
PLUTO 52369
PLUTO 96554
PLUTO Nb 53′
POACHER 61798
POACHER 79849
POACHERS MOON 74323
POACHERS MOON 79259
POCAHONTAS 73751
POCHARD Tug 5.9m BW-NE
POCKET 52553
PODLER 69375
POETS DAT 66377
POGI 66892
POGLESWOOD 51438
POISON DWARF 68622
POL 6160 NbC 40′ grn/red. B: 1975(?) Colecraft, f/o Fenny Compton Marina (?). Yanmar 12hp 1 cyl. Base Lower Heyford, S.Oxford canal. 23535
POLAR 70412
POLARIS Sm Woolwich Star Cl butty. Ex GUCC
POLBATHIC 47023
POLEIDON 65580
POLE POLE 50818
POLE POLE 71269
POLÉ POLÉ NbT 60′ blue/red
POLGARA 50656
POLKADOT PANTS 30130
POLLY 60929
POLLY 62574
POLLY 64770
POLLY 66561
POLLY 100028
POLLYANNA 50447
POLLYANNA 51839
POLLYANNA 53534
POLLYANNA 97369
POLLY FOSTER 72777
POLLY HOLLYBUSH 46107
POLLY OTTER 73193
POLLY PERKINS 52358

POLLY PUGWASH 51010 BRAUNSTON NbT 50' grn. B: 1991 R.S. Narrowboats, Thorne. 3 cyl Lister Alpha Canal Star. Base Braunston marina. 23669
POLLY VEE 61827
POL'N PEP 62191
POLYNIA 71213
POLYNOMIAL 74137
POMPOM 93040
PONDOKIE 50460
PONDSKATER JACKSON & Co HALESOWEN NbT 41' crimson/blue. B: 1994 Delph Marine, Brierley Hill, diy f/o. Lister ST2 air cooled. Base Halesowen off Dudley No. 2 canal. 21224
POOKA 74990
POPACATAPETL 62484
POP-A-LAY 97213
POPLAR 60170 MIDDLEWICH NARROWBOATS No 4 Hire. NbST 70' grn/red. B: Coles Moreton Marine, Whaley Bridge (year not known), refit 1994/95 + converted to semi-trad Middlewich narrowboats. BMC 1.5. Ex Clare Cruisers Northwich (Trad); originally called *Middlewich*. 028734
POPPIES 71436
POPPY No.3 53849 P.G. & G. NORTH BRAUNSTON NbT 60' Donegal grn/Mauritius blue. B: 1993/4 Marque Narrowboats, Eccleshall, f/o by owner at base, external painting Utopia Unlimited, Braunston. Mitsubishi FMK 4. Base Braunston marina. Example of modern fully fitted narrow boat: Geko generator, Atlas Combi 800 watt inverter, solid chestnut t&g cladding above gunwhale, oak 'cathedral' doors to cupboards, Eberspacher heating/radiators, Squirrel stove, turned chestnut posts, chesnut table in dinette, "one poster" fixed double bed, hand made sofa and matching soft furnishings, 13 amp ring main, large fitted kitchen, dog kennel! Very quiet propulsion, minimal wash. 24836
POPPY 54023
POPPY 60430
POPPY 62941
POPPY 67007
POPPY 102107
POPPY Hire. NbC 48' blue/red. Base The Wyvern Shipping Co, Linslade, GU 00452
POPPY *NbC 40' red/bl*
POPPY HIL 52218
POPPY NICOLA B1062
PORCUPINE PIE 95645
PORJON 78238
PORTA COELI 45989 HARWICH NbT 50' apple grn/holly grn. B: 1988 RW Davis, Saul, Gloucester -hull no. 828. Thornycroft 4 cyl. Base Whilton marina, GU. Latin name meaning Gate of Heaven. 22490
PORTHCERI 51819 *NbT 45' red*
PORTIA *NbC 50' mar/wh*
PORTREE 64152
PORT SUNLIGHT 75295
PORT SUNRISE No.1 *Trip boat*
POTTER 48787

POTTER 73276 139 STOKE ON TRENT NbT 50' deep royal grn/green paddock. B: 1985 Stoke-on-Trent Boatbuilders. BL 1.8/Thornycroft. Base Festival marina, Stoke-on-Trent. If not the first, then very close, shared owner Nb on canal system. Featured Waterways World in 1985(?). 25932
POTTERING 52224
POTT LUCK 65311
POTTSONN 45195
POTWESHERS ONLY 46702
POVERTY STREET 64059
POWYS 500878
POYNTON Motor vessel BW-NW
PRAVEEN - Lady of Fiji *103420 Grp Waverider*
PRECIOUS MOMENTS 53835 B.G. & M.A. TAYLOR MIDDLEWICH NbT 60' blue/ sandpiper. B: 1989/90 Chappell & Wright, f/o Lofthouse & Wilson. BMC/Thornycroft 1.8, PRM gearbox, Aqua-drive. Base Middlewich. Extended forward well deck used for entertaining with patio type garden furniture. 25961
PRELUDE II 102778
PREMIER CRU 103212
PRESIDENT No 195 REGISTERED AT BIRMINGHAM 1212 FELLOWS MORTON CLAYTON LTD 1396 *(Watermans Hall number)*. Floating museum piece. Iron side, elm bottom Josher in original 1909 format. 71'6", b 6'11", d 3'4" bl/red/crm. B: May 1909 FMC Yard at Saltley, Birmingham at a cost of £600. One of 31 steamers built by the company between 1989 and 1931. Steam - coal fired cochran dry back boiler powering a contemporary (1900) simple twin cylinder engine driving 33" propeller. The power unit took up much valuable cargo space for which there was room for only 12 tons. Operated 'fly' to timetable between London and the Midlands (54 hours London-Birmingham using 1 ton of coke). Base Black Country Museum, Dudley. Converted to diesel (Bolinder) 1925. Sold to Ernest Thomas, Walsall 1946. Sold or leased to George Matthews 1948; to Docks & Inland Waterways Board 1948. Sold as wreck 1973 to Malcolm Braine who restored it to steam. Now owned by Black Country Museum and maintained and operated around the system by the Friends of *President*. 261074
PRESIDENT II Motor vessel Mtce boat BW-NW
PRESTIGE 49776
PRESTIGE Hire. NbC 66' red/grn. Base Rose Narrowboats, Brinklow, N.Oxford canal. 026716
PRESTONIAN Motor vessel BW-NW
PRIAM 73445
PRIDE OF ALFION B1224
PRIDE OF CILAN 74120
PRIDE OF COLLINGHAM Crane boat 32m BW-NE
PRIDE & JOY 500047
PRIDE & JOY G11588
PRIDE OF HENLOW 63499
PRIDE OF HOLDERNESS 73800
PRIDE OF LINCOLN Crane boat 21.34m BW-NE
PRIDE OF LONDON 82189 BW-LON
PRIDE OF NORWOOD BW-LON

137

WHAT MAKES THE STEAMERS STEAM?

If *President* and *Kildare* hold you up at busy Summer locks you could fume but more likely you will find them a fascinating piece of living history. Here's the insides of *President*, a proud survivor of a fleet which did the 'fly' runs from London to the Midlands early this century, carrying a relatively small payload because of the space needed for engine and fuel.

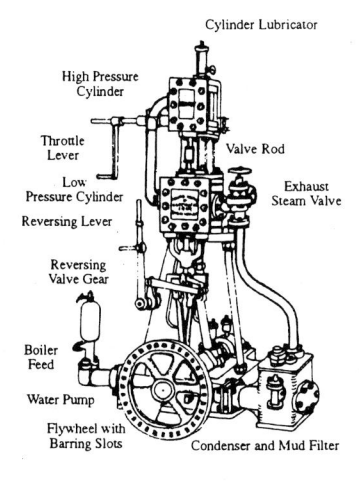

President's original compound steam engine built by Fellows Morton and Clayton to a design by W.H. and A.H. Haines of Birmingham. Engine 11 bhp at 200 rpm.

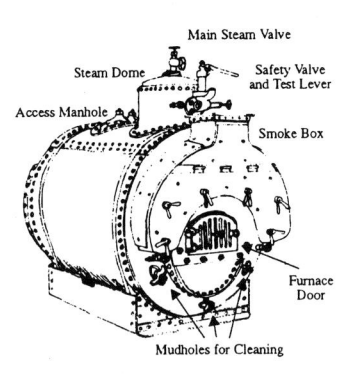

President's original riveted 'Scotch' return tube boiler built by Ruston Proctor and Company of Lincoln. Boiler Pressure 150 psi.

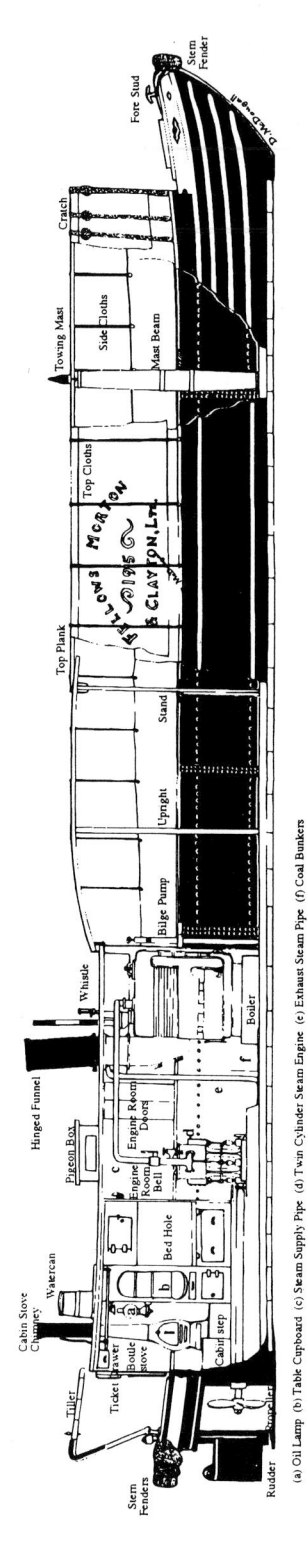

(a) Oil Lamp (b) Table Cupboard (c) Steam Supply Pipe (d) Twin Cylinder Steam Engine (e) Exhaust Steam Pipe (f) Coal Bunkers

Reproduced from leaflet about *President* and *Kildare*

[courtesy The Friends of *President*]

PRIDE OF PENSBY 64045
PRIDE OF SANDWELL 75768
PRIDE OF SEFTON 76785 Hire for day trips and holidays for handicapped passengers. Wide beam steel with large teak deck forward, 38 tons gross, 60', b 11', d 2'8" blue/bl. B: 1982 British Shipbuilders Birkenhead. Perkins 4.108. Base Haskayne L&L canal. All ramps on board - no steps; 2 passenger cabins and 1 for crew; all facilities for passenger comfort and welfare. Operated as independent charity with help and financial support from public & private benefactors. 2011
PRIDE OF SUZANNE 48577
PRIDE OF THE MIDLANDS 64169
PRIDE OF WALES 51373 No. 1 S & E WILLIAMS ANGLESEY NbT 50', d 30" royal grn/cr. B: 1991 TT Marine Doncaster. Lister Petter Alpha 3 cyl 30hp 3000rpm. Base Golden Nook Farm, SU canal. Colours and finish of external paintwork attract favourable comment from passers by. 23651
PRIMERO 69168
PRIMO 47183
PRIMROSE Hire. NbC 40' blue/red. Base The Wyvern Shipping Co, Linslade, GU 00458
PRIMROSE 49891
PRIMROSE 54567
PRIMROSE 64707
PRIMROSE 72088
PRIMROSE 72164
PRIMROSE LEAGUE *500378 NbT 40' yel/bl*
PRIMULA 77109
PRINCE No 1 63983 Motor. Ex Barlow
PRINCE ALBERT 48250 BRAUNSTON NbC 52' red/blue/cr. B: 1990 Pat Buckle, Stibbington, part f/o by original owner. 1.5 BMC CB Marine. Base Braunston marina. 2086
PRINCE ALBERT No 2 52054
PRINCE CASPIAN 54596
PRINCE HENRY 54878
PRINCE REGENT 45967
PRINCE RUPERT 74540
PRINCE RUPERT *NbC 50' wh/blue*
PRINCESS 53910
PRINCESS 61370
PRINCESS 73257
PRINCESS 77049
PRINCESS 91121
PRINCESS No 5 52180
PRINCESS ANNE 74860
PRINCESS ANNE 78460
PRINCESS CATHERINE 75601
PRINCESS OF CHILTERNS 71944
PRINCESS REBECCA 61097 NbT 48' grn/burgundy. B: 1970 Les Allen & Sons, Oldbury (having ordered boat in 1969, Les Allen unfortunately died before completion). Lister SR2 (original). Base Middle Level Navigation. 25926
PRINCESS SOYARA 50109
PRINCETHORPE 75059
PRINCE WILLIAM 52098
PRINTERS DEVIL 51459
PRINTERS DEVIL 79004

PRINTERS END *NbC 35' blue*
PRIORY 53611 NbC 36' dk blue/mar. B: 1994 Springer. Base Linslade, GU. This was the very last boat built by Springers before they collapsed - it was put on the water by them 48 hours before the receivers moved in. Built essentially as a "marketing tool" for owner's company, Priory Records, a specialist classical recording company. Maiden trip was Debdale Wharf to Hopwas laden with recording equipment to be used at Lichfield Cathedral. Pictures taken of choristers on roof, after recording, used in hi-fi publications. Now used to take clients for lunch at The Globe in Linslade. 25944
PRIVATE DANCER 97008
PROBATICA 71159
PROCRASTINATION 76634
PROCYON 72460
PROGRESS 47413
PROGRESS 62714
PROGRESS 76267
PROGRESS Wide motor. Ex GUCC
PROGRESS *NbT 70'*
PROMISE Hire. NbC 40' grn/yel. B: 1980 Godalming Narrowboats on Colecraft hull. BMC 1.5. Base Farncombe Boathouse, R.Wey. 00379
PROMISE No. 4 74799 G & G WHITTLE PYRFORD NbT 58' Mauritius blue. B: 1988 David Piper, Stoke on Trent. Vetus Mitsubishi 4. About half way through 5 year cruise of the system. 23753
PROMISE ME TOO 53443
PROPER JOB 52209 ROGER & ANN HAYES KNOWLE HALL WHARF NbT 60', d 2'7" grn/red. B: 1992 Les Allen Shell, f/o Stephen Goldsbrough. National DM2, circa 1936 and original apart from oil pump and gearbox. Base Braunston marina. Bow thruster, interior well equipped inc deep freeze. 24807
PROSPECT 50202
PROSPECT 67659
PROSPECT OF BRADWAY 79084
PROSPERO 48917
PROSPERO 67517
PROTEA *NbT 45' blue*
PROTEAM 31146
PROTEMPORE 49719
PROTEUS 45417
PROTEUS 61416
PROTEUS 64336
PROTEUS *NbT 60' red*
PROTO 3 71107
PROVIDENCE 45428
PRUDENCE 47074
PRUDENCE 62242
PRUDENCE 74646
PRUDENCE B8000
PSALM 31475
PSALM 50811
PSALTER 76252 SHARDLOW Nb 57' dk blue/red. B: 1982 (at 45') Sagar Marine, Brighouse; f/o by first owner; extended and additional f/o 1992 by Dobsons of Shardlow. BL 1500cc. Base Wheaton Aston, SU canal. Name

derived from lane in Sheffield in which present owners used to live. 22418
PSMITH II 500963 M C SMITH CALF HEATH NbC 57' grn/blue. B: 1996 John White, f/o Triton. Lombardini 4 cyl. Base Staffs & Worcs canal. Two matching electric/instrument panels dual senders from engine for temperature, oil pressure, etc. Named after a P G Wodehouse character (silent 'P'). 23694
PTARMIGAN 69966
PTARMIGAN 74955
PTARMIGAN *NbC 40' grn/crm*
PUB CRAWLER 48877
PUB CRAWLER II 46315
PUB CRAWLER No 4 53440
PUB CRAWLER 5 500359
PUDDING 69097
PUDDING No 2 75407
PUDDLE 71682
PUDDLE DUCK 77630
PUDDLEDUCK Steel day/weekend boat 18'6" blue/wh. B: 1990 Bead Engineering Kings Lynn. 15hp Suzuki 2-str ob. Base Hartford marina, Huntingdon. One of 3 small craft with distinctive appearance designed by original owner - see also *Pipit* and *Mega Pipit*. 00790
PUDDLEDUCK 47319
PUDDLEDUCK 60618
PUDDLEDUCK 79332
PUDDLEDUCK 100089
PUDDLEDUCK 104001
PUDDLE JUMPER 51182
PUDDLE JUMPER 60939
PUFFIN 52994
PUFFIN 62357
PUFFIN 64710
PUFFIN 64930
PUFFIN 65921
PUFFIN 71785
PUFFIN 73754
PUFFIN 74930
PUFFIN 93073
PUFFIN 103713
PUFFIN X713 Grp 16'6", b 6', d 9" blue/wh. B: 1976app. Microplas Ltd, Mitcham. Honda 10hp ob. Trailed - used on Broads. Serial no. 23. 20197
PUFFIN N2305   054625 NbC 23' blue/red. B: 1990 Springer (Waterbug) 9.9hp Honda 4-str ob. Base Ely, R.Great Ouse. 23648
PUFFIN No 35 47828
PUFFIN *NbT 35' red/grn*
PUG 48874
PUG 63401
PUGWASH *NbC 30' red/blue*
PULEKA 46234
PUMPERNICKLE 54624
PUPPIS 64042 Sm Northwich Star Cl butty. Ex GUCC/BW/WW
PURBECK Motor vessel Mtce boat 38'9" BW-NW
PURBECK PRINCESS 49879
PURE GENIUS
PURTON 47039
PURTON Lg Northwich Town Cl. motor

PUSSKA III 91544
PUSSYFOOT 96812
PUTNAL FIELD 71658
PUT PUT 97936
PUZZLE 97390
PYGMALION 46578
PYMMA 103151
PYRITES 62983
PYTHON BW-LON

Is Your Boat In It?
Is the Entry Accurate?
Please see page 12 to find out how to get included or amended in the next edition

---

Q

A well travelled Queen in much royal company, a conversion and Quiet Quests

QE III 65041
QH II 78935
QUACKERS 52359
QUACKERS 66346
QUAIL 500048
QUANDO B0129
QUANTOCK 75250
QUARK 500692
QUARRY BANK MILL 68419
QUASI 53573
QUAYS 75679
QUEEN 76499
QUEEN *(class)* Hire fleet (12 boats) NbC 40-54' B: 1988 onwards S W Durham Steelcraft, f/o Simolda Ltd. Base Simolda Ltd, Basin End, Nantwich, SU canal. All have front galleys. 205
QUEEN ANGELA 52944
QUEEN ANNE *see FAVERSHAM*
QUEEN B 46598
QUEEN BEE 50435
QUEEN BEE 103353
QUEEN BOADICEA 50076
QUEENBOROUGH 53584
QUEEN CAROLINE 48520
QUEEN DEBORAH 45816
QUEEN HALEY 53884
QUEENIE 103730
QUEEN IONA 75200
QUEEN JANE 45815
QUEEN JEAN 50126
QUEEN JUNE AMELIA 54146
QUEEN LUCIA 46743
QUEEN MICHELLE 47608
QUEEN MOLLY 75776
QUEEN OF CUMBRIA 72925
QUEEN OF HEARTS 100445

QUEEN OF SHEBA 52661 ALAN & SARAH PADWICK NbC 61' navy blue/yel. B: 1992-93 Marque Narrowboats Eccleshall, f/o Stephen Goldsbrough. Mermaid Meteor II based on Ford XLD 1.8. Base Devizes, K&A. Portraits of Sheba, owners' former golden retriever on each side. Just about every corner of connected system covered between 1993-96 (4500 miles) with only a few bits left to do! But now bought a house! Featured in many magazine articles. Story of name in Waterways World Oct 95. 22515

"portraits of Sheba on each side"

QUEEN OF SHEBA 67610
QUEEN SAMANTHA 48519
QUEEN SARAH 74032
QUEENSTOWN 500830
QUEEN VALERIE see GENISTA No.3
QUENTA 69077
QUERCUS 75172
QUESLET 71945
QUEST 51364
QUEST 53641
QUEST 70166
QUEST 78204
QUEST 78783
QUEST II 70522
QUEST III 60573
QUEST IV 60319
QUESTOR 54639 Motor vessel BW-NE
QUESTOR THEWS 73946
QUICKLY 75196
QUIET WATERS 73170
QUIET WATERS 75037
QUINCE 75962
QUINQUERENE 61591
QUINTESSENCE 47851
QUINTET 52677
QUINTET II 70849
QUINTONIA 65858
QUO VADIS 70527 Nb 54'7" red/grn. B: 1976 Ted Farr. Perkins 3HD 46 / Newage hydraulically operated reverse reduction, 23" prop. Originally built as a steamer, converted to diesel. 21308

R

Panoramic views on this Trip, a not-so-humble mini fleet, fitting out instructions here. Meet "Otis". A campaigning diminutive Josher, true pioneers, a bespoke new hull, disabled people welcome on board these craft and a circumnavigation of East Anglia

RA II 65493
RABBIT 45906
RABBIT 80029 BW-
RABLE 101927
RABOSA B1783
RABY ENTERPRISE 51388
RACHAEL ROSE NbC 45' blue
RACHEL 053616 Wide beam 40', b 10'6" dk grn/red. B: 1987 Springer. Base Lower Foxhanger Wharf, nr Devizes, K&A canal. Initially called the *Irianne* and operated on R.Thames by Iris and Mike Harvey who fitted her out to a high standard especially for families with a wheelchair user; has wide access ramps, lift, etc. Now operated by the Bruce Charitable Trust. 00561
RACHEL 70216
RACHEL 72348
RACHEL 84781
RACHEL B1592
RACHEL NbT 50' blue
RACHEL Barney(58) 1976 52' (ex Muskoka and Queen of the Nile)
RACHEL II NbT 30' red/grn
RACHEL II 49212
RACHEL CATHERINE 54977
RACHEL CATHERINE NbT 70' grn
RACHEL E 63959
RACHEL & EMILY 84652
RACHEL LOUISE B0751
RADIANCE M 74275
RADIANT Mid Northwich motor. Ex GUCC/BW
RADIO HAM 71227
RAFFETY 65271
RAFFLES 62192
RAFIKI 49164
RAFT OF CHORES 52058 K R & C A HILL NbST 46' dk blue/mar. B: 1992 Colecraft, owner f/o. Beta BV 1505 35hp. Base Crick marina, GU-Leics. 2084
RAGAMUFFIN 45641
RAG DOLL 52021 NbT 25' red/grn
RAGGED ROBIN 65923
RAGGED ROBIN 71681
RAGGY CASTLE 77672
RAGLAN 60650
RAGLAN CASTLE Hire. NbC 45' grn/yel. Electric propulsion. Base Castle Narrowboats, Gilwern. 00215
RAGMAR ONE 60129
RAGTIME DANCER B0625
RAILWAY INN 60760
RAINBIRD 65359
RAINBOW 63238
RAINBOW 66526
RAINBOW 76082

RAINBOW Hire. NbC 60' red/grn. Base Rose Narrowboats, Brinklow, N.Oxford canal. 026711
RAINBOW *NbT 20' red/grn*
RAINBOW II 68461
RAINBOW II B0190
RAINBOW COVENANT 47117
RAINBOW QUEST 75048
RAINBOWS END 74467
RAINBOWS END N5102
RAJAH BROOKE 070771 NAPTON NbC 42' dk blue/crm. B: 1984 Springer. BMC 1.5. Base Napton, Engine Arm, S.Oxford canal. 23655
RAKES PROGRESS 73971
RALEIGH 49937
RALFRED 67098
RALLI-ROUND 71380
RALPH *Nb 26'*
RALWYN 69001
RAM Mtce boat dumb 9.15m BW-NW
RAMBLER 45721
RAMBLER 61961
RAMBLER 64109
RAMBLER 69039
RAMBLER 71274
RAMBLER Hire. NbC 50' red/grn. Base Rose Narrowboats, Brinklow, N.Oxford canal. 026708
RAMBLER I 85040
RAMBLING ROSE 45201
RAMBLING ROSE 61415
RAMBLING ROSE 68944
RAMBLING ROSE 71823
RAMBLING ROSE 91200
RAMBLING ROSE Barney(12) 1972 50'
RAMILLES 73319
RAMLAITUI 71738
RAMONA 51751
RAMSDALE 71665
RAMSGATE 073235 CLIFTON CRUISERS Hire. NbC 41' grn/crm. B: 1986 R&D Fabrications, f/o Clifton Cruisers. BL 1.5. Base Clifton Wharf, Rugby, N.Oxford canal. 025678
RANA FELIX 47841
RANBER 67524
RANBY Weedcutter 5.5m BW-NE
RANGER 46413
RANGER Patrol craft 30' BW-OGU
RANGER I Patrol craft BW-NW
RANNOCH B0006
RAPSCALLION 45676 WELTON HYTHE Nb 48' grn/crm. B: 1988 Colecraft/Rory Marine. Isuzu/Beta 1524cc 3 cyl. Base Weltonfield, GU-Leics. Traditional f/o. 22400
RARE AULD TIMES 79177
RASCAL 80118
RASCAL B1205
RASTEAU *72549 Nb 30' grn/red*
RATTIE 100209
RATTY 62398
RATTY 65506
RATTY 98632
RAVEN 49825
RAVEN 49845
RAVEN 65085
RAVEN 68142

RAVEN 73839
RAVEN 74503
RAVEN 77346
RAVEN *Nb 40' blue*
RAVENSWOOD II Barney(36) 1974 35'
RAWLINSON END 54545
RAY 63503
RAY Motor. Ex Ovaltine
RAYMOND 78921 Butty. Ex Barlows
RAYNARDINE 75394
RAY OF LIGHT 71497
RAZZLE 93227
RBOTE 67928 BRAUNSTON Nb 28' grn/red. B: 1974 Springer, family f/o. Lister 2 cyl ST2. Base Braunston marina. New hull needed in 1992 - Springer made new bottom section and dropped boat into it - welded all together and now very satisfactory and solid. 20104
REA Motor boat 12m BW-LAP
REALITY 70737
REALTA 61809
REARSBY 62301
REASON HILL 74402
REBECARR *NbT 50'*
REBECCA 047504 Hired to groups of disabled people with their carers. Wide beam 61', b 10'6" dk grn/red. B: 1988 Steelcraft, Old, Northants. Lister. Base Great Bedwyn, K&A canal. Especially built for comfort and convenience of disabled people. Operated by the Bruce Charitable Trust. 00562
REBECCA 68572
REBECCA 72234
REBECCA LOUISE 66566
REBEKAH No 2 75691
REBEL 73290
REBEL LEADER 48028
RECALDE 48159
RECKLESS TOAD 74668
RED ADMIRAL 63607
RED ADMIRAL 74926
REDBEARD 65346
RED DOG 65233
RED DRAGON 75470
RED DRAGON 102662
REDFERN 71608
REDFERN 76371
RED JASMINE 500375
RED LADY 84852
RED LADY 101528
RED MIST *48387 NbT 50' blue*
RED MOUSE 31636
REDNECK *NbC 20' red*
RED OTTER 53742 NbT 57' blue/red. B: 1995 Evans & Company, Hixon, Staffs. Kingfisher 26. Base South Island marina, Enfield, R.Lee. Internal refurbishment proceeding plus external re-paint incl. boatman's cabin panels. 251009
RED ROSE 79787
REDSANDS LADY 66106
REDSKIN 79603
RED SQUIRREL 46619
REED 53383
REEL CASTLE 64430
REEVE 46235

142

REFLECTED SUN 51326 THE KENYON FAMILY BRAUNSTON NbST 20m grn/red. B: 1992 Colecraft. 1.8 Thornycroft. Base Braunston marina. Name from a poem ... "If all reflected sun was truely silver upon the sea, we would be rich from travelling". 25935
REFLECTIONS *NbT 40' blue*
REFLECTIONS 45757
REFLECTIONS 46814
REFLECTIONS 54891
REFLECTIONS *75965 NbC 50' blue/crm*
REFLECTIONS 78010
REFLECTIONS II 53865
REGAL AN 69495
REGAL STAR 046161 Hire. NbC 63' grn/red. BMC 1.8. Base Evesham Marina, R.Avon. 0371040
REGAL STAR 54028
REGENT 50042
REGENT 70259
REGENT Tug
REGENT Motor vessel 52'6" BW-OGU
REGGIE GEORGE 73878
REGULUS No 343 Mid Northwich Star Cl butty. Ex GUCC
REINA DEL MAR 50909
REIVER 53806
RELAINE 74432
RELIANCE 53627
RELIANCE *Wey barge preserved*
RELIANCE No 6 Butty
REMEDIS 52932
REMIND ME 50090
REMUS 79406
RENAISSANCE 66738
RENDEZVOUS 53143
RENEBECCA 70874
RENEE 53821
RENFREW Lg Woolwich Town Cl motor. Ex GUCC/BW/BL
RENHOLD 71186
RENOWN Butty
RENTON 80577 BW-
RENTON Lg Woolwich Town Cl motor. Ex GUCC
REPTILES 66348
RESOLUTION 073380 NbC 46' blue/red. B: 1986/87 Colecraft. Thornycroft. Base Stenson marina, T&M canal. 22523
RESOURCE Flat 21m BW-LAP
RESURGENT 80485
RESURGENT Flat 8m BW-LAP
RETREAT 47179
RETURN 31642
REVALINA G11401
REV CATHY MILFORD 47774 CATHERINE AND DAVID APPERLEY BRIDGE NbC 56' grn/red. B: 1989/90 South West Durham Steelcraft, f/o Baltimore Boats, Todmorden. Lister Petter 1.4 3 cyl. Base Snaygill Boats, Skipton, L&L. 23540
REVELLER 64100
REVENGE 65572
REWARD 80496 Flat 11m BW-LAP
REWARD 104300

REYNARD 70626 NbT 48' midnight blue/mar. B: 1984 Ward, Lancashire, f/o unknown. Arona 295 2 cyl 1356cc (Italian). Base Greenwood, Calder & Hebble Navigation. One of the very few boats to cruise newly re-opened Rochdale Canal, Sowerby Bridge to Littleborough, present limit of navigation (8-10 July 96). 22486
R G BAR G 52786 LYDIATE NbC 41' navy blue/bl. B: 1993 John White, Garston, Liverpool, self f/o. Beta BV 1205 1200cc 30bhp @ 3600rpm, Hurth HBW 100 gearbox. Base MMBC Lydiate, L&L. Open plan, Mikuni skirting board central heating. 20149
RHAPSODY 53224 R & R PICKFORD ADLINGTON BRAIDBAR BOAT SERVICES No.18 NbT 50' Donegal grn/bl. B: 1993 Jonathan Wilson, f/o Braidbar Boat Services, Poynton. Thornycroft 1800cc. Base Lyme View marina, Adlington, Macclesfield canal. Trad roses/lettering on sides. 21210
RHAYADER 099535 GOYTRE Grp 20' crm. B: early-1970s Norman (North Manchester Plastics). Mercury ob. Base Goytre Wharf marina. First boat through Cwmbran tunnel in about 50 years (1st Apr 1995 in a sponsored bow haul) to reach the lowest end of the Mon/Brec canal at "5 locks" (furthest navigable at present). Hoping to be first cruiser to use the Crumlin Arm from Pontywaun (scenic drive) to the "Darren" at Risca. 20164
RHIANNON 47488
RHIANNON 71527
RHIANNON *NbT 50' blue/brown*
RHIANNON JANE 70729
RHONDA 75285
RHONWEN 48758
RHUM ONE 77508
RHYDDID 50972
RHYTHM ON THE RIVER 51390
RIA II 70926
RIBBLE 76401
RIBBLE VALLEY 79209
RIBBY 078188 Restaurant Boat. NbT 55' red/grn. B: 1989 Hancock & Lane kit - built and f/o by owner. 2.5 BMC. Base The Old Wharf, Tevor, Llangollen canal. 01123
RICHARD ARKWRIGHT 61914
RICH JIM 53456
RICHMOND 63170 FOXTON BOAT SERVICES LTD Hire. NbST all steel (now) 54' rotavator orange/dk admiralty grey. B: 1976 Fernie Steel (special). Lister SR3. Base Foxton bottom lock. 0381078
RICHMOND CASTLE 71489
RICKMAN B1445
RICOLA 67630
RICOLA *NbT 50' crm*
RIC-SHER-MARDA 51063
RIDGEWAY 62051
RIGAL 45919
RIGAL 69363
RIGHTEOUS 50576
RIGSBY 48363
RIMA 71762
RINGWRAITH 85288

Rallies ... Large ... Medium ...

The IWA National Festival at Waltham Abbey, River Lee

Annual Ashby Canal Rally at Sutton Cheney Wharf

and Small

Local event at Hickling on the restored section of the Grantham canal which has yet to be re-connected to the River Trent

RALLIES - Either love 'em or stay well away. But there's no denying their effectiveness at campaigning and bringing the cause of our waterways to public notice

RIO No 1 B1501
RIO GRANDE 102185
RIOS 45634
RIPON Motor vessel + crane !4.95m BW-NE
RIPPLE 102460
RIPPLES 45310
RIQUET 78648
RISI 71398
RITE OF SPRING 75197
RIVENDELL 46396
RIVENDELL 71132
RIVER & CASTLE 52445
RIVERDALE 78691
RIVERDANCE B1869 NbC 25' Oxford blue/gold. B: 1992 Venetian, f/o Mick Sivewright. Vetus 10hp. Base "Ye Olde No. 3" (Coaching house near Lymm), Bridgewater canal. Can often be seen during extensive cruising in the Cheshire area with "Otis" the parrot who sits in his cage hanging in the well deck. 22470
RIVER KING 61404
RIVER LADY NbC 50' navy blue. B: 1978 Springer, Mkt Harborough. Petter PH2 air cooled, Petter/Newage 2:1 g'box. Base Middle Level Cruising Club, R.Nene. "Bog standard". 22485
RIVERMEAD 49789
RIVER PRINCESS see *OCEAN GYPSY*
RIVER PRINCESS see *WAYFARER*

RIVER RANGER 70685 Motor vessel BW-NE
RIVER ROSE 67280
RIVER SCOUT 78793
RIVERTON 68089
RIVER VOLE 75004
RIVERWEED 51414
RIVETS 5000 EDWIN W FASHAM BIRMINGHAM Small open boat - half scale Josher Nb hull constructed of aluminium on cast aluminium frame 10', b 3'6", d 12" (loaded). B: 1966-67 in owner and brothers garage in Birmingham. Petter AA1 single cyl diesel mounted inboard on a quick release system for ease of transport: ahead only clutch drive, 2.5:1 red. on 12" prop. Base Birmingham or Huntingdon. Fore end and stern are to half scale but length $^1/_7$th scale to make it practical for trailing. Believed unique. Constructed on traditional lines - all rivetted (5000 rivets - hence name) but aluminium used for portability and durability. Has been on many restoration campaign cruises in late 60s/early 70s, e.g. Pocklington and Caldon canals and bits of BCN. 22498
R.KNOBBY 47257
ROACH 72958 Yarwoods Fish Cl motor. Ex FMC/BW
ROACH Motor vessel BW-NW
ROACHES 65481

ROAD RUNNER 71022
ROALD AMUNDSEN 72141
ROAMA 68038
ROAMA 78073
ROAMA Ex LMS
ROAMER 45748
ROAMIN IN THE GLOAMIN 75167
ROANOAKE 45567
ROBANNA 103990
ROBBO II 46902
ROBELLE 67458 *NbT 30' red/grn*
ROBERT 60971
ROBERT Tug. Ex BCN
ROBERTA 50709
ROBERT AICKMAN Purpose built welded steel hopper barge with removable 20 ton capacity hold. Used for navigation maintenance by the Lower Avon Navigation Trust Ltd. 40', b 10', d 9". B: 1982 Watercraft, Evesham. Propulsion by Tug "City" *(see entry)*. Base Mill Wharf, Wyre Piddle, R.Avon. 033910
ROBERT MYLNE 64941
ROBERT WALPOLE 64404
ROBIN 45880
ROBIN 46452
ROBIN 71142
ROBIN HOOD 65435
ROBIN HOOD 67191
ROBIN HOOD 74289
ROBIN HOOD Tug 11.58m BW-NE
ROBINS NEST 52731
ROBLLOYDLOUI 54240
ROBYN 68889
ROCHDALE 70698
ROCHESTER CLIFTON CRUISERS Hire. NbST 60' grn/crm. B: 1996/97 Southwest Durham Steelcraft, f/o Clifton Cruisers. BL 1.5. Base Clifton Wharf, Rugby, N.Oxford canal. 025686
ROCHESTER CASTLE 65315
ROCKINGHAM 60703
ROCKINGHAM 75420
ROCK N ROLL 50794
ROCK PARTRIDGE 52780
ROCKY 63025
ROCKY 77600
ROCKY RACOON 62952
RODANNA 30854
RODESSA 66865
RODING 79882
RODMELL No 3 72198
RODNEY II 64370
ROEBUCK *NbT 40'*
ROGER Motor. Ex Harvey Taylor/BL
ROGUE III 74237 *NbT 35' grn*
ROISIN DUBH B1685
ROJANE No.3 *68529 NbT 40' blue/mar*
ROLASSE 61136
ROLLYBRICK 50665
ROMA 47536
ROMA 68744
ROMA 80950
ROMA 102288
ROMA II 78226

ROMAJEAN 68741 D & J HALL BARTON NbC 48' grn/red. B: 1981 Colecraft. BL/CT Marine 1.8L keel cooled. Base - bottom of garden. Designed/built for comfortable extended cruising. Small steel mast mounted aft of accommodation. Named after sons in chronological order: Rodney, Martin, Jeremy, Andrew. 20116
ROMAN LADY 72563 DJ & JM SAADY & FAMILY GREENHAM LOCK NbC 60' red/grn. B: 1985 Colecraft, f/o not known, completed by present owner. Thornycroft 108. Base Cottage Basin, Greenham Lock, K&A canal. Standard Colecraft cruiser bought semi-derelict in 1988. Attended many important events, e.g. re-opening and back-pump opening of Caen Hill. 22428
ROMANY 50485 SSR 60822 Drascombe "Coaster" Grp yawl rigged, used with ob on canals 21'9", b 6'8", d 1' to 4' (with centreplate) wh/lt blue. B: 1991 Honnor Marine, Totnes, Devon. Honda 4-str 8 hp ob (+ sails and oars). Base Coventry Cruising Club, Wyken Arm, N.Oxford canal. Has circumnavigated East Anglia (R.Nene, The Wash, North Sea, R.Thames and GU). Easiest boat to steer on canals with centreplate half lowered. Difficult to use sails on canals (it's either dead against, dead before or missing altogether) but elsewhere the small fishing boat lines, the main lugsail, jib and bermudan mizzen offer good sailing. Invites favourable comment everywhere. 22393
ROMANY 75341
ROMANY GIRL 053795 NbT 42' dk grn/mar. B: 1994 Midland Canal Centre, Stenson. Lister LPWS 3. Base Stenson marina, T&M canal. Photograph frequently seen in MCC advertising for their 'Sapphire' class narrowboat. 23551
ROMANY PRINCESS 71796
ROMAR II 46187
ROME 51028 GR & EM BOOTH WOLVERLEY NbT 60' red/grn. B: 1991 Les Allen & Sons, Oldbury, f/o Graham Booth, Wolverley. Lister HW2. Base Wolverley, S&W canal. Fitting out featured in "The New Narrow Boat Builders Book". *(An admirable introduction and inspiration for many amateur fit-outs, certainly mine - compiler).* Exhibited at the first inland Boat Show at Nottingham in 1993. Won the Marion Munk Rose Bowl at 1995 National Festival, Chester. 23595
ROMNEY 54822
ROMULUS 45798
ROMULUS 65690
RONALDSWAY 61657
RONCHER 71523
RONDO 47106
RONDO 103358
RONELEAN 45975
ROOK 49834
ROPE 51281
ROSABELLA 48204
ROSA CANINA 70555
ROSALYN 77723
ROSAMUND THE FAIR *Restaurant boat*
ROSAN *NbST 50' mar/blue*

146

ROSANNA 68494
ROSANNA 76333
ROSANNE 46043
ROSE 45913 THE ASHBY TRIP Trip/restaurant boat. NbT 72' navy/burgundy. B: 1988 Steelcraft, Northants. BMC 1.8. Base Sutton Cheney Wharf, Ashby canal. This trip boat features 12 windows each side + 2 portholes. 015287
ROSE 65872
ROSE 70167
ROSE 71972
ROSE 73058
ROSE 75005
ROSE 94013
ROSE B1395
ROSE 61364 Hotel
ROSE III 61334
ROSE-AL 500080 *NbT 50' grn*
ROSE ALICE 78768
ROSE ANNE 65235
ROSEATE TERN 51462
ROSEBAY 79676
ROSEBERRY 47571
ROSEBERRY 54864
ROSEBUD Waterbus
ROSEBUD 47206
ROSEBUD 80324
ROSEBUD II 47296
ROSE CLEMANSON No.1 77894 *NbT 42' grn/red*
ROSEDALE 65011
ROSEDALE *NbC 40' blue/grey*
ROSEDENE 74303
ROSE EMILY 049991 Hire. NbST 50' navy blue/lt blue. B: 1991 Brummagem Boats. Lister LPWS. Base Sally Boats Bradford on Avon marina. 013229
ROSELLE 71264
ROSEMARY 49103
ROSEMARY *63151 NbT 50' crm/grn*
ROSEMARY 69755
ROSEMARY 75429
ROSEMARY *NbT 50' grn*
ROSEMARY ANNE
ROSE OF BRECON (hotel boat pair) - 018422
  see ABERGAVENNY CASTLE
ROSE OF HUNGERFORD KENNET AND AVON CANAL TRUST Trip boat - 50 seats. Wide beam 65', b 9' red/grn. Base Hungerford, K&A raising funds for K&A Trust. 030802
ROSE OF LOTHBURY 76784
ROSE OF PARBOLD 52331
ROSE OF SHARON 63987
ROSE OF SHARON 76642
ROSE OF THORNE 50768
ROSE PIPER 51536
ROSE QUARTZ 47792
ROSETTA 100578
ROSETTA *NbC*
ROSETTA SAVORY 62557
ROSETTE Day hire. NbTug 60' red/grn. Base Rose Narrowboats, Brinklow. 026948
ROSEWEED 76679
ROSEWIL 52353
ROSEWOOD Dayboat

ROSIE 46613
ROSIE 66508 No.2 WELTON HYTHE NbT 46' blue/red. B: 1978 David Jones of Chester, lengthened in 1996 by 2m by Weltonfield Narrowboats, steelwork by Mike Gration, Greentour Ltd. and refitted forward of engine room. Lister ST2. Base Welton Hythe, GU-Leics. 23614
ROSIE 76964
ROSIE 79664
ROSIE II 73346 SAUL JUNCTION NbT 62' dk grn. B: 1986 Mike Heywood, Hoo Mill. BMC 1.5 Calcutt Boats. Base Diglis Basin Worcester. 21345
ROSIE II 73644
ROSIE 3 *46915 NbT 50' blue*
ROSIE & JIM 54579
ROSIE LEE 71078
ROSINA 61541 Nb 35' grn/crm. B: 1975 Dobsons, Shardlow. Lister SR2. Base Hopwas, Birmingham & Fazeley canal. Double chine hull. 24787
ROSINA 71675
ROSS 78322 Ice breaker
ROTHEN *NbTug 20' grn/red*
ROTHERHAM Motor vessel + crane 17.85m BW-NE
ROTHESAY 65696
ROUGH & TUMBLE 71520
ROULETTE 69147
ROULETTE 98890
ROULETTE II 62837
ROVER 50161
ROVER SWAN 63472
ROVER T 97424
ROWAN 45321
ROWAN No 10 69911
ROWAN BERRY 67968
ROWANNA 72553
ROWN 500767 IAN & SUE LOUGHBOROUGH NbST 70' dk blue/antique gold. B: 1996 R&D Fabrications, Notts., f/o Willowcraft (owners' company). BMC 1.8. Base Loughborough. Many years planning providing a real "home" with all comforts and space! Visitors/prospective customers welcome. 21266
ROXANNE 97603
ROYAL FALCON 73464
ROYAL FLUSH 70451
ROYALIST 64481
ROYCE 74055
ROYDON Motor
ROYDON Crane barge BW-L&S
ROZINANTE 64978
ROZINANTE 77965
ROZINANTE B1238
R THYME 54550
RUBY Hire. NbC 52' blue/red. Base The Wyvern Shipping Co, Linslade, GU 00446
RUBY 31058
RUBY 45090
RUBY 49378
RUBY 64704
RUBY 74950
RUBY 84312
RUBY II *Trip boat*

147

RUBY BRYNE 76673
RUBY ELISE 64264 R G COLOMB & CO STRETTON STOP NbC 42' dk grn/lt grn. B: 1974 Mindon Engineering, Pinxton, Notts. Lister SR3. Base Stretton Stop, Rugby. Built by Mindon as demonstration or show boat, hull no. ME 597. 23549
RUBY MOON 82512
RUBYANN 74405
RUDD No 323 80849 Yarwoods Fish Cl motor. Ex FMC/BW
RUDD 89175 Mtce boat 9.2m BW-
RUDDIGORE 62411
RUDDS ROGOZA 50036
RUDDYARD Barney(20) 1972 45'
RUDDY DUCK 70232
RUDDY DUCK 88767
RUDSTY 75084
RUDYARD 67253
RUFF 54014
RUFFORD No 166 GRAND UNION CANAL CARRYING COMPANY LIMITED Full conversion of ex GUCCCo "Big Northwich Town Class" working boat 71'6", d 3' sapphire blue/bl/wh. B: 1936 Yarwood, Northwich; conversion late 1960s ME Braine. Petter-McLaren 2PDM air cooled gas oil. Base Willow Park marina, Ashby canal. Back cabin and engine hole are as built; false counter fitted conversion is plywood skinned in aluminium. GUCCCo Ltd cabin side lettering is unique - "ROYALTY" scrolled signs. 23663
RUGRAT 77774
RUISLIP Tug BW-LON
RUMBA 71667
RUMBA Hire. NbC 60' red/grn. Base Rose Narrowboats, Brinklow, N.Oxford canal. 026713
RUMBLE 089102 Day Hire. Nb-style purpose built 22'6", b 6' red/grn. B: 1970ish, believed by Kingfisher Hire at Hoo Mill; lengthened at Sileby Mill 1991/92. Originally powered by Stewart Turner petrol engine - now by small 2 cyl diesel. Base Sileby Mill Boatyard, Soar Nav. See also *Fumble* and *Jumble*. (Also in original fleet were *Mumble* (now in Birmingham) and *Bumble* (now near Tring). History of this mini fleet being researched *(see page 14)*. 032887
RUMBOW 53189
RUM DO TOO 49708
RUMPEL TEASER 68369
RUMPOLE 47568 KS & JM HUDSON & DAUGHTERS NbTug 38' dk grn/dk red. B: 1990 Springer. Thornycroft Mitsubishi. Base Gayton marina, GU. 21279
RUMPUS 78643
RUM RUNNER 67897
RUMTUB IV 73004
RUM TUM 78278
RUM TUM II 74684
RUM TUM TUGGER 50291
RUN COMMON 50959 DF & LR BALL BLETCHLEY NbT 60' red/grn. B: 1991 Gary Gorton, f/o Warwickshire Narrowboats. Russell Newbery DM2. Base Crick marina. Full specification to enable two to live aboard in comfort including "lived-in" boatmans cabin using cross bed and vanity unit in cupboard. 12/24/240v system. 21286
RUPERT *50255 NbT 28' grn/red*
RUPERT 64293
RUPERT X 73127
RUSHALL SALLY 45483 *NbT 40' grn/red*
RUSKIN *NbT 20' wh/bl/grn*
RUSKIN JOHN 49003
RUSPER 077382 CLIFTON CRUISERS Hire. NbC (square stern) 48' grn/crm. B: 1982 Calcutt Boats (as *Wild Chervil IV*), re-fit 1990. Base Clifton Wharf, Rugby, N.Oxford canal. 025674
RUSSE II 50666
RUSSET *NbC 42' red/grn*
RUSTY B0345
RUTH 047833 Hire. NbT 43' navy blue/lt blue. B: 1990. Lister LPWS. Base Sally Boats, Bradford on Avon marina. 013227
RUTH 54302
RUTH 91033
RUTH CAROL 49150
RUTH LOUISE 51030
RUTILUS 54312
RUTILUS *NbC 60' blue*
RUTLAND WATER 65596
RYANS LASS B1701
RYE 051514 CLIFTON CRUISERS Hire. NbC 26' grn/crm. B: 1993 Arcrite Fabrications, f/o Clifton cruisers. Lister SR2 air cooled. Base Clifton Wharf, Rugby, N.Oxford canal. 025672
RYE 78183
RYLSTONE 69446
RYTHM GYPSY 67903

Sainsbury Shuttle awaiting passengers for a cruise on the short restored section of the Huddersfield Narrow Canal at Marsden Tunnel End (Standedge tunnel entrance to left of picture)

S

Far and wide - visiting the Emerald Isle, across Britain's second largest aqueduct and "at home" by the Grand Western. A family joke and a TV star. Piper apprenticeship, an ultimate restoration, sweeping curves, working ventures, recalling the earliest navigations. Knights feature strongly and an ancient custom survives. A Hire boat with no engine and a farm tractor engine to "high tech". "Silver" is precious to many

(St. listed with Saint)

SAABIAR 72140
SABAI-SABAI 50059
SABINA 63863
SABINA 1 77270
SABINA II 70567
SABLE 64311
SABLE ANNE MARIE 64503 *NbC 50' grn/mar*
SABRE 62932
SABRE 64969
SABRINA *Nb 56'*
SABRINA ROSE 74244 WORCESTER NbST 40' Mauritius blue/Bounty. B: 1988 Colecraft/ Tom Preen, Worcester. BMC 1.8. Base Venetian marina, SU canal. Port holes throughout.   23656
SABRINA SWAN 47112
SADIYAT 71834
SAFFINA 500386
SAFFRON 49852
SAFFRON 53929
SAFFRON 65761
SAFFRON No 2 76107
SAGA II B1232
SAGE 82884
SAGE 500089
SAGITARIUS 67587
SAGITTA 526
SAGITTA 45619 RATAE CORITANORUM Wilderness Beaver 23' red/grn.   B: 1989 Wilderness Boats. 4-str ob. Base Soar Navigation. Arrow on nameboard has owners' and their son's Christian names hidden in it.   21314
SAGITTA 80 Sm Northwich Star Cl motor. Ex GUCC/BW. See *SCULPTOR*
SAGITTARIAN 73959
SAGITTARIUS 46093
SAIEDA 65470
SAILOR VEE 46665
ST. ALEXANDER 54451
ST. BASIL 45544
ST. BEUNO 52221
SAINT CATHERINE 500665
SAINT CHAD *NbT 45' mar/blue*
ST. ELIAN 67169

149

SAINT FLORIAN 52179 NbT 72' grn/yel. B: 1992 M+N Narrowboats, f/o continues. Lister Canal Star 36 4 cyl. Base Lock 95 Hanwell flight, Southall, GU. *Saint. Florian* is believed to be the Patron Saint of chimney sweeps. 22491
ST. GEORGE 62930
ST. GEORGE 63180
ST. HELEN Trip boat - 25 seats. Grp workboat 20' wh/bl. Lister 2 cyl. Base Sankey canal. Built for St. Helens Council to operate on Taylor Park boating lake. 261071
ST. ITA 86639
ST. JOANNA 67713
ST. JOHN 83132
ST. KILDA 65133
SAINT MAGDALENE 51434 Trip boat (Linlithgow Union Canal Soc.) 45', b 8', d 2'6" red/wh. B: 1990 Millsteel Fabrication, Abergavenny. 72volt 7.5kw electric propulsion. Base Linlithgow, Linlithgow Union canal. Very quiet! Environment friendly. "Saint Magdalene" has long associations with Linlithgow; there was a convent and latterly a distillery of that name to the east of the town. Weekend cruises across the second largest - the Avon - aqueduct in Britain. 023532
ST. MAWR 82227
ST. TERESA 75283
SAI WEN TWO 63909
SALACIO N6403
SALAHAH 64557
SALAMANDA 62039
SALAMANDER 68281
SALAMINA B0958
SALAMIS 47737
SALAR 48960
SALAYNE IV 62646
SALFORD QUAYS B0030
SALIZARAH 74014
SALLY 50786
SALLY 51195
SALLY 61878
SALLY 64213
SALLY 66105
SALLY 102920
SALLY JANE 057679 Hire. NbT 40' navy blue/lt blue. B: 1990. Lister LPWS. Base Sally Boats, Bradford on Avon marina. 013226
SALMON 71749
SALMON Mtce boat 9.6m BW-
SALOME 100987
SALON 48741
SALTAIRE 68648
SALTAIRE 73979 EREWASH CANAL TRANSPORT LANGLEY MILL No. 167 Working Nb used occasionally for commercial carrying 71'6" blue/grained border. B: 1936 WJ Yarwood & Sons Northwich. Lister HR2. Base Langley Mill. Built for GUCCCo; passed to BW on nationalisation, later used for maintenance purposes. Private ownership 1987 and restored to carrying condition. 261064
SALTAIRE *NbTug 60' bl/grey*
SALTEN FJORD 76368
SALTERHEBBLE 78886

SALTHEART 97 72986 Motor
SALTINA 72130
SALTY 31555
SALTY DOG 93458
SALUKI 64271
SALWARKE Motor boat 21m BW-LAP
SAM 73829
SAMALI 61124
SAMANTHA 62825
SAMANTHA 93015
SAMANTHA KATE 96741
SAMARA 79666
SAM FISH 78291
SAM GANGEE 75734
SAMHACH 68756
SAMMY B 54145
SAMMY-JO 51509
SAMMY JOE 101442
SAMPAREIL 53665
SAMPSON Lifting barge BW-NW
SAMS DOING 76072
SAM TOO 63066
SAM TOO 69655
SAMUEL 49932
SAMUEL HUNTER B0872
SAMUEL JAMES 72726
SAMUEL OLDKNOW 77135
SAMUEL PEPYS 47739
SAMUEL SIMCOCK 64038
SANBEC 52466
SANCERRE G14223
SANCTUARY 68300
SANCTUARY 69928
SANDALWOOD 53511
SANDBACH 500527
SANDBACH 89278 BW-
SAND DOLLAR 77532
SANDE FJORD 47635
SANDMARTIN 70987
SANDPIPER *51542 Grp Ensign crm/brown*
SANDPIPER 53804
SANDPIPER 54728
SANDPIPER 64746
SANDPIPER 65398
SANDPIPER 67642
SANDPIPER 68124

Where Is It?
Look it up in the Location Glossary

SANDPIPER 74079
SANDPIPER 79505
SANDPIPER 85176
SANDPIPER 86077
SANDPIPER 102678
SANDPIPER II 75523
SANDPIPER Tug 18' BW-BBC
SANDPIPER Tug 5m BW-LAP
SANDPIPER *NbC 50' blue/red*
SANDRINGHAM 50262
SAN DURANGO 79291
SANDWICH TERN 51463

SANGOHMA 51605
SANJO 80449
SAN MIGUEL 46630
SAN MIGUEL 47895
SAN MIGUEL 74579
SAN PIERE 69635
SANS SOUCI 46793
SANS SOUCI 49045
SANS SOUCI 49231
SANS SOUCI 63460
SANS SOUCI 76798
SANS SOUCI 100245
SANTA CLAUS 65022
SANTANNA 52386
SANTE 52709
SANTEE 47634
SANTELIA *47415 Nb 25'blue*
SANTOLINA B0543
SAN TOY 60020 KINTBURY Steam launch 32', b 7', d 2'6" varnished.   B: 1901 by unknown builder. Coal fired steam engine - twin 3^1/$_2$" x 3^1/$_2$" x 4" (stroke). Base Kintbury. Aft cabin plus forward canopy. Reputedly first owned by Marie Tempest who played in the musical San Toy at Daly's theatre. Hull is the only original item; cabin and machinery fitted on restoration. 24855
SAPPHIRE Hire. NbC 52' blue/red. Base The Wyvern Shipping Co, Linslade, GU. 00447
SAPPHIRE 45051
SAPPHIRE 50030
SAPPHIRE 52484
SAPPHIRE 70097
SAPPHIRE 70645
SAPPHIRE 76335
SAPPHIRE 79204
SAPPHIRE 80665
SAPPHIRE 95124
SAPPHIRE Nb. Boat Museum
SARA No 5 51033 HR & SM DAVIS MARSWORTH NbTug - replica Josher, 40' dk grn/red.   B: 1991 Simon Wain Boatbuilding, Stretton Wharf, SU canal, f/o and decoration by owners continuing, signwriter Dave Moore. Russell Newbery DM2, PRM160 g'box. Base Dunstable & District Boat Club, GU. Traditional boatmans cabin, central engine room. 23642
SARA 62472
SARABANDE Hire. NbC 42' red/grn. Base Rose Narrowboats, Brinklow, N.Oxford canal. 026700
SARABANDE 79137
SARABELLE 50158
SARAGRAE 49123
SARAH 31558
SARAH 66007
SARAH 72400
SARAH *see FORGET ME NOT*
SARAH ABBOTT Workboat unpowered. Boat Museum
SARAH ANN B1552
SARAH BEATRICE 50296
SARAH BEATRICE No.2 *NbT 50' blue*
SARAH-DAVEY 45480 PEWSEY VALE CHARTER CRUISES Trip boat. Nb 65' blue/bl. B: 1988 David Piper Boatbuilders, Stoke-on-Trent.

1.8 Thornycroft. Base Pewsey Wharf, K&A canal. Name derived from 1988 BBC TV programme "The River" starring David Essex as the lock keeper; filmed at Wootton Rivers, K&A canal. BBC gave permission for the names of the stars to be used. 21297
SARAH ELIZABETH 100869
SARAH ELLEN 53378
SARAH ETHEL 74542
SARAH H 31210
SARAH HOMERA 75364
SARAH JANE 61767
SARAH JANE 64174
SARA JANE 72367
SARAH JANE 101163
SARAH JANE B1791
SARAH K 103173
SARAH LOUISE 53900
SARAH LUCY 68739
SARAH MARIE 50510
SARAH THOMAS 50368
SARAH Z 72874
SARA JANE *NbC 50' grn/red*
SARA LOU 95000
SARA LOUISE 53270
SARA-LOUISE 61718 NbC 46' burgundy/French grey.   B: 1974 Calcutt Boats. 1.5 BMC. Base Market Drayton, Shropshire. Big well deck able to feed four people. All varnished wood in cockpit fitted by owners. 20160
SARANE 68032
SARCELLE 63501
SARD II 68122
SARK 52396
SARNI Mini-steel NbTug 18', b 4', d 19". B: 1988 Adelaide Dockyard, Middlesex. Yanmar PMX8. Trailed southern England, R.Wey. Probably smallest "narrowboat" in UK. 21220
SARNIA 49371
SARNIA 72294
SARNIA TOO 47252
SARPETAINE B1703
SARUM 47860
SATISFACTION
SATISFACTION No.2 *Nb blue/red*
SATURN 52258
SATURN *see SYMBOL*
SAUCY SUE 71185
SAUL 92223
SAUROS 66442
SAUTE 100909
SAVANNAH 66922
SAVERNAKE TUNNEL 72921
SAVILE 500756 CALDER NAVIGATION SOCIETY Passenger day boat 32' blue/crm. B: 1995 Tayberg Steel Boats, Brighouse, f/o by Society members. Lister Canal Star 3 cyl. Base - anywhere on Calder & Hebble Navigation. Open front, rear cabin. Replacement for ex Windermere launch *Doreen* which was owned by the Society for 25 years. 22415
SAVOY 501063
SAVOYARD 46211
SAVOY HILL 50069

151

SAVOY HILL 77577
SAWLEY MIST 49671
SAXON 45499
SAXON 48125
SAXON 49113
SAXON 64099
SAXON 77018
SAXON 77534
SCAFELL PIKE 79179
SCALES B0449 GUCCC No 191 (type E). Residential. NbT butty 71'6", b 7'0$\frac{1}{2}$", d 2'6" mid blue/pale blue. B: 1936 Yarwoods, Northwich. Base Bedford Basin, Bridgewater canal. *Scales* is sheeted, is a middle Northwich, distinguished by steel strip handrails on back cabin. Rounded bilges and vee bottom with 4'6" sides. 261086
SCALLYWAG 72656
SCALLYWAG 96287
SCALLYWAG II 100645
SCAMP 54517
SCAMPI 93035
SCANDALOUS 104085
SCARAB 52223
SCARAB 52846
SCARAB 53305
SCARAMOUCH 102158
SCARISBRICK Rope crane dredger BW-NW
SCARLET 54645
SCARLET *NbC 40' mar*
SCARLET LADY 45741
SCARLET PIMPERNEL 45805
SCARLET POPPY 71664
SCARLETT 73648
SCHANDELLE 94509 4052 (Windermere) Grp trailable cruiser 16', b 6'6" orange/wh. B: 1972 Microplus 501 explorer. Honda B100 4 str. Trailed from home. Subject of "Schandelle visits ..." series in Waterways World. 22484
SCHARNEBEK 69585
SCHEHERAZADE 46278
SCHIFFCHEN 61763
SCHIPPERKE 60041
SCHNAPPS 80552
SCHNUCKI 51412 THURMASTON NbST 41' Mercedes red/midnight blue. B: 1991 R&D Fabrications/Trafalgar Canal Boat Co. Sheffield, self f/o; 10' extension 1995 by Nimbus Narrowboats. Lister Alpha Canal Star 2 cyl 18bhp. Base Nimbus Narrowboats, Thurmaston. 23591
SCHOLAR SHIP 50745
SCHUBERT 61401
SCINFLINT *Nb*
SCIPIO 73226
SCOLAR SHIP 74915
SCOOBY II 68637
SCORPIAN Open motor boat, welded/rivetted alu-minium hull, grp decking, stainless steel/aluminium windscreen, wheel steered 14', b 5'2", d 10" wh/blue. B: 1978 "Pearly Mist" believed at Wroxham, Norfolk. Honda 5hp 4 str ob. Trailed, used on day licence basis on Yorks, Notts, Lincs, Norfolk waterways. 25924

SCORPIO 53787 NbC 50' bl/grey. B: 1993 Arcrite/Ashby Canal Centre. BMC 1.8. Base marina. 261023
SCORPIO 67502
SCORPIO 72501
SCORPIO 86395
SCORPIO 92164
SCORPIO I 65940
SCORPIO Traditional maintenance boat 21.8m BW-
SCORPIO Workboat unpowered. Boat Museum
SCORPIO *see SCULPTOR*
SCORPION 63974
SCORPION 65058
SCORPION 74548
SCOTIA 45358
SCOTSON B1503
SCOTTISH QUEEN 64765
SCOTTY 72027
SCOUT 70134
SCOUT Tug 6m BW-NW
SCOUT OWL 53152
SCRAPWOOD III 49401
SCRUFFY FOX II 51174
SCRUMPY 61779
SCRUMPY 96806
SCULPTOR G.U.C.C.Co. LTD 82 Small Northwich ex working narrowboat 71'6", b 7'0$\frac{1}{2}$" red/blue. B: 1935 Yarwoods, Northwich composite construction, riveted iron sides, elm bottom, steel cabin and engine hole. Lister air cooled HA2 (originally Russell Newbery water cooled twin cylinder). Based as exhibit at Canal Museum, Stoke Bruerne. One of the large fleet of boats built for the newly formed Grand Union Canal Carrying Co. Ltd in the mid 1930s. In 1949, after nationalisation, *Sculptor* and sisters *Scorpio* and *Sagitta* were sent to the Shropshire Union canal as maintenance boats. *Sculptor* has been restored to original condition (apart from engine type) and now appears in the utility wartime livery of the G.U.C.C.Co. Ltd. 2065
SEA DANCER 48812
SEA EAGLE 48469 Broads cruiser, carvel 28', b 9'4" grn/brown. B: 1949 Wards of Thorpe, Norwich. BMC 1500. Base Sileby Mill, Soar Navigation. Of 4 built this is the only one left. Having been sunk at Thurmaston she has been completely renovated to original condition, other than engine. 24791
SEAFORD 168 Lg Woolwich Town Cl motor. Ex GUCC
SEA FOX B7514
SEAGULL 52940
SEAGULL 66216
SEAGULL 73798
SEA HAWK N7790
SEAHAZE 76430
SEA HUNTER 51745
SEA JAY 50233
SEALANDER *51631 NbC 50' blue*
SEALAND PRINCESS 75389
SEA LEGS 76384
SEAMALAIR B1571

152

SEA MIST 45140
SEA MIST 61285
SEA MIST 71579
SEA MIST 100542
SEA MOON 82617
SEAMUS 63834
SEANDER 100428
SEA PANDA 76172
SEA PRINCESS 45991
SEA SCOUT B0482
SEASONS 64560
SEASONS No. 3 500509 J & D WHITTLE MILL HILL LANCS NbT 53' navy blue. B: 1991 Johnathan Wilson/Midland Canal Centre. Perkins P3 152. Base Mill Hill Blackburn, L&L. 23576
SEASONS No 3 B1407
SEA SPEED 93735
SEASPRAY 31608
SEASPRAY 100889
SEA SPRAY 64644
SEA TALE 103253
SEATREK 78574
SEA WOLF 103224
SEB 49430
SEBASTIAN 49148
SECOND ATEMMPTE 54024 NbST 50' grn/mar. B: 1994 Shepley Bridge Marina Ltd., Mirfield. Lister LPWS4. Base Shipley Wharf, L&L. 23691
SECOND CHANCE 50210
SECOND LOVE 50261
SECOND MEADOW 47072
SECOND TO NUNN 54409 NbST 50' blue. B: 1994 Orchard Marina Northwich T&M. Beta. Base Orchard Marina, T&M. Features 'L' shaped sofa across front door - middle seat lifts out for access. 20128
SECOND VENTURE 45559
SECTION VII 91404
SECUNDUS NAVIS 48174
SEEBURGH 50495
SEEKER 60042
SEELYBROOK 47787
SEFTON 46859
SEKIM V 73145
SELBOURNE 50788
SELBY Motor vessel 14.95m BW-NE
SELENA 71851
SELENE 47576
SELENE 68726
SELINA 70340
SELINA WOOD 45629
SELWORTHY 54387
SENCE 81702 Grab dredger 16m BW-NE
SENORITA 46595
SENTINEL 045949 Hire. NbC 40' grn/red. BMC 1.5. Base Evesham Marina, R.Avon. 0371033
SENTINEL 49087
SENTINEL 50285
SENTINEL 70584
SENTINEL No 344 73327
SEPOY 70061
SEPTEMBER LADY 73630
SEPTEMBER MORN 73194

SEPTEMBER MORN 073254 AUSTCLIFFE NbT 52' mar/bl. B: 1997 David Piper, Red Bull Basin, Church Lawton. Mitsubishi. Base Austcliffe. 24863
SEPTEMBER MORN 77781
SEPTEMBER SONG 51216
SEPTEMBER SONG Barney(19) 1972 32'
SEQUEC 69380
SEQUOIA 68336
SEQUOIA 69999
SERENADE 49656
SERENADE 51305
SERENADE 54242
SERENADE 69843
SERENADE Hire. NbC 60' red/grn. Base Rose Narrowboats, Brinklow, N.Oxford canal. 026712
SERENDIPITY 45622
SERENDIPITY 47485
SERENDIPITY 047763 RAH SMH (in logo form) NbC 50' Oxford blue/pillar box red. B: 1990 North West Narrowboats Jack White, Liverpool. Mitsubishi 1.4, Newage PRM gearbox. Base bridge 165 L&L canal. Helical stern, 6 cut away fender ports, mast step 12' aft from bow. 20131
SERENDIPITY 51420
SERENDIPITY 52147
SERENDIPITY 52517
SERENDIPITY 62811
SERENDIPITY 65622
SERENDIPITY 70976
SERENDIPITY 76671
SERENDIPITY 79459
SERENDIPITY 80602
SERENDIPITY 98956
SERENDIPITY II 78443
SERENDIPITY VI 48645
SERENE LADY 48309
SERENE LADY 48505
SERENE LADY 54431
SERENGETI 73785
SERENITY 46430
SERENITY 47315
SERENITY 61631
SERENITY 65401
SERENITY NbST 50' blue
SERENITY NbT 42' red/grn
SERENUS 61926
SERESHA 50334
SERPENS Sm Northwich Star Cl butty. Ex GUCC/BW
SERUWA III see NATTAJACK
SESH 79831
SEVENOAKS 054555 CLIFTON CRUISERS Hire. NbC 60' grn/crm. B: 1995 South West Durham Steelcraft, f/o Clifton Cruisers. BL 1.8. Base Clifton Wharf, Rugby, N.Oxford canal.025683
SEVEN YEAR ITCH 101276
SEVERN B1487 Commercial use. L&L canal 'short boat' 62', b 14'3", d 3' grn. B: circa 1931 Pimblott of Northwich, refurbished Lorenz & Co. Lister HA3M 3 cyl air cooled. Base Bridgewater canal. The last traditional short boat owned and operated on L&L canal by British Waterways. Purchased in a very run down condition, she has

Shackleton at Windmill End National IWA Festival 1996

been restored and is now available for cargo again.
0351007
SEVERN BELL 74658
SEVERN DOLPHIN Motor. Ex Severn CC
SEVERN MIST 71542
SEVERN RAMBLER ONE 46037
SEVERN RAMBLER TWO 50060
SEVERN ROAMER 49998
SEVERN ROAMER ONE 49999
SEVERN SECRETS 52750
SEVERN SECRETS TWO 54611
SEVERN SERENE 1 75456
SEVERN SERENE TWO
SEVERNSIDE 72478
SEVERN SPLENDOUR 53882
SEVERN SPLENDOUR 53883
SEVERN SUPREME 500590
SEVERN SWALLOW 73350
SEVERN TRAVELLER 61328
SEVERN VOYAGER 67444
SEVERN VOYAGER ONE 46039
SEVERN WANDERER II 47921
SGT. PEPPERS 66202
SHAD Yarwood motor. Ex FMC/BW/WW. Boat Museum
SHAD Motor vessel BW-NW
SHADOW 500024
SHADOWFAX 61422

SHADOW FAX *64596 NbT 30' red/grn*
SHAKALENE 102598
SHAKA ZULU 51506
SHAKESPEARE 48384
SHAKY 77367
SHALIMAR 49823
SHALIMAR 96596
SHALLOW 101157
SHALOM 92278
SHALOM II 101041
SHAMANDE 64603
SHAMARIN II 78400
SHAMBLES 45058
SHAMROCKIWI 64966 WOODHAM JUNCTION NbC steel/wooden top 36' mar/crm. 1976 Springer. Lister SR2. Base R.Wey - New Haw. 2'x1'6" panel on each side with distinctive signwritten shamrock and kiwi bird (owners from Dublin and New Zealand). 25960
SHAMU 74725
SHAMUS 64969
SHANANDOA 50664
SHANE 83571
SHANGRI-LA 64446
SHANGRILA 67970
SHANKLEY 76472
SHANNON 79764
SHANTA 68597

SHANTY MAN 45500
SHAP FELL 65727
SHARASUN Grp cruiser/dayboat 14'9", b 6'6", d 9" wh. B: 1973 Headline hull & superstructure from Midland Marine/Heads Boatyard Stourport-on-Severn. Penta 2-str 12hp ob. Base Wyre Mill, R.Avon. Sliding side windows, unlike standard production boat. Ravaged by mink (only claim to fame!) and completely refitted 1995. A family joke when boat being built concerned "Charabang Sunday" which led to "Sharasunday", thence to name. 25977
SHARE B1330
SHARE DEAL 73501
SHARIAN 70512
SHARIMA 104420
SHARK 54129 Ex BWB working barge 57'6", b 14'2", lightship draught 2'6" beige/grn. B: 1967 JS Watson, Gainsborough Shipbuilders, owner currently fitting out for residential use. Lister HB2 2 cyl (original). Base BW wharf, Doncaster, Sheffield & S.Yorks Navigation. 24874
SHARON 52593
SHARON 62152
SHARON LYNN 69560
SHARPNESS 62650 Ice breaker/Tug 45' crm/blue. B: 1908 Abdella & Mitchell, Brimscombe Port, Thames & Severn canal, Gloucestershire. 1928 Gardner 4L2 40hp. Base Red Hill marina, Ratcliffe-on-Soar, Notts. One of 3 built for the Worcester & Birmingham Canal Co for tunnel work and the only one to be built as an ice breaker. 20146
SHAWFORD LILY *NbT 50' grn*
SHEANDEE 86550
SHEARWATER 52789
SHEARWATER 68832
SHEBA *NbT 50' blue/mar*
SHEBDON 65175
SHEBOB *52621 Grp 30' mar/wh*
SHEBROKUS *Nb blue/grey*
SHEENA 72278
SHEENA *97528 Grp Shetland*
SHEEPSHEAD 49881
SHEER FOLLY 31405
SHEFFIELD 61238
SHEFFIELD Motor vessel 15.55m BW-NE
SHEILA 50328
SHEILA ANNE 68050
SHEILA J 49604
SHEKINA 45980
SHELANE 82340
SHELDRAKE II 500151 REACH OUT PROJECTS Hire (groups with young people inc. disabled/disadvantaged and others in community). Wide beam boat 64', b 10'8" burgundy/grn/bl. B: 1996 Greentour Ltd., Daventry. Lister Canal Star 3L 4 cyl. Base Nash Mills, GU. Facilities incl. 10 berths and full facilities including space for 6 wheelchair passengers. 029746
SHELDUCK 81621 BW-
SHELEAN 61279
SHELENU 60488
SHELLAN 65931

SHELLEY 45377
SHELLEY ANNE 51386
SHENDAM 75022
SHENGHAM 62246
SHENTON 81704 Power boat 6m BW-CATM
SHEPHERDS HEY 49556
SHEPPEY 66774
SHERBOURNE 67987
SHERE KHAN 067929 NbC 40' dk grn/pale yel. B: circa 1974 Foxton Boat Services. Lister SL3 air cooled. Base Warwick, GU. Heating by 1^1/$_2$" copper pipe radiator for full boat length from Ellis Heatmaster gas boiler. Domestic water via Godwin pump. 21358
SHERIAN 70512 NbT 45' grn/grey. B: 1981 Les Allen & Sons. Sabb 2HG. Base Langley Mill.21320
SHERMINI 70546
SHERRYBEE 51198
SHERWOOD 49293
SHERWOOD 80178 Crane boat 21.34m BW-NE
SHE'S-A-B 48723
SHETLAND 85430
SHETLAND 88120
SHEZOURS 62338
SHEILA ANN 75546
SHEILA MAY (OR MAY NOT) 65069
SHIKARA 49714
SHIKARA 74036
SHIKARA B1578
SHILLING 69453
SHILLING No. 2 51209 NbTug 31' bl/crm. B: 1991 Mike Heywood, f/o Stan Yorke -Redcraft. 500cc 2 cyl Vetus. Base Venetian marina. 23603
SHILOH 77459
SHILONA 53515
SHIMMER 46282
SHIPLEY Motor vessel 14.95m BW-NE
SHIRALEE 79187
SHIRE OAK 68314
SHIRL 50760
SHIRLEY 68572 GRAND UNION CANAL CARRYING CO. 169 Nb - converted Large Northwich Town Class Motor 71'6", b 7'0^1/$_2$", d 3' navy blue. B: 1936 W J Yarwoods & Sons, Northwich. National DM2 (1930s 2 cyl 18hp water cooled. Not the original but is the original type and of contemporary age). Base GU canal. Probably named after Shirley near Solihull in Warwickshire which was the only Shirley with a railway station: one theory is that GUCCCo got the town class names from railway directories of the time. One of the many boats passed into the hands of the British Transport Commission in 1948 on nationalisation and regularly carried cargoes on the GU until well into 1960s, incl period on loan to Willow Wren Transport. Converted to residential use early 1970s. 23580
SHIRLEY B 50521
SHISARS 76443
SHORE LARK 52187
SHOREWEED 60875
SHORT CONTRACT 47148
SHORTER 31045
SHORTWOOD 49709

SHORTY 61451
SHOTTERY BELLE *NbT 56' grn/red*
SHOVELLER Tug 6m BW-CATM
SHOWBOAT B8084
SHREW 45547
SHREWLEY TUNNEL 77103
SHROPPIE LASS 61073
SHROPSHIRE LAD 50404
SHROPSHIRE LAD 52867
SHROPSHIRE LASS *77722 NbT 60' grn/red*
SHUCKBURGH 74363
SHUGLEY 51671
SHUNDRAW 51753
SHURRAM *NbC 50' mar/grn*
SHY TALK 46558
SHY TALK 63856
SIAMESE GIRL 61063
SIAN 68060
SIANSUN 85252
SIBERIA 61799 UXBRIDGE WHARF NbTug BCN style 45', d 2'10" mar/dk blue. B: 1977 Water Travel, Autherley Junction, Wolverhampton. Gardner 2L2 (1942) hand start, direct drive, pre-war U.S. box. Base Braunston, GU. 20127
SICKLE 80575 Motor vessel 13.6m BW-
SIDE BY SIDE 48659
SIDEWINDER 69550
SIDNEY 54519
SIESTA *54400 NbST 50' blue*
SIET up ow SELVEN *Dutch sailing barge*
SIGNUS 77151
SIGNWRITER 76280
SIG OF SARUM 73682
SILAS 51083
SILEBY SWALLOW 77375
SILECIA 54800
SILENT LADY 104459
SILENT SWAN 45338
SILHOUETTE 53482
SILHOUETTE 61068
SILHOUETTE 68138
SILHOUETTE 71870
SILHOUETTE 81728
SILK DREAM 50886
SILMARIL 73908
SILOAM 97130
SILVA ANDERIDA 68359
SILVER ANN 79199
SILVER ANN II 72824
SILVER BIRCH 71145
SILVER BIRCH 72577 NbC 30' sharkskin grey (looks pale cream)/grn. B: 1986 Springer. Vetus/Mitsubishi 3 cyl 20hp. Base Braunston marina. 20103
SILVER BOND 78761
SILVER CHASE 60198
SILVER CLOUD 97378
SILVERDALE 70397
SILVER DAWN NN6267 Grp 25' wh. B: Dawncraft design. 15hp ob. Base Oundle marina, R.Nene. 20117
SILVER DEW 50756
SILVER DREAM 46970
SILVER DREAM 47572

SILVER DUSK 47733
SILVER FIR *see WALNUT*
SILVERFISH 52725
SILVER FOX 69299
SILVER FOX *NbT 60' grn*
SILVER GLEN 31790
SILVER HERON 77623 Marine ply on mahogany cruiser 24'6" wh/varnish. B: 1955 Canal Pleasurecraft, Stourport-on-Severn. Engine originally Austin 7/Coventry Victor outdrive then Coventry Victor 'N' type (now at Boat Museum, Ellesmere Port), now Nanni 3 cyl/Enfield outdrive. Base Fazeley. Earliest surviving 'CPL' cruiser by Holt Abbott; some were used as hire craft - this one went into private ownership. Recent partial rebuild and preparation for another 40 years - a substantial feat for a plywood cruiser. Full history, including that of the builder, in Canal & Riverboat, July and August 1995. 24894
SILVER JUBILEE 52393
SILVER JUBILEE B1731
SILVER JUNE 75369 Grp 26', b 6'6" crm/chocolate. B: 1984 "Classic" Ensign. Honda 10hp ob. mounted inboard of transom. Base Retford & Worksop Boat Club, Clayworth, Chesterfield canal. 20150
SILVER LADY 47330
SILVER LADY 74140
SILVER LADY 74480
SILVERLEA 61071 Admiralty Pinnace 50', b 9'6", d 3'6" blue. B: 1918 Gosport. Unpowered - towed to dry dock. Based, residential, GU canal. 23597
SILVER LEAF 101173
SILVER LYNX 50571
SILVER MIST 73808
SILVER MOON 74463
SILVER REED 47899
SILVER SAIL 77268
SILVER SALMON 47905
SILVER SAND 51723
SILVER SATIN 49903
SILVER SATURN 75477
SILVER SHADOW 51989
SILVER SKY 71458
SILVER SPRAY 45038
SILVER SPRAY 54668
SILVER STONE 75481
SILVER SUN 45626
SILVER SWALLOW 52739
SILVER SWALLOW B0473
SILVER SWAN 52095
SILVERWEED 62329
SILVER WIND 53864
SILVER YEAR *84926 Grp 18' wh/blue*
SILVIE 46759
SIMBA *98399 Grp 18' red/wh*
SIMMERDOWN 54736
SIMON D 73790
SIMON-DE-MONTFORT 049822 Hire. NbC 68' grn/red. BMC 1.8. Base Evesham Marina. 0371046
SIMPKIN 65181
SIMPKISS 46561 NEW CANAL CO. PYRFORD No. 211 NbT 50' grn/red. B: 1988

The Wolverhampton Narrowboat & Canal Carrying Company Limited (their last boat), f/o Bettisfield Narrowboats. Perkins 4108. Base Pyrford, R.Wey. Named after former well known Midlands brewers; it is believed that the builders occupied - or were close to - the former brewery site. 25957

SIMPLY JANE 49690
SINBAD 69914
SINGING SWAN 72163
SINITTA 65883
SINKIN 65883
SIPSWIM 63114
SIR ALISANDER 45621
SIR BELIN 47688
SIR BENFRO 72052
SIR BERT NbC 30' grn/red. B: 1985 Jondeblin Marine, Avon Canal Boat Centre, refit by present owner 1988. Vetus 2 cyl plus emergency backup by electric ob. Base Basingstoke canal. 20186
SIR BLAMOR 51501
SIR DANIEL GOOCH 45147 NbT 70', d 2'8" - unballasted weighs 23 tons, 21' swim and box rudder - dk blue/lt blue. B: 1989-90 Brummagem Boats. 2.4 Thornycroft mounted transversely with hydraulic drive to 20"x15" prop and second hydraulic drive to 5kva generator. 12v + 24v alternators. Base Braunston marina. F/o in solid Brazilian mahogany and koto. Shower and full size bath and jacusi in bathroom. 25975
SIR EDMUND HILARY 48014
SIR ERNEST SHACKLETON 72809
SIR FERGUS 49853
SIR FRANCIS DRAKE 46246
SIR GUYUS 71731

SIRIUS 50777
SIRIUS 62760
SIRIUS 76648 (REG AT RICKMANSWORTH 29) FLEET No. 358 (GUCCC) Wooden Small Ricky butty, converted under canvas 70' bl/graining. B: 1934 W H Walker Bros, Rickmansworth. Base GU canal. Butty to *Electra* (see entry). First butty built for the Grand Union Canal Carrying Co. Built with the motor boat *Arcturus*. Subsequently used as a horse drawn maintenance boat for the LMS Railway on the Llangollen canal. 24842
SIRIUS 77510
SIRIUS B7900
SIRIUS 80253 BW-
SIR JASPER 50372
SIR JOHN 61157
SIR KAY 46207
SIR LADINOS 47687
SIR LAMORACK
SIR LANCELOT 75519
SIR LANCEOR 73915
SIR LAVAINE 45620
SIR MORDRED 70731 NbC 48' blue/red. B: 1984 Arcrite, f/o Countrywide Cruisers, Brewood, SU canal. Thornycroft Mitsubishi 4 cyl. Base Cooks Wharf, Cheddington, Bucks. Operated by Countrywide Cruisers as hire boat 1984-93. Two large pale blue diamonds on roof. Bridge guards fitted. 22464
SIR PELLEAS 76389
SIR PEREGRINE 70335
SIR RICHARD GRENVILLE 49258
SIR ROBERT CLIVE 61735
SIRS 73568

Ice breaker/tug *Sharpness* on the bank

SIR STANLEY FREDERICK 79680
SIR THOMAS 72693
SIR THOMAS BROCKLEBANK 78449
SIR TOBY 62201
SIR TRISTRAN 77045
SIR ULFIUS 46405
SIR ULFIUS 53755
SIR WALTER 71054
SIR WALTER RALEIGH 46614
SIR WILLIAM STANIER 47734
SISKIN 49996
SISKIN 51590
SISKIN 61556
SISKIN 65195
SISKIN 65716
SISKIN 82778
SISKIN Tug 5.9 BW-NE
SISKIN *NbT - 70' replica Lg Northwich butty grn/red*
SISSY JUPE 77679
SISTER ELIZABETH 65845
SIXPENCE 48227
SIXPENCE 51298
SKAIDIE 65803
SKANGA 65159
SKARA BRAE 72680
SKEBRAKE 53484
SKIDADDLE 68041
SKIDBLADNIR 47019
SKIMBLESHANKS 68371
SKINTUS 52413
SKIPTON Motor vessel BW-NW
SKIRR 47038
SKIRRIA 81850
SKUA 103426 'MAYLAND' Grp 14' yel/wh. B: 1983 Mayland Marine, Essex, f/o by owner, 1995/96 modification to cabin. Yamaha 4hp ob. Base R.Trent, Nottingham area. This small craft is fitted with a full length berth (for one person) which dismantles. 23558
SKYBOW 72347
SKYE 52598
SKYE *NbC 35' grn*
SKYLARK 46434
SKYLARK 64860
SKYLARK 76447
SKYLARK Motor. Ex Cowburn & Cowpar
SKYLARK *Dayboat*
SKYMISE 103767
SLAINTE MHATH 99825
SLAVE TO LOVE 47075
SLAVIC 103322
SLEEPY OWL 51608
SLENDER 103924
SLIEVEBLOOM 47802
SLIM JIM *NbC 60' blue/mar*
SLINGSBY 61594
SLINGSHOT 101032
SLIPPER *101710 Grp 20' wh*
SLOLEY No 1 (male and lady snails depicted) NbST 60' bl/crm/red.   B: 1996 Bridgewater Boat Builders, Astley Green. Lister Classic CRK3. Being built for continuous cruising. Features boatman's cabin, bedroom at front. Owner's first boat was *Sloley* after village in Norfolk, his wife's home village; used as a nice play on words to suit a narrowboat's pace. 21373
SLOOPE 46650
SLOOPY 75115
SLOOPY 103360
SLOTH 46879
SLOUGH 64147
SLOUGH 81064 Tug 8m BW-
SLOWCOACH 70787
SLUG 44318
SLYBURN 49460
SMALL COPPER 063104 Hire. NbT blue/red. BMC 1.5. Base Evesham Marina, R.Avon. 0371042
SMALLEY Dredger 34'9" BW-OGU
SMALL FRY 52329 NbST 30' royal blue/red. B: 1992 by owner with assistance of craftsman joiner. Kubota 3 cyl ex Beta Marine. Base Fallwood marina, Bramley, Leeds, L&L canal. 21248
SMALL WORLD 49620 NbC 60' grn/red. B: 1989 Colecraft, f/o Morse Marine. BL 1.8. Base Stanstead Abbotts, R.Lea. 24900
SMART LADY 61514
SMEATON 79630
SMEEDGIN 63080
SMETSTOW 81695 Piling boat 16.2m BW-
SMEW 61088
SMEW Tug 20' BW-NW
SMIFFY 101493
SMIFTER 67256
SMILE 54330
SMILES 104456
SMILEY 64012
SMILEY 95270
SMILLIE MAY 65831
SMITE 81711 Power boat 16m BW-CATM
SMOGS 46221
SMOKEY JOE B0873
SMOKEY RAY 88736
SMOKEY STOVER 45340
SMOKY OWL 500435
SMOO 61690
SMUDGIE 70603
SMUGGLER 74369
SMUGGLS 47974
SNAFU 82992
SNAIL 67641
SNAILS PACE 61612
SNAPDRAGON 48889 JIM & ANNE LINDOP MARKET DRAYTON NbST 52' Rochelle red/Donegal grn. B: 1990 R&D Fabrications, f/o by previous owner. 1.8 BMC. Base Market Drayton, SU canal. 24898
SNAPDRAGON 71984
SNAPE Tug 6m BW-NW
SNARESTONE TUNNEL 73888
SNARK 52803
SNIPE 68435
SNIPE I 47480
SNIPE No 4 69745
SNIPE *Hotel boat red/bl*
SNIPE *see KILDARE*
SNOOPY 45466
SNOOPY 89547

158

SNOOPY 91767
SNOOPY 94292
SNOOPY B7552
SNOOPY 4 51535
SNORK MAIDEN *52703 NbC 30' blue*
SNOWBIRD 45404
SNOWBIRD 53508
SNOWBIRD 65637
SNOWBIRD II 75101 B1013
SNOWBIRD VII 78795
SNOW BUNTING 50503
SNOWDON Mtce boat BW-NW
SNOWDROP Hire. NbC 42' blue/red. Base The Wyvern Shipping Co, Linslade, GU. 00456
SNOWDROP 72641
SNOWDROP Tug 13.6m BW-
SNOWFLAKE 80105
SNOWFLAKE *Grp Rowancraft*
SNOWGOOSE 61783
SNOW GOOSE 67272
SNOWGOOSE 68696
SNOWGOOSE 71338
SNOWGOOSE 72974
SNOWGOOSE 73844
SNOW GOOSE 75372
SNOWGOOSE 77613
SNOWY OWL 46105
SNUBNOSE 70019
SNUG 48066
SOAR Motor vessel 10.97m BW-NE
SOAR VALLEY 65765
SOFF 71786
SOGGIES PRIDE 79203
SOJOURN 53723
SOL 66555
SOL 103635
SOLACE 46247
SOLACE *NbC 40' red/bl*
SOLAREX 90333
SOL-DE-MER 70205
SOLDONELLA 64429
SOLENT 71688
SOLENT TEMPTRESS 100498
SOLITAIRE 046477 E J & C M MOUNTFORT HAZLESTRINE Nb 50' dk fawn/lt fawn. B: 1990 (launched) - 5yrs to build - second steel boat to be entirely built by owner, John Mountfort, in spare time. 1.5 Leyland (Thornycroft). Base Stafford Boat Club, S&W canal. 24757
SOLITAIRE 51607
SOLITAIRE 54126
SOLITAIRE 74088
SOLITAIRE 78039
SOLITAIRE No 1 70580
SOLITON 73025
SOLITUDE 46617
SOLITUDE 52636
SOLO 71980
SOLOMON No. 255 *77295 NbT 45' red/grn*
SOLVA 90367
SOLVEIG 69205
SOL-Y-MAR 103062
SOMBONG 50802
SOMERTON 79649
SONATA 54061
SONG THRUSH 95810
SONIA MARIE 100679
SONORETTE "Short" double skiff, clinker mahogany on oak timbers 20', b 4', d 6" varnished. B: 1900 Bathursts of Tewkesbury. Sculls provide propulsion. Base Henley on Thames. Built as hire boat. Restored late 80s. 21291
SONSKIT 69033
SOPHIA GINGER 54847
SOPHIA GRANTHAM 48843
SOPHIE 45506
SOPHIE 70572
SOPHIE B0973
SOPHIE B7875
SOPHIE No 2 72418
SOPHIE *see CYPRESS*
SOPHOMORE 49924
SORCERER 047830 NbT 60' blue/grn. B: 1990 GT Boatbuilders, self f/o. Beta BD3. Base Birmingham & Fazeley canal. Domestic tilt and turn double glazed windows (a "first" - featured in Aug 1992 Waterways World); Esse Sovereign diesel cooking range supplies cooking and heat to whole boat (also a "first"). Also first to fit Beta BD3 in canal boat. 22417
SORCERER 74864
SORCERESS *NbST 55' grn/mar*
SORREL 47589
SORREL 49398
SORREL 66356
SORREL 67512
SORREL 67691
SORRY II 52437
SOURNOIS 50707
SOUTH CAPE 50225
SOUTHERN COMFORT 46165
SOUTHERN COMFORT 48809
SOUTHERN COMFORT 62440
SOUTHERN STAR 74338
SOUTHERN STAR 76616
SOUTHLAND 54807
SOUTHMILL 71279 BISHOPS STORTFORD NbC 60' red/grn. B: 1985 after 4 years building by owner, evenings/weekends (in "Southmill" Road, Bishops Stortford). Ford Supermajor from farm

---

Whether you own a boat or hire one
WE WANT TO HELP YOU!
We hire small narrowboats, for 2 to 12 persons, by the day and larger ones (up to 6 berth) for longer. We also offer a full range of services for the boat owner. You name it, we'll do or get it! We're just below Sileby Lock on the River Soar.

SILEBY MILL BOATYARD
Mill Lane, Sileby, Leics. LE12 7NF
Tel: 01509 813583

tractor (simple old engine, reliable, economical, rebuilt by friend - tractor cost £300, rebuild £400), PRM gearbox. Base Hardmead Lock, Gt. Amnell, R.Lea. Solar panels charge batteries, 7 roof lights provide light airy interior, self-build wood burner, digital panel, gas alarm, burglar alarm, etc. Total cost to build about £7000. 22420
SOVEREIGN Hire. NbC 62' blue/red. Base The Wyvern Shipping Co, Linslade, GU. 00434
SOVEREIGN 51132
SOVEREIGN 52159
SOVEREIGN 54967
SOVEREIGN 67671
SOVEREIGN NbT 50' blue
SOWENA NbC 50' mar/blue
SO WHAT 74543
SPADE 67648
SPANISH LADY 60289
SPANISH LADY Grp wh/turquoise
SPARKBROOK 75994
SPARKENHOE 61659 NbC 50' wh/grn
SPARROWHAWK 47709
SPARROWHAWK 76701 NbC 60' mar/blue
SPARTACUS 68978
SPARTACUS 73880
SPARTH 73505
SPECK 72554
SPECTRA NbT 50' blue/crm
SPECTRE 45677
SPEEDSPOT 53006
SPEEDWELL Restaurant boat. Wey Barge 56', b 9' red/wh. B: 1987 Colecraft, f/o by Ian Causton. Vetus 65hp. Base Farncombe Boat House, R.Wey. 00370
SPEEDWELL 46426
SPEEDWELL 47677
SPEEDWELL 49005
SPEEDWELL 50598
SPEEDWELL 61477
SPEEDWELL 65241
SPEEDY 46291
SPEEDY 66574
SPEEDYGREEN 52460
SPEEDY GREENFLAG 73104
SPELLBINDER B1660
SPELL BROOK BW-L&S
SPERLING 74826
SPEY No 88 69372 FMC Motor. Ex T.Clayton
SPHINX 31768
SPIDER 76181
SPIDER Mtce boat 30' BW-NW
SPIDER see WASP
SPIFIRE 61108
SPINDRIFT 61106
SPINDRIFT Grp 25' wh
SPINEL 47789
SPIRIDON B0676
SPIRIT OF FREEDOM 72648 NbC 40' grn/mar
SPIRIT OF FREEDOM II 52671
SPIRIT OF NOVA SCOTIA 101371
SPIRIT OF THE NIGHT J & M PENFOLD NbC 38' Mauritius blue/gold. B: 1996 Liverpool Boats, self f/o. 34hp Lombardini. Base Farncombe Boat House, R.Wey. F/o proceeding; motif featur-

ing wolf's head in moon is intended feature. 20180
SPIRIT OF YOUTH 70813
SPLENDID Hire. NbC 62' blue/red. Base The Wyvern Shipping Co, Linslade, GU. 00435
SPLENDID 76445
SPLENDOUR 51818
SPOOK B1403
SPOTTED CRAKE 51471
SPRAY 72725
SPREE 52324 NbST 40' blue/red
SPRING GARDEN 65149
SPRING HARMONY 50676
SPRUCE 72837
SPRY CHEPSTOW 1894 Severn trow 71'6", b 18'3". B: 1894 by William Hurd at Chepstow. One of many such vessels plying the R.Severn when river routes for trade were still important. First owner, William Davies, was a 'stone' merchant. Then various uses until ignominious retirement in Digbeth Canal basin. Recovered from the mud in 1983 by Upper Severn Navigation Trust and extensive restoration started. Now on display at Ironbridge Gorge (Blists Hill) Museum. Sole survivor of her type. Full history in various publications from Museum. 20101
SPRY-JAZÉ 80867 Grp 20'
SPYDER 46183
SQUIDGE 86430
SQUIL 45432
SQUIRE No 2 69497 Ex S&L/BCN
SQUIRE TRELAWNEY 65180
SQUIRREL 49917 LONDON NbT 40'6", d 2'9" blue. B: 1991 Associated Cruisers, Victoria Basin, Wolverhampton. Lister Alpha 4. Base St. Pancras Cruising Club. Added ostec bow. 23538
SQUIRREL 71055
SQUIRREL 75104

(St. listed with Saint)

STABOARD LIST 67542
STACCATO 31287
STAEDY 46248
STAFFORD 61113
STAFFORD 61673
STAFFORD 79285
STAFFORDSHIRE 69708
STAFFORDSHIRE 80141
STAFFORDSHIRE KNOT 70610
STALWART 45775
STAMFORD Lg Woolwich Town Cl motor. Ex GUCC/BW
STANDEDGE No 1 72672
STANDEDGE TUNNEL 74879
STANLEY 80254 BW-
STANLEY Tug
STANLEY CHARLES B1279
STANNEY 89241 Motor vessel BW-NW
STAN'S WAY 50335
STAPLETON 72252
STARCROSS 50504
STARDUST 70094
STARFIRE 48389
STARFIRE 79144
STARGAZER 63500

STARLIGHT 63533
STARLIGHT 78403
STARLING 51272
STARLING 71696
STAR PRINCESS 100407
STARRY STARRY NIGHT 76343
STAR TREK 47033
STEADFAST *49052 NbT grn*
STEADFAST 61603
STEADFAST 500653
STEALAWAY 50010
STEELAWAY 48006
STEELAWAY 50319 REACH OUT PROJECTS Hire (groups with young people inc. disabled/ disadvantaged and others in community). Nb 65', b 7' blue. B: 1992 Steelcraft. Lister ST3. Base Nash Mills, GU. Includes full access and facilities for disabled people. 029745
STEELAWAY 66703
STEEL RIGG *NbT 60' grn*
STELFOX 53605
STELLA MARIA 77737
STELLA MARIS 47447
STELLERN 68158 STAFFORD NbC Fibre glass roof on steel hull/sides 40' pale blue. B: 1975 Brian Artis as hire boat - with fibreglass sides; called a Trentham 40 design. Present owner refitted and replaced sides with steel. Lister SR2. Base Stafford Boat Club, S&W canal. Built for 1975 Earl's Court boat show - taken there on low loader (owners have even met the driver who discovered boat had been finished in 2 shades of blue - one each side!). Original name *Marauder* then sold to hire company in Wales and renamed *Viola*. Has much admired galleon done in stained glass in one porthole. 24876
STEMMA 80437
STENSON BUBBLE 77196
STENTOR 72253
STEPHANIE ANNE 51361
STEPHANN 48129
STEPHANO 78936
STEVADORE 63864
STEVEN B1640
STEWPONEY 60466
STILL FRISKY B0298
STILL MAGIC 54961
STILL THINKING 69079
STILLWATER 70206
STILTER 64620
STIRRINGS 62294
STOAT 62251
STOAT 89069 Dredger (hydraulic) 43' BW-NW
STOAT *NbT 30' red*
STOAT Barney(55) 1976 35'
STOKER 73631 PA GAMBLE & Co KILBY BRIDGE WHARF NbT 48' Oxford blue/ burgundy. B: 1986 Ironwork, Nazeing, Essex, f/o by owner. Hercules 2-127 (1942). Base Kilby Bridge, GU-Leics. 21245
STOKIE No. 1 53212 TRADITIONAL CANAL CARRIERS KENNET & AVON Commercial carrying Nb, blue sheeted hold, 72', d 30" (empty) 3'8" (fully loaded) red oxide/ blue/red. B: 1991/93 John Pinder, Stoke Prior, f/o

Pinder & Son + the late David Sharman and Brioni Sharman. Ruston Hornsby (India) 2YWM 15hp at 1000rpm. Base K&A canal. Carries coal, steel, wood, etc. up to 23 tons. Distinguished as last working boat built and history made as the first to deliver a load (of wood) at Bradford on Avon wharf for 50 years. This done in 1995 by Brioni and John Chard following her husband David's tragic death before he could see his ambition realised. Space saving arrangements include kitchen sink in engine room and shower fitted between engine room and hold. In Summer of 1996 travelled delivering charcoal for IWA barbecues and joined in on BCN Explorer Cruise (winched by BW off shallow object in middle of Walsall canal); followed this by winning 'Cressy' award for best all year live aboard boat at IWA Windmill End Festival in 1996. First working boat to win the Silver Buckby Can. Owner/operators welcome carrying enquiries *(see page 14).* 251016
STOLEN MOMENTS 45877
STONECHAT 45940
STORK B0740 REGISTERED AT MANCHESTER No. 1123 W.H. COWBURN & COWPAR Ltd. MANCHESTER NbT motor, steel rivetted, round bilge, pointed stern 72', b 7', d 3' mar/graining/grn. B: 1934 W.J. Yarwood, Northwich. Still powered by original single cylinder 4 VT 2-str - hot bulb diesel started by blowlamp and brass retracting pin in flywheel; 12.6bhp at 475rpm through a Ferry gearbox. Controlled either in engine room or at steering position. Base Lorenz Boatyard, Barton, Bridgewater canal. Carried chemicals in carboys (continued as working boat till 1951) - now preserved with hold clothed up. Used for exhibit and pleasure. Has 100 gal diesel tank with 10 gal gravity feed tank mounted over the top. Relevant historical accounts of the company, W.H. Cowburn & Cowpar and its boats in Waterways World Jan 86 and Feb 92. 24915
STORK Tug 6m BW-CATM
STORM 69471
STORM 74769
STORM 101024
STORM PETREL 49840
STORMY WATERS B1607
STORNAWAY 46329
STORNOWAY *NbT 50' bl/wh/red*
STOUR No 87 FMC motor. Ex T.Clayton
STOUR 81823 Mtce boat 16.9m BW-
STRATFORD 500578
STRATFORD Motor. WW
STRATFORD Iceboat. Boat Museum
STRATHMORE 79870
STRATTOCRUZ 46833
STRATUS 77120
STRAVAIG 75106
STRAVAIG 77493
STRAW BEAR 77877 WHITTLESEA NbT 46' bl/red. B: 1980ish Original Boat Company. Lister FR2. Base Whittlesea - and all over European canals including UK. Prior to 1987 known as *Pensylvania Yankee*. Present name after ancient

Cambridgeshire Fens custom in which 'Plough Boy' dressed in straw dances in the streets following the dressed plough, on Plough Sunday early in January; now unique to Whittlesea. 22424
STRAWBERRY CLOVER 62078
STRAWBERRY FIELDS 48078
STREAK 46281
STREATLEY Restored Salter Bros. steamer
STREET GIRL NbC 50' blue
STRETTON 79741
STRIDER 48642
STRIDER 51601
STRIKER 73775
STRIP THE WILLOW 071600 ND & MF PANZETTER NbC 40' dk grn/old gold. B: 1984/5 Colecraft, f/o Mick & Tony George, Boat Breakdown Co., Fenny Compton. BL 1.8. Base Braunston. 23611
STROLLER 68044
STROLLING BONES 74795
STRONGBOW 50926
STRUGGLE 63514
STRUMBLE 72732 NbT 32' bl/red. B: 1983 Doug Moore (when trading at Riley Green as J.J. Crook Boat-builder). Barnes Leyland 1.5. Base L&L and S&W. Lots of sweeping curves typical of Doug Moore boat. Debut at IWA National Rally at Wigan as trade exhibit attracting lots of attention. 25952

STUART 048057 Hire. NbC 63' navy blue/lt blue. B: 1990 Lister LPWS. Base Sally Boats, Bradford on Avon marina. 013237
STUART STEVENS 85277
STUDELEY CASTLE 71753
STYRBORN 86846
STYVRA III 75375 NbT 40' grn
SUE 83736
SUEBRYAR 53127
SUE ELLEN 70806
SUKI JAYN 63787
SULBY BW-L&S
SULCATUS 68003
SULIS 054211 DEVIZES NbST 55' dk blue. B: 1994 John White, f/o Triton Boats. Lombardini 1204. Base Hilperton, K&A canal. 24806
SULTAN FMC Saltley steamer
SULTAN NbT 50' blue
SULTANA 68125
SULTAN SENTINEL 53743
SUMMER 103041
SUMMER BREEZE 46605
SUMMER BREEZE 64162
SUMMER LADY 65176 NbC steel/grp 60' red/grn. B: 1974 approx - no history available but several different owners and refits. Lister SR3 air cooled. Base Cooks Wharf, Cheddington, GU. 25937
SUMMER PLACE 73288 NbC 30' blue

Stowe Hill Marine

Constructors of Quality Narrow Boats

We are specialists in the building of totally unique narrowboats. Every boat is carefully planned to suit your own individual requirements.

We are one of only a very few companies to undertake all aspects of the build. Established in 1983 since when we have created many superb craft.

Our product is designed for the more serious, elitist boater. If you demand the best then you need look no further.

Full colour brochure on request.

Stowe Hill Wharf, Weedon, Northamptonshire NN7 4RZ
Telephone (01327) 341365

British Marine Industries Federation

SUMMER WINE 50479
SUMMER WINE 76996
SUMMER WINE 77242
SUMMER WINE B0164
SUMO 80831
SUN 80251 Motor vessel 15.24m BW-NE
SUNBAR M20301 Grp 16' brown. B: 1978 Mayland, Essex. Mercury 75 (7.5hp) ob. Base R.Medway. 20202
SUNBEAM 60048
SUNBIRD 60299
SUNBIRD *NbT 50' mar*
SUNBURY 69266
SUNDANCE Hire. NbC 60' red/grn. Base Rose Narrowboats, Brinklow, N.Oxford canal. 026717
SUNDANCE 53874
SUNDANCE 54454
SUNDANCE 102247
SUNDANCER 50493
SUNDAY GIRL 72979
SUNDOWNER 45101
SUNDOWNER 45773
SUNDOWNER 60074
SUNDOWNER 83452
SUNDOWNER 91612
SUNDOWNER 49617
SUNFISH EXETER SR No. A5312F Grp 5m, b 1.9m, d 0.25m yel. B: circa 1985 Microplus 502. 50hp Mercury ob 2-str, electric start. Trailed from home alongside Grand Western canal. 23610
SUNFLOWER 75249
SUNFLOWER *103786 Grp yel*
SUN KING 48037
SUNLIGHT 31116
SUN & MOON 77520
SUNNYBROOK 49827
SUNNY VALLEY / NORTHOLT Nb Commercial carrying working butty - forecabin boat - in livery as formerly operated under Captain Cargo Ltd. - red/grn/yel; iron composite construction. B: 1897 (believed correct) for Fellows, Morton & Clayton Ltd. Base Coventry & GU canals. 031819
SUNRAY 48208
SUNRAY 48420
SUNRAY 88182
SUNRISE 46494
SUNRISE 49874
SUNRISE 62576
SUNRISE 73663
SUNRISE 74606
SUNSEEKER *NbST 55' grn/red*
SUNSET 45782
SUNSET 61134
SUNSET *62287 Grp 35' bl/wh*
SUOA NOVA 68264
SUPERB OWL 50104
SUPER SKIFF
SUPER STAR 85861
SUPERSTAR 79141 J & S GUNNING / C & J GIBBS BEAMINSTER NbC 58'6" red/grn. B: 1981 Hancock & Lane. Volkswagen Golf 1600. Base Gayton marina. Ex Cowroast hire fleet. 21456
SUPER TROOPER 60718

SUPREME Hire. NbC 60' blue/red. Base The Wyvern Shipping Co, Linslade, GU. 00436
SUPREME 54934
SUPREME 64698
SURDRAW II 102468
SUREETA 77541
SURONDA II 73268
SURREY Hire. NbC 50' red. B: 1980 Godalming Narrow Boats, Colecraft hull. BMC 1.8. Base Farncombe Boat House, R.Wey. 00375
SURVEYOR 74885 NI Registration: 3590 NbT 50' blue/wh. B: 1988 Canal Craft Boatbuilders, Coven, Staffs., f/o by 1990 by owner with professionally fitted services. Thornycroft 1800cc. Base (currently - 1996 - at The Moorings, Bellanaleck, Co. Fermanagh, N.Ireland). *Surveyor* was freight shipped to Republic of Ireland in May 1996 and took part in the Shannon-Erne 150 Rally and the 36th IWA Ireland Shannon Rally. 22480
SURVIVOR 65862
SU SA LU TU B1657
SUSAMIS 85983
SUSAN 75107
SUSAN BELLE 66927
SUSAN MARY 46314
SUSANNE II *79365 Grp 20' wh*
SU SIAN 74869 NO. 8 BUILT NORBURY JUNCTION 1967 NbC steel/wood cabin. 42' grn/grey. B: 1967 Shropshire Union Boatbuilders, Norbury Junction; cabin - built by David Piper as an apprentice - mahogany framed, marine ply exterior, pine interior. Re-fitted 1989. Lister SR2 (1967 original), manual change fwd/rev gearbox. Base Llangollen canal. Distinctive curved lines to cabin, mahogany handrails on roof. 25964
SUSIAN 97270
SUSIE - B 50297 SAWLEY NbT 50' aircraft blue. B: 1991 R&D Fabrications, Ollerton, f/o Anchor Boats, Eastwood. Perkins 4108. Base Sawley marina. 24766
SUSIE Q
SUSIE-Q *NbC 45' red/grn*
SUSIE TOO 92057
SUTHERLAND 67737
SUTTON 52778
SUTTON 177 71965 Lg Woolwich Town Cl motor. Ex GUCC/BW
SUTTON STOP Barney(53) 1975 35'
SUTTY 77209
SUZANNA GLOYN 70362
SUZANNAH *65194 NbC 45' red/grn*
SUZANNAH LUCY 76014
SUZANNE 65983
SUZANNE 78447
SUZIBELLE 77681
SUZIE 76140
SUZIE B 46885
SUZIE B 62559
SUZI-JO III 97078
SUZY 62559
SVEN 73535
SWAGMAN 66317
SWALE II Tug 10m BW-NE
SWALLOW 46931

163

SWALLOW B1218 MANCHESTER 1121 Commercial carrying. NbT round bilged 72', b 7'1", d 3' mar/bl. B: 1934 Yarwoods of Northwich, restored Lorenz & Co. National 2DM twin cyl., built circa 1935. Base Bridgewater canal, Barton Aqueduct. Originally built to carry chemicals for Cowburn & Cowpar Ltd. Entered maintenance fleet as a dumb workboat and was then purchased and fully restored by present owner to original working order and arrangement. The Cowburn & Cowpar fleet of narrow boats traded from Trafford Park to Coventry and Wolverhampton with chemicals for the various Courtauld factories. Loads were not excessive as speed was essential to keep plants supplied. 10 days allowed for return trip to Coventry, 7 to Wolverhampton, inc loading/unloading. Eight motor boats were built in mid 30s, all named after birds having initial 's' and having a cut out of the bird on cabin side. All 8 motor boats still extant, most are painted in their original livery.   0351005
SWALLOW 54895 STOURPORT NbC 46' red/grn.   B: 1986 Severn Valley Cruisers, Stourport. Thornycroft/Mitsubishi. Base Stourport Basin. Has cruiser style fore end incorporating bedroom cabin (no open deck or cratch); also sliding steel roof.   24824
SWALLOW 053917 NbST 58' blue/gold. B: 1994 Pat Buckle, Stibbington. Mitsubishi/Boatserve 1.4 4 cyl. Base Blue Lias marina. An Ownerships, shared ownership scheme boat.   24839
SWALLOW 65782
SWALLOW 65998
SWALLOW 67265
SWALLOW 71843
SWALLOW 71884
SWALLOW N7286
SWALLOW RETURN 73424
SWALLOWTAIL II 69945 GRANTHAM NbST (Northwich) 60' dk blue/straw. B: 1979 Rugby Boatbuilders on Colecraft shell. J G Meakes BMC 1.5. Base Sawley marina, R.Trent.   23544
SWAN 48891
SWAN 49775
SWAN 51531
SWAN 52998
SWAN 74185
SWAN B0659
SWAN Motor. Ex Cowburn & Cowpar
SWAN Tug 19'6" BW-OGU
SWAN LAKE Hire. NbC 56' red/grn. Base Rose Narrowboats, Brinklow, N.Oxford canal.   026715
SWANSCOMBE 500584 CLIFTON CRUISERS Hire. NbC 40' grn/crm.   B: 1995 Club Line, Coventry, f/o Clifton Cruisers. BL 1.8. Base Clifton Wharf, Rugby. Diesel c/heating.   025670
SWAN SONG 45134
SWAN SONG 103305
SWAN SONG No 1 45091
SWAZI CHIEF No 3 76310
SWEDEN 887
SWEDEN NbT (motor) red/grn
SWEET BRIAR B1659
SWEET DREAM 54230

SWEET GEORGIA BROWN 65605
SWEET JENNY 46982
SWEET LIFE B0963
SWEET PEACE 52581
SWEET SENSATION 101934
SWEET SOUND 49256
SWEET SUCCESS 62267
SWIFT 1119
SWIFT 50152
SWIFT 81822 Motor vessel 52'6" BW-OGU
SWIFT 84912
SWIFT 91813
SWIFT 101230 Grp Norman 20
SWIFT Motor. Ex Cowburn & Cowpar. Heritage craft: BW-BBC
SWIFT No 2 71004
SWILLER 62388
SWIMP 70171
SWINTON Motor vessel BW-NE
SWISS COTTAGE 69439
SWN-Y-DWR
SWN-Y-PDRAIG 52263
SWN YRAFON Nb 60' red/grn
SWORDFISH 45482
SWORDFISH Grp 20'
SYBARIS 60058
SYCAMORE 69913 MIDDLEWICH NARROWBOATS No. 9 Hire. NbT. trad built wooden cabin, 70' grn/red. B: (year not known) Hancock & Lane, Willow Wren cabin. Lister SR3. Base Middlewich. Classic "Willow Wren" style hire boat.   028733
SYCAMORE 74360
SYLKE 70869
SYLPHIDE 65520
SYLVARNA 47228
SYLVIA ANN 500507 Bridgewater 1863 WINCHAM WHARF BOATBUILDERS Nb 35' dk blue/lt blue. B: 1996 Colliery Narrow Boat Co. Wincham Wharf. Beta Marine 20hp. Base Preston Brook marina. All steel cabin at rear.   23654
SYLVIANNE 62599
SYLVIAS GIRL 78512
SYLVIE III 84608
SYLVIRIS KILDWICK 67802
SYMBOL 698 (SU fleet no.) REGISTERED AT CHESTER No. 732 BCN No 771 SHROPSHIRE UNION R & C Co. Traditional wooden Nb - Shropshire Union fly boat. 71'6", d 1' (unladen), 2'9" (laden) bl/wh. B: 1914 Shropshire Union Railway & Canal Carrying Company (owned by London & North Western Railway Co.), Trefor Dock, Llangollen canal. Horse drawn. Base Trefor Dock, undergoing restoration by the Symbol Restoration Society Ltd., by remarkable coincidence, in the dock by the Pontcysyllte Aqueduct where she was built. *Symbol* is one of the only two remaining Shropshire Union Fly boats left in the world (the other is *Saturn*) and the only one in original condition; probably the last - as far as is known - narrowboat left built in Wales. The Society's intention is to restore and operate this boat as closely to the original as possible. As a complete working unit of boat, crew, horse and

164

cargo moving through the canal and its architecture, it will directly explain, as a complete mobile canal museum, the first principals of the collaboration between man and natural forces. Support and membership of the Society sought *(see page 14).*   22519

SYMBOL No 2 53292
SYMI 46887
SYMPHONY 53760
SYMPHONY 64011
SYMPHONY 103967
SYNERGY 50099
SYON 78485
SYRIAN PRINCE 47344
SYRINX 65692

Symbol undergoing major restoration in the dock at Trevor where she was built.   [Harry Arnold, Waterway Images

T

If agitated or disturbed it will suck in air and blow itself up, unique Nb power, Indian connections and a Ragdoll Duke. Half a Joey with model railway, an electrical pioneer, a Black Country hammer and a hair-raising name. Top marks for Malcolm. Spare "Coventry" steel turned into 70' Nb and Rolt encouraged hire boating here

TA'BITHA MICK AND MARY HUTT FENNY STRATFORD NbST 70' grn. B: 1995 Mel Davies Boat Builder, Tuxford, nr Newark, self f/o 1996. Beta BD3 Tug. Base Fenny Stratford, GU. Steel roof over foredeck and forecabin. 21269
TABLEYMERE 48240
TACET II *Grp Madeira 21' wh*
TACWOOD II *NbT 50'*
TADWORTH 178 69771 Lg Woolwich Town Cl. Ex GUCC/BW
TACWOOD II 47979
TADPOLE 68400
TAFELBERG 101326
TAFFY 69935
TAFFYTOO 73620
TAHELIA 45971
TAI-PAN *NbT 60' blue/red*
TAKE FIVE 52633
TAKE FIVE *NbT 50' mar/blue*
TAKE IT EASY 49354
TAKE TWO 49549
TAKITEASY 101780
TAKORADI No.2 *NbT 55' blue/crm*
TALACHARN 47412
TALANA II N7652 Grp 27' wh/blue. B: 1980 Nauticus. 1.8 BMC, Enfield Z-drive (swivel type). Base Billing Aquadrome, R.Nene. 23598
TALESIN 74313
TALIESIN 79270
TALISMAN 45617
TALISMAN 45873
TALISMAN 67741 NbC 40' red/grn. B: 1976 Canal & Rivercraft, Sowerby Bridge. Lister 2 cyl SR2 air cooled. Base Milton Keynes, GU. Former name *Whistler*. 24768
TALISMAN No 3 46615
TALISMAN IV 71490
TALISMAN VI 67785
TALONS VENTURE 46900
TALPA 60500
TALYLLYN 79864
TAMAH 47540 STOCKTON NbC 45' mid coach grn/ayes red. B: 1989 R&M Burden, Blue Lias Marine (No. 5), private f/o. BMC 1.8, PRM gearbox. Base Gibralter bridge, Stockton. 24792
TAMAR 66883
TAMAR B0888
TAMARA LOUISE 77796
TAMARIN 85969
TAMARIND 46962
TAMARIND 51490
TAMARIND 66620 NbT 35' grn. B: 1980 Canal Transport Services. BMC 1.5. Base Latham Marine, Burscough, L&L canal. Wooden top, Masonite, steel hull. 23641
TAMARINDA 73848
TAMARISK 30767
TAMARISK 67266
TAMARISK 68244
TAMARISK 70600
TAMARISK 71854
TAMARISK B0373
TAMARIU 74948
TAMASANA 64382
TAMBOURLAINE 60890
TAME 81713 BW-
TAME VALLEY 71463
TAMER 75459
TAMILY 53371
TAMINA 70519
TAM LIN 070564 G.O. & J.C. WATSON MANCHESTER NbTug 47' red/bl. B: 1983 Barry Jenkins. Coventry Victor HDW3 twin cyl, horizontally opposed 28hp. Base Grindley Brook, Llangollen canal. Full length recessed panelling, tug style with distinctive fine bow shape. 24832
TAMLIN 66727
TAMMI TROOT 81833
TAMSIN CRICK MARINA NbST 58' dk blue/mar. B: 1997 Tim Tyler, f/o Barry Hawkins Narrowboats. Beta BV1903. Base Crick marina. Large sliding steel hatch covering the semi-trad area and folding lockable steel shutters covering windows. 24826
TAMSIN 72906
TAMWORTH 65172
TAMWORTH 72678
TANA FJORD 62089
TANA FJORD 76367
TANBEES 49099 WILLINGTON NbT 47' grn/red. B: 1990 Colecraft. Thornycroft 80. Base Braunston marina. 2082
TANDE 53183
TANDEL 103593
TANDEL II 30540
TANDY 62351
TANELORN 50797
TANGERINE 67258
TANGLE 102357
TANGLEWOOD 47647
TANGLEWOOD *Nb 30' mar/grn*
TANGO 78857
TANGO 97434
TANIWHA 79078
TANTO 80969
TANUK 54842
TANZANITE 49947
TAPESTRY 52383
TAPYNOT 78477
TARA 52290
TARA TOO 82498
TARA ROSE 70056 Nb 35' red/grn. B: 1976 Springer. 1.5 BMC, PRM 101 gearbox. Base Hallingbury Mill, R.Stort. Name on black oval name boards, named after granddaughter of first owner. 23559
TARDEBIGGE *74740 NbC red/grn*

166

TARDIS   49186
TARDIS   88989
TARDIS   99670
TARDIS   B0931
TARDIS II   73168
TARDY   49026
TARKA   51639
TARKA   52475
TARKA   62849
TARKA   65427
TARKA   69987
TARKA   75775
TARKA   B0290
TARKA XII   68631
TARN Mtce boat 70' BW-BBC
TARNHELM   69598   H&E MEANWELL BREWOOD NbT 58' red/grn. B: 1974 Malcolm Braine, Norton Canes. Captain 1500. Base Country Wide Cruisers, Brewood. Bought by present owners from Malcolm Braine in 1977; "our floating cottage - a particularly handsome Malcolm Braine product!"   261055
TARNWOOD   78506
TAROPAKA   54341
TARPORLEY   64483
TARRY AWHILE   76277
TARRY DANCER   104248
TARYN   67810
TASELYN   79309
TASHA-LEE   49780
TASHO   101531
TASSELWEED   61848
TASSY   47764
TASTOMA   52859
TAT   63106
TATLA   97326
TATTIE BOGLE   65612
TAUNTON   60782
TAUPIO   50590
TAURUS   49177
TAURUS   53357
TAURUS   60029 Mid Northwich Star Cl butty. Ex GUCC/BW/Threefellows
TAURUS   54980 POTTAGE AND CO CANAL TOWAGE HUDDERSFIELD No 1 NbTug 59' grey/red. B: 1995 Kenfield Boatbuilder, self f/o. Gardner 3LW. Base Calder & Hebble Navigation. Low in water, deep draught, recessed panels, tug deck, rivets, etc.   25997
TAURUS   67194
TAURUS   68436
TAURUS   71576
TAURUS   74504
TAURUS *Hotel boat (butty) red/bl*
TAVY CLEAVE   96315 Cabin cruiser, marine ply 36' mahogany/blue.   B: 1964 Holt Abbott, Stourport. 3 cyl Vetus. Base Hermitage marina, Earith, R.Great Ouse. Holt Abbott was the first builder to make purpose built hire boats for canal hire, encouraged by Tom Rolt.   22527
TAWNY OWL   49974 NbC 31' blue/mar. B: 1991 Mick Sivewright, Barbridge Marina, Wardle, SU. Vetus 10.5hp. Base Newbury, K&A canal.   20184
TAWNY OWL   73891

TAWNY OWL   75996
TAWNY PIPIT   49842
TAY No 90 FMC River Cl. motor. Ex Clayton
TAYGETA *BW heritage boat 70'*
TAYLOR MADE   75970
TCHAIKOVSKY   68159
TEAL   45659
TEAL   49040
TEAL   52422
TEAL   61858
TEAL   B1712
TEASEL   82816
TEASEL   500167 RYTON NbT 70' British racing green/post office red.   B: 1995 Warble, Hyde, Cheshire. Beta BD3 Tug. Base T&M canal. Warble's 50th boat, first with true engine room. Serious kitchen (3-person). Integral bicycle stowage in engine room! Featured in Canal & Riverboat Aug 1996 article with full details of the high specification.   23601
TECKEL   46029
TEDDY   49429 NbT 40' royal blue.   B: 1990 Liverpool Boats, f/o various - completed 1995 by owner and Streethay Wharf. BMC 1.5. Base Middlewich. Cratch board has teddy bears painted by Dusty Miller; coach lines with leaf patterns in corners, two cast plaques with boat name in floral surround.   23652
TEE CEE   63081
TEE JAY   31617
TEIDE   65184
TEILA   47489
TEINPEACE Motor vessel BW-NE
TELCREST   51190
TELEMACHUS   66584
TELFORD   70178
TELFORD   68660
TELFORD   70178
TELFORD Grp 40' wh/navy. B: 1969. Perkins 4,107. Base Lechlade marina.   24822
TELSTAR   71464
TEME   82375 BW-
TEMERAIRE   51623
TEMPO COMMODO   52220
TEMPTRESS TOO   67223
TEMPUS LENTEM   64138
TEMPUS LENTEM Barney(47) 1975 35' *(ex Fenners)*
TEMUJIN   65700
TANACITY   46260
TENCH 326   62812   Yarwoods Fish Cl motor. Ex FMC/BW
TENDER   88744
TENNIAD   62904
TE PU   66740   PUGSONS OF DERBY   NbC Grp superstructure 45' bl/wh/grn. B: 1975 Greaves Engineering, Derby, f/o by original owner, Swan Line, Fradley Junction. Lister SR2. Base Bond End canal. Cratch added (which seems unusual for grp superstructure type). Hull has very pleasing longitudinal curve (sheer) of gunwale. Article about this class of boat in Waterways World October 1972.   23730
TEQUILA IV   45119

TERESA 66545
TERESA III 61178
TERMITE Mtce boat, flat, powered 30' BW-NW
TERN 45658
TERN Mtce boat 9.6m BW-
TERNDALE 71493
TERPSICHORE II 64009
TERRYANN 74507
TERSHALL Barney(33) 1973 35' *(ex Muskoka)*
TESA 50556
TESLA 52129 RADCLIFFE CARRYING OXFORD ENGLAND Nb 70' mar/blue. B: 1992 Graham Edgeson, Norton Canes Boatbuilders. Kobota governed to 2100rpm, hydraulic propulsion to prop. Base Thrupp. All 240v power from 9kw generator or 4kw inverter - very quiet, smooth in use. *Tesla's* owner works in the field of magnetic resonance imaging and created the boat in recognition of Nikola Tesla's contribution to science, engineering and humanity. Tesla, born Croatia 1856, emigrated to America. He was obsessed with concept of electrical resonance and made many discoveries in fields of electricity and magnetism. Invented alternating current electric motor; most importantly his inventions led to generation, transmission and consumption of alternating current in our homes and factories. 22440
TESS 46988
TESS 52153
TESS *74783 NbT 60' blue*
TESS 96186
TESS B1568

TESSA 054410 LONGPORT WHARF No. 193 NbT 46'10" mid coach grn/Dovedale grn. B: 1994/5 Stoke on Trent Boatbuilding. Beta BD1305. Base Chirk marina, Llangollen canal.
24780
TESSA 500846
TESS ADVENTURE 101178
TETRAD 49649
TEUFLIN 63402
TEWITFIELD Motor vessel flat, powered 35' BW-NW
TEWKESBURY 47731
TEWKESBURY 52489
TEXAS STAR *53210 NbC 40' mar/blue*
TEZZERA 47931
THAI *Nb 70'*
THALIA 68846
THAMZON 62306
THANE 74305
THARK 69330
THAXTED 66235 Lg Woolwich Town Cl motor. Ex GUCC/WW/UCC

Boat names including the word "the", when clearly given, are listed as such. It is possible that "the" may have been excluded, therefore check for next word alphabetically.

THE ADMIRAL 500498 J.P. & T.J. OWEN AND MATES NbC 45' mar/navy blue. B: 1996 B.K. Stokes, Bettisfield Boats, Whitchurch. Bukh. Base GU canal. Many people ask who the "Mates" are - this refers to the two dogs. 22511

The Bodger: half a Joey, awaits slipping for regular maintenance

168

THE ANGRY BULL 65650 DAY-STAR THEATRE AUDLEM Travelling theatre NbT 60' burgundy/dk blue. B: 1976 David Piper, Red Bull Basin, Kidsgrove; extended 45' to 60' by Keith Humby, Minerva Wharf, Wolverhampton. BMC 1.5. Base Old Stables, Audlem, SU canal. Used since 1983 by Day-Star Theatre for Summer boat tour. 21343

THE BODGER AUDREY & TEDDY BOSTON CADEBY NbST converted Birmingham Joey boat 40' grn/red/yel. B: 19-- John Vernon, converted 1976 by Audrey & Teddy Boston. BMC 1.5 (originally Armstrong Whitworth single cylinder with 4-1 reduction). Base Sutton Cheney. Purchased from British Steel (fleet no. 113) at Coombswood in 1976 for £500. Bow hauled down Farmers Bridge and Aston locks and ultimately, through frozen canals, to the Ashby canal in Nov 1976. Winched out of water on Boxing Day, cut in half on the spot and taken to Church Farm, Newbold Verdon (Leics.) where, for 3 years, the 2 boats were completed using recycled materials. For example, the solid fuel stove found by the railway line near Nuneaton, near a cemetery, while attending a funeral! Named *Bodger* after Teddy's first model railway engine.
Boats were towed by road with a pair of wheels converting them to portable wheelbarrows, to be re-launched at Sutton Cheney Wharf in 1979. Unfortunately engine was so slow (1mph) so *Bodger* taken out of water next year to have BMC 1.5 fitted.
Teddy naturally wanted it powered by steam (having a steam museum at Cadeby *(unmissable! - compiler)*) but Audrey had no intention of putting more muck and grime on the boat. However she allowed him a model railway on board - narrow guage - 'N', to satisfy his steam interest. 25981

THE BOWMAN *NbC 25' ob*

THE CASTLE *NbT 60' grn*

THE CITY OF SHEFFIELD *Nb 70'*

THE COUNTESS 51575 ALVECOTE No. 16 NbT 55' mar/crm. B: 1992 Narrowcraft, Alvecote. Ford XLD/Thornycroft. Base Whilton marina, GU. 202

THE DUCHESS No.14 *NbT 60' mar*

THE DUKE OF BRIDGEWATER 66593 LEICESTER BOAT CO. LTD. THE WATERSIDE CENTRE Trip boat - 48 seats. Nb 70' red/grn. B: 1963 Hancock & Lane. 2 cyl Lister. Base Waterside Centre, Abbey Meadows, Leicester. The only boat licensed by Ragdoll Productions Ltd to operate themed Rosie & Jim trips in conjunction with Rosie & Jim Waterside Experience. 2030

THE ELECTRIC FERRET *Grp 15' wh/blue*

THE EMPRESS AND THE SAVAGE 46798 D.J. COOPER - LONDON NbT 70' red/brown. B: 1989 Jonathon Wilson. De Havilland 50hp. Base London, GU canal. 24882

THE FLOSS *70401 NbC 30' red/grn*

THEFOUROFUS 65505

THE GO-BETWEEN Barney(26) 1973 32'

THE HARGREAVES 65314 REGISTERED CHARITY NO 1037467 Trip boat. Nb 70' blue. B: 1976/77 by apprentices at Cammel Laird Ship Builders, using steel surplus from the building of *HMS Coventry*. Lister twin, air cooled. Base Boot Inn, Nuneaton, Coventry canal. 12 passenger trip boat with large windows equipped for disabled passengers but offering the whole Nuneaton/ Bedworth community the opportunity of enjoying their local waterway. Operated by volunteers of The Hargreaves Narrowboat Trust. 23583

THE HEMING WAY 75297 SURREY NbT 62' blue/red. B: 1984 Colecraft, f/o at Norton Canes. Bukh 3 cyl 36hp. Base Glascote Basin, Tamworth, Coventry canal. 22398

THE HORNY TOAD 51653 TEAPOT ROW BUGSWORTH NbT 40' red/grn. B: 1992 John White, f/o by North West Narrowboats. Mitsubishi /Boatserve 3 cyl 979cc. Base New Mills marina, Upper Peak Forest canal. The Horny (or Horned) Toad is native to the southern staes of America; if agitated or disturbed it will suck in air and blow itself up. 22473

THE IRON GOOSE *64318 NbT 60' blue*

THE JAMES BRINDLEY B1681 NbC 42' chocolate brown/crm. B: 1985 Eggbridge, Chester. BMC 1.5. Base Lymm C.C. Bridgewater canal. Painted in Great Western Railway livery. 25974

THE JUGGLER *NbC 55'*

THE KOOKABURRA N7477 Midway 235 Nb 23'5" red/French blue. B: 1993 Midway Boatsales. Honda 9.9hp ob electric start. Base Stanground marina, R.Nene. 25946

THE LADY ALICE N6769 Victorian launch 60', b 6'10" blue/crm. B: 1989 Branson Boats, Crowland, Peterborough. 35hp Isuzu. Base Oundle marina, R.Nene. 20107

THE LADY LIZBETH 65842 NbT 38' burgundy/grn. B: 1977 builder not known but possibly Springer, re-fit by present owner. BMC 1500. Base Waterside, Leicester. 21209

THELEMA 64729

THELMA 63957

THELMAE 67529

THEMA 52720

THE MARYLEBONE LIGHT 45726 R SPENCE & CO LONDON Nb 71'8" navy/red. B: 1988 Black Country Narrowboats, Stourton, W.Midlands. 12.6L 'Van Rennes' semi planked built 1937 Utrecht, Holland. Base Cassio Bridge, Watford, GU. Black Country 1930's tug style hull. 24770

THEMIS 70037

THE NEW WORLD Nb 34' red/wh. B: 1986 Springer. Mitsubishi 3 cyt. Base Pyrford marina, R.Wey. 22482

THE OLD VICTORIAN 72260 NbT 45' grn/red. B: 1984 Stowe Hill Marine. BMC 1.5. Base Hampton Hall Farm, Batchworth, GU. Named after former pupils of 'Queen Victoria School', Dunblane, Scotland, a military boarding school and Scotland's memorial to Queen Victoria. 22388

THE OSTRICH 072490 NbT 35' red. B: 1986 Springer. Base Venetian marina, SU canal. 2098

THE OTTER NbT 60' mar/blue
THE RAVER 50161 NbT 50' blue/crm
THERE'N'BACK 84161
THERESE 71931
THERMOPYLAE 66902
THE RUFF Nb blue/red
THE SAUCY MRS FLOBSTER 79390 HNBOC REGISTRATION Ex-working wooden Joey Nb 48', b 6'6", d 2'10" poppy red/blue. B: 1920s/30s (probably) BCN. Heavy oil P4. Base Ellesmere canal. Converted to houseboat in 1970s. Hull disintegrated: replated using reclaimed steel in 1980s. 25929
THESEUS 91749
THE STOKIE No 1 see THE STOKIE No 1
THETA 50095
THETA 78164
THE TERRY ANN NbST 37' red/grn
THETIS 103596
THE WAKEMAN Nb Estuary tug 57' blue/red
THE WAY AHEAD NbC 40' grn/mar
THE WIZARD 51320 NbST 60' mar/crm. B: 1991 GT Boats, f/o South Shore Narrowboats. Ford 1.8/Thornycroft. Base South/Midlands canals. Built as 12 share boat, now private. "Wizard & wand" motifs painted on each side. 23550
THESEUS 91749 Cruiser - plywood/wood 20' blue/wh. B: about 1967 Brooklands Aviation Ltd., Northampton (serial no. 2270). Johnson 20hp Seahorse 2 str unleaded petrol ob. Base Old Junction Boatyard, Syston, R.Soar. 24912
THESEUS 78232 NbC 45' brunswick grn/lt grn. B: 1984 Hancock & Lane. Lister SR3. Base Fenny Compton. Formerly named *Goldstone*. 24850
THIN LIZZIE 48233
THIN LIZZY 500631
THIN LIZZY NbT 60' blue/red
THIRZA 48310
THIS ENGLAND 68921
THIS IS IT 50186
THIS'L DO 65934
THISTLE 47600
THISTLE 049025 JOE & BETTY OTTEWELL LANGLEY MILL NbTug 47' dk grey/lt grey. B: 1990 Barry Jenkins, f/o Carlin/Ottewell. Lister STW2M, prop shaft inclined down at 10°, Aquadrive deep sea seal. Base Langley Mill, Erewash canal. Last one of only 5 built, all panels recessed, all brass external fittings, all solid hardwood or pine internally, sprayed foam insulation. 22508
THISTLE 61881
THISTLE 68607
THISTLE 74428
THISTLE 77624
THISTLE 500639
THISTLE B1793
THISTLE DEW 77068
THISTLE DO 54702
THISTLE DO 88265
THISTLE DOO 61856
THISTLEDOME 52463
THISTLEDOWN 50945

THISTLE-DOWN 79198 Hire. NbC 45' red/yel. B: 1984 Les Allen, Birmingham, re-fit 1994. Lister 4 cyl. Base Linlithgow, Union Canal, Scotland. The ONLY holiday hire boat on the Edinburgh and Glasgow Union Canal. 261062
THISTLE VENTURE III 47711
THOMAS 45653
THOMAS 71930
THOMAS COVENANT 45823
THOMAS DADFORD Trip boat. NbST 22' red/grn. B: 1990 Watercraft, Maesyscwmmer. Ob. Base Resolven, Neath canal. Public trip boat on newly restored Neath canal. Named after original Engineer/Surveyor of canal in 18th Century. 22383
THOMAS FREDERICK 53832
THOMAS FRIAR 51813
THOMAS GORDON 52984
THOMAS HARRIET 48441
THOMAS LAWTON 45490
THOMAS RYAN 51743
THOMAS TELFORD 51889
THOMAS TELFORD 66979
THOMAS TELFORD see VICTORIA
TH'OMMER 71904 B.D. BULLOCK, CHURCHBRIDGE NbC 72', b 7', d 2'9" blue/red. B: 1986 Allen & Co., Oldbury, f/o Teddesley Boat Co. Air cooled Lister. Base Stafford Boat Club. Designed for two people to a personal spec. Teak interior. Named after Black Country for hammer (owner's factory makes hammers) 251021
THOR 46572
THOR 66281
THOR 71545
THOR 73835
THOR I 81549
THOR No 2 Tug
THORIN 65995
THORIN 72811
THORN No 1 67010
THORNBIRD 49864
THORNBIRD 77248 RS & MM THORNE NbTug 38' grn/red. B: 1982 Colecraft. Lister ST2 Canal Star. Base Wyre Piddle, Lower Avon Navigation. Folding cratch board design protected by patent 8500014 taken out by previous owner (see Narrow Boat Apr 1985). Stylized image of a bird on large aluminium plaques. 22506
THORNBIRD NbC 40' red/blue
THORNBURY 44758
THORNBURY 45080
THORNE Motor vessel 14.95m BW-NE
THREE DEES 66473
THREEFELLOWS 62370
THREE OF CLUBS 66846
THREE PIPS 83891
THREE-WAY-CUT 500411 ALVECOTE No 25 FENN, EDWARDS AND CLARK NbT 57' azure blue. B: 1995 Colecraft, f/o Narrowcraft Ltd, Alvecote. Kingfisher KD26. Base Alvecote, Coventry canal. 22419
THROSTLE No 3 53717
THRUPENCE 48446
THUMP 49926
THUMPER 64459

Tenacity - elegant traditional cruiser

THUMPER 66262
THUNDER see *CHUG*
THUNDERCHIEF 70826
THUNDERBALLS see *CHUG*
THURLESTONE 47459 NbC 64' blue/mar. B: 1989 Colecraft, f/o 1990 Warwickshire Narrowboats. Reconditioned Thornycroft 1.8 BL. Base Chirk marina, Llangollen canal. Originally 54' but lengthened/additional f/o by above firms. 22416
THURLWOOD 63937
THURLWOOD 72475
THYME 45604
THYME 53766
THYME 79077
THYME Barney(35) 1974 32' *(ex Galka II)*
THYME II 46252
TIBET 48886
TICHITORO 72371
TICKEY 69853
TICONDEROGA 066824 Nb 55'6" lt blue/dk blue. 1976/77 Tolladine Boat Services Ltd, Stoke Prior. 4 cyl water cooled Thornycroft 90. Base Stratford marina, Stratford upon Avon. Name from Iroquois Indian: "between two lakes" and town in New York State, USA. 21363
TIDDLEY JOSSMAN 45715
TIDDY OGGY III Grp Thames cruiser 35' wh/blue
TIDOS Barney(2) 1969 50' *(ex The Fossa)*
TIG NbT 18' mar/blue
TIGER 72977
TIGER CUB 53022
TIGER CUB 74112
TIGER LILY 53467
TIGER LILY 68743

TIGER M 49414 WA & E HOLMES & CO. WYKEN NbT 50', d 2'6" dk red/dk blue. B: 1990 Graham Edgson, Norton Canes, f/o Blue Haven, Stockton. Ruggerini 2 cyl 1700cc water cooled (24hp @ 2000 rpm). Base Wyken basin, N.Oxford. 24881
TIGERMIST I 94483
TIGER MOTH NbT 70' blue/crm
TIGGER 45301
TIGGER 70432
TIGGER 75675
TIGGER II 45167 Grp 8.18m wh. B: 1982 Norman Cruisers. 25hp Mariner ob. Base Whilton marina, GU. 23661
TIGHT ALNWICK 79987
TILBURY 74617
TILLER GIRL 51213
TILLEY 51213
TILLEY 62597 NbC, grp top, 35' Bounty mar/crm/Donegal grn. B: 1971 Atlas Cruisers Ltd, Batley, Yorks. 1.5 BL taken from J4 van and rebuilt, gearbox originally from a fish & chip van but now replaced with Newage hydraulic. Base Waterside Moorings, Marple, Macclesfield canal. 24914
TILLEY 2 62821
TILLEY FLOSS 52518
TILLINGBORNE II 67334
TILLY 62619
TILLY 84396
TILLY MINT B1003
TIMARU 73527
TIMBERS 73411
TIM BOBBIN 68513

TIME 72830 Nb 40′, d 3′ red/grn. B: 1964, new bottom/top 1991. Lister 15hp. Base Robinsons Boatyard, Dewsbury. Counter stern. 23606
TIME No 1 74349
TIME MACHINE 50667
TIMES MANY 77377 *NbT 50′ grn/red*
TIMEWARP 67068
TIMONEER 46621
TINA 78218
TINA 1 64607
TINA II 74219
TINA II B0183
TINCA 103066
TINKER 60762
TINKERBELL 49324
TINKERBELL 73695
TINKERS LEEN 67719
TINKERS WOOD 48315
TINTAGEL B1271
TINY 80016
TINY PURPLE 53869 AITKEN-GRANGE CRUISING COMPANY Hotel boat. NbT 60′ Oxford blue/mar. B: 1994 Harboro' Boats, f/o 94-96 Aitken-Grange Cruising Co. Perkins MC42 (transverse in mid engine room), VOAC hydraulic drive 3:1 reduction, Crowther high efficiency 19x14 prop. VOAC/Markon 5kva variable hydraulic generator driven from power take off on main engine (only one of type installed in Nb?). Designed as hotel boat with all modern comforts for single party charter, operating most of year. Base Sheffield + Summer cruising. 261058
TINY TOO G10633 Grp 23′, b 8′6″, d 2′9″ wh/buff. B: by owner over 4 years - launched 1982. Vetus 414, Hurth 2:1 gearbox & aquadrive. Colin Mudey design - only 6 made - some for Nigerian patrol service. Heavy hull layup. Oak keel and stem. 24759
TIOLA 103999
TIOLA B0541
TIO PEPE 71482
TIPTON Lg Northwich Town Cl motor. Ex GUCC/BW
TIPTON 50054
TIPTON 74977 No. 1 M & RR HEREFORD NbTug 45′ bright red/royal blue. B: 1988 Gary Gorton, Pipe Gate, Mkt. Drayton (his first tug). Kingfisher type 26hp 2 cyl water cooled. Base top lock, Tardebigge. Trad back cabin, engine room, cabin all scumbled, roses & castles by Malcome Ward. 24773
TIP TOP 97743
TIPSY ANNIE 51619
TIPSY LIZZY 45411
TIREE 86175
TIRNANOG 71273
TISHOMINGO 52229
TISMYNE TOO 74362
TITAN 69930
TITAN 70854
TITCH 51143
TITCH 84583
TITLOIT 76046
TITTER NOT 66071

TITTLEMOUSE *Nb 55′*
TITUS 49383
TITUS *Nb25′*
TITUS II 47601
TIT WILLOW 68928
TIT WILLOW N7423
TITW-TOMOS 60605
TIVIDALE 69246 D BATCHELOR & FAMILY STOURBRIDGE NbC 40′ bl/wh. B: 1972 Simolda, Nantwich. Lister SW2. Base Stourbridge - Navigation Trust. 20114
TIVOLI 71059
TIXALL 52810
TJALK 500087
T'MORA 45963
TOAD 67379
TOAD 83506
TOAD 96368
TOADFLAX 63977 STOURPORT Nb 45′ red/grn. B: 1975 Hoo Mill Boats, f/o and lengthening by Teddesley Boats. Petter PH2W. Base Stourport basin. Mild steel "wind shield" around 8′ cruiser stern. Was hire boat *Morwenna*. 22382
TOAD HALL 30541
TOAD HALL 52300
TOAD HALL 60441
TOAD HALL G1108
TOBAR MHOIRE 54877
TOBAR MHOIRE *NbT 60′ grn/red*
TOBERMORAY B1424
TOBERMORY 67547 WBC *(Wheelton Boat Club)* Grp 27′ wh/blue. B: 1976 Norman Cruisers Ltd. AMC diesel 1.5L + Transadrive outdrive. Base Wheelton, L&L. 25988
TOBIAS 74563
TOBY 49795
TOBY 52049
TOBY 68348
TOBY 69271 NbST 30′ bl. B: 1982 BMC 1500. Base Ring-o-Bells, Lathom, L&L canal. "Tatty but friendly". 24793
TOBY JUG 64383
TOCSA 66705
TODACASU MASO 49536
TODDER 65423
TODDLING FOURTH 50704
TODDY 50343
TO & FRO 77427
TOM 71890
TOM 101254
TOMADOR 45210
TOMADORO 64646
TOMBEE TOO 51453
TOM BOMBADIL 64637
TOM BOMBADIL 71818
TOM BOMBADIL II 46751
TOMBOY 101999
TOMCAT 52823
TOM COBLEIGH 63716
TOM PAINE 73918
TOM THUMB 50373
TOM THUMB 63070
TOM TIDDLER 15 45368
TONANJO 62909

172

TONBRIDGE 076390 CLIFTON CRUISERS Hire. NbC 41' grn/crm. B: 1983 Colecraft, f/o Clifton Cruisers, refit 1991. BL 1.5. Base Clifton Wharf, Rugby. Sister boat to *Ramsgate*. 025679
TOODLE-OO 52877
TOOTING 50995
TOOWONG 75132
TOP BUZZ 104294
TOP CHEQUERS 51978
TOPAZ 52401
TOPAZ 77161
TOPAZ 83302
TOPAZ II 75192
TOPERU 75857 NbC 33' dk blue/gold. B: 1988 Colecraft, f/o Warble Narrowboats, Hyde. Mitsubishi/Thornycroft 80D 28hp. Base Fradley, T&M canal. 23644
TOPSHAM 71291 NbT 60' bl/red. B: 1984 Colecraft. Lister ST3. Base Cowroast, GU. 24847
TOPSY 63981 POYNTON CHESHIRE NbT 40' grn/red. B: 1981 Hancock & Lane (Norseman). BL 1.5. Base Dobsons, Shardlow, T&M canal. 21271
TOPSY 69417
TOPSY 80391
TOPSY TOO 45465
TOR 46345
TOR 53829
TORANAGA 72466
TORBURN 500550
TORIA 76810
TORKSEY Tug 8.46m BW-NE
TORLIEF 78619
TORMUND 54537
TOROK 65501
TORRICELLI 64617
TORTOISE 70850
TOSCA 74265
TOSHER 76232
TOSKA 47602
TOTAL ANARCHY 74735
TOUCAN 70557
TOUCH & TELL 77095
TOUCHWOOD 116 Ex dayboat
TOUJOURS No 3 74788
TOULKALOT 46661
TOUSLEHEAD 45772 CR & HM BARNACLE NAPTON JUNCTION NbT 48'6" red/grn. B: 1987 Club Line Coventry, f/o by owner 1987-91 in cherry and oak ply. BMC 1.5. Base Napton junction. Named after owner's wife's hair first thing in the morning. Glazed cratch, removable trad painted panel. Cockpit used as extra room when required. Now fitted helm shelter for weather & cold protection *(ageing owner)*. VHF fitted for R.Severn estuary cruising. 24919
TOWCESTER No 1 68397 Lg Woolwich Town Cl motor. Ex GUCC/BW/WW
TOWNSCLIFFE 78347
TOWY 93 63553 FMC River Cl motor. Ex T. Clayton
TOWYN 79937
TRAA DI LIOOAR 49016
TRAA DY LIOOR 52399

TRAA-DY-LIOOAR 52779
TRACYAN 97287
TRAFALGAR 63024
TRAMONTANA 69823
TRAMP 99279
TRAMPS RETREAT 48707
TRANQUILITY 68312
TRANQUILITY 91314
TRANQUILLITY 61292
TRANQUILLITY 67646
TRANQUILLITY 68920
TRANQUILLITY 71310
TRANQUILLITY 75273
TRANQUILLITY 75983
TRANSFORMER 49052
TRANSPORTEUR 76217
TRANTER REUBEN *76350 NbC 50' red/grey*
TRAVELER PEACE *see KATHLEEN*
TRAVELLER 45799
TRAVELLER 73998
TRAVELLERS JOY 46696
TREACLE BOLLY 45015
TREBALISA 53602
TREBLE JOY 54445
TREBLE JOY *Grp 39'6" wh*
TREEFROG 68297
TREE PIPIT 49833
TREE SPARROW 45593
TREFALDWYN 64921
TREFOIL 50732
TREFOR 73851
TREJOCO 69470
TREKKER 51721
TREKKER II 76053
TRELAWNY No 5 46046
TRELEASE 77740
TRELYSTAN 63211
TREMAR 78829
TREMBLER 77490
TREMYRANN 50196
TRENDIS Suction dredger, dumb BW-NE
TRENOY B1629
TRENT 5 Ex tar boat
TRENTHAM B0898
TRENT LADY 52694
TRESCO 61189
TRESKELLY 52856
TREVOR F Barney(8) 1971 44'
TRIANDA 46206
TRIANGULUM
TRICANN 54477
TRICIA 70867
TRIDENT 62035
TRIFFIC 49340
TRIGGAN *Nb 30'*
TRIKIMIKI 71770
TRILOGY 46059
TRIMELIDIT 73022
TRIMPLEY 77232
TRIN 61424
TRINARY VENTURER 49877
TRINCULO 67575
TRING Motor vessel 13.6m BW-
TRINITY 68666

173

TRINITY *NbT 35' grn/red*
TRIO 75713 NbC 50' Danube blue/bounty. B: 1988 Narrowcraft, f/o Weltonfield Narrowboats. Volvo 3 cyl 2003. Base Welton Hythe. 206
TRIO 81614
TRISCA 85464
TRISKAR 78887
TRITON 52077
TRITON 70277
TRITON 79157
TRIUMVRIATE 68901
TRIVIAL PURSUITS 51877
TRIVONA 65936
TRIXIE 72123
TRIXIE 89210
TROJAN 49680 NbST/Tug 57' burgundy/lt grey. B: 1990 Colecraft, f/o by owners during following 4 years. Perkins D.3152 3 cyl 2.5L / RZ Marine. Base Wheaton Aston, SU canal. 24804
TROJAN 73051
TROLL 49713
TROODOS 51047
T ROSE 101076
TROUT 45160
TROUT 327 61197 Yarwoods Fish Cl motor. Ex FMC
TROWLIN ALONG *NbST 55' mar/grn*
TROY 72092
TRUDGE 47676
TRUDIE ANNE 46304
TRUDY 67574
TRUE BLUE B1065
TRUE BRIT 85598
TRUMPETER B1486
TRUNDLE 69984 Nb 45' burgundy red/dk blue. B: 1973 Davisons Bros, Long Eaton. 16hp Lister air cooled. Base R.Loddon, Wargrave. Tapered stern for ease of passage through locks, transom seat in well and distinctive design of windows are hallmarks of Davison-style narrowboats of early 1970s. 25958

TRUNKLES 52184
TRURO 78339 LEEDS & LIVERPOOL NbT 60' grn/red. B: 1920s(?) Harris of Netherton (?). Perkins 4108 in bows - hydraulic transmission to conventional prop. Base L&L canal. 22509
TRUSSEL Mtce boat, flat, dumb 30' BW-NW
TRYOMAY 99973
TRYPHINA 65364
TRYST 64184
TSAI-CHIN (Sea flower) B7129 Grp 20', b 8' wh/bl hood. B: 1974 Norman Cruisers. Honda 75 4-str ob. Base Worsley Cruising Club Patricroft moorings. Large opening sun roof to main cabin. 25963
TSALENO 100342
TSARA 52248
TSARA NbT 53' grn/blue. B: 1991 Gary Gorton, owner f/o. Perkins D3 offset in rear engine room driving prop via C/V joints (allows for necessary easy access via stairway to rear deck). Base Chirk marina, Llangollen canal. 20148
TSAREVNA 65717
TUDOR LADY *87938 Grp 20' wh/blue*
TUDOR PRINCE 80003
TUESDAY NIGHT II 52599
TUFFITOO 48997
TULIP Hire. NbC 46' blue/red. Base The Wyvern Shipping Co, Linslade, GU. 00453
TULIP 71971
TULKAS 49750
TULLAMORE 70312
TUMBLEHOME 71921
TUMBLEWEED 45537
TUMBLEWEED 49583
TUNA 85695
TUPELO HONEY 52057
TUPILE 67201
TUPPENCE 50004
TUPPENCE 67021
TUPTONIA 77454
TURNSTONE 52782

TURRITELLA 68492
TURTLE 61199
TUSCANY OWL 47782
TUSCARORA 78126
TUSH 47767
TUTTI 75340
TUTTSIE TOO 75969
TWEEDLEDUM 80162
TWICE AS NICE 76229
TWILIGHT 500028
TWILIGHT *NbT 40' mar/blue*
TWINING SPIRIT 77932
TWINKLE 53879
TWO BREVITS 63630
TWOCAN *49489 Nb grn/graining*
TWO CHICKS 71839
TWO MOONS 71323
TWO ROSES 69425
TWO-TONE TIKI *NbT 55' brown*
TWO WATERS 500980
TYCHO Ice breaker. Ex GUCC
TY DDEWI 501148 Nb 60' blue/red.   B: 1996 Warble Narrowboats. Lister Canal Star 36. Base Stanstead Locks. Name = St. Davids.   24786
TYKE 75863
TYNE LADY 51545 Grp 24', b 9' wh.   B: 1990 Kite Cruisers, Essex (floataway), owner f/o on R.Tyne. 30hp Mariner ob; originally 75hp (overpowered!). Base Naburn marina.   23552
TYNTESFIELD B0090
TYNWALD 48574
TYPSY TWO 66383
TYSELEY No. 183 67840 Lg Woolwich Town Cl motor. Ex GUCC. *Mikron Theatre*
TYTAS 54073
TYTHERLEY 65642
TY-TWT 61203

U

Under-represented, this letter. A floating classroom with lots of bookshelves and a Classic recalling the Senior Service

UB60 69747
UBIQUE 52154
UDDERS 80586
UFTON 78932
UGLY DUCKLING 06265 SSR66343 Grp 24', b 8'6" wh/red.   B: 1970 Senior Marine Southampton, f/o Eastwood Yacht Co. Ltd., Walton-on-Thames. Ford Watermota - petrol. Base Elmhaven marina, R.Medway. Regularly cruises to R.Thames.   21375
UGLY DUCKLING 72389
UGLY DUCKLING 77838
ULAN 69988
ULTIMA 51205

ULYSSES 65017 NbC 42' red/grn. B: 1975 Harborough Marine. Lister SR2 air cooled with Lister gearbox & reduction. Base Llangollen canal. Carries hand painted emblem of the destroyer *HMS Ulysses* (1943-66) after which it is named as previous owner served on her. Listed with Harboro Classic Boat Owners' Club.   21355
UMBRIEL 63618
UMEA No 3 61204
UNANIMOUS 45291
UNCHAINED MELODY 53544
UNDECIDED 500353
UNICORN 68945 Hotel (Guest house?) NbT 70' grn/red.   B: 1974 Braunston Boats Ltd (Chris Barney(41)). Sabb 2 cyl 18hp. Base Swallow Cruisers, N. Stratford canal. Designed as floating class room, hence large saloon with book shelves for several hundred volumes.   22524
UNICORN 85903
UNILEC B1269
UNION JACK 92717
UNION JACK Motor. Ex FMC
UNION MAID 63206
UNION ROSE 63496
UNITY 47632
UNITY 54144
UNSPOILT BY PROGRESS I 53880
UNSPOILT BY PROGRESS II 53881
(Black Country to Black Sea pair)
UNUS 64284
UNWYND 49127
UP SPIRITS 51403
URANUS 70916
URANUS   80194 Tug 8.77m BW-NE
URCHEON D'OR 51242
URCHIN 61952
URCHIN 66494
URE 89700 Grab dredger 17.3m BW-NE
URICON 81364
URSA 69007
URSULA 47531
URSULA 71645 RS & M SMITH SAWLEY NbC 45'3" red/grn.   B: 1985 Les Allen, Oldbury, f/o Teddesley Boats. BMC 1.5. Base Sawley marina. Pre-1992: *Gailey Wayfarer II* (Gailey Marine).   21223
URSULA IV 96177
UTOPIA 51344
UTOPIA 75435
UTOPIA *NbT 60' blue/grn*
UTOPIAN 51664 BRADFORD ON AVON NbT 60', b 6'6" dk blue/crm. B: 1992/93 Heritage Boatbuilders, f/o Bob Harris. Thornycroft 1.8. Base K&A canal.   20102
UZEZENA 68519

V

Recognise this one instantly. Sparky tales and a replica Victorian. Who's the builder? An FMC restoration. And hoping for total silence (!)

VADER 93050
VAGABOND 46647
VAGABOND 061309 Tripper. Pitch pine, carvel, ex-harbour launch 40', b 8'6", d 11" wh/dk blue. B: Year and builder not known but at least 100 years old. Lister SR2 Base Foxton bottom lock. Originally (or previously) called *Little Eastern* and a tripper on the Lancaster - then owned by Harborough Marine. 0381081
VAGABOND 76946
VAGABOND 77056
VAGRANT BROOMSQUIRE 79095
VALDEN 45258 Nb 40' red/grn. B: 1988 M Heywood, diy f/o. Thornycroft type 80. Base Sawley marina. 21374
VALE OF SAFFRON 75275
VALENCIA 102903
VALERIE 45308
VALERIE ANN 78337
VALERY 104580
VALETA 73320
VALFREDA 52185 NbC 42' grn/crm. B: 1992 Blue Water, Thorne. Mitsubishi/Thornycroft. Base Stanilands, Thorne. 21367
VALGRIVE 41962 NbC birch plywood skimmed with glass fibre top cabin 46' Sherwood grn/lime grn. B: 1977 Canal & Rivercraft, refit 1987. 1500cc BMC Leyland Thornycroft, PRM hydraulic gearbox. Base Marsh Lane bridge, S&W canal. Previously hire craft for 6 years. Name = valley thrush (French). 22504
VALHALLA 73701 RH & R TINSLEY NbTug 40' mar/crm. B: 1986 Peter Nicholls Napton. Mitsubishi 1100cc 3 cyl. Base Dunstable & District Boat Club, Cheddington, GU. 22395
VALHALLA 76769
VALHALLA 77052
VALIANT 50833
VALIANT 67178
VALIANT 74089
VALIANT 76020 MIKE DEX - WEEDON NbTug 48' red/blue. B: 1982 GM Engineering, Black Country; f/o Chris Lloyd, Atherstone. Vintage Lister JP2. Base GU-Leics. 21213
VALKYRIE 51179
VALKYRIE 64958
VALLE CRUCIS ABBEY 45842
VALOUR 63544
VAMOS 80565
VANESSA 61033
VANGUARD 67465
VANGUARD No. 214 *NbT FMC*
VARDO 68004
VARLEBENA 46472
VARNA 52259
VARRIUS 102873
VAVLIDIS 72301
VAVRONE 62875

VAYN CON DIOS 46796
VECKS 69312
VECTIS ROSE 67106 SANDOWN (in Isle of Wight outline) NbC 40' lt grey/dk grey. B: 1974 Colecraft - originally 30', lengthened by Colecraft 1994; f/o Waterways Services, High House Wharf, Weedon. Vetus 3.10. Base Gayton, GU. Originally built for Fenny Boats, Fenny Compton as one of 40/50 of its type. Instantly recognisable with distinctive canoe bow. 24883
VEE JAY 30980
VEE JAY 60950
VEELACE 51964
VEGA 070777 AUDLEM NbT 50' red/grn. B: 1986 Mike Heywood; amateur f/o. 1.5 BMC /Thornycroft. Base Audlem, SU canal. 23586
VEGA II 83629
VEINARDE B1561
VELA No 383 64831
VELLENDER ROSE 99049
VENETIAN 51817
VENETIAN PRINCESS 103282
VENETIAN QUEEN 72007
VENICE 67516
VENICE Mtce boat, flat, dumb 30' BW-NW
VENICE *ex FMC butty*
VENTS 76182
VENTURA 80411
VENTURE 67532
VENTURE 85226
VENTURE B0982
VENTURE B1652
VENTURER 63461
VENTURER 75709 NbC 48' blue/red. B: 1988 Springer. BMC 1.5. Base Loveys Marina, Ely. 25953
VENTURER 77096
VENTURE TWO 73033
VENUS 47743
VENUS 49711
VENUS 500330
VENUS Motor
VERA B 49239
VERANDA 91860
VERAY 65697
VERBENA Grp 23' wh/bl. B: 1983 Viking. Yamaha 4-str 9.9 ob. Base Lower Avon. Named after Flower class corvette, *HMS Verbena*. 24775
VERBENA 74068
VERDEGRIS 76860
VERDUN II 78191
VERITYS SHADOW 52765
VERONDIL 47599
VERULAM 65942
VERULAM 60000 BW-
VESPA 52817 NbT 50' blue. B: 1992 Shotbolt Engineering. Isuzu 3 cyl. Base Highline Yachting, Cowley Peachey, Uxbridge, GU. 25968
VESPER 60388
VESTA No 3 Motor
VIA CON DIOS 500758 Nb 45' grn/red. B: 1966 Liverpool Boats. Lombardini. Base Braunston Marina. 21353
VIANNA 74330

176

VIC 99 76722
VICEROY 196 FELLOWS MORTON & CLAYTON Nb Wrought iron hull, wood topsides, restored to FMC steamer type 70′, d 3′ traditional FMC colours. B: 1910 FMC Saltley, Birmingham as steamer within 6 months of the well known *President* (consecutively numbered 195 and 196). Now powered by Lister HB2. Base GU canal. Worked originally between London, Braunston, Birmingham, Leicester. Was apparently last steamer to be converted to motor boat in 1927. Working life ended after 1939-45 War and might have finished her days submerged at Braunston. Restored late 1970's, used as trip boat on K&A near Bath. Refurbished by present owner to include cabin, bathroom and unusual "bed 'ole" retaining clear centre passageway. Boatmans cabin unaltered as compromise to retain trad appearance with reasonable comfort. Externally sheeted over original carrying hold of which 14′ remains. 22468
VICEROY 79705
VICKIE VI 48031
VICKY 72385
VICON 62688
VICTOR 76294
VICTORIA 46657
VICTORIA 46685
VICTORIA 49923
VICTORIA 50038
VICTORIA Royalty Cl motor. Ex GUCC

VICTORIA 66078 Butty
VICTORIA Trip. Replica Victorian steam inspection launch 37′ red/wh. B: 1965 Braunston Boats. Single cyl 10hp Sabb. Base Linlithgow. Yellow funnel, semi-open wheel steering from midships. 023531
VICTORIA 69466 Nb 40′ grn/red. B: 1976 approx Dartline. Lister SR2. Base Rainsway, Thurmaston. Steel top fitted over fibre glass top. Originally *Thomas Telford* and formerly *Adams Apple*. 22460
VICTORIA 52342 NbT 62′ mid blue/lt oak scumble. B: 1992 Midland Canal Centre, Stenson. Lister Petter 4 cyl 36bhp. Base midland/southern canals and rivers. 22526
VICTORIA *65544 Grp 20′ wh/blue*
VICTORIA 64065
VICTORIA 82105
VICTORIA Barney(10) 1971 36′
VICTORIA II 83003
VICTORIA EUGENE 46349
VICTORIA LEE 88160
VICTORIA LOUISE 54910
VICTORIA LOUISE 78564
VICTORIANA 67144
VICTORIA PLUM 53003
VICTORIA PLUM 54804
VICTORS NEW HOME 54063
VICTORY 47626
VICTORY 66489
VICTRIX 65502

VIRGINIA CURRER MARINE
INLAND WATERWAY SPECIALISTS

B U Y I N G

- Specialist Inland Waterway Brokers •
- Narrowbeam and Widebeam •
- Cruising and Residential •
- Large Selection of Craft Available •
- Part Exchanges Considered •
- Convenient West London Base •
- Twenty Years Broking Experience •
- Insurance and Finance Available •
  (written details on request)

100% BROKERAGE 100%

- Craft Always Needed for Clients
- No Sale - No Fee - No Hassle
- Free Collection and Mooring
- Craft Bought Outright for Cash
- Nationwide in Depth Advertising
- Accompanied Viewing
- Professionally Qualified & Insured
- We Only Sell - So We Must Sell!

S E L L I N G

01753 832312

VIENNA 64169
VIENNA 72851
VIENNA 203 Butty Ex FMC
VIENNA 102554 PACIFIC 550 Grp 19'10" wh/grn. B: 1980 Builder not known *(owner would like to know - see page 14)*. Mercury 9.9 ob. Rishton, L&L. 20105
VIGEOIS III 61423
VIGILANTE 74526
VIKING Hire. NbTug 40' grn. B: 1980 Godalming Narrow Boats on Harbour Marine hull. BMC 1.5. Base Farncombe Boat House, R.Wey. 00372
VIKING 50111
VIKING 77183
VIKING 103320
VIKING B0531
VIKING LASS 49210
VIKTORIA *(& Ambush) Commercial boats*
VIMY 79160
VINCENT 47129
VINCENTIO 49463
VINDI 73216
VIOLA *see STELLERN*
VIOLET 047680 Hire. NbC 54' navy blue/lt blue. B: 1990. Lister LPWS. Base Sally Boats, Bradford on Avon marina. 013232
VIOLET 61872
VIOLET CLAIRE 76981
VIOLET ELSIE 54187
VIOLET MAUD 65926
VIRAGO 66267
VIRAGO 69387
VIRAGO 103060 BW-
VIRGINIS 061587 FOXTON BOAT SERVICES LTD Nb Small Woolwich butty, unconverted, composite steel and elm 71'6", d 3' dk admiralty grey/orange. B: 1935 Harland & Wolff. Base Foxton bottom lock. Towed by motor *Coleshill* but not used much at the moment, previously for camping/winter carrying. 0381083
VIRGO 78106
VIRLEO 74615
VISCOUNT 51529
VISCOUNT 69046
VISCOUNTESS BURY *former Thames passenger launch undergoing restoration*
VITAL LADY 78633
VITAL SPARK No.2 45685 I & E SUTHERLAND CHANDLERS QUAY NbTug 47' bl/deep red. B: 1988 Dartline, f/o by owners and friends. BMC 1.8. Base L&L canal East. Named after the ficticious Puffer made famous by Neil Munroe in the "Para Handy Tales" 25959
VITESSE 46050
VIVID 500668
VIVID II 53922
VIVIEN ANNE *NbC 35' red/grn*
VIXEN 66230 NbT 45'9" Bounty red/Donegal grn. B: 1971 M E Braine, 1986 cabin top rebuilt by Davison Bros., f/o D E Crossland. Petter P4Z WM(RMR) 2 cyl. Base Beeston Lock, Notts. 23545
VIXEN 61876 STONE NbC 40' Donegal grn. B: 1977 Hancock & Lane. BMC 1.5. Salt Moorings, nr Sandon, T&M. Ex hire boat from L&L canal. 21351
VIXEN 048971 FOXTON BOAT SERVICES LTD Horse-drawn Tripper Nb modern "butty" 30' dk admiralty grey/orange. B: 1990 Harborough Boats. Base Foxton bottom lock. 0381080
VIXEN 89540 Motor vessel mtce boat 51' BW-NW
VIXEN 60424
VIXEN 60984
VIXEN 62478
VODAR 46137
VOYAGE OF DISCOVERY *10291 Grp 20'*
VOYAGER 46972
VOYAGER 47108
VOYAGER 47479
VOYAGER 52891
VOYAGER 60079
VOYAGER 69940
VOYAGER 71559
VREDE 501600 STAMHAVEN Nb Dutch Barge - Luxe Motor 60' mar/grey. B: 1995-97 David Harris, Dadsford Wharf, Stourbridge. Gardner 4LK encapsulated in midships engine room driving main propeller and bow thruster via proportional hydraulic system (VOAC from A.R.S.). The aim is total silence at wheelhouse - time will tell! Base Marineville, Higher Poynton. Hull features vee bottom, round bilge, full counter up from keel (not a false one above waterline). Folding wheelhouse with vertically sliding side doors. Electro/hydraulic steering by lever (mini-tiller) in "wheel" house. 23563
VULCAN 45057
VULCAN 183 63361 Motor. Ex FMC
VULPUS 61224
VYMOND *NbT 40' mar/blue*

A poignant and stirring tale of chilling but beautiful Winter, offered here as a counterpoint to those who are concerned with life on the cut in other seasons and who enjoy just the warm rain of Summer cruising.

ICY CHRISTMAS
by Mary Matts
of Foxton Boat Services
(first published in *Union*, the journal of the Old Union Canals Society, December 1996)

Most of us send and receive many Christmas cards depicting the countryside and its watercourses picturesquely frozen and covered with snow. We don't actually expect our festive season surroundings to look like that, but for the second year running they have, and the photogenic and delightful scene on the mantelpiece is not so easy in real life.

I set off two days before Christmas to retrieve our work flat, cut off at Kibworth by the demolition and re-building of bridge 74. There wasn't much ice at Foxton, but round the corner, long lengths had frozen over, some to a good 2" thick. Our little day-boat *Foxy* isn't really designed to go ice-breaking in, but luckily a sturdier hire boat had gone through ahead and forced a channel. It was still very heavy going as the splintered broken chunks piled up under the bow, and more worryingly, under the stern and prop. The strong north-easterly wind swiped mercilessly across the fields, unbroken by the leafless skeleton trees and naked hedges, but a vibrant setting sun turned the world red-gold and chillingly beautiful.

The hire boat gave up the struggle by Smeeton winding hole, and I battled on alone into Saddington tunnel cutting, where on full revs poor *Foxy* just stopped dead at the narrow sheltered solid slab of ice that the canal had become. At one point she actually rode up onto it and slithered about like a spun stick. Eventually we forged a way through and in the lowering light surprised the navvies still working at Ross Bridge (74). I think this must have been the first boat they had seen through, because they all stopped and hung over their half-finished parapets for a better look. I seemed to detect an element of resentment, possibly because most of the building trade get a full fortnight off over Christmas, but they were working to a tight deadline, as the farmer must sow his field in Feb.

Dawn, Christmas Eve, I set off back with the flat, and anybody who has towed one of these solid square-ended craft knows that they tow like a brick; when there's a strong wind, a lop-sided brick. The ice broken the day before had knitted back together with extra strength, due to the severely sub-zero temperatures with added wind-chill and it was obviously going to be more stop than go. I was accompanied by a daughter with the flu, huddled and shivering in the cabin, and even the dog, normally game for anything, was not amused. The unforgiving wind managed to still be in my face and down my neck, but in the way of these things a truly magical scene unfolded: a glorious golden sunrise poured reams of light directly through Saddington tunnel, the rays investigating every section of irregular brickwork, and dazzling the eyes. No need of a headlamp, just keep going. The bats, presumably woken by the phenomenon, flickered around in the powerful beams, and no elaborate special-effects department could have created anything more impressive.

Emerging, I looked back and the whole tunnel bore, the portal and surroundings were floodlit as I have never seen them before, and probably won't again. A car screeched to a halt on the road bridge, and a muffled figure with a camera must have obtained some dramatic shots as we hammered through, silver slabs bouncing out from the hull sides, the whole scene lit by this exotic rising sun. Pity he could not capture the accompanying sounds - the vibrating ice whistling until it cracked like gunshots, and then crashing and clattering up and under the boat and banks. The hire boat had turned round and retreated the day before, so we were into virgin ice, coming to a standstill at regular intervals (at which point the flat rides up and rams you up the back end). The photographer and the bats were the only moving life we encountered, and the snowy landscape had a primeaval silence and power. "Goode's Mountain", the huge spoil heap dug out in the making of the new Debdale marina, imitated a volcano with its dark clodded clay topped by the fiery sun. The Van Gough-like sunflowers planted round the dredging tip were charred black, their giant seed-heads bent over and withered, silhouetted against the bright cold sky. An abandoned BW mud pan leant over at an alarming angle, locked solid in an icy grasp. In the evening a huge luminous full moon rose in a perfect negative of the sunrise, and bathed the steely canal surface with chilled spilt cream. None of the fancy Christmas lights came near to competing with nature's free show that day.

The grip tightened, and intrepid boaters out for the holiday were thwarted in their attempts to get beyond Foxton junction. A large Boxing Day turnout of visitors was entertained for several hours by two boats trying to smash their way back through Bridge 62, their bow-thrusters - ie person perched precariously on bow with boat pole, jabbing at ice - working overtime. A hotel boat attempting to turn towards the village had the misfortune to tip a duck off an ice floe into the propeller, where it was instantly decapitated and flung up across the surface, much to the horror/delight of the kiddywinks clutching their bags of bread.

Next day a friend managed to force her tug down towards Leicester, only to be stumped at Bush Lock for lack of water, frozen or otherwise. Of course holiday time means fewer BW staff in evidence, so I was asked for some contacts: "you know the local blokes". Some North Kilworth hirers were distressed by frozen water points (I filled their proffered saucepans), frustrated by bored kids, and disgruntled by frozen and immovable lock gates. "What can you do about it; we're having a sense of humour failure". They weren't the only ones.

The old year dead, the New Year sun rose blood red from behind the incline hill and bathed Gumley in horizontal ruby light, pink-painting the snow-covered ridges of the ridge and furrow, and making me curse another lost photo-opportunity (too busy with the boats at Saddington, camera failure at Foxton). The side-pond-dwelling mink showed up well against the snow and Sam kept his gun handy. Anybody who is uneasy about that should come and watch the mallard mothers proud with their new-hatched broods: next day they have two less, then three, then one, until they swim around alone, forlorn and uncomprehending. Crows have short legs and walk with an ungainly shuffle which in snow means they shovel it up underneath, their glossy black chests scarring the soft surface. Good title for a poem - "Crows in Snow".

By the butt end of the holiday the ice was entrenched and immutable. Nobody was going anywhere - boats abandoned in places friendly and not-so-friendly. Tracks and towpaths were packed down and treacherous, casualty departments over-stretched, purses empty, festive spirit evaporating and the January landscape left dull, dank, depressing and dangerous.

ONWARDS!! Boats moored at the "dead end" at Snarestone, Ashby Canal, on the occasion of the celebration of the 200th anniversary of the first sod cutting simultaneously with the sod cutting for the restoration to Measham, Moira and beyond(?)

W

A "cauldron" conundrum, wheelchairs at speed, an amazing history, some BIG dimensions, soft water, a converted tanker, a Wise One Ernie and Barrington's Bashers are here. Plus much "Wild", "Wind" and "Wood"

WADHAM 46383
WAGGONER 76363
WAGTAIL 218C (Broads Auth.) 30322 Grp 6m, b 2m wh. B: 1977 Leisurecraft Marine, Wolverhampton. Honda 9.9hp 4-str. Base Wroxham Norfolk. Exceptional headroom below for such a small craft. 21330
WAGTAIL 30322
WAGTAIL *46233 NbTug 40' wh/bl*
WAGTAIL 72715
WAGTAIL 76223
WAGTAIL 84210
WAIMARAMA 500917 NbST 57' aircraft blue/ Oxford blue. B: 1996 Midland Canal Centre, Stenson. Lister 36hp 4 cyl. Base Stenson marina, T&M. Name is Maori for moonlight water. 22430
WAINSTONES 72452
WAITAMARA 100796

WAI-WURRY 64730
WAKANUI 54854
WAKA ROA 67385
WAKEMAN 72380
WALLABY 89229 Mtce boat 15.6m BW-
WALLY ONE 54138
WALLY ONE 74075
WALLY ONE *Nb 50' grey/red/bl*
WALNUT 63691 Nb 56' grn/red/yel. B: 1974 (stated on Cert. of British Registry from Hull dated 4.2.75) Roger Barrington Wright on Springer hull. Sabb 2HG 16/18hp. Base Calcutt marina. Ex-hire: 10 boats were built - 6 at 56' and 4 'shorter' ones. They operated out of Stenson from 1975 to Aug 1981; known locally as "Barrington Bashers". Roger sold them all in Aug '81 when *Walnut* was acquired by present owner. The other 5 long ones were: *Grey Poplar, Hornbeam, Silver Fir, Juniper, Maple* - one short one was *Holly*. 20201
WALRUS 45439
WALSALL ENTERPRISE 65339
WANAPITEI
WAND 99172
WANDERER 45396
WANDERER *48762 NbC 30' red/grn*
WANDERER *52281 Nb 50' mar*
WANDERER 54903

WANDERER   64048
WANDERER   64358
WANDERER   65093
WANDERER   71736
WANDERER   78018
WANDERER   87533
WANDERER   90758
WANDERER   94827
WANDERER III *53913 Nb 35' grn*
WANDERER B   52528
WANDERING STAR   31443
WANDERING STAR   45806
WANDERING STAR   64766
WANDLE *Grp 30' wh/blue*
WANDLEKIND   52532
WANGANUI   73514
WAPPENSHALL Iceboat. Boat Museum
WARBLER   65503
WARBLER   66767
WARBLER   74969
WARBLER Motor
WARBY   52680
WARBY   B1778
WARDE ALDHAM Motor vessel BW-NE
WARDIE   72181
WAR'ORSE   71416
WARREN CASTLE   49851
WARREN CASTLE   73969
WARRIOR JA & AL SHOTBOLT RAMSEY NbTug 54' midnight blue/crm.   B: 1995 Shotbolt Engineers Ltd. Ramsey. 1938 3 cyl National. Base Bill Fen Marina, Ramsey, Middle Level Nav. 23692
WARRIOR   46084
WARWICK   53213
WARWICK   63255
WARWICK CASTLE   72675
WARWICKSHIRE LAD Barney(25) 1973 35'
WASP   51314 NbTug 62', d 2'6"(minimum) bronze grn/red. B: 1991 Gary Gorton, f/o Nimbus Narrowboats, painting and signwriting by Beryl McDowall. Lister SR4M in engine room mounted starboard side with universal joints in shafting beneath boatman's cabin floor; 182 gal diesel tank under back cabin floor. Base Mill Lane Boatyard, Thurmaston. 20-8-4 steelwork: thick baseplate eliminated ballast apart from trimming. Internal headroom 6'10". 300 gal water tank under tug deck. Owner's previous boat was *Spider*, after the Blisworth tunnel tug of which it was a replica, then theme was continued with *Ant*, then *Wasp* and *Moth*.   25955
WASP *100981 Grp 15' grn*
WASP   89007 BW-
WATCHET *NbC 50' grn*
WATCHET   79768
WATCHTOWER   54491
WAT DABNY   76089
WATE   84614
WATER ADMIRAL   79891
WATER AVENS   45209
WATER AVENS *NbT 60' grn/red*
WATERBABY   48314
WATER BARON   52889
WATER BEAR   67931

WATERBED   76037
WATER BOWMAN   52735
WATER BRAMBLE   72058
WATER BUFFALO   64204
WATER CHERRY   72828
WATER COMMANDER   60419
WATER CRACKER   69537
WATERCRESS Grp 25' crm. B: 1983 Microplus - Buckingham 25. Ob. Base Abingdon.   22433
WATER DAMSEL   52453
WATER DAMSON   73245
WATER EMERALD   50569
WATER FERN   65900
WATER FERN Motor vessel BW-NE
WATER FLEA   64168
WATER GIPSY *91607 Grp 18' wh*
WATER GLIDER   49093
WATER GYPSY   74719
WATER GYPSY   96607
WATER HERON   78565
WATER JESTER   51630
WATERJET   45520
WATER JOKER   51319
WATER KNIGHT   53891
WATER LADY   61229
WATER LILLY   52443
WATER LILLY   77146
WATER LILY   45554
WATERLILY   60264
WATER LILY   64906
WATER LILY   69821
WATER LUPIN   B0529
WATER MAIDEN   48730
WATERMAN   71657
WATERMARK   71768
WATERMARK   B0048
WATERMARK *NbT 60' grn/mar*
WATERMARK *see MILLSTREAM*
WATER MILLER   52558
WATER MINSTREL   50349
WATER MOLE   76463
WATER MUSIC   052244   NbST 60' dk grn/burgundy.   B: 1992 G.T. Boatbuilders, f/o South Shore Narrow Boats Ltd. Kubota Beta. Base Nantwich Canal Centre.   24764
WATER MUSIC   94331
WATER NAVIGATOR   54650
WATER NAVIGATOR   63711
WATER NYMPH   65028
WATER ORCHID   48218
WATER OUZEL   61368   *Trip boat*
WATER PRINCE 061277 APPOLLO CANAL CRUISES LTD   SHIPLEY WHARF Trip/Restaurant boat. L&L 'Short Boat' - iron/steel 57', b 14'3", d 3' grn/red.   B: 1937 Isaac Pimblott, Northwich. Perkins 4236 + Lister generator ST2. Base Shipley, L&L canal. Originally *Wharfe*. Shortened and converted by British Transport Waterways in 1958 based Leeds/Wakefield. To York circa 1964 and to Apollo Canal Cruises 1975 where re-fitted.   01019
WATER RAIL   52172
WATER RAIL   64396
WATER RAT   75971

WATER REED II 67508
WATER ROSE 46489
WATER ROVER NbC 30' blue/grn
WATER ROVER I 69879
WATER ROVER II 70954
WATER SABLE 60692
WATER SAGE 72057
WATER SAPPHIRE 49872
WATER SAPPHIRE Motor vessel BW-NE
WATER SATIN 45705
WATERSHED 77046
WATERSHIP UP 76298
WATERSHRIMP 70441 DM & J WILSON NbT steel hull, wooden top 70' flame red/dk blue. B: 1975 Chris Barney, Braunston(54). Twin cyl 18hp Sabb. Base Devizes marina K&A. Originally built as restaurant boat for R.Wey during Winter months so has large well equipped galley and large open plan lounge with de-mountable tables; used to cruise with 4 paying guests in Summer. Original owners name "Shrimpton", hence *Watershrimp*. 23546
WATER SILK 72056
WATER SNAIL 47562
WATER SNAIL 62548
WATER SPRITE 64125
WATER SPRITE 079249 Hire. NbC 45' grn/red. BMC 1.5. Base Evesham Marina, R.Avon. 0371049
WATER THISTLE 72059
WATER TRAVELLER 62749
WATER TRAVELLER I 60522
WATER TROUBADOR 53366
WATER VELVET 71799
WATER VOYAGER 61672
WATER WAGTAIL see *COROLLA*
WATERWAY DOLLY 67804
WATERWAY LASS B0602 Nb/river & estuary cruiser - steel hull/sides, wood/fibreglass roof 45' blue/yel. B: 1966 Pimblotts of Northwich, f/o Davisons, Sawley Bridge. Perkins 4-107 mounted transversely; hydraulic pump control and motor mounted on top of bevel gears driving propeller in well at stern. Base Pyranha, Preston Brook. Only 4 to this design for BWB, high prow, compact 3 cabins, 6 berths, small seating area in bow, cockpit and raised area on stern. 20187
WATERWILLOW 50723
WATER WIND 99874
WATERWITCH 45526
WATER WITCH Trip boat NbT 26'
WATER WIZARD 51320
WATERWORKS 74843
WAT TYLER No. 91 SAUL JUNCTION NbT 62' mar/dk grn. B: 1990 Phil Trotter, RWD Marine, Saul Junction. Indian import Ruston Hornsby YD2. Base Midlands and South. Named after leader of peasants' revolt during construction - one of the boatyard staff protested about paying poll tax (would rather go to jail, etc.) and "Wat Tyler" was chalked on the steelwork; owner also a fan of Fairport Convention who had recently released a song about "Wat Tyler". 261087
WAVE CREST 88169
WAVELENGTH 60356

WAVELENGTH 85917
WAVERLEY 48763
WAVERLEY 68619
WAVERLEY 71220
WAVERLEY No.1 NbT 50' mar/grn
WAVERTON MILL 51303 CHESTER NbC 40' blue/yel. B: 1991 Mancunian Narrowboats on Liverpool Boats hull. Vetus 310. Base Bridge 119 SU canal. 22434
WAVES 101700
WAXWING 48288 NbT 45' red/mar
WAXWING 71614
WAY AHEAD 49712
WAYFARER 78667
WAYFARER M20422 Cruiser 30', b 8'3" varnished wood. B: 1928 Salters of Oxford. 1.5 C.T. Marine Mitsubishi. Base Yalding, R.Medway. This Dunkirk Veteran has a history which could fill a small book. As far as the present owner is concerned it all started in 1975 when he and his wife discovered on the bank of the R.Medway near Tonbridge an iron hull. The wooden superstructure was in the last stages of decay but she had super lines. The owner (who had previously lived on board with 27 dogs) was traced and the sum of £27.50 paid. The receipt shows the boat's name as *River Princess*. The long process of restoration began involving replacement steel plates, 500 rivets, hand fitted with much elbow grease, the discovery - under layers of paint - the original name *Wayfarer*, engine replacement with a £160 Perkins P3 from fishing boat (originally in Trojan van), design and construction of superstructure with secondhand timbers, windows and roof lights from old buses and lorries. Engine fitting, plumbing, etc. continued and a search for the boat's history was started. Discussions at the Thames Conservancy stand at the 1981 Boat Show led to Salter Bros; Mr A Salter remembered *Wayfarer* being built when he was a boy - subsequently details found of original specification and that she was built for £250 for Salter's hire fleet where she remained till 1953 when sold to a private owner. Refurbishment complete after 5 years but due to extent of corrosion a fibreglass sheath put on. Engine replaced with Mitsubishi in 1982 (no more vibration!). Not till 1990 was it discovered by chance that *Wayfarer* had been one of the Little Ships of Dunkirk, this being confirmed by the Archivist of the Association of Dunkirk Little Ships. Now, as members of the Association, the owners proudly fly the flag of St. George defaced with the arms of Dunkirk and a brass plate on the front of the wheelhouse which says 'Dunkirk 1940'. 2029
WAYFARER Grp 30' wh/turquoise
WAYFARERS ALL 51447 NbC 40' bl/crm
WAYFRONT OWL 45996
WAYLON 65788
WAYNDALE 78578
WAYZGOOSE 47660
WAYZGOOSE 73401

184

WEASEL 47902
WEASEL Dredger 45' BW-BBC
WEASEL *Nb 45'*
WEASEL Barney(56) 1976 35'
WEAVER *72276 NbT conversion*
WEDGE B1182
WEE CUTLER 54452
WEEDRAM 79003 NbC 42' blue. B: 1981 P. Nicholls Napton; owner f/o. BL 1.5. Base Clock Warehouse, Shardlow, T&M canal. 21332
WEEKEND LADY 67119
WEEKEND LADY 90002
WEE WILLIE 76834
WEEZEEANNA 68703
WEIRBIN HULL Cruiser 44', b10', d 3'6" ivory/ grn. B: 1942, Yarwoods & Sons, Northwich. Two diesel engines. Base Lincoln residential moorings. Built as RAF tanker for sea plane refuelling; rebuilt 1950 as cruiser low enough to cruise inland waterways and French canals. Maximum air draft 8' incl. fly bridge, $^1/_4$ deck, fore mast for sail. Has lain derelict for 10 years but re-engined and refitted over 3 years, now used residentially. 24761
WELFORD 78391
WELL OVER 65746
WELLAND 72297

Using the *Listing*
A "how to use" guide is on pages 13-14
Frequent abbreviations inside front cover
Full list of abbreviations included in
Location Glossary at end of book

WELLAND VALLEY 72305
WELLEC 30023
WELLINGTON 65239
WELLINGTON 68088
WELSH POPPY 61756
WENDA 51772
WENDOVER 67513
WENDOVER 82166
WENDOVER Motor vessel 15m BW-
WENHAM 52908
WENLOCK 50123
WENSLEYDALE HEIFER 73781
WENTWOOD 100293
WESTAR 61235
WESTERING HOME Barney(39) 1974 28'
WESTERN APPROACHES 49695
WESTERN ROSE 50815
WESTERN SKY 61363
WESTERN STAR 51905 Hire. NbC 45' blue/yel. B: John South, f/o Starline Narrowboats. Lister TS2, Hurth HBW150 g'box. Base Starline Narrowboats, Upton marina, Upton upon Severn. 008110
WESTFALIA 66973
WESTHORPE 60591
WESTMORE 53696
WEST STOCKWITH 75999
WEST WIND II 51297
WEYFLOWER 79425

WEYFLY 54741 NbC 55' burgundy/midnight blue. B: 1988 Brummagem Boats. BMC 1.8. NT moorings, Addlestone, R.Wey. 21221
WEY WITCH
WHALE Motor vessel 18.34m BW-NE
WHALLEY BRIDGE Boat Museum
WHARFAGE 74497
WHARFE *see WATER PRINCE*
WHARFE II Tug 10m BW-NE
WHARNCLIFFE 53858
WHEATSTON BRIDGE 50169
WHEELBARROW 61788
WHEELOCK 76923
WHERNSIDE 52766
WHETTY WITCH 49332
W.H. GILLOTT 76237
WHICH ONE B0175
WHIMBREL 45589
WHIMBREL 51323
WHIMBREL 53569
WHIMBREL 63434
WHIMBREL 79510
WHIMBREL 91740
WHIMBREL *Grp 27' crm/brown*
WHINCHAT 74971
WHINCROFT 52922 S & S BURNETT & CO SKIPTON No 4 NbT - Josher style. 52', d 2'9" red/ dk blue. B: 1993 Tim Tyler, Hixon, Staffs., owner f/o. Vintage Lister JP2 (1950). Base Snaygill moorings, Skipton, L&L canal. 22528
WHIPORWILL 60363
WHIPPET 61273
WHISKEE II *79189 Grp 20' bl/wh*
WHISKEY GALORE 45208
WHISKEY GALORE 54208
WHISKY 54457
WHISKY GALORE 54917
WHISKY MAC 51571
WHISKY P B1361
WHISPER 68079
WHISPER 74345
WHISTLE No 1 72287
WHISTLEDOWN 79212
WHISTLER 048450 S & M MOTE PEAK FOREST Nb 56' dk grn. B: 1989 Chappell & Wright, f/o Lofthouse & Wilson. Thornycroft. Base Northamptonshire. 24844
WHISTLER 48617
WHISTLER 51628
WHISTLER 53918
WHISTLER *see TALISMAN*
WHISTON 89313 Mtce boat 15.6m BW-
WHITBY 62495
WHITBY 185 Lg Woolwich Town Cl motor. Ex GUCC/BW/WW
WHITE ADMIRAL 046132 Hire. NbT blue/red. BMC 1.5. Base Evesham Marina, R.Avon. 0371044
WHITE CRUSADER 51129
WHITE CRUSADER 100762
WHITE CRYSTAL 049821 Hire. NbC 54' grn/red. BMC 1.8. Base Evesham Marina. 0371045
WHITE ELEPHANT 72608
WHITE FLASH 66033
WHITE FOX 62526

185

Commerce Continues on the Waterways

Commercial carrying is certainly not entirely a thing of the past as there are many boats able and willing to carry your cargoes anywhere on the connected system.

Many regularly trade fuels to canalside properties and passing cruising boats can re-fuel from them too. But of course the golden years of commercial carrying is unlikely to return. Instead, there are numerous boats which carry passengers - trip boats (motor and horse drawn), water buses, floating restaurants and hotels. Also shops and workshops - large and small - to supply many needs. Souvenirs, traditional painted ware, model making, ropes and fenders, chandlery, music, pictures, photography and entertainment. Help keep the colour, atmosphere and economy of the waterways alive by supporting the water-borne traders when you can.

WHITE GULL 97083
WHITE HARRIET B1420
WHITE HART 500119
WHITE HEATHER 63946 Tug. Ex Borough of St. Marylebone
WHITE LADY 49596
WHITE LADY 66657
WHITE QUARTZ 64917 *NbC 45' red/grn*
WHITE RABBIT 63692
WHITE ROSE II 71044 D & L HELLIWELL Nb - Butty type stern 41' mar/grn. B: 1982/84 Whittle Boats Ltd., f/o by owner, engine installed by David Piper Boatbuilders. Vetus M 4.14. Base Sowerby Bridge Basin, Calder & Hebble Navigation. Not many 'Butty' type sterns about - rudder and tiller decorated with ropework in trad butty style. Won awards at Peterborough 1993, Waltham Abbey 1994 and Chester 1995. 20158
WHITE SATIN 47352
WHITE SPEEDY 61853
WHITE STICK 68216
WHITE STORK 74729
WHITE SURREE 49810
WHITE SURREY 60981
WHITE SWAN 47965
WHITE SWAN 49995
WHITE SWAN 52907
WHITE SWAN B1439
WHITEWAYS II 71192
WHITEY 97594
WHITLEY 80266 Motor vessel 17.55m BW-NE
WHITSTABLE 051655 CLIFTON CRUISERS Hire. NbC 45' grn/crm. B: 1993 Arcrite, f/o Clifton Cruisers. BL 1.5. Base Clifton Whf, Rugby. 025675
WHITSUNNBROOK 49786
WHIXALL 64990
WHIZZ 71029
WHOOPER SWAN 52797
WHOOPPEE 74713
WHY NOT 53978
WHY NOTTE 75458 *NbST 55' mar/grn*
WHY WORRY 69508
WIBBLE WOBBLE 45894
WICKED LADY 50087
WICKFORD 74392
WICKHAM 70922
WIDCOMBE 67860 BATH NbT 45' mid grn. B: 1979 (f/o complete) Hancock & Lane, owner f/o. Lister SR2 drive via offset propshaft under double bunk in aft full headroom cabin. The drive comprises two heavy duty toothed belts and a torque limiting clutch, set at 10% above engine max. torque. Weed hatch area sealed from rest of hull by complete bulkhead for better safety. Base Bath area. 24861
WIDDERSHINS 72311 *Nb 40' mar/grn*
WIDGEON 45832
WIDGEON Tug 5m BW-LAP
WIDGEON *NbT 45' blue*
WIDGEON see *THAXTED*
WIGAN Motor vessel 17.85m BW-NW
WIGFORD 77261
WIGLET 47891
WIGRAMS 46023

WIGRAMS TURN No.1 *NbT blue/wh*
WILD BURDOCK III 74995
WILD BURDOCK IV 51482
WILD CHERVIL X 72251
WILDCOOT 101386
WILD DUCK 65040 *NbC 60' grn*
WILDEN 45530
WILDE ROSE 71777 *NbT 60' grn*
WILD FLOWER 77637
WILD GARLIC 51782
WILD GOOSE 54358
WILD GOOSE 61523
WILD GOOSE 61800
WILD GOOSE 70239
WILD GOOSE 70276
WILD GOOSE 101769
WILD HEATHER 68416
WILD HEMLOCK II 47554
WILD HEMLOCK VII 73542
WILD HEMLOCK VIII 73910
WILD HEMLOCK X 45670
WILD IRIS 78277
WILD LADY B0110
WILD MINT 66407
WILD OATS 49389
WILD OATS 64282
WILD ORCHID 48190
WILD POPPY 60690
WILD ROSE 53351
WILD ROSE 76055
WILD ROSE 101314
WILD ROSE B1665
WILD SWAN 77316 NbC 50' blue/dk blue. B: 1982 Colecraft, extended 1989. 1500cc BMC. Base Kegworth, R.Soar. 22390
WILD TANSY IX 47621
WILD TANSY X 49751
WILD THYME 48820
WILD THYME 52768
WILD THYME 72734
WILD THYME 77383
WILD TORMENTIL 74993
WILD TURKEY 66126
WILFORD WREN 60053
WILFRED 68254
WILL 75840
WILLEYMOORS OWL B1482
WILLIAM 48297
WILLIAM 49385
WILLIAM 051430 Hire. NbC 69' navy blue/lt blue. B: 1992. Lister LPWS. Base Sally Boats, Bradford on Avon marina. 013239
WILLIAM 69542
WILLIAM 78239
WILLIAM B0141 REGISTERED AT MANCHESTER No 1165 Nb 70', b 7' red/grn. B: 1932 Yarwoods, Northwich. Bolinder semi diesel. Base Moore, Warrington. Grand Union Royalty class boat. 23571
WILLIAM BENJAMIN 72985
WILLIAM CLARK 71573
WILLIAM CLIFTON 75189
WILLIAM GLADSTONE see *LADY JUNE*
WILLIAM HENRY 66518

WILLIAM JESSOP 63874
WILLIAM JESSOP   89701 Grab dredger 21m BW-NE
WILLIAM PAGE 72399
WILLIE 64403
WILLIE No 2 45675
WILLINGTON 45652
WILL O'THE WISP 51031
WILL O' THE WISP 500027 NbT 57' mar/grn. B: 1995 Stenson Boatbuilders. Lister 4 cyl Canal Star. Base Stenson T&M. "Just a Nice Boat!" 22465
WILLOUGHBY 70744
WILLOUGHBY 75810
WILLOW 42524
WILLOW 47090
WILLOW 49350
WILLOW 51909
WILLOW 53705
WILLOW 64703
WILLOW 68916
WILLOW 71232
WILLOW 71609
WILLOW 74965
WILLOW 75517 MIDDLEWICH NARROWBOATS No 6 Hire. NbT 56' grn/red. B: 1988 Ivy Bridge Marine Braunston, f/o Middlewich Narrowboats. Lister SR3. Base Middlewich. Boatman's cabin; traditional engine room and controls; exhibited at IWA rallies: Netherton and Chester.   028738
WILLOW 76857
WILLOW B1006
WILLOW Hire. NbC 45' blue/red. Base The Wyvern Shipping Co, Linslade, GU.   00450
WILLOW 6 46548
WILLOW EMPEROR 45742
WILLOWVALE 78357
WILLOWWEED 73801
WILL POWER 66787 NbC 50' grn/red
WILL SCARLET 79855
WILL SCARLET Tug 7.01m BW-NE
WILL STUTLEY 80184 Tug 7.01m BW-NE
WILL-TRY 76124
WILLY NILLY 74878
WILLY NO-NAME 53654 DAVE AND JANE GREEN WARINGS GREEN WHARF NbT 62' red. B: 1994 Norton Canes Boatbuilders, f/o Stephen Goldsbrough Boats. 26hp 2 cyl Kingfisher. Base Warings Green Wharf, N.Stratford canal.   25962
WILLYTEE 64659
WILSON 48567
WILWYN II 51442
WIMOPSON 53831
WINCHCOMBE 64907
WINCHESTER 69691
WINDALE 66149
WINDERMERE 64141
WINDFALL 50063
WINDFLOWER 46676
WINDFLOWER 52900
WIND FLOWER 61678 NbC 50' red/grn
WINDHARP 73967
WIND IN THE WILLOWS 47916

WIND LASS V 49320
WINDMILL 63956
WINDRUSH 61253
WINDRUSH 64469
WINDRUSH 72945
WINDRUSH 75373
WINDRUSH 94334
WINDRUSH 96113
WINDSONG 50110
WINDSONG 51059
WIND SONG 67718
WINDSOR 48013
WINDSOR 52552
WINDSOR 63757
WINDSOR 64599
WINDSOR VIII 62419
WINDSOR NbST 50' blue/red
WINDWHISTLE II 72241 SYMONDS & McCOOEY (on plaque with painting of boat) NbC 56' grn/red. B: 1984 Stoke-on-Trent Boatbuilders (No.21), f/o John & Jenny Howncel at owners' home 1984. Lister Canal Star 3. Base Bridge 94, L&L canal. Sleeps 9 in 4 cabins - top bunks become settees.   261057
WINDWILLOW 67468
WINDY BLOW 77302
WINDYMILL 61474
WINE & ROSES 61854
WINGLETANG 54572
WINGLETANG NbT 50' grn
WINGS OF THE MORNING 45430
WINIFRED 102193
WINJIN POM 50183
WINNEBAGO 74389
WINNIE 66551
WINNIE B 72567
WINROSE 79516
WINSFORD 60385 BATTYEFORD NbT - all steel hull, elm wood bottom 44', b 7', d 2.5' grey/bl. B: 1898 Fellows Morton & Clayton at Saltley Dock No. 1007. Converted by M. Braine, Norton Canes in 1970 from 70'6". Petter air cooled PJ2 22½hp, Borg-Warner hydraulic gearbox. Base South Pennine Boat Club, Calder & Hebble Nav. Converted from working Nb using fore end which is rivetted puddled iron.   21311
WINSHILL 77986
WINSLOW REVIVAL 52840
WINSTON 66129
WINTERBURN 74870
WINTER MOSS 63552 NbST steel hull, wooden top 52', b 7' dk grn. B: 1970 Harborough Marine; refit by previous owner including conversion from cruiser stern. Lister SRM3. Base Nantwich. In previous ownership a compressor was fitted in forward end for a mobile shot-blasting business - now removed. Present owner, since 1996, seeks information about history, especially photos showing boat in original state (see page 14). 23668
WINWOOD 61759
WIRRAL B0438
WIRRAL WANDERER 53848
WIRRAWAY 64047
WISECRACK 60097

WISE CRACK BROOM 30 MK III Cruiser 30', b 10'4" wh/grn.　B: 1974 Broom. Single 4.1L Perkins. Base Wyre Mill Club. Originally commissioned by comedian, Ernie Wise.　25930
WISH ME LUCK B7314
WISONS B0420
WITCHCRAFT *45132 NbT 70' bl*
WITCHCRAFT 60884
WITCHCRAFT 67324
WITCHCRAFT *NbT 70'*
WITCHINGTON 45150
WITCH OF OSIER 52537
WITCH OF THE NORTH 103482 PRESTON LAKE DISTRICT REGISTERED　Grp day cruiser 16', b 6' blue/wh.　B: 1970 Yeoman, Personally fitted out, slatted timber design. 4hp Mariner single cyl 2-str ob. Base Jolly Roger Boatyard Adventure Cruisers. Trailed - has been to Poole and Menai Straits, Anglesey and used off shore.　23537
WITCH WAY　52929　HUGHIE & GAIL LANCASHIRE NbT 60' bl/wh. B: 1992 Billington Dewhurst, West Houghton, Lancs., f/o North West Narrowboats, Preston. Lister Alpha Canal Star 4 cyl. Base Red House moorings, Adlington, Lancs. Shell is replica of steam boat *President* with Josher bow and long swim. Name decided as boat fitted in Houghton where the Lancashire Witches were held before going to trial; L&L canal on which boat is based also passes through heart of pendle witch country; the witch used for logo holds a certain mystery - if you look at her cloak it forms another face so 'which way' is she facing!!?　20181
WITCHWAY 74682
WITCOMBE 45337
WITER 65208
WITHYMOOR 50077

WITS END 49948
WITTON Dredger. Boat Museum
WITTON BEAVER 50680
WIZARD `B1234　STOCKTON HEATH WARRINGTON　Trip boat for disabled.　Nb Inspection launch 38'3", d 3' blue/wh.　B: 1987 Sagar Marine, Brighouse; f/o Hesford Marine, Lymm.　Vetus 3 cyl.　Base London Bridge, Bridgewater canal. Open bow section. Fitted with floor lift for wheelchair access. Bows concave and slipper stern designed for speed.　261069
Wm SCORESBY 3　66015
WOBBLY WOB 46945
WODEN 61257
WOL 47101
WOL 49176
WOL 69491
WOL *NbT 55' blue*
WOLF-PAC 62102
WOMBAT 79175 Grp - Stirling 26' crm/blue. B: 1983 Lincoln (?). Yanmar 2 cyl. Base Strawberry Island, Doncaster. Grp swinging lid to open cockpit, wooden supports and windscreen.　21312
WOMBAT 101945
WOMBLE 77914
WONBLE II 46348
WONDERFULL 74996
WONOFF 51747
WONTHAGGI 68361
WOODBINE 500703 STAVERTON MARINA Nb style inspection launch 49'9" blue/ivory. B: 1996 Thorne Boatbuilders, owner f/o in hand. BMC 1.8. Base Staverton marina, Trowbridge, K&A. Forward steering, large windows at front, vertical stem, double chine.　2097
WOODBINE 79627
WOODBURY 68081

WOODCOCK 45599
WOODCOCK Tug 5.9m BW-NE
WOODCOTE 75821
WOODEND 66930
WOODENTOP 67436
WOODENTOP 69876
WOODIE'S 98259
WOODLARK 47717
WOODPECKER 66603
WOODROLFE 50400
WOODRUFF 47883 S & J McGUIGAN THRUPP OXON. NbT 54' grey/blue. B: 1989 Delph Marine to design by Criterion (Engineers) Swindon, f/o C T Fox, March; lengthened 1995 by S G Priest, Stockton. Lister CE16(1948), ex GPO generator, marinised Criterion (engineers). Base Thrupp, Oxford canal. Low wash hull design, vee-bottomed, aerofoil rudder. 21214
WOODRUFF No 1 46455
WOODSMOKE 76910
WOOD SORREL 73500
WOODSPRIDE 80542
WOODY 69339
WOODY 100807
WOODYS QUANDRY 71234
WOOKEY HOLE BW-
WOOLEY TWO 101895
WOOLWINDER 50101
WORCESTER 60686
WORCESTER 66228
WORCESTER 67744
WORCESTER 69803
WORCESTER 71723
WORCESTER Tug. Boat Museum
WORCESTER BAR No.10 NbTug 47' blue
WORDSLEY LASS 64845
WOTAN 51811 NbT 40' bl/red. B: 1992 White Bear Marina, f/o W M Booth, Wigan. Lister LPWS3, PRM gearbox. Base Toms Mooring, Penkridge. 22426
WOT ME WORRY 46849
WOULD CREUSE 102461
WOVEN GRASS 53222
WOYAYA 45406
WRANGER 49677
WREAKE Motor vessel 11.8m BW-NE
WREKIN NbT 35' grn
WREN 66370
WREN 74006
WREXHAM 64993
WROE 75151
WRYNECK 48635
WYCH 89325 BW-
WYCHDON PRINCESS 68255
WYCHWOOD 75307
WYE Motor. Ex BW
WYE ROSE 96211
WYEVALE 77239
WYE VALLEY 75548
WYLDE ROSE 66375
WYLO 79665
WYNN DIXIE 51941
WYNWOOD 48187
WYRE LADY Trip vessel red/wh

WYSIWIG 45948
WYTON 78989 NbC 60' grn/yel. B: 1978 Hancock & Lane, f/o Orchard Cruisers, Oxford and owner. BMC 2.5L underfloor (i.e. sloping to stb'd). Continuous cruising. Sides and top continued to cover in front well; rear deck covered with folding hood attached to folding windscreen; water softener for domestic water. Cruised much of Irish waterways May-Oct 1996. 23750
WYVERN 65328
WYVERN 68503

X

Xtra effort required here.

XAI XAI 65972
XANADU 60722
XANADU III 79242
XANTHUS 74921
XAROSHARE 53921
XENOPUS 74483
XERXES 51237
XYST 72495

Y

Camping in town and sisters in reflection.

YABBA DABBA DOO 45570
YALDING 500321 CLIFTON CRUISERS Hire. NbC 60' grn/crm. B: 1996 South West Durham Steelcraft, f/o Clifton Cruisers. BL 1.8. Base Clifton Wharf, Rugby. Sister boat to *Sevenoaks* but internal layout is mirror image. 025685
YALIKAVAK 47437
YANA 61264
YARMOUTH 62442
YARROW 80013 Motor vessel Mtce boat 50' BW-NW
YASMAR 50674
YAVANNA 76836
YAVANNA 500557
YELLOW COCKATOO 78933
YELLOWHAMMER 45588
YELLOWTAIL 52446
YELLOW WAGTAIL 51465
YELTSA B0169
YEOFORD BIRMINGHAM & MIDLAND CANAL CARRYING Co. No.3 "Town" class commercial Nb, all steel riveted. Camping boat ("Camping Afloat") 70' b 7' coach grn/chrome yel. B: circa 1937 W J Yarwood & Co. Northwich for GUCCCo., adapted for camping 1978. Armstrong-Siddeley AS2 twin cyl 20bhp. Base Birmingham Gas Street basin. Exterior preserves original look. Interior provides sleeping, cooking and living accommodation for up to 12 people "under canvas". Operates mainly on long circuits from Birmingham through Midlands. 034995

YEOMAN 52418 J S and J HOBSON 818 WYRE MILL NbT 45' dk grn/yel. B: 1988 R W Davis & Son Ltd, Junction Dry Dock, Saul, partial self f/o. Vetus 414. Base Wyre Mill Club, R.Avon.   25941
YEOMAN   67462
Y'GENNI   74608
Y-GENNI DAN   54350
YIANNI   74936
VOCKER II   53453
YOLKULUKLAR   48484
YOR-A-DOL   31960
YORK   73622
YORK   500678
YORK No 47   71188
YORKIE   79661
YORK ROSE   49770
YORK ROSE   69080
YORKSHIRE LASS   62501
YORKSHIRE LASS   73219
YORKSHIRE ROSE   52074
YORKSHIRE ROSE *54772 NbC 40' blue/grn*
YOUTHFUL ADVENTURE   71990
YOUTH REACH   45443
Y-ROVI   73810
YVONNE   30955

Z

A lonely tripper, a multi-purpose launch and on acquaintance with the gods

ZACHARIAH KEPPEL WEY AND ARUN CANAL TRUST Trip boat, 30 seats Nb 50' red/grn. B: 1973 Springer, converted 1992/3 by Trust volunteers. Lister SR3. Base Loxwood, Wey & Arun canal.   This is the only boat on the unconnected Wey and Arun canal. Named after the local building contractor who built canal in 1813-16.   20161
ZAKAMI *NbT 40' blue*
ZAKI B7168
ZAMBRA Hire. NbC 60' red/grn. Base Rose Narrowboats, Brinklow, N.Oxford canal.   026714
ZANADU   31145
ZANDER   64067
ZANY   49147
ZAUN KONIG   69423

ZAVALA   54719
ZAVALA   N7453
ZEALLA   77981
ZEBEDEE   45823
ZEFFIRO   47762
ZELENA LEGUNA   73498
ZELUS   91603
ZEMMA B   46505
ZENITH 46474 NbT 50' dk grn. B: 1989 Richard Wilson, Midland Canal Centre, Stenson, f/o Robert Ford, Boatworkers, Stratford-on-Avon. 1.8 BMC. Base Little Venice, Regents Canal.   22533
ZENITH   67855
ZENOBIA   65726
ZEPHYR   52482
ZEPHYR   65418
ZEPHYR   65537
ZETA   74778
ZEUS   52828
ZEUS   74828
ZEUS *NbT 40' grn*
ZIDON   45720
ZIDON   50863
ZIDON No.2 *NbT 55' blue/red*
ZIGENHER   48449
ZILLAH   64003
ZINGARO   50407
ZINGARO   79670
ZINO   52760
ZIPPORAH   103252
ZIZETTE   61037
ZODAM   49027
ZODIAC Motor. Ex GUCC
ZOE   61119
ZOE   76044
ZOE PERKINS   74925
ZOHECA   54722
ZOZA   71401
ZULU   63148
ZULU CHIEF   84840
ZUNGERU   B0009
ZUNGERU *NbT 60' mar/graining*
ZUSAMMEN   67577
ZYPHER RED HILL MARINA Used for advert/ exhibit/pleasure Thames Launch 20', b 5' olive grn /mahogany deck. B: 1922 Snercold Engineering Co Ltd. 4 cyl Gains petrol. Base Red Hill marina, Ratcliffe-on-Soar.   2066
ZYRA   69857

The "List Man" Strikes Again ...

In course of preparation ... a brand new offering from the publishers of INLAND WATERWAYS BOAT LISTING

.. INLAND WATERWAY PLACES ..

Of course, YOU know where to find (and name) every junction, every bridge, lock, wharf, every watery nook and cranny, every abandoned arm or creek, every significant pub, yard, dock, warehouse and other building ... Don't you?
And every long forgotten boatman's name for them, every alternative name, a bit of history about them and exactly where they all are. Not just the ones you can look up in any guide book. That's too easy!

Well, whether you're an expert or not, you will probably know a good many of them very well, especially around your own bit of canal or river.

Would you, please, consider sharing some of your knowledge so that, from all the bits of information supplied, the publisher can compile a truly comprehensive

"INLAND WATERWAY PLACES"

We'll all pool our knowledge - it's going to be a great game - everyone supplying a few bits of the jigsaw puzzle. The resulting book will be a handy companion full of interest and knowledge.

To take part simply ask us for details about exactly what is required. We'll send full information about what you can get out of it as well as what you can put in. Just send or phone your name (ask for details about "Places") to:

Inland Waterways Books
8 Clover Close, Narborough, Leicester LE9 5FT
Telephone: 0116 - 2750746

LOCATION GLOSSARY

It must be noted that this Glossary supplements the information about places, boat builders, etc. for the entries in this book only. It is not intended as a list of all waterway locations (see opposite). Many of the entries give the full location anyway, especially when they occur only once or twice. The Glossary also incorporates the abbreviations used. Where references are made to boat builders, etc. this does not imply that a firm still exists or is still in the same location; such references are in the context of the entries.

ABBOTT, H E of Canal Pleasurecraft (Stourport) Ltd.
ABINGDON R.Thames, Oxon.
ADLINGTON Macclesfield canal, nr. Higher Poynton, Cheshire
ALLEN, LES & SON, Valencia Wharf, Oldbury
ALVECHURCH BOAT CENTRE W&B canal
ALVECOTE Coventry Canal, nr. Tamworth, Staffs.
ANDERTON T&M / R.Weaver, Cheshire
ARCRITE FABRICATIONS, Corby, Northants.
ANSTY N.Oxford canal nr. Hawkesbury, Warwicks
ASHBY NARROWBOAT CO. Willow Park Marina, Stoke Golding, Ashby Canal, Leics.
ATHERSTONE Coventry canal, Warwickshire
AUDLEM Shropshire Union canal, Cheshire
AUSTCLIFFE S&W canal, nr. Kidderminster
AUTHERLEY JUNCTION S&W / SU canals, Wolverhampton
AYLESBURY / AYLESBURY ARM GU, Bucks.
AYNHO / AYNHO WHARF S.Oxford canal
b = beam (width of craft at widest point), given if other than narrowboat dimension (6'10" - 7')
B: = followed by year built/builder/fit-out/etc.
BANBURY S.Oxford canal, Oxon.
BANTOCK T. Ltd. Oldbury, BCN
BARBRIDGE at junc SU main line and Middlewich Branch, Ches.
BARLOW, SAMUEL etc. *see page 41*
BARNEY BOATS Ltd., Braunston (see following)
Barney - followed by build number in brackets, then year, length and any known previous names. Taken from a reasonably up-to-date list supplied of boats built by Chris Barney of Braunston Boats Ltd.
BARROW UPON SOAR nr. Loughborough, Leics.
Base = where boat is normally kept, either specifically or a general area as indicated by owner
BATTYEFORD Calder & Hebble Nav. W. Yorks
BCN = Birmingham Canal Navigations
BEDFORD R. Great Ouse, Beds.
BENSON R.Thames, Oxon.
BERKHAMSTED Grand Union Canal, Herts.
BETTISFIELD PLEASURE BOATS Clwyd
BILL FEN MARINA Ramsey, Middle Level Nav.
BILLING AQUADROME R.Nene, Northampton

BINSEY, R.Thames, Oxon.
BL = (in context) either Blue Line or British Leyland
BLABY GU-Leics., nr Leicester
BLISWORTH TUNNEL BOATS GU, Blisworth, Northants.
BLUE HAVEN MARINE Hillmorton, Rugby, N.Oxford canal, Warks.
BLUE LIAS Stockton, GU canal, Warwickshire
BLUE WATER MARINA Stainforth & Keadby canal, Thorne, S.Yorks.
Boat Museum = the Museum at Ellesmere Port
BOSSOMS BOATYARD R.Thames, Binsey Oxon
BOURNE END MOORINGS GU canal, Berkhamsted
BRADFORD ON AVON K&A canal, Wilts.
BRADLEY BCN, Wednesbury Oak Loop
BRAINE, MALCOLM E. Norton Canes, BCN
BRAMWITH BRIDGE Sheffield & S. Yorkshire Navigation
BRAUNSTON Grand Union/Oxford canals, Northants.
BRAUNSTON BOATS Ltd. see Barney Boats
BRAYFORD POOL Fossdyke/R.Witham, Lincoln
BREWOOD Shropshire Union canal, Staffordshire
BRIAR COTTAGE MOORINGS Lapworth, North Stratford canal
BRIDGEWATER BOATBUILDERS Worsley
BRIGHOUSE Calder & Hebble Nav. W.Yorks
BRINKLOW N.Oxford canal, Warwicks. ("Stretton Stop")
BROMSGROVE Worcs.
BROMSGROVE BOATBUILDERS W&B canal, Hanbury Wharf, Droitwich Spa
BRUMMAGEM BOATS BCN
BUCKLE, PAT Stibbington, R.Nene, nr. Peterborough
BUMBLE HOLE arm off Dudley No2 canal BCN
BUNBURY SU canal, north of Barbridge, Ches.
BURDEN BROS. Blue Lias, Stockton, GU canal
BURGHFIELD K & A canal, nr. Reading, Berks.
Butty = Working boat towed by horse or Motor

BW - British Waterways
The following indicate in which region or area the listed BW workboats operate:
BW-BBC   Birmingham & Black Country
BW-CATM Coventry, Ashby,Trent/Mersey
BW-LAP   Lapworth
BW-LON   London
BW-L&S   Lee & Stort
BW-NE   North East Region
BW-NW   North West Region
BW-OGU   Oxford & Grand Union
BW-   location not indicated
CADEBY nr. Market Bosworth, Ashby canal, Leics.
CALCUTT Grand Union Canal nr. Napton junction
CALCUTT BOATS GU canal, nr Napton junction
CANAL TRANSPORT SERVICES Norton Canes
CARABOAT Ltd. Sutton-in-Ashfield, Notts.
CATTESHALL LOCK R.Wey
CHEDDINGTON GU, Bucks.
CHESHIRE STEEL CRAFT Widnes, Lancs.
CHESTER Shropshire Union canal
CHIRK Llangollen canal
Cl = Class (e.g. as in Star Class)
CLIFTON WHARF / CRUISERS
N.Oxford canal, Rugby, Warks.
CLUBLINE CRUISERS Coventry canal, Coventry
COLECRAFT Long Itchington, GU canal, Warks.
COLES MARINE N.Oxford canal, Rugby, Warks.
Colours - frequent colours given as:
    bl = black   crm = cream
    dk = dark   grn = green
    lt = light   mar = maroon
    wh = white   yel = yellow
COSGROVE GU canal, Northamptonshire
COWROAST GU canal, nr. Berkhamsted, Herts.
CREIGHTON BOATBUILDERS Cheshire
CRICHTONS Saltney Dock, nr Chester
CRICK G U canal, Leicester section, Northants.
CROSSFLATS L&L canal
d = draught (depth of boat below waterline), given if exceptional for type of craft, e.g. very shallow or over 30" in the case of a narrow boat
DAVIS, MEL, BOATBUILDERS Tuxford, Notts.
DAVISON BROS Trent Lock, Erewash canal
DEBDALE WHARF Grand Union canal, Leics. Section, nr. Market Harborough, Leics.
DELPH MARINE Brierley Hill, BCN
DERBY NARROWBOATS Littleover, Derby
DEVIZES Kennet & Avon Canal, Wilts.
DEWSBURY Calder & Hebble Nav.
DOBSONS BOATYARD
T&M canal, Shardlow, Derbys.
DROITWICH W&B canal, Worcs.
DROITWICH BOAT CENTRE
Hanbury Wharf, W&B canal, Worcs.
EASTINGTON Stroudwater Nav.
EASTWOOD ENGINEERING
Owston Ferry, R.Trent
EATON HASTINGS
R.Thames, nr. Lechlade, Oxon.
EGERTON NARROWBOATS
Castlefield, Manchester
ELY R.Ouse, Cambs.
ENSLOW Oxford canal, nr. Kidlington, Oxon.

EVANS & SON Hixon, Staffs.
EVESHAM R.Avon, Worcestershire
FARNCOMBE BOAT HOUSE Catteshall Lock
FAULKNER, G Cosgrove, GU canal, Northants.
FAZELEY junc. Coventry / Birmingham & Fazeley canals near Tamworth, Staffs.
FELLOWS, MORTON & CLAYTON LTD.
see page 41
FENNY STRATFORD GU canal, Bucks.
FERNIE Market Harborough, Leics.
FMC / FM & C see Fellows Morton & Clayton Ltd.
F/o = fit-out
FOX'S MARINA / BOATYARD
March, Middle Level Nav.
FOXTON / FOXTON BOAT SERVICES
GU Leics. Section
FRADLEY JUNCTION T & M / Coventry canals
FRENCH AND PEEL
Thorne, Stainforth & Keadby canal, S.Yorks
FRY'S ISLAND R.Thames, Reading, Berks.
FULWOOD CRUISERS Ltd.
Sutton in Ashfield, Notts.
GAILEY WHARF S&W canal
GAYTON Grand Union canal near Northampton
GILWERN Mon & Brec canal
GODALMING R.Wey, Surrey
GODALMING NARROWBOATS R.Wey, Surrey
GOLDSBROUGH, STEPHEN, BOATS
Knowle, GU, W.Midlands
GORTON, GARY nr. Stoke on Trent, Staffs.
GOYTRE Mon & Brecon canal
GRANBY BRIDGE L&L canal
GREAT HAYWOOD
junc. Staffs & Worcs / T&M, Staffs.
GREENTOUR Weltonfield, GU-Leics.
Grp - boat or part of boat made of this material, generally one of the many types of canal and river cruisers; sometimes the cabin top of an older narrow boat, etc.
G.T. BOATBUILDERS Stafford
GU or GUC = Grand Union canal
GUCCC = Grand Union Canal Carrying Co.
GU-Leics. = Leicester Section of the Grand Union Canal (could be the whole section from Norton Junction to the R.Trent but usually when referring to north of Leicester the R.Soar or the Soar Navigation is used).
GUILDFORD R.Wey Navigation, Surrey
GUILDFORD BOAT HOUSE
R.Wey Navigation, Surrey
HAINSWORTH BOATYARD Bingley, L&L
HANBURY WHARF Droitwich Spa, W&B canal, junc. Droitwich Junction canal, Worcs.
HANCOCK & LANE Daventry, Northants.
HARBOROUGH BOATS /
HARBOROUGH MARINE Market Harborough
HAREFIELD GU canal, Middlesex
HARGRAVE SU canal, south of Chester
HARLAND & WOLFF *see page 41*
HARRIS BROTHERS Bumble Hole, Dudley
HATHERTON S&W canal north of Wolverh'pton
HATTON GUC nr. Warwick Warks.
HAWKESBURY JUNCTION N.Oxford/ Coventry canals nr. Coventry, Warks. ("Sutton's Stop")

HAWNE BASIN Dudley No. 2 canal, Halesowen
HEBDEN BRIDGE Rochdale canal
HENWOOD WHARF Solihull, W.Midlands
HERITAGE BOATBUILDERS Evesham, R.Avon
HESFORD MARINE Lymm   *
HEYWOOD, MIKE Hoo Mill, later Evans & Son
HIGHER POYNTON Macclesfield, Cheshire
HIGH LANE ARM Macclesfield canal, Cheshire
HIGH LINE YACHTING Cowley Peachey, GU
HIGH ONN SU canal, Staffs
HILLMORTON nr. Rugby, N.Oxford canal, Warks
HILPERTON K&A canal, Wilts.
HINCKLEY Ashby canal, Leics.
HIXON Staffordshire
hNBOC = Historic Narrow Boat Owners Club
HOO MILL T & M canal, nr. Great Haywood
HOPWAS Coventry
  (B'ham & Fazeley) canal nr. Lichfield
HUCKER MARINE
  GU-Leics. at North Kilworth, Leics.
HUDDLESFORD Coventry canal
HUDSON S M
  Glascote Basin, Coventry canal, Tamworth
HURRANS WHARF Banbury
HYDE Lower Peak Forest canal, Cheshire
INGLEMERE
  T&M canal (bridge 70 - Colwich lock)
IWA = Inland Waterways Association
HUNTINGDON R.Ouse
Italics are used either to give estimated information in one-line entries or for any comments added by the compiler.
IVYBRIDGE MARINE Braunston, Northants.
IVER Slough Arm, GU canal, Bucks.

JD BOAT SERVICES Gailey, S&W canal
Joey - refers to working day boat, generally without cabin in original forms
JOSHER *see page 41*
K&A = Kennet & Avon canal
KATE BOATS Warwick
KEADBY Stainforth & Keadby canal, junc. R.Trent
KEAY, PETER & SON Walsall
KEGWORTH Soar Navigation, Leicestershire
KENFIELD BOATBUILDER Aldridge, W. Mids.
KIDDERMINSTER S&W canal, Worcs.
KINTBURY K&A canal, Berks.
KLONDYKE BOATBUILDING
  Ashby de la Zouch, Leics.
LANGLEY MILL Erewash canal
LAPWORTH North Stratford canal
LARGE WOOLWICH *see page 41*
LAROSE NARROWBOATS Rochdale, Lancs.
Lg = Large (e.g. as in Large Woolwich)
LIMEKILN NARROWBOATS
  Compton, S&W canal
LINLITHGOW Union canal, Lothian
LINSLADE Grand Union canal, Bucks.
LITTLE HALLINGBURY R.Stort
L&L = Leeds and Liverpool canal
LIVERPOOL BOATS Liverpool
LONG ITCHINGTON
  Grand Union canal nr. Rugby, Warks.
LORENZ & CO. Barton, Manchester
LOUGHBOROUGH Soar Navigation, Leics.
LOWESMOOR WHARF Worcester
LYME VIEW Macclesfield canal, Cheshire
LYMM Bridgewater canal, Cheshire
MACCLESFIELD Macclesfield canal, Cheshire

An unexpected inclusion in this book is the *Colonel Baldwin*, the trip boat which gives Summer rides on a restored section of the Middlesex Canal at Woburn, north of Boston, Massachusetts, USA. The canal interested the compiler on a visit as it is to much the same scale as our own narrow canals

M&N BOATBUILDERS Mansfield, Notts.
MARCH Middle Level Nav., Cambs.
MARINEVILLE
   Macclesfield canal, Higher Poynton, Ches.
MARKET HARBOROUGH
   GU Leicester Section, Leics.
MARQUE NARROWBOATS Eccleshall, Staffs.
MASSEY, DAVE Wincham Wharf, Northwich
MAYORS BOATYARD
   Tarleton, Rufford Branch, L&L
MIDDLEWICH at junc. T&M canal and SU
   (Middlewich Branch), Cheshire
MIDLAND CANAL CENTRE
   Stenson, T&M canal, Derbys.
MIKE GRATION GREENTOUR Ltd. Welton
   Hythe, Grand Union canal, Leics. Section
MILL WHARF
   Wyre Piddle, Lower R.Avon, Worcs
MILTON KEYNES Grand Union canal, Bucks.
MON & BREC Monmouthshire and Brecon canal
Motor =Working boat with engine to distinguish
   from Butty without engine
M.S.C. = Manchester Ship Canal
NABO = National Association of Boat Owners
NABURN R.Ouse, N.Yorks
NANTWICH SU canal, Cheshire
NAPTON / NAPTON JUNCTION
   Grand Union / S.Oxford canals, Warwicks.
NARROWCRAFT Ltd. Coventry canal, Alvecote,
   nr. Tamworth, Staffs.
NAV. = Navigation(s)
Nb - Narrow boat. Used specifically or if type
   not known
NbC - Narrow boat, Cruiser style, i.e. usually
   with large open aft deck area and without
   attempts to achieve "traditional" lines
NbST -Narrow boat, Semi-Traditional style, i.e.
   composite of "traditional" lines and larger
   semi-open area aft
NbT - Narrow boat, either an original "traditional" preserved boat or original but
   converted, retaining much of the former
   style. Or a modern replica - either for
   working (rarely) or fitted out for cruising
   or residential use; always featuring motor
   or butty style aft deck, hatches, lines, etc.,
   reminiscent of traditional working boats.
NbTug - As for NbT but Tug or Tug-style with
   distinctive shape, long foredeck, high
   cabin sides on low freeboard, deep
   draught and powerful machinery
NENE MARINE Whittlesey, Middle Level Nav.
NETHERTON Dudley No.2 canal, BCN
NEWBURY Kennet & Avon canal, Berkshire
NEW MILLS Peak Forest canal
NICHOLLS, PETER
   Napton, S.Oxford canal, Warwicks.
NIMBUS NARROWBOATS
   Thurmaston, Soar Navigation
NORMAN CRUISERS Ltd. Shaw, Oldham,
   Lancs. (*orig:* NORth MANchester Plastics)
NORTH WEST NARROWBOATS Riley Green
NORTHWICH T & M canal / R.Weaver, Ches.

NORTON CANES BOATBUILDERS /
NORTON CANES Cannock Extension canal, BCN
Ob = Outboard engine
OLDBURY BCN
OWSTON FERRY R.Trent
OXFORD CANAL BOAT Co.
   Little Chesterton, Oxon.
PELSALL Wyrley & Essington canal, BCN
PENKRIDGE Staffs & Worcs canal, Staffordshire
PEWSEY K&A canal, Wilts.
PHOENIX NARROWBOATS
   Coventry, Coventry Canal
PICKWELL & ARNOLD Todmorden, W.Yorks.
PILLING, GEOFF Cheshire Steel Craft, Widnes
PIMBLOTT Northwich, Ches.
PINDER J L & SON Bromsgrove, Worcs.
PITSTONE WHARF GU canal, Bucks.
PRESTON BROOK T&M/junc Bridgewater canals
PYRFORD R.Wey Navigation, Surrey
R & D FABRICATIONS Ollerton, Notts.
RAMSEY Middle Level Navigations
RHODES, MALCOLM Shardlow, T&M, Derbys.
Ricky - Boat built at Walkers of Rickmansworth
RILEY GREEN L&L canal, nr. Blackburn, Lancs.
ROBINSONS BOAT YARD
   Saville Town, Dewsbury
ROCHDALE Rochdale canal, Lancs.
ROSE NARROWBOATS
   Stretton Stop, N.Oxford canal, Warks.
RUGBY BOATBUILDERS
   Hillmorton, N.Oxford canal, Rugby, Warks.
RUGELEY Trent & Mersey canal, Staffordshire
SAGAR MARINE
   Brighouse, Calder & Hebble Nav., Yorks
SALTLEY Birmingham boat building base of FMC
SANDON T&M canal, nr. Stone, Staffs.
SAUL JUNCTION Gloucester & Sharpness canal
   / Stroudwater Arm
SAVILE TOWN BASIN
   Dewsbury, Calder & Hebble Nav.
SAWLEY/SAWLEY BRIDGE/SAWLEY
   MARINA R.Trent, Derbys.
SCCCo - Severn & Canal Carrying Co.
SHARDLOW T&M canal, Derbys.
SHEPLEY BRIDGE
   Mirfield, Calder & Hebble canal, Yorks.
SHIPLEY / WHARF L&L canal, nr. Bingley
SHERBORNE WHARF Birmingham
SHOBNALL BASIN T&M, Burton-on-Trent
SHOTBOLT ENGINEERING Ltd.
   Ramsey, Middle Level, Cambs.
SHROPSHIRE UNION BOATBUILDERS
   Norbury Junction, SU
SIMOLDA Ltd.
   SU canal, Basin End, Nantwich, Cheshire
SILEBY MILL / BOATYARD Soar Navigation
SIVEWRIGHT, MIKE Middlewich, T&M canal
SKIPTON L&L canal, Skipton, W.Yorks
Sm = Small (e.g. as in Small Woolwich)
SNAYGILL L&L canal, Skipton, W.Yorks
SOUTH, JOHN Garston, Liverpool
SOUTH SHORE NARROWBOATS
   S.Oxford canal, Aynho

196

SOUTH WEST DURHAM STEELCRAFT
Bishop Aukland, Co. Durham
SOWERBY BRIDGE Calder & Hebble Nav.
SSY = Sheffield & South Yorkshire Navigation
STAFFS & WORCS (S&W)
= Staffordshire & Worcestershire canal
STANILAND Thorne, Stainforth & Keadby canal
STANLEY FERRY Aire & Calder Navigation
STANSTEAD R.Lee
STAR CLASS *see page 41*
STARCRAFT Ilkeston, Derbys.
STARLINE NARROWBOATS Upton on Severn
STEELCRAFT Old, Northants.
STENSON BOATBUILDERS Stenson T&M canal
STENSON Trent & Mersey canal, nr. Derby
STIBBINGTON R.Nene, nr Peterborough
STOCKTON GU, Warwickshire
STOKE GOLDING Ashby canal, Leicestershire
STOKE ON TRENT
Trent & Mersey / Caldon canals, Staffs.
STOKE PRIOR Worcester & Birmingham canal
STONE Trent & Mersey canal, Staffordshire
STONE BOATBUILDING Ltd. Stone T&M canal
STOURBRIDGE Stourbridge canal, Worcs.
STOURPORT R.Severn / Staffs &Worcs canal
STOWE HILL Weedon, GU canal, Northants.
STOWE HILL MARINE Weedon, GU canal
STREETHAY WHARF
Coventry canal, nr Lichfield, Staffs.
STRETTON STOP
N.Oxford canal, Brinklow, Warwicks.
SU = Shropshire Union canal
SUTTON CHENEY Ashby canal, Leicestershire
SUTTON-IN-ASHFIELD Notts.
SUTTON'S STOP =
Hawkesbury junc. Coventry/N.Oxford canals
S&W = Staffordshire & Worcestershire canal
SWANLINE Fradley junc. T&M/Coventry canals
SWARKESTONE T & M canal, nr. Derby
SYDNEY WHARF K&A canal, Bath

TARDEBIGGE W&B canal, Worcestershire
TAYLOR, J H Chester
TEDDESLEY BOAT Co.
Park Gate Lock, S&W, Penkridge, Staffs.
TEWKSBURY R.Avon / R.Severn, Glos.
THOMAS, DAVE Braunston, Northants.
THORNE Stainforth & Keadby canal
THRUPP / THRUPP WIDE
South Oxford canal, nr. Oxford
THURMASTON nr. Leicester, Soar Navigation
TIXALL / TIXALL WIDE
S&W canal nr. Great Haywood
T&M = Trent and Mersey canal
TONBRIDGE R.Medway, Kent
TOWN CLASS *see page 41*
TRENT LOCK
Erewash canal at junc. with R.Trent & R.Soar
TREVOR Llangollen canal
TT MARINE Thorne, Stainforth & Keadby canal
TUNNEL MARINE Foulridge, L&L canal
UCC - Union Canal Carriers
UPTON-ON-SEVERN R.Severn
UXBRIDGE GU, Middx.

VALENCIA WHARF BCN, Oldbury
VENETIAN MARINE
SU canal, Cholmondeston, Cheshire
W&B = Worcester & Birmingham canal
WAIN, SIMON Stretton Wharf, SU canal
WAKEFIELD Aire & Calder Navigation
WALKER, W H, BROS. Rickmansworth *see p. 41*
WALSALL BCN
WALTHAM ABBEY R.Lee, Essex
WARBLE BOAT BUILDERS Hyde, Cheshire
WARGRAVE ON THAMES nr. Reading, Berks.
WARINGS GREEN North Stratford canal
WARWICK Grand Union canal
WARWICKSHIRE NARROWBOATS
Stretton Stop (Brinklow)
WATER-CRAFT Maescwmmer, Mid Glamorgan
WATERCRAFT BOATS Ltd. Newport Pagnell
WATERINGBURY R.Medway
WATER TRAVEL
Autherley junc., SU canal, Wolverhampton
WATFORD GU canal, Hertfordshire
WAVE RIDER Malden, Essex
WEEDON Grand Union canal, Northants.
WELFORD Welford Arm, GUC, Leicester Section
WELSHPOOL Montgomery canal, Powys
WELTONFIELD NARROWBOATS /
WELTON WHARF / WELTON HYTHE
Grand Union canal, Leics. Section, Northants.
WESTON FAVELL R.Nene, nr. Northampton
WEST RIDING BOAT Co.
Wakefield, Aire & Calder Nav.
WHEELTON L&L canal, nr. Chorley, Lancs.
WHILTON Grand Union canal, Northants.
WHITTLE BOATS
Whittle-le-Woods, Chorley, Lancashire
WHIXALL Llangollen canal
WILDERNESS BOATS Corsham, Wilts.
WILLMINGTON, RICHARD
Hoo Mill Lock, T&M canal nr. Gt Haywood
WILLOW PARK MARINA
Stoke Golding, Ashby canal
WILLOWTREE MARINA
GU canal, Paddington Arm
WILLOW WREN Rugby Arm, N.Oxford canal,
Warks. (formerly Braunston)
WINCHAM WHARF
Northwich, T&M canal, Cheshire
WOLVERHAMPTON NARROWBOAT &
CANAL CARRYING COMPANY LTD., The
Minerva Wharf, Wolverhampton
WOLVERLEY S&W, nr Kidderminster, Worcs.
WOOTTON WAWEN Stratford on Avon canal
WORSLEY Bridgewater canal
WYKEN Old Pit Basin, N.Oxford canal, Coventry
WYRE PIDDLE Lower R.Avon, Worcs.
WYVERN SHIPPING CO. Ltd., The
GU canal, Linslade
YARWOOD, W J Northwich, T&M / R.Weaver,
Cheshire *see page 41*
ZOUCH north of Loughborough, Soar Navigation

197

SOME LAST THOUGHTS

It's a fact ... to seek entries for this book, about 20,000 Information/Questionnaire sheets were distributed in a big operation during the second half of 1996; by inclusion in magazines; by circulation to just about every waterway and boat club, society, branch, etc; by circulation to hundreds of appropriate waterways businesses (boatyards, marinas, chandlers, hire fleets, etc.); by circulation to navigation authorities and museums and directly in response to announcements and advertising in the waterways press. The invaluable assistance of everyone who has helped to spread the word is acknowledged elsewhere. It might be needed again for future editions!

Entries to the *Listing* were still being received at the last minute. There had to be a final, final cut-off date otherwise the book would never get printed. Everyone disappointed has been assured that their entry will qualify for any subsequent edition which may be produced.

Frank Munns' line drawings (the main ones) have been taken from photographs of real places and things around the waterways. You could try to identify them. Some are sure to be easier than others!

Most narrow boats - old or modern - are constructed using fairly "low-tech" methods. In sympathy with that thought, this book could also be said to be "low-tech" in its basic construction (though the actual printing and binding will use the latest technology). The components comprising the pages have been put together using tried and tested old methods: paper, knives, glue, much time, dedication and back ache. Like the occasional imperfection which gives the hull of a boat a certain "character", the occasional "rough edge" may show within these pages. I hope the reader will regard them with similar kindness.

The gang which was busy dredging a section of the Chesterfield Canal in the summer of 1978 found an obstinate piece of heavy chain along with the rusting bicycles and discarded refrigerators. They heaved the chain out with the dredger, along with a block of wood on the end. This was the plug which James Brindley had put in 200 years earlier. Now, the millions of gallons of water in one and a half miles of canal drained into the River Idle nearby.

It is hoped that the mistakes which keen boat spotters are sure to find in this book will not be quite as serious as this. Inevitably there will be duplications, discrepancies and inaccuracies despite the endless checking which has been done. Please help the *Listing* Project by letting the publisher know. More information on pages 12 & 13. Thank you.

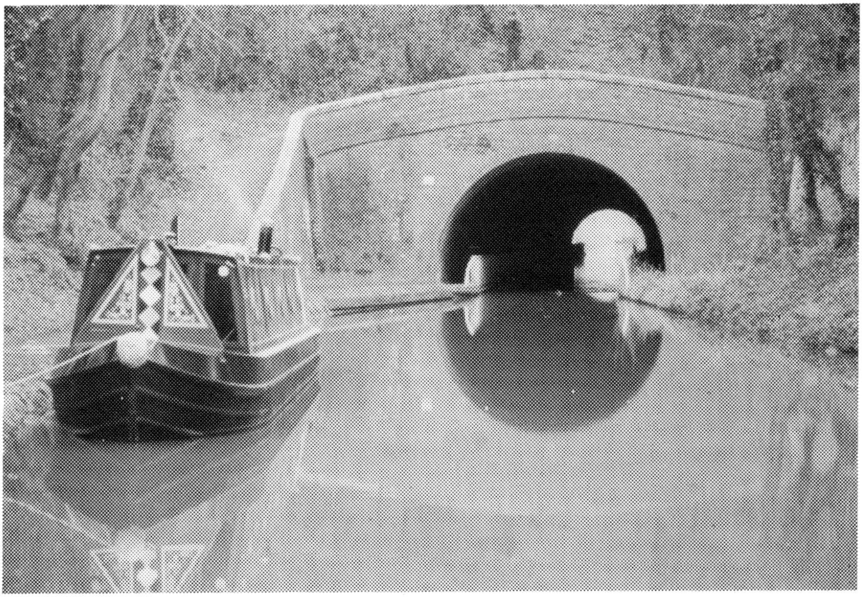